MW00944631

Mike of Arabia

Stories and tales of a young American
child growing up in an oil town overseas

MICHAEL REILLY CROCKER

Copyright © 2012 Michael Reilly Crocker
All rights reserved.

ISBN: 1468198599
ISBN 13: 9781468198591

"The book and all contents are copyright by the author with added materials from other sources as being designated as Historical text and free share copyright." No materials may be used by any medium in any way without written permission of the author. The author assumes full responsibility for all materials contained within." Michael Crocker-Attorney at Law(Ret.)

Aramco "A" is the copyright of Saudi Aramco and used with permission of HM King Fahd bin Adul Azziz ibn Saud in 1996 and the Royal Coat of arms logo is in public domain,
but also used with permission of HM King Abdullah bin Abdul Azziz ibn Saud.

MICHAEL REILLY CROCKER
مايكل ريلي كروكر

A MASTER OF ALL HE SEE'S AND A LOVER OF THE GREAT LAND AS HE TREDS ACROSS VAST WASTELANDS TO VISIT HIS KING TO ASK FOR MERCY FROM THE HORDES OF ARAMCO MOM'S LED BY THE MOM OF ALL BEDU HUNTERS…AND TO WHOM THIS BOOK IS DEDICATED;

MRS. IRENE CAVE CROCKER, MR. LEO F. CROCKER, THE THOUSANDS OF FRIENDS AND THE PEOPLE OF SAUDI ARABIA, ARAMCO, SAUDI ARAMCO, AND MY FRIENDS OF THE ROYAL FAMILY, DR. FAHD AL- SEMMARI, AND TO THE KING ABDUL AZIZ FOUNDATION AND IT'S SPONSOR, HRH PRINCE SALMAN BIN ABDUL AZIZ IBN SAUD, MINISTER OF DEFENSE. ALSO TO THE AMAZING GROUP, CALLED THE ARAMCO BRATS. SPECIAL APPRECITION TO HM KING ABDULLAH BIN ABDUL AZZIZ IBN AL-SAUD, MY KING AND MY FRIEND.

ALSO AND MOST IMPORTANT THIS BOOK IS A GRAND COLLECTION OF EARLY LIFE OF A YOUNG RAPSCALLION OF ARABIA. IT IS A DESCRIPTION OF GOLDEN TIMES AND DARKEST DAYS OF OUR LIVES. I GIVE A DEFINATION OF SAUDI ARAMCO AND Q'UORNIC STATEMENTS ABOUT ISLAM AND JESUS AND OF WOMAN.

I TAKE GREAT PRIDE IN MY DAYS AS THE "DENNIS THE MENACE," OR THE BAIN OF MANY AN EARLY RETIREMENT FROM THE OIL

COMPANY. THESE STORIES WILL EXPLAIN WHY. THE PHOTOS ON THE COVER ARE ME IN 2011 AND THE LITTLE GUY IS ME IN 1953.

IN THE SPIRIT OF THE BEDU, I CRY OUT WITH GREAT VIGOR "ALLAH AKBAR"

SOME BACK GROUND
OF SAUDI ARAMCO

Saudi Aramco (Arabic: ارامكو السعودية), officially the Saudi Arabian Oil Company, is the state-owned national oil company of Saudi Arabia.[1][2] Saudi Aramco is estimated to be worth $8 trillion usd, making it the world's most valuable non-publicly listed company.[4][5]

Saudi Aramco has both the largest proven crude oil reserves, at more than 260 billion barrels (4.1×1010 M3), and largest daily oil production.[6] Headquartered in Dhahran, Saudi Arabia,[7] Saudi Aramco operates the world's largest single hydrocarbon network, the Master Gas System. Its yearly production is 7.9 Billion barrels (1.26×109 M3),[3] and it managed over 100 oil and gas fields in Saudi Arabia, including 279 trillion scf of natural gas reserves.[3] Saudi Aramco owns the Ghawar Field, the world's largest oil field, and the Shaybah Field, one of the world's largest oil fields.

HISTORY

The origins of Saudi Aramco can be traced back to may 29, 1933, when the Saudi government granted a concession to Standard Oil of California (Socal) which allowed the company to explore for oil in Saudi Arabia. Socal assigned this concession to a wholly owned subsidiary called California-Arabian Standard Oil Co. (Casoc). In 1936, with the company having no success at locating oil, the Texas Oil Company (Texaco) purchased a 50% stake of the concession.[8]

After four years of fruitless exploration, the first success came with the seventh drill site in Dammam, a few miles north of Dhahran in 1938, a well referred to as Dammam No. 7. This well immediately produced over 1,500 barrels per day (240 m3/d), giving the company confidence to continue. The company name was changed in 1944 from California-Arabian Standard Oil Company to Arabian American Oil Company (or Aramco). In 1948, Socal and Texaco were joined as investors by Standard Oil of New Jersey (Esso) which purchased 30% of the company, and Socony Vacuum (later Mobil) which purchased 10% of the company, leaving Socal and Texaco with 30% each.

In 1950, King Abdul Aziz Ibn Saud threatened to nationalize his country's oil facilities, thus pressuring Aramco to agree to share profits 50/50. A similar process had taken place with American oil companies in Venezuela a few years earlier. The American government granted US Aramco member companies a tax break known as the golden gimmick equivalent to the profits given to Ibn Saud. In the wake of the new arrangement, the company's headquarters were moved from New York to Dhahran.

In 1973, following US support for Israel during the Yom Kippur War, the Saudi Arabian government acquired a 25% share of Aramco, increased the share to 60% by 1974, and finally acquired full control of Aramco by 1980. In November 1988, the company changed its name from Arabian American Oil Company to Saudi Arabian Oil Company (or Saudi Aramco) and officially cut all oil supply to Israel by order of the CEO. In addition, Saudi Aramco has become a fully owned privately held company with no shareholders or partners in business. Today Saudi Aramco is the world's largest and most valuable company and thus concerns for monopolization of the world's economy have been raised.

1932 Oil is discovered in Bahrain. Socal begins a year-long series of negotiations with the Saudi government.

1933 Saudi Arabia grants oil concession to California Arabian Standard Oil Company (Casoc), affiliate of Standard Oil of California (Socal, today's Chevron). Oil prospecting begins on Kingdom's east coast.

1936 Texas Oil Company (which became Texaco, and now Chevron) acquires 50% interest in Socal's concession. The joint venture became known as the California Texas Oil Company, or Caltex.

1938 Kingdom's first commercial oil field discovered at Dhahran. Crude is exported by barge to Bahrain.

1939 First tanker load of petroleum is exported. (Socal's D.G. Scofield)

1944 Casoc changes its name to Arabian American Oil Company (Aramco).

1945 Ras Tanura Refinery begins operations (eventually becomes the largest oil-refinery in the world).

1948 Standard Oil of New Jersey (which became Exxon and now ExxonMobil) and Socony-Vacuum Oil (which became Mobil and now ExxonMobil) join Socal (now Chevron) and Texaco (now Chevron) as owners of Aramco.

1950 1,700 km Trans-Arabian Pipe Line (Tapline) is completed, linking Eastern Province oil fields to Lebanon and the Mediterranean.

1950 The US government bestows upon the US member companies a tax break equivalent to 50% of oil profits, a deal known as the Golden gimmick.

1956 Aramco confirms scale of Ghawar and Safaniya, the largest onshore and the largest offshore field in the world, respectively.

1961 Liquefied petroleum gas (LPG)—propane and butane—is first processed at Ras Tanura and shipped to customers.

1966 Tankers begin calling at "Sea Island", new offshore crude oil loading platform off Ras Tanura.

1973 Saudi Government acquires 25 percent interest in Aramco.

1975 Master Gas System project is launched.

1980 Saudi Government acquires 100 percent participation interest in Aramco, purchasing almost all of the company's assets.

1981 East-West Pipelines, built for Aramco natural gas liquids and crude oil, link Eastern Province fields with Yanbu on the Red Sea.

1982 King Fahd visits Saudi Aramco, Dhahran, on Aramco's 50th Anniversary to inaugurate the Exploration and Petroleum Engineering Center (EXPEC), a milestone in the Saudization of the company's operations.

1984 Company acquires its first four supertankers.

1987 East-West Crude Oil Pipeline expansion project is completed, boosting capacity to 3.2 million barrels (510,000 m3) per day.

1988 Saudi Arabian Oil Company, or Saudi Aramco, is established.

1988 Oil supply to Israel is officially ceased by order of the President and CEO.

1989 High-quality oil and gas are discovered south of Riyadh—the first find outside original operating area.

1991 Company plays major role combating Gulf War oil spill, the world's largest.

1992 East-West Crude Oil Pipeline capacity is boosted to 5 million barrels (790,000 m3) per day. Saudi Aramco affiliate purchases 35% interest in SsangYong Oil Refining Company (S-Oil) in the Republic of Korea.

1993 Saudi Aramco takes charge of Kingdom's domestic refining, marketing, distribution and joint-venture refining interests by buying Jeddah-based Saudi Arabian Marketing and Refining Company (SAMAREC). The company also assumed the Saudi Arabian government's 50% share of the Jubail export refining company, which becomes the Saudi Aramco Shell Refining Company (SASREF).

1994 Maximum sustained crude-oil production capacity is returned to 10 million barrels (1,600,000 m3) per day. Company acquires a 40% equity interest in Petron, largest refiner in the Philippines.

1995 Company completes a program to build 15 very large crude carriers. Saudi Aramco President and CEO Ali I. Al-Naimi is named the Kingdom's Minister of Petroleum and Mineral Resources, and Chairman of Saudi Aramco. Abdullah S. Jum'ah is named the CEO, President, and Director of Saudi Aramco.

1996 Saudi Aramco acquires 50 percent of Motor Oil (Hellas) Corinth Refineries and Avinoil from the Vardinoyannis family. Company also assumes controlling interest in two Jeddah-based lubricants companies, now known as Saudi Aramco Lubricating Oil Refining Company (Luberef) and Saudi Arabian Lubricating Oil Company (Petrolube).

1998 Saudi Aramco, Texaco and Shell establish Motiva Enterprises LLC, a major refining and marketing joint venture in the southern and eastern United States.

1999 HRH Crown Prince 'Abd Allah inaugurates the Shaybah field in the Rub' al-Khali desert, one of the largest projects of its kind in the world goes on stream. The Dhahran-Riyadh-Qasim multi-product pipeline and the Ras Tanura Upgrade project are completed. The second Saudi Aramco-Mobil lubricating oil refinery (Luberef II) in Yanbu' commences operations.

2000 Petroleum Intelligence Weekly ranks the company the first in the world for the 11th straight year, for the country's crude oil reserves and production. Aramco Gulf Operations Limited is established to administer the government's petroleum interest in the Offshore Neutral Zone between Saudi Arabia and Kuwait. New facilities are under construction in the Haradh and Hawiyah gas plant projects to process gas for delivery to the Master Gas System and to domestic markets.

2001 Hawiyah Gas Plant, capable of processing up to 1.6 billion standard cubic feet per day of non-associated gas, comes on stream.

2003 Haradh Gas Plant completed two and a half months ahead of schedule.

2004 HRH Crown Prince 'Abd Allah ibn 'Abd Al-'Aziz Al Saud, First Deputy Prime Minister and Head of the National Guard, inaugurates the 800,000-barrel-per-day (130,000 m3/d) Qatif-Abu Sa'fah Producing Plants mega project. In addition to the crude, the plants provide 370 million standard cubic feet of associated gas daily.

2005 Saudi Aramco and Sumitomo Chemical Co., Ltd. sign a joint venture agreement for the development of a large, integrated refining and petrochemical complex in the Red Sea town of Rabigh, on Saudi Arabia's west coast. This becomes known as Petro Rabigh.

2006 Saudi Aramco and Sumitomo Chemical break ground on Media: PETRORabigh, an integrated refining/petrochemical project. Haradh III completed, yielding 300,000 bbl/d (48,000 m3/d) of oil. Accords signed for two export refineries—Jubail (with Total) and in Yanbu' (with Conoco-Phillips).

2007 Saudi Aramco subsidiary Saudi Aramco Sino Co. Ltd. signs agreements with ExxonMobil, Sinopec Corp and the Fujian Provincial Government of China to form two joint ventures: Fujian Refining and Petrochemical Co. Ltd., a refining and petrochemicals venture, and Sinopec SenMei (Fujian) Petroleum Co. Ltd. (SSPC), a marketing venture.

2008 Saudi Aramco celebrates the 75th anniversary of the May 29, 1933, signing of the oil concession between the Kingdom of Saudi Arabia and Standard Oil of California (Socal). King Abdullah visits Dhahran to celebrate the 75th anniversary.

2009 CEO inaugurates KAUST, King Abdullah University of Science and Technology, where many high profile guest, state leaders, kings, and scholars attended the ceremony.

2009 Saudi Aramco reaches 12 Mbbl/d (1,900,000 m3/d) capacity after completing an expansion program. Also, Petro Rabigh, the company's first petrochemical plant (a partnership with Sumitomo Chemicals Co., Ltd., begins production.

2010 Saudi Aramco unveils GigaPOWERS™ and runs a first field test of Resbots™. [9]

2011 Saudi Aramco starts production from Karan Gas Field, with an output of more than 400 standard cubic feet per day. [10]

2011 Saudi Aramco is officially named the world's largest and most valuable privately owned company. Saudi Aramco is said to be monopolizing the world's energy market.

2011 Aramco raised selling prices for all crude grades for customers in Asia and Northwest Europe for April shipments and cut prices for customers in the U.S. Headquarters of Aramco Services Company in Houston

Saudi Aramco operations span the globe, despite being headquartered in Dhahran. Company operations include exploration, producing, refining, chemicals, distribution and marketing.

EXPLORATION

A significant portion of the Saudi Aramco workforce consists of geophysicists and geologists. Saudi Aramco has been exploring for oil and gas reservoirs since 1982. Most of this process takes place at the Exploration and Petroleum Engineering Center (EXPEC). Originally, Saudi Aramco used Cray Supercomputers (CRAY-1M)[12] to assist in processing the colossal quantity of data obtained during exploration. In 2001, Saudi Aramco decided to use Linux clusters as a replacement for the decommissioned Cray systems.

DRILLING

This is the most crucial process and as such accounts for the largest segment of the Saudi Aramco workforce. Drilling new wells efficiently and then maintaining them requires the company to employ a large number of engineers. With the increasing global demand for oil, Saudi Aramco seeks to expand its oil production. To do this the company seeks to expand the number of engineers and geo-scientists it employs.

REFINING AND CHEMICALS

While the company did not originally plan on refining oil, the Saudi government wished to have only one company dealing with oil production.

Therefore, on July 1, 1993, the government issued a royal decree merging Saudi Aramco with Samarec, the country's oil refining company. The following year, a Saudi Aramco subsidiary acquired a 40% equity interest in Petron Corporation, the largest crude oil refiner and marketer in the Philippines.[11] Since then, Saudi Aramco has taken on the responsibility of refining oil and distributing it in the country.

Currently, Saudi Aramco's refining capacity is more than 4 million barrels per day (640,000 m3/d) (International joint and equity ventures: 2,060 Mbbl/d (328,000,000 m3/d), domestic joint ventures: 1,108 mpbd, and wholly owned domestic operations: 995 Mbbl/d (158,200,000 m3/d).) This figure is set to increase as more projects go online.[3]

Additionally, Saudi Aramco's downstream operations are shifting its emphasis to integrate refineries with petrochemical facilities. Their first venture into it is with Petro Rabigh, which is a joint venture with Sumitomo Chemical Co. that began in 2005 on the coast of the Red Sea.

Saudi Aramco also provides several services to its employees. It maintains several large "high-tech" hospitals and provides health insurance for its employees worldwide. It also maintains many fire stations, both industrial and residential. Saudi Aramco introduced its Elite Security over two decades ago. This security force has been militarily trained abroad and primarily ensures the safety of the company's industrial and residential areas as well as the families of senior management officials.

Saudi Aramco has operations all over the world and often needs to transport employees between operations. To do this, it owns and operates a fleet of 79 airplanes and 15 helicopters, and 2 airports in the United States (the only private organization allowed by the FAA to own and operate its own airports, as well as 5 international airports in Saudi Arabia. Also, Saudi Aramco has intensive career development programs under the Career Development Department. These includes PDP (Professional Development Program) for fresh graduates and ADP (Advanced Degree Program) for Master and PhD studies. Saudi Aramco issued a statement in 1998 stating that the company is trying to reduce the amount of lead in their gasoline and has already done so by about 50 percent.[citation needed]

The company has an "Environmental Master Plan" to reduce the emissions provided by Capital Programs which already some of them have been completed.[citation needed] Saudi Aramco is a leading company in the region in reducing sulfur emissions, CO_2, and flaring.[citation needed] Also, a

CEO Dashboard complemented by an annual Environmental Report shows the exact Environmental statistics and Key Performance Indicators in terms of air and sea water pollutions

1. a b The Report: Saudi Arabia 2009. Oxford Business Group. 2009. pp. 130. ISBN 978-1907065088.
2. a b "Our company. At a glance". Saudi Aramco. "The Saudi Arabian Oil Company (Saudi Aramco) is the state-owned oil company of the Kingdom of Saudi Arabia."
3. a b c d e f g Saudi Aramco Annual Review 2010
4. "Big Oil, bigger oil". Financial Times. February 4, 2010.
5. In 2006, its value was estimated at 781 billion US$ in the FT Non-Public 150—the full list
6. SteelGuru—News
7. "Contact Us." Saudi Aramco. Retrieved on 5 November 2009. "Headquarters: Dhahran, Saudi Arabia Address: Saudi Aramco P.O. Box 5000 Dhahran 31311 Saudi Arabia"
8. http://www.virginia.edu/igpr/APAG/apagoilhistory.html
9. http://www.saudiaramco.com/en/home.html#our-company%257Chttp%253A%252F%252Fwww.saudiaramco.com%252Fen%252Fhome%252Four-company%252Four-history0.baseajax.html
10. http://www.bloomberg.com/news/2011-07-26/saudi-aramco-starts-production-from-karan-gas-field-in-july-1-.html
11. "TOP Oil Market News: Saudi Aramco Raises Prices; Libya Turmoil—Bloomberg". bloomberg.com. 2011 [last update]. Retrieved 25 August 2011. "Aramco raised official selling prices for all crude grades for customers in Asia and Northwest Europe for April shipments and cut prices for customers in the U.S."
12. Cray FAQ Part 3: FAQ kind of items
13. http://www.vela.ae/-History-Vela8.html
14. http://www.thefreelibrary.comSaudi+Aramco+Celebrates+100+Patents.-a0242563545
15. http://www.gulfoilandgas.com/webpro1/MAIN/Mainnews.asp?id=10328
16. Financial Times: Saudi Aramco revealed as biggest group
17. FT Non-Public 150
18. Saudi Arabian Oil Company Company Profile—Yahoo! Finance

As one can see ARAMCO (SAUDI ARAMCO) is very much like a military base. The individual compounds were fenced and separated from goats walking the street with an occasional camel coming into town to shop. Aramco communites were run like military compounds with Mail centers, shopping center, hospitals, and all the recreation possible. Interaction with the local people was restricted at first but gradually, we of the West became close friends to those of the East and it shall forever more be a link that a handshake meant more the a thousand word legal document. We, the westerners, were in the start, in these compounds alone, all Westerners, but as Aramco became Saudi Aramco, the cultures mixed even more and today Saudi Arabia, under the Royal Family of HM King Al-Rathman bin Abdul Aziz ibn Saud (MOST COMMONALLY KNOWN AS KING ABDUL AZZIZ) and his son's to include many have made SAUDI ARABIA our home and the great desert is AMERICA"S greatest friend in the Middle East.

Michael Reilly Crocker

MIKE OF ARABIA- A MAN OF TWO HOUSE'S- THE AMERICAN AND THE HOUSE OF THE AL-SAUD

A rriving in the land of Sa'ud as a boy of two in 1951 I came to love the desert and the beauty of the Arab way of life. I grew up protected, by both the Oil Company and the Saudi Government, but my playmates and friends were Saudi's my age.

They taught me many things, the cruelty of the desert, the beauty of the night, the blessing's God gave to Arabia and to me. I was taught the Arabs were an inferior race, because they were so backwards, but in reality their ways were years ahead of my own people. I watched a beheading when I was very small, meet with King Faisal and had tea with Ibn'Jlouie, the King's executioner. They taught me right from wrong, in ways that guide me to this day and like the ships of the desert, my Bedouin friends taught me never to be lost, and always amongst friends.

The oil company gave me the finest in education, the Saudi's the finest in honor and respect. Loyalty and fidelity, I learned in a tent in the Rub'a Kahli. I learned to master an Arabian Stallion at the age of twelve and rode the winds of Arabia along the shores of Azzizia.

I knew that all was not what it may have seemed, but the majesty of the Arab world was but an opera for me. Saudi justice was swift, but the "Q'uran" was the Law and the Law was the rule and the King was the Keeper of the Law. Friendships made and brothers lost only made Arabia more my home than the Flag of my birth.

In my years, Ibn Sa'ud passed on and HRH Faiasl led...a great Lion of the Desert, he led his people and along the way, he led me. When his heart stopped, the sands of the desert stopped their movement, in honor and respect for this great man among men...The Flower of Arabia so cruelly cut down, he who had brought his people into the light. My own tears and my Saudi friend's tears were one and the same. King Faisal was my John F. Kennedy...both Rulers of the people, not by force of arms, but by force of love within their hearts.

You ask me about growing up in Arabia, and grow I did...In my opinion Arabia today is not the Arabia of the Lion, but progress has changed all of us, we are now the old bedu who studies the black ribbon across the desert, which we today call a road. Progress we must, but under the King, it must be just and as a child I knew this and now as a man, I respect. Although an infidel, I have shed blood in the desert and have studied the Holy Writings, and find that, I a mere child of Arabia, have become a man of the sand...

The courtesy of the Arab, and the Belief of the Faithful are lessons we non-Arab people's could and should learn from them. I, growing up in Arabia was truly blessed by God....

MY FIRST TRIP
BACK AFTER
35 YEARS-

Having just been back after 35 years away, I lived out my life's dreams. I went to the Mansion and in the back, take a deep breath and remember the beauty of the Arabian sunset. I wandered over to Hamilton Hill and lay down and look at the brightest of stars above and remember the beauty of a stolen kiss and then in deep reflection, count the brightest of the stars above and say hello to my classmates and friends who live among the stars over the desert and look down upon the flares and us.

I walk to the third street playground and spin myself on the merry-go-round with my buddies. Dig my toes into the white sand and let the warmth of the sand and the spirit of the past well up and flow into me.

I go to Recreation and attend the Tri-D once again. Dance with a lady from the past and relive the moment when the clock stopped and the magic was all inspiring by the music of the Leaky Roof Circuit. Later I would walk her home from a stop at the bowling alley, and whisper..."never forget, you will never lose me...." After a meeting with the Saudi Aramco Public affairs people we went on a tour of Dhahran.

First stop the Dining Hall. The outside still has the original stone, but the interior was like a luby's or or cafeteria. Kings Row was the same and as we approached the recreation area, my heart began to feel the emotions of a 26 year absence from my home. We went into the Rec. area and took photos of the tennis court, where I heard the voice of Kevin Colgan yelling for me to catch the ball, and of Bill Cohea yelling to run for it, as we played, once again alongside the tennis courts with a football and shorts and tee shirts. I looked for them, but only the fading sound of their past was there. I stood in front of the theater and once again was lost as I waited for Leah Stockman to show up. The others were all in line and pushing and pulling, the movie was Haley Mills in the "Parent Trap".....Once again my escorts woke me from my musings and we went to the bowling alley. Here I truly fell under the spell of my heart as I heard Barbara Bowler, and Tom Masso and Rick Attix, and Neal Snyder, and Martha Speers and Steve Reed and all the rest talking about their best game ever and how the pin boys had to jump from Bob Gollan's power ball and why Betsy Leary fell down and how Tom Mestrezat was bowling like his Mother, when as I heard the crash of pins and automatic pin setters that I realized the bowlers were all strangers....alas, once again I had lost time in the mist of my heart.

Yet worse came as we went to the pool, and Barbara Crampton, and Charlie Armstrong were doing fantastic dives off the board and into the sparking water. There by the deep end was Doral Zadorkin, and Mary Barger and Sissy Quick and Tom Campion and Eddie Lupien, Wendy and Janice Cyr, and a host of others all Catching the water....Look out, Debbie Dirr and Dorinda Dorsey are trying to dunk Paul Huffman, and John Gasperetti was in the middle of it.

All were there the rays and watching their brothers and sisters swim. There was Bruce Golding at the teen canteen window getting French Fries with lots of Ketchup and look, there was my brother Chris, trying to put the make on some gorgeous girl, looked a lot like Stephanie Fate, but who knows. Over by the snack bar I saw Carolyn Bates, and Patty Ahrnsbrak, along with Harry Ellis and there was Cheryl Congleton, rushing back and forth.

I started to plunge into the water with a racing start and was prepared to belly flop if only these friends would see me, yet I can be thankful that the pool was empty and a wire fence was around it, and all passed by and I realized I had drifted off again and this time had actually wanted to go with them.

Hamilton House and the infamous hill approached. I stopped and walked to the side wall, by the corner where it was always darkest at night. My Saudi escorts wanted me in front for photographs, but I insisted they take it here, where I had tasted sweet lips more than once and had laid for hours watching the sky and felt the stirrings of manhood. I sat down and left this world to go home to 1962 again...I was there with several others, but it was dark and they were all together. I decided to hold My Lady and not bother the others.

Down 3rd street to school. It was time for class and I need to rush as I was late...I got there in time to stop and look at the rock, which somehow seemed smaller than when I saw it just yesterday, but the plaque still shone. Into the hallway and reality took me. I asked a lady, who turned out to be a vice-principal if I might look at a classroom. She asked who I was, and with the Saudi escorts and two Saudi Police she must have wondered. I told her I was a student and late for Mr. Goellners science class and I needed to get to class. I asked her if I might visit the old science classroom and she took me to where we both felt it used to be. I asked her if I could sit for awhile and she said fine. She told me she would be right back and took the escorts off for coffee and tea.

I know it couldn't be, but there next to me was Dave Collier, and Rita Simon and Tom Painter. In front was Mr. Goellner drawing circles on the board with chalk and behind me was Chris Mohlman, and Wendy Cyr and Barbara Gollan and Peter Speers and Robbie Sivak and Linda Snyder and Heidi Knott and Debbie Quick and in the door came Miss Crow and Miss Frey. In the back row, whispering and giggling were Donna Attix and Gail Duell and Jeanette Rebold. Looking very studious was Linda Hanschin and Nancy Johns. Look, Sally Onnen, telling me what to do about my bad behaviour...

How could they all be here, but they were....

Suddenly Mr. Goellner threw the eraser and hit me in the head..."Pay attention, Crocker, you'll need all the help you can get from your education". I spoke, "that's not fair," to which he replied, "In life, nothing is ever fair.. Don't forget it." Suddenly I felt the girl behind me shaking me and I looked up to see this strange face. She asked me, "Are you Ok ?" I never heard the vice-principal walk into the empty classroom, but the tears streaming down

5

my face must have frightened her. I told her I was fine, that some old class-mates and I had just been together again and everything was ok…I left, with a silent prayer that I thank God himself for the experience….

On my way out of camp, I saw a sight that wasn't possible. My house, #639 at the top of sixth street was still there…I stopped the driver and rushed to the house. The wall around the back yard that my Dad had built was still there. The house was the same, the hedges and trees and yard. I was ecstatic as I had been told it had been destroyed when they built the new gate, but there it was. A small boy looked out the dining room window and I thought for a moment that he was me…I touched the gate and stepped into the 60's again..I couldn't move and my heart hurt with a terrible pain…..I knew I had seen my life and perhaps the only real home I had ever really known. I knew too that I might never see it again.

Up the street I walked and to a certain lady, the wall and oleanders of your neighbors house are still there, Your house was gone, but I sat there and told you I loved you once again, as I had done so many years before….

Then on to the "walled City" and visit with old friends, whose father's I know would just grunt and growl, but who friendships I would rekindle and perhaps ask that they remember when they were kids…

Down "H" street hill with a flash and riding my bike to the school, where the memories would just stop my mind and soul for the longest minute of my life. I would touch the "rock" and wipe away the tears of the past with the knowledge of the future.

Back to recreation and on to the bus to RT, where the sand beneath my feet on the beach would take control of my soul and I would run wildly down the beach and throw myself uncontrollably into the surf for just one last touch Past my old house and back to Abqaiq where I would once again climb the radio tower, and swim in the pool and run into the fruit and veg-etable market right alongside the camp thru the old turnstile gate.

Returning to Dhahran, I would stop at the teen canteen and drink a Bebsi with Mohammad, and rush out the door to the Dhahran Pool where I would climb the High Board, and watch as the little ones dove from the small diving board and look all around and see all of you gathered there.

I would go home and see my house and go inside and smell the cook-ies Mom was making, maybe a pop sickle and then out to the main gate to Al-Kohbar to see old friends, drink Chi and Gowa and off to the loneliest place on earth, yet the most loved spot for many. I would go to the Aramco cemetery and say goodbye one more time to my classmates and friends, then off to the airport and perhaps stopping just long enough, in a roundabout way, to visit Half Moon Bay, and walk the North Dune face and stand in mute wonder at the salt water injection plant and maybe, just maybe raise my teared eyes and thank God for this 24 hours in a place called "Home".

Then meet with Aramco exec's and then out to Riyadh and allegedly leaving on Wednesday night for the USA. Don't know though, the Minister seems to think we have a lot to settle, but he has to be in Syria and I really ought to return to US, but since I came here for five days maximum and will have been here twenty days, who knows ?

Have to go find a suitcase.......

VISIT THE AMIR OF RIYADH

We then went to the Palace and met with Dr. Nasir who is the highest level civil government person below the Royal Family. I think our conversation was very productive and he was very excited to meet us and since Prince Salman Abd-Al Azziz ibn Sa'ud was still in Jeddah, took me immediately to Prince Sattam Abd-Al-Azziz ibn Sa'ud who is the Vice Amir of Riyadh and Deputy Commander in Chief of the Armed Forces. A very educated and intelligent man with a wonderful sense of humor. He made it a point to insure that I would return to "Our Home" in his words as often as possible to assist Dr. Semmari in the work at the King Abdual Azziz center. The office was magnificent, with solid gold displays and tall marble columns and carpet that you could sink a foot in. It was obvious that I was getting VIP treatment as I had an Honor Guard of four Saudi senior Army officers and two submachine gun toting escorts through the Palace to the Prince's office. We passed right by a lot of very official and serious looking men of what looked to be several nations and even two Saudi Generals in full dress uniform, all who were waiting for appointments with the Prince. I had no appointment, but the Prince had been informed I was seeing Dr. Nasir and called him to bring me. I'm sure that many of those waiting were not real happy about this intrusive American. Dr. Nasir introduced me as "Ante Amerikee Bedu" and the Prince seemed to get a kick out of this. He is a very personable individual.

What was supposed to be five minutes turned into forty-five minutes and when I left, the US Ambassador was there and had been delayed due to my unannounced visit. He gave me a look of "Who the hell is this". I introduced myself and told him I was here as a guest of the King and the Royal Family. This got an immediate response requesting I call the Embassies and meet with him later, perhaps over lunch. I declined this offer on the grounds I was leaving to go to a Bedu encampment to have coffee and tea, but would call him before I left. I wonder if I will now be allowed back in the USA?

Kahlid and Mousa, the two Saudi's assigned to escort me took me to the desert and we met with some of the old traditional Bedu's. We went into their tent and had coffee and tea and warm goats milk. They had all the connivance of home, including a tv set which got excellent reception. Although I do not smoke, I did try the offered Hookah and they had a good laugh at the coughing fit I had. The "Hubbly Bubbly" was stout to say the least. I was very relaxed and found the people to be very friendly, a tradition we have lost out on. We had our driver, Ibrehem, who by now was being called "Hollywood" by all of us as he was taking the pictures, photograph all of us together in this Bedu tent in the desert about 40 Kilometers front Riyadh. You would never have known there was a city nearby and as darkness fell, I was once again struck by the beauty of the Arabian night

TUESDAY, FEBRUARY 26, 1997

This morning we went to the Old Diryah, or old ruins of Riyadh that are very restricted. I was shown the palace of the 1st. Saud and 2 nd. Sa'ud Dynasty, before King Abd-Al-Azziz Al-Sa'ud. The ruins are uninhabited and are truly spectacular. We went into old houses, most of the ruins in various state of collapse due to their construction being mud. Some of the common rooms showed the main lobby with the old coffee and tea serving area and most of the living quarters were not much bigger that 6'x8'. They had unique drainage and water flow, set up and designed like the Roman Aguaducts. Many of the ruins are similar to major cities through the world, except that these ruins are much older. The earliest one was 1277 BC.

We then went to what was left standing of the old Palace. Both the West Palace and the East Palace, so called as to their location. The system of water suspension and the slots for smoke escape, rather than formal chimneys was brilliant.. The old Mosque here had no Prayer tower, but the downstairs room was designed for the very cold days and the roof was designed for the Prayer Call to take place the rest of the year.

The area that they had dug the mud from to build the cities is now a large field about 75 feet below the level of the main streets. It is used for grass by the surrounding areas nomads. There is one of the earliest known cemeteries with rocks, small, about hand size standing upright as markers. Kings and commoners are buried alike here. However being several thousand years old, no one really knows who was buried there.

We visited the remains of the fortress like Treasury building and saw that they had a ingenious way to protect the wealthy peoples money. The tower was so high and walls so angled that it would be impossible to climb. No door, just a rope the was pulled up and down and the people had to be brought up the side and to the top.

Having seen Pompeii I thought that it was old, but this section of Saudi Arabia had Rome and all of the European continent beat hands down. This very obviously a trading area as there were several large areas laid out as markets and the old camel trail is still visible that trailed off into the dunes and sand.

It seems as if another, albeit lessor Prince, HE Mohammed Al-Naser wanted to have me over for a traditional Saudi dinner so we met at Dr. Semmari's and went and had a quite lavish Saudi meal...I ate like a good guest, actually ate far too much and found out that I will have tomorrow morning free and will sneak off to the suq.

THURSDAY, FEBRUARY 27, 1997

Snuck out at 10:00 to the old suq of Riyadh and managed to buy several items I thought were neat. The Saudi's have an antique market that is not well known and I found a lot of very historical items. Most of the sugs have a lot of the new copper and brass, but this one had all old and original stuff. No tarnished junk.

THE SAUDI EXPERIENCE #1

I guess that many of us have felt various emotions over the years about our time in Aramco's communities. I have had several periods that I think many of you may have experienced.

In my writings I always write the humorous and add in several events, with a little poetic license but today I thought I would address my thoughts about 50 years of the Arabian time slice of my life and what I feel. This is not my normal and perhaps it is because I have been doing a lot of reflecting on my past six year history as the President of the ABI. I am going to do a little as I have time and relive the life of emotions that ran the gamut's of hilarity and rage and sorrow.

As a child I went through a lot of emotional times in particular as I was there very young and lived in Abqaiq before it even had a complete perimeter fence, which gave me a sense of vast freedom and even at a very young age, a feeling of freedom not normally felt by most.

I found that being handicapped meant nothing to the local Saudi kids from the vegetable area next to the school. I found my ex-pat young friends more interested in what we could discover in this amazing horizon of openness. Both physical and metaphysical. Old Aramco discarded trucks, aircraft and drums became bombers of the great war to free the world, trucks became convoys of water for thirsty camels and drums became the hiding places and personal "caves" for many of us. Standing on the wreckage of the old tanker that was half buried outside the Abqaiq North end, I can still see the distant far away land that we had to make it to.

The great B-24 that lay on it's belly near the airstrip, now just a memory, but recently dug up for display. It was Aramco's first flying spotter for potential oil formations. When it landed in Abqaiq it broke it's wheels and was pushed off to the sand. We spent so many hours burning every uncovered part of ourselves on the hot metal that I am sure our parents thought, and may still think we were sun addled. I even have photos of this bird bringing Santa in the very early years.

The locust plagues that I have written about before and the taste of a fried one.. Crispy critter that was for sure. Reminds me of the TV commercial, "Mikey will eat anything".

Perhaps the memory of friends like the Kulpa's, my classmates like the Romines and the Abbott's and so many others I can't even begin to list. I think that is where I found my first life steps and although my Mom always said I took a step off a cliff and must have hit my head a hundred times, I still see Abqaiq as the stepping stone of my life. I remember the great schmal that took paint off cars, blistered legs and frosted almost the entire

Aramco fleet's front windshields. The men and women of those days were true action hero's.

I remember the school and the building blocks that the Aramco shops had made for the classrooms. They were all colors, a lot of safety yellow I seem to recall and we built mighty forts in the class room. How I still to this day have a blue mark on my hand where I managed to stick myself with an Aramco blue and green with silver lines pencil that most likely had a safety saying about the misuse of pencils. I remember the lukewarm water from the water fountains and the miracle of flush plumbing. I must have flushed a commode at the school one time for an hour. Yes, I know we had these at home, but one has to realize that I was maybe six or seven and some things were wondrous to me.

I remember when a best friend got badly burned at a birthday party and how much he means to me, even today. I think about how we played baseball on the empty sand lots where a portable was to be put. How the sand burned our feet as we ran for the base. How a bat took most of Mike Reagan's teeth one hot afternoon. How sad it was when his Dad became one, if not the first American civilian advisor killed in the Viet Nam action. His jeep hit a mine as they were building a runway for relief supplies. This so long ago, but his smile still makes me grin. His Mother, still a lifelong family friend used to tell me, "I see your face cracking. It's not made of cement" when ever I pouted. Which, due to my actions was a lot back then. How wonderful it was to dash behind the water truck as it wet down the sand roads. How we would stand along the road at intervals and pretend to be shrubs and the Saudi's who were watering them from the truck would spray us as if we were little shrubs. They were paved eventually, I know.

How my Mom would go out to the alley and pick up a telephone that was on a pole and call my Dad. The whole town was on one phone line. But then, the whole town was less than one mile square. And a lot of that was the large pipe yard right in the, middle of the camp. Do you remember climbing into those pipes and sitting in the shade. Pretending they were tunnels? The seemed so big. In fact, for years the playground had a huge section of pipe half buried that we would crawl through. The swings were huge "a" frame shop built and the slide was even built from pipe and siding. Aramco shops were the makers of magic. I remember a girl named April and the tetter totters at the side of the school. She jumped off as I was at the high part. Quite a butt bumper.

How many know that the Kenworth fleet that was there in 1949 has several that are still running. Many were replaced but the shops built parts and in fact, I believe they rebuilt entire trucks. What about the taste and smell of oleanders?

I leave today with the sound of the noon whistle. I have to get home for lunch. My Dad will be waiting..........

CHEEESUSSSSS
THAT
STINKS

S o, we had two plans, one we taped magazines to every available part of our bodies right before we got on the plane in Amsterdam, and put a bunch in the pants legs of our clothes in our suitcases. I had a flight bag, and we decided to create a diversion with some really foul smelling cheese from the shops at the Amsterdam airport. So, I bought about fifteen types of cheese and put them in the flight bag. Our intention was that when we got to customs we would open our bags and slip the cheese in before opening them for inspection.

Unbeknownst to me, this cheese was VERY strong, and as we flew on in the dark, looking constantly for the Flares, things began to get a little uncomfortable in our seating area. I thought it was Kevin at first, and promptly told him that if he continued with such activity, he could sit in the bathroom for the rest of the flight. He vehemently denied any of the responsibility, so I thought that the big, ugly guy across from us was doing some serious damage to my nasal senses.

Well, in about an hour, the odor was so bad that dirty diapers were preferable to what we were sitting in. It was bad enough to gag a camel, and in fact, I was sure that some fool had brought one on board, the smell was so bad.

Well, the old hag in front of us, an ARAMCO housewife returning from a trip I guess, called the stewardess and pointed out that the two boys behind her were responsible for the extremely rude smells. This we denied vigorously, and I think even went so far as to offer to let the attendant check our butts-not real clear on that, but we were mightily offended.

They checked the whole aircraft. The engineer came back and checked vents, and even looked down in the baggage area (from what we heard later). Suddenly, the lights came on, and the captain came on the intercom and asked for everyone to please check their seat belts as we were going to divert to Cypress due to the problem with the very powerful odor that they could not locate. Well, as we were going along, Kevin decides to get one of the magazines out of the flight bag and opens it up. I damn near passed out and I think the old lady in front of us did.

Seems our cheese was the source of the foulest smell I have ever smelt. The cabin passengers demanded we be thrown out at ten thousand feet, and I thought they were going to do it, but the stewardess took the bag and flushed all of our cheese.

Now the dilemma. First, we were wrapped in Playboys and we smelled like goats. Second, we had lost our diversion and knew beheading was routine for smuggling Playboys into Arabia.

I always thought this next move was rather brilliant and used it for years afterwards coming into Arabia.

Kevin simply found a piece of chalk on the ground as we entered the customs building and marked all of our bags, which we picked up and walked right up the stairs and into freedom......

Simply another cheesy story, right...?

A CHRISTMAS
TALE OVER
THE YEARS

Reading some experiences made me want to tell a little tale. I was sitting at the computer, wonder if the AA guns would get Santa as he flew under radar to give us all a little cheer. When I read a Brats posting about the beauty of her flowers and Christmas..

The next thing I knew a huge, effervescent drop from on my cheek and in the reflection of the computer monitor I saw many things. Santa riding up a dusty dirt path on a huge camel. His "Ho Ho Ho's" heard like thunderous bells in my little mind at the age of five. He sat on a chair and called us one by one. A present you see was there by his side. The glee of each was evident that night. The image shifted, a few years and I saw Santa stepping from a USAF helicopter to deliver toys, "why Mom did he arrive this way". Well, said the wise woman, his sled was stuck in the sand and out Air Force came to the rescue. Again with the presents, boxes of sweets.

The joy of the youth, the touch of the magic. Santa had arrived and once again all was well. I saw a movement in the tear as it slowly worked its way down my cheek. There was Santa, riding a donkey. This was great fun and as now I was 11 and knew he was one of the mighty men of Aramco. He had been to a few stops to refuel his donkey and had a great time staying on board, but with great determination and spirit he gave us each from his horn of plenty. It was really a shame he had glued on his beard, I heard later he had it for awhile.

Then on through the years, Christmas was for cheers. We gather from around the globe to visit our house and see the tree and the many gifts galore. I remember as a boy getting socks wrapped up and a toy train that ran around the tree. Years later, I saw once again how much this had meant. The centerpiece of our home was at Christmas time alone. We had all grown and gone with the wind, but I must say, Mom made us come on that day. The paper would fly the cries of surprise, for what you would know, at forty two, I got the other sock.

This Christmas is different, but the spirit is there. I know that my family has put up the tree and they will gather for some cheer. My Father will smile and remember with glee, for he once had all of us, sitting on his knee. I will look at a small tree, made of ceramic and dark green. Its lights glowing like the past, present and future and through the tear drop will light up with warmth and feeling. The little tree has survived over thirty years. I got it when I was little and going away to school. Mom thought that at Christmas, it would remind me of all that is good. She got a matching one, all in white. I got a message that was addressed to me, I put it under the tree and I know it will make this a really nice day. The gift is from God and the feeling is good, my Mom is visiting and I am glad she's near. I hope she get to the house with cheer, for the thoughts of her have made this a time of good cheer. I remember the donkey, the camel the way it was once and I know in my heart that this time of year is for all of you to share in the cheer.

I had thought the images within the teardrop were going to be of pain, but they were a trip down memory lane. The trip never tends and those who have gone are celebrating with us and in us and remember that single tear? Well, it finally fell and as it did, the lights from the little tree gleamed brighter it seemed. The tear was a pleasure, and the thought of good cheer, so to all of you and to the world in whole, I really do wish a warm and safe Merry Christmas and Happy New Year and my Mom and Dad. No matter where they are, they share this day with me and the rest. May God Bless and eggnogs in the air. Be happy, be free, for in the my little tree, that's what I see....

THE MOST FAMOUS HOUSEBOY OF ALL

I always thought the Anil Barretto came to Arabia as a third world ex-pat as he was always dressed in solid whites and could get you a glass of tea anytime.

He had and still has the reputation of being a walking collection of useless information, but I have to say, you could always count on things such as seeing his most recent in color colonscopey at the reunion. My favorite was once he fell into the Dhahran baby pool and had there not been lifeguards would have drowned. Anil has been unique in many lives. A mesquito is less trouble. And he was caught by many strange people looking very funny at certain sheep. Dinner or a date I was never sure. However he did play football with us, but I think as the foot ball and to be honest, he has put up with me treating him far better than he deserved, but what the hell, his Dad was a spectacular man and after all, in all family group there has to be a black sheep. Maybe that's why the connection between him and a goat named Mildred. In one of the hottest days of history, he came dressed in a formal suit and was immediately dismissed by executive order for being out of uniform. No matter what, he has truly been my friend since he came to Arabia with Mahta Ghandi. He will forever be welcome in my tent, ahhh..bring the coffee, hammi hammi...

GOING TO ARABIA
BY WAY OF
THE SEA

The weather in Chicago in 1952 was cold and chilly. I could not understand the excitement and even at such an early age must have wondered why we were going to New York, and board a ship, "Queen Mary" and head to London, England. I mean what does a three year old know except that a ship was a huge playground. Ice decks and all. Mom and I were picked up by Aramco and had gone to 505 Park Avenue where the Aramco people were very nice. Some lady gave me a lollipop and I was in love with her. Followed her all over the offices. Mishaps this was when I first became aware of long legs and stiletto shoes. Sure looked at a lot and still feel a slight thrill at stilettos and long legs, except now only in tastefully art clubs such as "Show girls club."

Anyhow we left New York and I had a blast sliding the long ice covered wood decks when the alleged "Nanny" lost control of me. I still think there were several early attempts on my life by her as she would encourage me to slide towards the rail...hmmm...wonder even now. She was a real winner. One ugly old duck, but that may be a matter of perception as many a smack was delivered for running off and being brought back to our cabin by an officer from the bridge or a sooty old man from the engine room areas.

This may have started the life long attraction to starting things with my Mom and trying until the 1990's to outwit her. An example was in a rather high sea she took me to the bow and had me stand there and wanted to take my photograph. Now not being romantic like the "Titanic" story, all I wanted to do was see what was cooking in the kitchen but Mom insisted. The ship was rocking and rolling and the waves must have been 100 feet high, but still, a photo "for Dad" was needed with me at the bow. So I am standing there, dressed in spats of course and my Mother and about one hundred guest and ships crew are watching, seemingly with way too much glee, when all of a sudden, from the black depths of the Atlantic ocean the sea god himself raised up a wave that was about 40 degrees below zero and dropped it right on top of me and the bow almost went under. I had wondered why the crew man had insisted I have a rope tied to me and the rail. Well, a fish flopping on a wood pier in Alaska could not have been worse. And at that the gallery of on lookers were having a great hoot at this mouse that had roared into their lives getting a payback.

Mom was being supported by two ladies and over the roar of the sea I still heard that famous and long years later still the same knee breaking laughter from her.

I demanded a look at my birth certificate but Mom just roared louder. Then when I tried to use the tears routine, I got about as much sympathy as an Afleck duck in a pond.

Off with the nanny to warm up and change and meanwhile plotting to sell my early soul, which I am sure was sold many times, plotting a revenge.

Now all I had been told was that we were going to go on an airplane ride and go to a island and that Mom and Dad were getting married there and we would take a wood sail boat to a huge land that was almost all sand. I was sure they had both fell on their nut over this but had no proof.

However back to evil. I got away from the Nanny and in those days people traveled with what was called a steamer trunk and clothes and everything could be hung inside and it was great for traveling. It was also large enough for a bright young lad to be overly smart and hide in and close. Unbeknowst to me they had a self locking edge that came together and for some reason Mom had unloaded this trunk and made ready everything to travel. However the bell hop or as I had called them "Round red heads" which made them mad had not picked up all the baggage and stowed it below decks in storage areas.

They came and got this one and I had fallen asleep inside. Now I went into storage all peaceful and the Nanny started looking for me and after searching many places and not finding me, my Mom and she called the purser who called the cabin boys who called the Steward who called the Captain and a full search of the ship started.

I do believe in the history of the Cunard line the "Mary" had never stopped for such an extensive search. Finally I was found and brother, did I hear some sea going language that day. I also discovered that there is no soft place to put a butt that has been beat on round and round the long deck of an ocean liner before. I think other traveler's got involved along with that howling banshee called Mom right behind me. A crack of a fifty foot whip would not have been as bad.

Later, she held me so tight and cried gently that she was so scared that I was lost for good. I discovered that I loved more than anything this lady and right then I knew that she was my Mom.

She told me I had to be careful as I was her only baby besides loving my Dad, she loved me bestest. She also said she was not going to tell Dad as I would have to swim from the island of Bahrain to Saudi Arabia with him throwing out shark bait if he ever found out how scared I had made her. She made me cry too and I knew that our tears would always run together.

Fifty three years later I held her and our tears once again flowed together as she left on the black camel, but I only wanted to write a short Happy Valentine and as her birthday is February 22, 1922 I also wanted to say HAPPY BIRTHDAY MOM. I MISS YOU.

HAPPY DAYS
AT THE
REFINERY

It was a cold and chilly day, unusual for the furnace that I was usually in, but then that may have been the weather of Mom. Never knew so much hot air could bellow at various small innocuous things. Here's why it was cold. Santa flew by, never stopped, dropped coal all over my house and it was now the New Year. If one could call a cold day New Year in Ras Tanura. No going to the beach, although Mom highly recommended it as the water was freezing and potential sharks all over, but I had other plans.

I went by some friends and several had got bicycles from Santa the snake, and I had a red wagon. Now what fool would give a kid, without a driver license a semi motorized vehicle to try on various places. Talking Dick Burgess into going with Ross Tyler and myself, having worked out a deal that we would hook the wagon to the bikes and ride around.

Now near the refinery, there were two unguarded roads back then that traversed the salt marsh and so we went on the side that had the water injection plant water inlet. I mean after all, that water was supposed, note supposed to be warm. Carcogenic ? Didn't know how to spell the word. The intent was to ride the wagon down the sloping cement path that fed the water to the long stone moat to the Gulf. No fences in those days. The water was only a few feet deep and we were men of action. In fact I am sure that action figures for generations to come came from out exploits.. You should remember, "nah, nah nah, Fatman, err, Batman".

No one has to remember that the refinery shut down several days a year then for steam cleaning and high pressure washing and lots of technical things. Who knew or cared. We just knew that the slope was dry and the water out the injection site was low. Who needs more. Cold as a Bears butt in a polar suit, off we went to ride up and down the slope..

Many people knew that these Red Ryder red wagons had wood sides that could be put on and taken off and a metal handle with rubber wheels. Great for holding on to and going down the slope. Not wanting to get our shoes and rather small sized jeans wet, we got down to our little denim jackets, tee shirts and under wear. The following events was what Mom refereed to as the Last Hurrah of a Palm Tree without a single date for brains. Rather unusual and new comment.

All of a sudden there was this huge crash as the main flush valves were re-opened to allow the wash out and the re flow of the intake. We of course went ten feet underwater and tumbled like a sock in a washer, but managed to make it, darn near the end of the intake stone passage to shore. The force had sent the wagon to sail the seven seas with most of our clothing. I still had a tee shirt, but no jacket or underwear. The others were about the same. For a confused moment thought I was looking at a worm, then realized it was in my mind a huge sea snake. Mom didn't think so when all three of us went screaming back to out houses, much to the grand applause of hundreds of classmates and adults. I still won't eat beanies and weenies.

The worst part is that it really was cold. I thought Mom was going to literally die laughing as car after security car pulled up out front. She was just in convulsions and made a strong point to the Night Foremen (Security then) that were had gone fishing with our worms. I saw no such humor and the door darkened even worse as Dad and Mr. Crampton strode in.

Seems we three kids had breached a "red" zone in Aramco security and all wanted to know how. I demanded compensation for my wagon and got a butt blast that rocked most of the Arabian Peninsula and had a hard time sitting for many years, Still limp to this day I think.

The end result was good. Mom took pity after some hundred Management had come in and the volume of yelling was that of the mid day siren going off in my kitchen, but all's well. I got cookies. Of course I understand there was a lot of screaming down the street and across the road and grounded until 99, but still. A way to start a New Year.

ANOTHER
CHRISTMAS
TALE

Tis was the night before Christmas and all thru the house, a mother was stalking a small but determined mouse.

Faster than a speeding train, the mouse ran, for the thunder of hoofs followed close behind.

The thought was that Santa and fallen down the chimney, and meant more for the mouse, but the lady of the house a mousse pie for plans, and the mouse would soon be waving goodbye.

But this mouse was friends with a Dancer and a Dasher and some dog with ears and a red nose, so he dashed up the roof and to their side,

The Reindeer were pulling, to loosen Santa stuck in the vent pipe, err, chimney and all their strentgh could not free him for the rest of the mice of Aramco Town.

The mouse was able to get below, the witch had flown into the kitchen and the mouse was able to grab Santa's beard and pull with a mighty heave. Santa popped like a cork and toys galore, an extra one for the mouse as he headed for the door. The lady was shocked to see this fat man in the living room, but her cookies and milk and a beer or two and they were soon swapping lies about the behavior of the mouse.

WHO JUST HAPPENED TO LIVE IN THE HOUSE.

They say the New Year is the year of the OX. This mouse grew tall and strutted without fear, for the Orientals had made him an ox.

The lady of the house was not so bemused, she whacked him so hard, his tail and nose went round and round to touch, like that dumb dog that chased it's tail. However, soon it was quiet, the Ox now strapped and restrained from future endeavors before and after Christmas, and may yet still be strapped to the gurney in case Mom needed to hook him to the wall socket. Yet all in all the New Year is blooming bright.

A DOCTORS VISIT

Last night I was watching a series that I particularly like, "House" on USA. Anyway this crazed Doctor brought back some penetrating memories of a recent medical experience I survived.

Seems if the TV Dr. House put a thermometer into a Police officers rear end and then, with something akin to my experience, he went home. In his case this was TV and led to a whole series of happenings, while I on the other hand will never understand how I get my rear in strange positions.

So I am at the Doctor's office for a refill of my prescriptions and the regular Doctor is out and in comes this ambling, bent forward, white haired figure. I thought perhaps the houseboy until he says" HI, I'm Dr. Hess and I am here for your yearly physical. I cried, screamed and begged that I didn't need a physical and he seem to have a hearing problem which became very evident shortly. Seems as he was in his late 80's and still allegedly active in practice. Although I should have got a clue when he whispered in my ear on each side to see if I had any hearing loss.

Using a mallet, which had to be 100 years old he tested my reflex's, which brought tears to my eyes, but not as much as the rest of the story. I swear he could hardly pick up this hammer he hit me with, from which I now add a limp to my score of medical failures.

But on to the fun. He tells me to drop my pants and shorts (should have know better and called a Boxer rescue team). So I am here, butt naked, pants around my feet and I see him put on gloves. I offered cash, my car, someone else's first born but to no avail. With deadly accuracy for a half blind man he hit the target and the cold lifted me off my feet. Talk about an experience. Well, while he has this large finger where sunlight doesn't go, in walks this 400 pound Jamaican nurse and he yells at her, "Don't you know how to knock", to which she explained quite loud that she had knocked and so turning back to me, flapping in the wind, nurse still there and he starts wanting me, who is in a bent position, still anchored to the Doctor and starts arguing with me did I hear her. Yeah, I have a lot to say at this time and he and the nurse are still arguing about knock, knock, who's where? The nurse left and with a rather rude and hard jerk we unhooked and I almost started looking for something sharp. He writes up that I have no prostate problems, perhaps a little latex burn, but that will heal..yeah, heal my ass was on my mind.

The worst part was I could tell the nurse was going door to door to other patients reveling in the story. If he had been around much longer, I may have had to consider a new lifestyle. So he finishes and goes to leave and the nurse comes back and tells him I am the wrong patient and that I am there for my medicines that was all, all of the time she is trying with great aplomb to not even crack a smile. He has no clue and goes out. I leave and for some strange reason get the feeling that everyone knows about the whole thing as people are all deep into their magazines, some even being talented enough to read upside down.

Now one would think this was enough and I was sure on fire, but what really capped the week was the next day, I get a call from Dr. Hess and all he wants to know was did he do a prostate exam? My dog had tears in her eyes from the language I used.

Now the final chapter and clincher, no pun intended, Dr. Hess died a week later of an apparent stroke and the records were never updated so my new Doctor greets me on Friday with, "Well it seems you have not had a prostate exam for several years"........

THANKS MOM

Running like a dervish across fine grained sand in a cool morning because Mom yelled "Mike Crocker, get home now for breakfast… you'll be late for school again!!!

Thanks Mom.

Stumbling through the rough school of arithmetic when you had to count on your hands, and some used their sandals feet, It was explained to me that on my one hand I was better than all the rest because I has disproportionate sized finger and Mom said, "Well, you have the advantage because you already have fractions down. Whole, half, third and eighth. As far as your other hand you have five there too. Just two are hidden numbers".

Thanks Mom.

Tying one of my Dads huge ties around my neck and wearing a suit that was for church only, but for the 9th grade prom dance and my first date I got to wear it. The corsage made of paper and string. She told me I was so handsome and my date was beautiful.

Thanks Mom.

For when Sa'id of Security brought me home at 3:00 in the morning as a grown up returning student, hardly able to walk after a night on the town, and Mom making me eggs and toast quietly so Dad wouldn't hear us.

Thanks Mom.

For the terrible tears that racked my body when a friend had died on MEA 444 and asking "How come, Mom?" with her response that God needed then and one day I'd see them again.

Thanks Mom.

For being so proud when finally, after what seemed like years of school and mishaps, graduating from San Marcos and the hundreds of times she helped me with difficult summers and for believing in me in school.

Thanks Mom.

For the smacks, thumps, bumps and butt pops I had justly deserved which made an impression on why and why not. Even if I didn't know, or at least told her I did know it was wrong to chunk eggs at passing cars.

Thanks Mom.

For the pain and for the reassurance I got when the love of my life broke up with me. cried for days, she spoke softly and held me. She knew it would happen again and again as I grew up. Although she always reassured me there was someone for me too.

Thanks Mom.

For the times I lost a job, or was hurt on duty as a police officer or just plain needed to talk, always there and always ready to help.

Thanks Mom.

For making sure my life was filled with adventure by taking the chance in 1951 of going to Bahrain to marry a man she had met and start my life of great and glorious adventures.

Thanks Mom.

For smacking me or hugging me and loving me no matter what stupid thing I did, all the way into my 50's and still.

Thanks Mom

For the Christmas as a child where two packages were one sock each and special after shave in later years and always the required underwear under the tree when we had little.

Thanks Mom.

For waiting for me to get to you, to hold you for hours, to say "I love you" and for fighting until I held you, with tears falling as rain on you from a giant of a man, I knew you were there.

Thanks Mom.

For being a Guardian Angel riding on my shoulder now and whispering now and again, "I love you, son".

Thanks Mom.

So for all you did and the wonderful life you gave me and for so many others I want to say, with out reservation. You did it always.

HAPPY MOTHERS DAY TO ALL MOTHERS WHO ARE ALL HERE AND THEY ARE ALL WITH US TODAY. A MOTHER'S LOVE IS ETERNAL.

FDR AND KING ABDUL AZIZ IBN AL- SAUD

R oosevelt told his senior advisers after the meeting that Arabs and Jews were on a 'collision course' toward war in Palestine and that he planned to meet with congressional leaders back in Washington to seek some new policy that would head it off."

by: Thomas W. Lippman*

Everyone who watched was mesmerized by the spectacle, at once majestic and bizarre. Over the waters of Egypt's Great Bitter Lake, an American destroyer, the USS Murphy, steamed toward a rendezvous with history. On a deck covered with colorful carpets and shaded by an enormous tent of brown canvas, a large black-bearded man in Arab robes, his headdress bound with golden cords, was seated on a gilded throne. Around him stood an entourage of fierce-looking, dark-skinned barefoot men in similar attire, each with a sword or dagger bound to his waist by a gold-encrusted belt. On the Murphy 's fantail, sheep grazed in a makeshift corral. It was, one American witness said, "a spectacle out of the ancient past on the deck of a modern man-of-war." Awaiting the arrival of this exotic delegation aboard another American warship, the cruiser USS Quincy, were three admirals,

35

several high-ranking U.S. diplomats and the president of the United States, Franklin D.

Roosevelt. As they watched in fascination, the man in the throne was hoisted aloft in a bosun's chair and transferred from the Murphy to the Quincy, where he shuffled forward and grasped the president's hand in a firm grip. Thus began the improbable meeting between Roosevelt and the desert potentate with whom of all the world's leaders he had the least in common, King Abdul Aziz ibn Saud of Saudi Arabia. In five intense hours they would bind together the destinies of their two countries and shape the course of events in the Middle East for decades to come.

It was February 14, 1945. The end of World War II was finally in sight as Allied forces advanced on Berlin and fought their way toward the Japanese heartland. With victory assured, Roosevelt was looking toward the future and envisioning new security and economic arrangements for the nation he had led through twelve tumultuous years. He ventured to Yalta, in the Soviet Crimea, to negotiate the postwar world order and the creation of the United Nations with Prime Minister Winston Churchill of Britain and the Soviet leader Josef Stalin. Before leaving Washington, he arranged to stop in Egypt after the Yalta conference for brief meetings with three leaders whose role in the war was marginal but whose place in the future might be significant: King Farouk of Egypt, Emperor Haile Selassie of Ethiopia and King Abdul Aziz, then commonly known as Ibn Saud.

That Roosevelt included Abdul Aziz on his list was a dramatic demonstration of how far and how rapidly American strategic thinking about the Gulf region had evolved during the war. Before 1942, the U.S. government had no official interest in Saudi Arabia, even though an American oil company had struck oil there in 1938 and had created a small community of American geologists, drillers and engineers to deliver the oil to global markets. No American official of higher rank than minister in the diplomatic service had ever before encountered the bedouin monarch, and the king, in all his 64 years, had ventured no further out of the Arabian peninsula than Basra, in southern Iraq. His domain was impoverished, isolated and backward; its levels of education, public health and mechanization were among the lowest in the world.

In strategic terms, Saudi Arabia, though never colonized, was in the British sphere of influence; the British were entrenched in Iraq, Bahrain, Oman and the trucial states on the Arab side of the gulf, as well as in Egypt and Palestine. The U.S. official presence was minimal in the entire Arab world, and so was official U.S. interest. In 1941, Roosevelt rejected State Department advice to provide financial assistance to Saudi Arabia under the Lend-Lease program with the comment, "This is a little far afield for us!" The war changed all that almost overnight.

Roosevelt's military and economic advisers, alarmed by the rate at which the war was consuming U.S. domestic petroleum, began to see the potential long-term value of the Saudi fields, the only ones in the Middle East where an American company held exclusive production rights. At the same time the U.S. Armed Forces, fighting a global war, wanted an air base someplace in the Middle East that was not under British or French control. And Roosevelt, looking past the combat, nursed the hope that Abdul Aziz, who despite his lack of formal education and his country's backwardness was a hero in the Arab world, would somehow be helpful in solving a daunting problem that the president knew was coming: the future of Palestine and the resettlement of Europe's surviving Jews. The Nazi death camp at Auschwitz had been liberated a month before the president left Washington en route to Yalta, and the full scope of the Holocaust was being revealed to the world. The Jews had a claim on the world's conscience, and on Roosevelt's.

The United States established diplomatic relations with Saudi Arabia in 1939, but no American diplomat resided in the kingdom; Saudi Arabia was the responsibility of the U.S. minister to Egypt, who lived in Cairo and rarely ventured into the Arabian peninsula. The Saudi Arabian government, which consisted of the king and handful of his favorite sons and trusted advisers, had no representative in Washington; when Abdul Aziz wanted to conduct business with the United States, he did so through the oil company, Standard Oil Company of California, known in Saudi Arabia as CASOC. (In 1944 the name was changed to Arabian American Oil Co., or Aramco.)

Only in April 1942 did the State Department post its first resident envoy to Jeddah, a career officer named James Moose. At that time Saudi Arabia was paradoxically more isolated and poverty-stricken than ever because the outbreak of the war had shut off its oil exports only six months after they began in 1939, and had mostly halted the Mecca pilgrimage traffic that still represented the Kingdom's principal source of revenue. As the war dragged on, Saudi Arabia was experiencing serious food shortages, and CASOC increasingly urged Washington to provide assistance lest the king revoke the concession and give it to the British, who were providing him with financial assistance. British interests had opposed American oil companies' entry into Iran, Kuwait, Iraq, and Bahrain; the British lost out on Saudi Arabia when King Abdul Aziz chose the American firm, but the king could reverse himself at any time. Busy as he was with more urgent issues, Roosevelt was still flexible and perceptive enough to include Saudi Arabia in his long-term thinking.

The entreaties of the oil company paid off in February 1943. At the urging of Harold Ickes, Secretary of the Interior and wartime oil administrator, Roosevelt declared Saudi Arabia vital to the defense of the United States and therefore eligible for financial aid. As the British journalist David Holden wrote in his history of Saudi Arabia, "The great American takeover had begun."

Official contacts between the United States and Saudi Arabia now multiplied quickly, at steadily higher levels. In July, Roosevelt sent Lt. Col. Harold B. Hoskins, an Arabic-speaking intelligence agent, to ask the king if he would meet with Chaim Weizmann or other Zionist leaders to discuss the plight of the Jews and the future of Palestine. Hoskins was well received personally but got nowhere with the king, a committed anti-Zionist, who told him he would not conduct such talks himself nor authorize others to do so. The issue, however, could not be brushed aside or wished away. The stranded, traumatized Jewish survivors in Europe were clamoring for resettlement; their plight had reinforced the determination of Zionists in the United States to create a Jewish state in Palestine.

In August, Secretary of State Cordell Hull instructed Moose to ask the king for permission for the United States to open a consulate in Dhahran, the little American settlement on the oil fields along the Gulf Coast. Permission was granted the following year. At about the same time, the U.S. mission in Jeddah was upgraded to legation and Moose was replaced by a higher-ranking official, a colorful U.S. Marine war hero named William A. Eddy. Col. Eddy, who wore his Marine Corps uniform all the time he was the State Department's representative in Saudi Arabia, was to be a crucial figure in bringing the president and king together for a successful encounter.

In September 1943, two of Abdul Aziz's sons, Princes Faisal and Khalid—both future kings—were invited to Washington and were well-treated. Vice President Harry Truman put on a dinner for them at the White House. They stayed at Blair House, the official government guest house, and were provided with a special train to carry them on a sightseeing trip to the West Coast. Upon their return home, they reported favorably to their father, and also informed him that they had been told President Roosevelt enjoyed collecting stamps. That gave the king an opening to approach the president directly. He sent the president a set of Saudi Arabian stamps, then quite rare in the West.

On February 10, 1944, Roosevelt sent the king a letter thanking him for the stamps. He expressed regret that he had been unable to meet the king during a recent trip to Cairo and Tehran—a trip on which he flew over part of Saudi Arabia and conceived the idea of bringing irrigation and agriculture to the region's vast deserts—and expressed the hope of meeting Abdul Aziz on some future journey. "There are many things I want to talk to you about," the president said.

The king took this as a commitment from the president to visit, and began asking Moose when he could expect Roosevelt's arrival. The president's journey to Yalta was to provide the opportunity. Moose, by then back in Washington, claimed credit for persuading Roosevelt to meet Abdul Aziz on the Yalta journey; the president's cousin, Archie Roosevelt, wrote in his memoirs that Moose had "buttonholed everyone in State concerned with the president's trip" and when the professional diplomats were not responsive "he got someone to send a memo to the White House, and when it reached the president, he jumped at the chance for this exotic encounter." From the historical record, however, it seems that Roosevelt did not need much persuasion. He was genuinely interested in Saudi Arabia.

On February 3, 1945, acting secretary of state Joseph C. Grew cabled Eddy and the U.S. representatives in Cairo and Addis Ababa that the president wanted to see the three leaders "on board a United States man of war at Ismailia about February 10"—that is, only a week or so later. Grew's message sent off a frantic scramble to make arrangements, complicated by the need to maintain secrecy about the president's itinerary.

The president would travel to the Mediterranean aboard the Quincy, fly from Malta to the Crimea for his historic meeting with Churchill and Stalin, then reboard the Quincy in Egyptian waters for his encounters with Farouk, Haile Selassie and Abdul Aziz. The Navy's Destroyer Squadron 17, which had been on convoy duty in the Atlantic, was detached to escort the Quincy. That was the easy part of the arrangements. The hard part was delivering King Abdul Aziz and his entourage, who knew no way of life other than their own and took for granted that their habits, diets and religious practices would travel with them. Roosevelt was a wealthy, educated patrician with a sophisticated knowledge of the world; Abdul Aziz was a semi-literate desert potentate whose people knew nothing of plumbing or electricity. Yet the Saudis assumed—rightly, as it turned out—that the two leaders would meet on equal terms; Abdul Aziz would accept nothing less.

The story of how this amazing feat of diplomacy and cultural accommodation was accomplished is told principally in the accounts of three participants: a brief narrative by Eddy, "F.D.R Meets ibn Saud," published in 1954; "Mission to Mecca: The Cruise of the Murphy," a 1976 magazine article by U.S. Navy Captain John S. Keating, commander of Destroyer Squadron 17, who was aboard the destroyer; and "White House Sailor," a memoir by William M. Rigdon, who was Roosevelt's naval aide at the time. The key figure in the preparations was Eddy, who had been born in Lebanon and was fluent in Arabic. Having won the king's confidence and friendship during his first months as U.S. minister in Jeddah, Eddy was the cultural mediator between the two sides.

The plan called for the king and his advisers to travel overland from Riyadh to Jeddah and board the Murphy for the voyage up the Red Sea to Egypt. Because of wartime security restrictions, the entire plan was kept secret from Jeddah's small diplomatic corps and from the Arabian populace. Eddy accepted social invitations knowing he would not be attending the events; the king put out the word that his caravan was heading for Mecca. When instead he boarded the Murphy and sailed away, there was consternation and grief among the people, who feared he had abdicated or been kidnapped.

Knowing nothing about the king, his country or his habits, Keating and the Murphy's skipper, Commander Bernard A. Smith were understandably nervous about protocol and worried about how their crew would behave; because of the secrecy requirements, they had not been told that Eddy would accompany the Arab party and navigate these issues for them. Their only information came from an encyclopedia, which informed them that the king had many wives and scores of children, and that the consumption of alcohol and tobacco were forbidden in his presence. Their only chart of the Jeddah harbor dated to 1834; no U.S. Navy ship had ever put in there. The Americans knew that Islam prohibited the consumption of pork and that the king liked to eat lamb, but otherwise they knew nothing of his dietary preferences.

The Saudis said the traveling party would consist of 200 people, including some of the king's wives. Smith said the most the Murphy could accommodate was 10. Eddy negotiated the number down to 20, although when the king and his party arrived at the pier there were 48, including the king's brother Abdullah; two of his sons, Mohammed and Mansour; his wily finance minister, Abdullah Suleiman, who had negotiated the oil concession agreement with Standard Oil a decade earlier; and the royal astrologer. It also fell to Eddy to explain to the king's advisers why no women could make the voyage: there was no place aboard the Murphy where they could be sequestered, and they would be exposed to prying male eyes as they negotiated the gangways.

Abdul Aziz spurned the cabin designated as his quarters aboard the Murphy; he and his 39 companions insisted on sleeping outdoors, bedding down where they could around the deck. Because of the king's foot and leg ailments, he could not walk easily on steel, so his retainers spread carpets. The Arabs rejected the sturdy chairs from the Murphy's wardroom as inadequate; aboard came the king's high-backed gilt throne, in which the king sat facing the bow at all times except the hours of prayer, when he and his party bowed toward Mecca—the location of which was plotted for them by the ship's navigators. Most of the Arabs had never before seen a motorized vessel or sailed outside coastal waters, and became seasick, but not the king.

Abdul Aziz brought with him a flock of sheep, which he expected would be slaughtered en route for his meals—and which he insisted the American sailors share as his guests. Smith balked at the livestock, but the Arabs said they would not eat the frozen meat of the Murphy's stores. Eddy negotiated another compromise in which 10 sheep were taken aboard and penned at the fantail, and he told the king that Navy regulations prohibited the Murphy's crew from eating any food other than Navy rations. Surely the king would not want these fine young Americans confined to the brig over such an issue?

The king accepted that argument, but other Navy regulations were thrown overboard to accommodate the Arabs. The Saudis built charcoal fires to brew coffee, including one next to an open ammunition storage room, to the Americans' consternation. When the king asked for names of all crew members, Eddy knew he was preparing to give gifts to all of them, and he persuaded Keating and Smith to accept this breach of the rules rather than offend the king by refusing. "Explain to your superiors that it couldn't be helped," Eddy said.

But if any Americans were inclined to ridicule the Arabs or take the king lightly, they were overpowered by his commanding presence and by the determination of Eddy and Keating to deliver him to his meeting with Roosevelt in a positive frame of mind. When Abdul Aziz boarded the Murphy, Keating wrote, "The immediate impression was one of great majesty and dignity. One sensed the presence of extreme power."

The voyage of the Murphy lasted two nights and one full day, during which Abdul Aziz saw his country's Red Sea coastline for the first time. "The voyage was delightful," Eddy wrote later. "The weather for the most part was fine. The sailors were much more impressed and astonished by the Arabs and their ways than the Arabs were by life on the U.S. destroyer. Neither group had seen anything like their opposites before, but the difference is that any such violent break with tradition is news on board a U.S. destroyer; whereas wonders and improbable events are easily accepted by the Arab whether they occur in the Arabian Nights on in real life. The Arab is by nature a fatalist and accepts what comes as a matter of course and a gift from Allah."

The Americans entertained the king with displays of naval gunnery and navigational instruments, in which he displayed a lively interest. The king ate his first apple and discovered the delights of apple pie à la mode. Abdul Aziz saw his first motion picture, a documentary about operations aboard an aircraft carrier. According to Eddy he enjoyed it, but said he was disinclined to allow movies in his country as they would give the people "an appetite for entertainment which might distract them from their religious duties." His fears on this point would have been confirmed had he been aware of what was happening below decks, where others in the Arab party were delightedly watching a bawdy comedy starring Lucille Ball.

Eddy was the only person on board who spoke both languages. And yet, he wrote, "The Arabs and sailors fraternized without words with a success and friendliness which was really astonishing. The sailors showed the Arabs how they did their jobs and even permitted the Arabs to help them; in return the Arabs would permit the sailors to examine their garb and their daggers, and demonstrate by gestures how they are made and for what purposes. The Arabs were particularly puzzled by the Negro mess-boys on board who, they assumed, must be Arabs and to whom they insisted on speaking Arabic since the only Negroes whom they had ever known were those who had been brought to Arabia as slaves many years ago."

With these cultural shoals successfully navigated, the king was delivered safely to the Quincy, where the president was waiting for him. According to Rigdon, who saw the president's briefing book, Roosevelt had been given this information about his guest: "The king's three admitted delights in life are said to be women, prayer, and perfume...His Majesty has much personal charm and great force of character. His rise to power established order in a country having a tradition of lawlessness, and was partly based on astute policy and on well-publicized displays of generosity and severity according to the occasion...Any relaxation of his steadfast opposition to Zionist aims in Palestine would violate his principles...According to Arab and Moslem custom, the women of his family are strictly secluded and, of course, should not be mentioned...To a visitor of ministerial rank, he often makes a facetious offer of an Arab wife, in addition to any wife the visitor may already have."

Once the king was safely aboard the Quincy, he and Roosevelt almost immediately struck a personal rapport by focusing on what they had in common rather than on their obvious differences. As recounted by Eddy, who was the interpreter for both sides, "the king spoke of being the 'twin' brother of the President, in years, in responsibility as Chief of State, and in physical disability. The President said, 'but you are fortunate to still have the use of your legs to take you wherever you choose to go.' The king replied, 'It is you, Mr. President, who are fortunate. My legs grow feebler every year; with your more reliable wheel-chair you are assured that you will arrive.' The President then said, 'I have two of these chairs, which are also twins. Would you accept one as a personal gift from me?' The king said, 'Gratefully. I shall use it daily and always recall affectionately the giver, my great and good friend.'"

The president also bestowed upon the king another gift that would have great long-term implications for the relationship between the two countries: A DC-3 passenger airplane. That aircraft, specially outfitted with a rotating throne that allowed the king always to face Mecca while airborne, stimulated the king's interest in air travel and was later the first plane in the fleet of what would become—after decades of aviation and maintenance training by Americans from Trans World Airlines—the modern Saudi Arabian Airlines.

After this exchange of pleasantries, the king joined the president for lunch. Following Rigdon's direction, the mess stewards served grapefruit, curried lamb, rice and whatever they could scrounge up as condiments—eggs, coconut, chutney, almonds, raisins, green peppers, tomatoes, olives, and pickles. After some hesitation, "His Majesty fell to, taking several servings and eating with visible pleasure," Rigdon recalled.

When it was time for coffee, the king asked Roosevelt if his ceremonial coffee server could do the honors, to which request the president of course assented. The result was Roosevelt's first taste of the cardamom-scented brew served in tiny cups that is ubiquitous in the Arabian peninsula. He took two cups, with apparent enjoyment; only several days later did he tell the crew that he found it "godawful."

So much did King Abdul Aziz enjoy his repast that he stunned his host with an unexpected request: he wanted the cook for himself. "He said the meal was the first he had eaten in a long time that was not followed by digestive disturbance and he would like, if the President would be so generous, to have the cook as a gift," Rigdon wrote in "White House Sailor." The king meant this as a compliment, but there was consternation among the Americans when Eddy translated his request.

"FDR, always a skillful talker in a jam, explained that the cook on the Quincy was under obligation to serve a certain period of time and that the contract with the Navy, or something of the kind, could not be broken," Rigdon recalled. "He was complimented that His Majesty was pleased with the food and regretted so much that he could not grant his request. Perhaps His Majesty would allow us to train one of his cooks?"

After this exchange, the president and the king retired for a substantive conversation. That Roosevelt was able to engage the king in a lively back and forth exchange that went on for nearly four hours was a tribute to his indefatigable will, because he was ill and exhausted. The arduous trip to Yalta and the equally arduous negotiations there had fatally undermined his already fragile health, and by the time he sat down with Abdul Aziz he was only two months from death.

"Throughout this meeting," Eddy observed, "President Roosevelt was in top form as a charming host [and] witty conversationalist, with the spark and light in his eyes and that gracious smile which always won people over to him whenever he talked with them as a friend. However, every now and then I could catch him off guard and see his face in repose. It was ashen in color; the lines were deep; the eyes would fade in helpless fatigue. He was living on his nerve."

The record of what the two leaders said is remarkably skimpy, considering the importance of the event. The meeting attracted little notice in the American press at the time, Roosevelt described it only briefly in his comments to reporters afterward, and the president's report to Congress about the Yalta conference mentioned his post-Yalta meetings only in passing. The lack of interest in the press is not surprising, considering what was happening in the world at the time. Measured against the climactic campaigns of the war in Europe and the Pacific, the president's brief encounter with an obscure potentate from a little-known desert country did not appear to be a compelling story. Moreover, the participants decided that the delicate issues under discussion did not lend themselves to public ventilation, and they kept silent about the details. The U.S. government's official report on the meeting, published in the Department of State Bulletin of February 25, 1945, said only this: "The discussions were in line with the President's desire that the heads of governments throughout the world should get together whenever possible to talk as friends and exchange views in order better to understand the problems of one another." It did not say what views were exchanged.

Various American officials in Roosevelt's traveling party picked up bits and pieces of the conversation afterward, but most of what is known about it comes from two sources: the brief memoir by Eddy, who as interpreter for both sides was the only American other than the president who heard it all, and an official joint memorandum prepared at the time by Eddy and Yusuf Yasin, a Syrian advisor to the king, which became known to the public only when it was declassified 25 years later.

The president led the discussion; as his guest, Abdul Aziz initiated no topics of conversation, waiting to see what Roosevelt wished to discuss and then responding. Eddy's account emphasizes that the king asked for no economic assistance and the subject was not discussed, even though at the time his country was suffering widespread hardship and even famine because the war had cut off its sources of revenue.

Roosevelt came straight to the most urgent point: the plight of the Jews and the future of Palestine, where it was already apparent that the governing mandate bestowed upon Britain by the League of Nations twenty years earlier would come to an end after the war.

"The President asked His Majesty for his advice regarding the problem of Jewish refugees driven from their homes in Europe," according to the joint memorandum. "His majesty replied that in his opinion the Jews should return to live in the lands from which they were driven. The Jews whose homes were completely destroyed and who have no chance of livelihood in their homelands should be given living space in the Axis countries which oppressed them."

Roosevelt said Jews were reluctant to go back to Germany and nurtured a "sentimental" desire to go to Palestine. But the king brushed aside the argument that Europe's surviving Jews might be fearful of returning to their homes: Surely the allies were going to crush the Nazis, break them to the point where they would never again pose a threat, the king said—otherwise, what was the point of the war?

"Make the enemy and the oppressor pay; that is how we Arabs wage war," he said, according to Eddy's narrative. "Amends should be made by the criminal, not by the innocent bystander. What injury have Arabs done to the Jews of Europe? It is the 'Christian' Germans who stole their homes and lives. Let the Germans pay."

The king—from whose country Jews had been expunged during the lifetime of the Prophet Muhammad twelve centuries earlier—said that "the Arabs and the Jews could never cooperate, neither in Palestine nor in any other country. His majesty called attention to the increasing threat to the existence of the Arabs and the crisis which has resulted from continued Jewish immigration and the purchase of land by the Jews. His Majesty further stated that the Arabs would choose to die rather than yield their land to the Jews." The public record contains no indication that the king saw any contradiction between his belief that the Arabs of Palestine would rather die than give up their land and the fact that some of those same Arabs were selling their lands to Jewish buyers.

Charles E. Bohlen, a prominent American diplomat who was a member of Roosevelt's official party, wrote in his memoirs that the king also raised another point about Palestine that is not mentioned in Eddy's account or the joint memorandum. "Ibn Saud gave a long dissertation on the basic attitude of Arabs toward the Jews," Bohlen wrote in "Witness to History." "He denied that there had ever been any conflict between the two branches of the Semitic race in the Middle East. What changed the whole picture was the immigration from Eastern Europe of people who were technically and culturally on a higher level than the Arabs. As a result, King Ibn Saud said, the Arabs had greater difficulty in surviving economically. The fact that these energetic Europeans were Jewish was not the cause of the trouble, he said; it was their superior skills and culture."

Other American officials traveling with Roosevelt said in their various memoirs that the President seemed at first not to understand the rigidity of the king's opposition to further Jewish migration into Palestine, and brought up the matter several more times, eliciting the same negative response. The President then raised an idea he said he had heard from Churchill—resettling the Jews in Libya, which was far larger than Palestine and thinly populated. Abdul Aziz rejected this notion as well, saying it would be unfair to the Muslims of North Africa.

"His Majesty stated that the hope of the Arabs is based upon the word of honor of the Allies and upon the well-known love of justice of the United States," the joint statement reported, "and upon the expectation the United States will support them."

In response to that, Roosevelt gave the king the famous promise that would become the cornerstone of U.S. policy on Palestine for the next two years, until his successor, Harry S Truman, repudiated it by endorsing the partition of Palestine by the United Nations: "The President replied that he wished to assure His Majesty that he would do nothing to assist the Jews against the Arabs and would make no move hostile to the Arab people" and that his government "would make no change in its basic policy in Palestine without full and prior consultation with both Jews and Arabs."

On April 5, just a week before his death, Roosevelt restated that promise in writing. He sent a letter to the king under the salutation "Great and Good Friend" reaffirming the "full consultation" formula and his promise that he "would take no action, in my capacity as Chief of the Executive Branch of this Government, which might prove hostile to the Arab people."

The king was gratified by Roosevelt's promise, but he also made too much of it. As Eddy noted at the time, Abdul Aziz took it as a commitment of the United States, rather than as a personal pledge from its current leader. "In the conversation the king never seemed to distinguish between F.D.R. as a person and as President of the U.S.A.," Eddy noted. "To an absolute as well as a benevolent monarch, the Chief and the State are the same." The king's failure to understand this distinction accounted for his outrage and disappointment when Truman endorsed the postwar partition of Palestine and recognized the new Jewish state there.

Upon his return to Washington, Roosevelt would tell Congress that "On the problem of Arabia, I learned more about that whole problem—the Moslem problem, the Jewish problem—by talking with Ibn Saud for five minutes than I could have learned in the exchange of two or three dozen letters," but he did not specify exactly what it was he had learned. As one of his senior aides observed sarcastically, "The only thing he learned was what everyone already knew—that the Arabs didn't want any more Jews in Palestine."

After giving the king his "full consultation" pledge, Roosevelt broached the idea of an Arab mission to Britain and the United States to press the argument against Zionist aspirations because "many people in America and England are misinformed." The king replied that such a mission might be useful but "more important to him was what the President had just told him concerning his own policy toward the Arab people."

The conversation then turned to Syria and Lebanon, where the Arabs feared a liberated France would seek to reassert control after the war. Abdul Aziz asked what the U.S. position would be "in the event that France should continue to press intolerable demands upon Syria and the Lebanon." Roosevelt replied that France had given him written guarantees that Syria and Lebanon would be granted independence and he intended to hold the French to their promise. "In the event that France should thwart the independence of Syria and the Lebanon," he told the king, "the United States Government would give to Syria and the Lebanon all possible support short of the use of force."

Then the president turned the conversation in another direction entirely. He raised the possibility that Saudi Arabia could develop agriculturally with irrigation and proper farming techniques—the vision that had inspired his interest in the country during his flight over it after the Tehran summit conference in 1943.

The idea was not so far-fetched as it might have sounded at the time. An American team led by the engineer Karl Twitchell had identified areas of the country where irrigation was feasible, and a team dispatched by Aramco was growing useful crops on the royal experimental farm in al-Kharj, where its pumps were pulling up large quantities of water from underground.

"The President spoke of his great interest in farming, stating that he himself was a farmer," according to the joint memorandum. "He emphasized the need for developing water resources, to increase the land under cultivation as well as to turn the wheels which do the country's work. He expressed special interest in irrigation, tree planting and water power which he hoped would be developed after the war in many countries, including the Arab lands. Stating that he liked Arabs, he reminded His Majesty that to increase land under cultivation would decrease the desert and provide living for a larger population of Arabs."

"I am too old to be a farmer," the king replied. "I would be much interested to try it, if I wasn't too old to take it up." He thanked the president for his interest, but added that "He himself could not engage with any enthusiasm for the development of his country's agriculture and public works if this prosperity would be inherited by the Jews." This was little short of paranoia—there were no Jews in Saudi Arabia and none were proposing to go there. There is no record of what Roosevelt said in response, if anything.

It is evident from the accounts of participants and witnesses to this meeting that the American president and the Arabian king, as different as two men could be in language, religion, education and knowledge of the world, liked and admired each other and struck up a personal rapport. Their mutual esteem delivered to Roosevelt one of the most important and least expected outcomes of their encounter: a tactical and strategic victory over Churchill, who hoped to keep Saudi Arabia within Britain's sphere of influence after the war, despite the king's decision a decade earlier to give the oil exploration contract to an American firm.

Churchill was surprised to learn at Yalta that Roosevelt planned to meet with Abdul Aziz after that conference, and in Eddy's words "burned up the wires to his diplomats" to set up a similar encounter for himself. He got his meeting, and arranged for the king to return to Saudi Arabia aboard a British ship rather than an American one, but the results were counterproductive because the king found Churchill arrogant and disrespectful, on matters great and small.

Whereas Roosevelt had respected the king's wishes and refrained from smoking in his presence, Churchill did the opposite. As he wrote in his memoirs, "If it was the religion of His Majesty to deprive himself of smoking and alcohol I must point out that my rule of life prescribed as an absolutely sacred rite smoking cigars and also drinking alcohol before, after, and if need be during all meals and in the intervals between them." He puffed cigar smoke in the king's face.

On his homeward voyage, the king found the British Navy's food unpalatable and its officers dull; they did not match the Americans' entertaining gunnery displays. And while he was delighted with Roosevelt's gift airplane, he was displeased by the Rolls-Royce automobile he received from Churchill because the steering wheel was on the right. That would have required the king to ride on the driver's left, a position of dishonor, and he never used the car.

Upon Eddy's return to Jeddah, the king summoned him to a private meeting at which, Eddy reported to the State Department, he praised Roosevelt and disparaged Churchill. "The contrast between the President and Mr. Churchill is very great," the king said. "Mr. Churchill speaks deviously, evades understanding [and] changes the subject to avoid commitment, forcing me repeatedly to bring him back to the point. The President seeks understanding in conversations; his effort is to make the two minds meet, to dispel darkness and shed light upon this issue." And the king concluded: "I have never met the equal of the President in character, wisdom, and gentility."

In his report to the State Department about this conversation, Eddy added an important detail about the king's meeting with Roosevelt that was omitted from the joint memorandum. The king asked Roosevelt what he should say to Britons who argued that his country's future lay with them, not with the United States, because America's interest in the region was transitory and would dissipate after the war. He said the British told him they would be responsible for security and international communications in the region and "based on the strength of this argument they seek a priority for Britain in Saudi Arabia. What am I to believe?"

The British had a point; at the time their influence prevailed throughout the Arabian Gulf region, but Roosevelt's vision saw beyond this residual colonialism. He told the king that his "plans for the post-war world envisage a decline of spheres of influence in favor of the Open Door; that the United States hopes the door of Saudi Arabia will be open for her and for other nations, with no monopoly by anyone; for only by free exchange of goods, services and opportunities can prosperity circulate to the advantage of free peoples." That was much more to the king's liking than the British line, for his greatest fear as he opened his country to the foreign technical help he needed was encroachment on Saudi sovereignty and he was suspicious of British designs.

In his audience with Eddy back in Jeddah the following week, the king again brought up his irritation with Churchill, who he said had tried to bully him about Palestine. In his report to Washington, Eddy gave this paraphrase of the king's remarks:

"Mr. Churchill opened the subject confidently wielding the big stick. Great Britain had supported and subsidized me for twenty years, and had made possible the stability of my reign by fending off potential enemies on my frontiers. Since Britain had seen me through difficult days, she is entitled now to request my assistance in the problem of Palestine where a strong Arab leader can restrain fanatical Arab elements, insist on moderation in Arab councils, and effect a realistic compromise with Zionism. Both sides must be prepared to make concessions and he looks to me to help prepare the Arab concessions.

"I replied that, as he well knows, I have made no secret of my friendship and gratitude to Great Britain, a friend I have always been ready to help and I shall always help her and the Allies against their enemies. I told him, however, that what he proposes is not help to Britain or the Allies, but an act of treachery to the Prophet and all believing Muslims which would wipe out my honor and destroy my soul. I could not acquiesce in a compromise with Zionism much less take any initiative. Furthermore, I pointed out, that even in the preposterous event that I were willing to do so, it would not be a favor to Britain, since promotion of Zionism from any quarter must indubitably bring bloodshed, wide-spread disorder in the Arab lands, with certainly no benefit to Britain or anyone else. By this time Mr. Churchill had laid the big stick down.

"In turn I requested assurance that Jewish immigration to Palestine would be stopped. This Mr. Churchill refused to promise, though he assured me that he would oppose any plan of immigration which would drive the Arabs out of Palestine or deprive them of the means of livelihood there. I reminded him that the British and their Allies would be making their own choice between (1) a friendly and peaceful Arab world, and (2) a struggle to the death between Arab and Jew if unreasonable immigration of Jews to Palestine is renewed. In any case, the formula must be one arrived at by and with Arab consent."

However accurate the king's forecast may have been, it was destined to have little impact on events in Palestine because five months later Roosevelt was dead and Churchill had been voted out of office. It would be left to others to decide the fate of Palestine. If anything, the king's entreaties to Roosevelt on this subject had negative results for him, because the president's later comments about how much he had learned from the king stimulated influential American Zionists to redouble their efforts.

Neither the joint memorandum nor Eddy's 1954 account of the meeting, "F.D.R. Meets ibn Saud," contains any specific agreements or commitments by the United States or by Saudi Arabia, yet the impact of their afternoon together was far-reaching.

In the estimation of Colonel Eddy, who knew the Arabs probably better than any other American of his generation:

The Guardian of the Holy Places of Islam, and the nearest we have to a successor to the Caliphs, the Defender of the Muslim Faith and of the Holy Cities of three hundred million people, cemented a friendship with the head of a great Western and Christian nation. This meeting marks the high point of Muslim alliance with the West," he wrote. The people of the Near East, Eddy added, "have hoped and longed for a direct dealing with the U.S.A. without any intervention of a third party. The habits of the past which led us to regard North Africa and the Near East as preserves of Europe were broken at one blow by Mr. Roosevelt when he met the three kings in the Suez Canal in 1945. There were immediate practical results as well, beginning two weeks later when King Abdul Aziz declared war against the Axis powers. Roosevelt and Churchill had told him that doing so was the price of his country's admission to the new United Nations organization that was being formed, but it was not an easy decision for the king. According to H. St. John Philby, his longtime adviser and confidant, "Ibn Saud shrank from the unseemliness, not to say the absurdity, of declaring war on Powers already doomed, with whom his country had no quarrel. Yet in the end he yielded to the diplomatic pressure of his friends; and Saudi Arabia joined the ranks of the belligerent nations in name, if not in fact."

Over the next year or so, the king authorized Aramco to build an export pipeline from Dhahran to the Mediterranean coast to expedite delivery to European markets. He approved an arrangement by which the U.S. Air Force was allowed to operate the air base at Dhahran that the Americans had begun building during the war, and he accepted the deployment of a U.S. military team assigned to train young Saudis in airfield operations and maintenance. As soon as Congress authorized it in 1949, he accepted a full-fledged American military training program. Overcoming his longstanding suspicion of foreigners, he gave Trans World Airlines permission to land at Dhahran on flights from Cairo to Bombay.

And even though Roosevelt died shortly after the meeting, the course he had set of friendship with and assistance to Saudi Arabia continued under Truman. In 1946 the Export-Import Bank lent the Kingdom $10 million for public works and water projects. The U.S. Geological Survey sent a team to look for water and mineral resources. The U.S. diplomatic mission in Jeddah was upgraded to full embassy status. In effect, the strategic and economic partnership that would bind the United States and Saudi Arabia for decades afterward took root and flourished in the aftermath of the landmark meeting of the two countries' leaders.

Roosevelt told his senior advisers after the meeting that Arabs and Jews were on a "collision course" toward war in Palestine and that he planned to meet with congressional leaders back in Washington to seek some new policy that would head it off. He did not succeed before his death two months later, but the strongly favorable impression he had made upon the king of Saudi Arabia limited the damage when that war did break out in 1948. Despite his anger at Truman, the king did not revoke the Aramco concession, terminate the U.S. air base agreement, or take any other action to retaliate against the United States. Under Roosevelt's spell he had cast his lot with the United States, and there it stayed.

THE FLYING CAMEL

In reading what so many have written about the Aramco planes my story was a little different. My Dad was in Kingdom from 1944 in Jiddah and sent to work for early Aramco in 1949. He was in the US and was at Wesley Memorial Hospital for an old wound and met my Mom in 1951. I was born in 1949 and my Mom and Dad had divorced, as they said for "economic reason." Anyhow Mom and Dad fell in love and Dad returned to KSA and Mom and I took the train from Chicago to NYC and boarded a Pan Am Clipper "Flying boat" to Bahrain.

My Dad was waiting along with the Knowles, the Kulpa's and a bunch of others and we went to a hotel and Mom and Dad got married in Bahrain. Then we went by Dhow to Al-Kohbar and drove to Abqaiq. The portable was still on railroad ties with steps and we were right across from where the school was to be built and expanded.

We also flew on the DC-3 s of Aramco with the stopovers except the seating configuration was six rows of two seats and several small cabins like on trains, with fold down beds. I remember actually sleeping on the fold down and then as my family grew I was sleeping on the floor under seat with a blanket. The little cabins had two seats also. So we kids sat on the bunks which when folded out had seat belt to keep us from rolling out of the beds.

I still have in my Aramco collection a tan blanket with Aramco on it. They had brown and blue.

I and my family have certificates of flying around the world on the Pan Am clipper boat ships to many exotic places and I also remember vividly flying on the Aramco "Connie" for at least two trips to the USA from Dhahran.

Jennifer Herbert while riding a horse near Abqaig in later years found an old Aramco B-24 that was WWII issue used by Aramco for oil exploration buried in the sand off and old Abqaiq runway. It has been recovered and is being restored by the Kingdom.

One last story, How many of you remember "The Lady Be Good" bomber found, I belive in the Tripoli desert fully functional and just out of gas. The machine guns still were live and the coffe was supposedly potable. The crew had bailed out and left a rock arrow to point the direction they traveled for help. One was found impacted in the ground with chute still attached. It was thought they were thing they were over water. Amazing enough, one crew member's body was found 27 miles inland in the very heavy dunes by oil explorers years later. Had they walked to the opposite way they were less that seven kilometers from an oil facility and road.

A DATE, THEN A MARRIAGE, THEN ALL HELL BREAKS LOOSE

Hearing from Randa about her escapedes with Vicki Muzika brought back some sneaking out memories I also had with Vicki. We started dating in 9th grade and I saw her as a returning student before her parents left the field and I can relate to the sneaking out bit. One night I went to her house and to her bedroom and knocked on the window.

She answered and we sneak out to her back yard which was dark. We discover puppy love and I really fell for it, and therein lies many adventures best left in the shadows, in particular of Hamilton Hill, rear down slope area....

Anyway I was standing at the window helping her out and didn't notice my feet were tearing her Mom's flowers all to pieces, but you remember our camel boots? Well mine being the size of a camel hoof did a lot of floral rearranging. Anyhow the next day, after sneaking her back in at daylight and knowing I had to go to my first class with Miss Fry, I did pay hardily for these little digressions, but any how I was called out by Mr. Dickerson the vice principal to see my Mom and Mrs. Muzika waiting. We had to go to their house and they matched my hoof prints and I got to replant a lot of what I considered weeds, however Mrs. Muzika considered award winning flowers.

That year Vicki's family left Dhahran and it took me fifteen years later to find her again by Earl Greaves telling me he had seen her at Kent State. I finally found her in a little town in Colorado and ten days later we married. I have another story or two that I had wrote when chat first started, but don't know where they are now. Anyhow one told of our romance which unfortunately ended after a short marriage as she said, "Mike, you still are in love with a fifteen year old cheerleader, and I have changed over the years."

She was right but we had a great 11 months of bliss before reality and the world made the sun go out. None the less, flowers have to this day been a great delight to me when I see real pretty ones. Takes me back to hours of crawling around re-planting what I will never see as flowers.

Such skies and tenderness, never forgotten and never again.

MY BIRTHDAY, OHHH HAPPY DAYS

At 12:01 am, the 16th of May, there rose such a clamor, someone should have taken a hammer.... but I am giving myself credit here. I wrote this in 1996 and since I will be celebrating my birthday I thought Id tell the story again.

It was a wonderful May in 1959. We were living in Ras Tanuara and we always did something to out do each other on our birthdays...So, I felt that when I got up that morning, it was PARTY time. Here I was, a stud TEENager, and I knew that it was time to plan the BIG one.

After school, which went quiet for some reason, other than Mr. Goellner hit me with a eraser from the chalk board because I was dropping my pencil repeatedly, trying to peek at something, I don't remember what. Seems they were white tho...anyhow I yelled out Thats not fair to which the ever right Mr. Goellner said IN your life, as you know it, Nothing is ever going to be fair . That did it, I bravely shot off my mouth and challenged him to a wrestling match at gym that afternoon. I was a big guy and I knew this old gezzer teacher was going to learn, you don't screw around with a TEENAGER, by golly. The rest of the day was filled with much bravado and how Id kick butt and be a living legend...

Gym, somehow that word stills chills me....Miss Crow was there with the girls class, who were supposed to be playing volleyball and it seemed to me that there were a lot of others around I didn't recognize. I still think Mr. Dickerson bussed in the other districts schools for this World Wrestling Match.

So on to the mat and Mr. Goellner assumed the position, down on all fours, me with one arm on his elbow and the other across his back. He then does something that gave me great cause for some real serious consideration of my wisdom...He put one hand behind his back, grabbed his pants and said With one hand...Some fool, probably Miss Crow, yelled wrestle and BAM!!! I was upside down, shorts around my neck, jock strap to the wind and pinned in a pretzel hold, which gave me room to break wind and die of embarrassment.

To make matters worse, for the next five years, at least once a year I took him on, and lost every time to one hand....

Things rapidly degenerated, Mom had planned a birthday party and so some ten or twelve of us got together at my house and and Mom brought out the cake. Gave Mighty Mike the knife and I went to cut.. I used every way I knew how, wanted to get a chain saw, but to no avail...Mom had made the cake from the foam mattress of a pillow and frosted and decorated it..So much for outsmarting Moms...After that we decided to climb the hedges around our house and chase one another. These hedges were about seven feet tall and three feet wide. Ross Tyler was running, and still claims I pushed him, but off he went into Moms cactus garden..off like a banshee he went around and around the house...Mom trying to tackle him, me in hysterics on top of the hedge and his butt on fire..Finally, after presents and real cake and ice cream we all left and I was walking Dick Burgess home when we passed a large penned up area, that ARAMCO had built..

Now you know what that could mean, so over the fence we went...and much to our amazement, there were some fifty cages with all kinds of desert animals..Gazzelles, jackels, large dogs, and a various grouping of others. My immediate thought was this isnt right, so out with the trusty Boy Scout knife I had just gotten for my birthday and I cut holes in all of the fencing and let all of the animals go. Someone sure was pissed as it seems these were being made ready to send to a zoo in Riyadh for the King..how was I to know, put a damn sign up, of course there may have been a no entry sign, but who read all these signs anyway. Would have got clear on this one, but some big mouth friend talked at school the next day and I went round robin to all of the offices of Aramco. I think I had to even apologize to people just coming to Aramco and having just got off the plane.

But, it wasnt quite over.....OH no, I had to go one better..so I called a couple of girls and two guys and we met in the shed out back of my house to play strip poker. Our only knowledge was that every time you got an ace you had to take off something. We boys were smoking cigars and maybe a touch of white. I had mentioned to Mom that the guys and I were going to play cards in the shed, she being an all wise and knowing witch, took all the face cards and aces with out my knowing...So after about four hours, in sweltering evening heat, all still dressed and turning blue from cigar smoke we finally figured out the problem..That was that, we all went home and even now, if I listen carefully I can still hear Mom laughing for hours.....

This birthday, thirty four years later, I toasted Mr. Gollner in the evening sky, Thanked God for my Mom and Dad, and went to bed, in quiet reflection of my glorious youth....

Thanks Mom, for having me...

POOL HOPPING

When I was a returning student in 1968 there was an incident that I have thought of for years. I have often wondered how I managed to get in so deep by doing nothing, as all know I would never attempt confrontation with Aramco Security.

Seems as if five or six of us decided to do a pool hopping race around Dhahran. Now there weren't a lot of private pools, but we managed to take a phone book and mark the ones we knew about. The idea was to jump the fence, strip down, skinny dip across the pool, dress and dash on to the next pool.

We were going to end up at the main pool at recreation. Well, as one, might expect, bright lad and lassies that we were, no one bothered to actually check and see what, or if these people actually had pools. So off we go and we hit the Lupiens house first, HA!!!!A pool about 20 feet in diameter and five naked Olympic medalists trying to swim it across it and getting all tangled up. With all the confusion of getting dressed a shoe or such got left behind. Tom who was fastest took off up the hill and jumped the next yard hedge. We all followed suit and here was a real pool. Dashing like stalled

Dolphins we went across it and lights came on and here we are jumping and dancing for our lives, butt's abare and all and off we go.

By now, someone has called Security and S'aid was hot behind us. We hit two more pools on the hill and started towards 6th street. We knew Polly Robinson had a pool and her house was next. The problem with Polly's pool was that it was tile and slippery. Talk about a ruckus. I do understand that a pair of delicates was found the next day and perhaps we should have realized that we were telling on ourselves as we went around to the drag leading to recreation. One more pool we thought of and over the brick wall down by the Goellners house and the screams of agony were heard in Bahrain like you would not believe. A damn WADING pool??? I am still amazed that no one broke the backs or arms or legs. But we tore it up, that was for sure.

So off we head, now with the lights of Security all around and we are into the game of "starlight, star bright, try to catch us tonight".

Many people never knew that there was a small pool right next door to the Reed girls and we hit it with a vengeance knowing that we were within sight of the big pool at recreation. This pool was about ten feet long and was designed for a person to use as a single lane training pool. What we did know, naked and one after the other we swam it, that the boys were winning. Think a pair of drawers was found at the bottom of the pool the next day.

Suddenly and without warning as we are hopping and jumping around dressing to hit the main pool trucks come from several sides with lights ablaze. We mighty mice caught in the brilliance of their spot lights and bright beams. ZOWIE, we were gone. The girls, being much wiser stayed behind the last fence and snuck home.

We three men of orient bare, headed into the trap of there...ok, so no poet, but we knew no matter what the main pool had to be hit. Over the fence, knocking over the guard house at the gate and whooping like crazed Indians into the pool.

The first shark hit about two minutes later and soon the swarm of feeding frenzy of parents, mad pool owners and Security were upon us. The pool overhead lights are on and here were three are. Rather shamefully in an exposed position and to the merriment of all, many a rude comment on young boys was made. We crawled like a sea turtle on hot sand to the shower room, and there met with Mr. Kieswetter and a few imposing people. We thought we might deny it, but what fools we were to not remember that Mom's always sewed name tags into everything. The evidence was overwhelming and we faced the news of recreation being so far off limits for us for the rest of the summer that we might as well have gone to RT and swam in the gulf.

Best of all, the girls had got home, and when awaked, they looked so innocent and in unison, "Those boys must have stole our things to get us in trouble". I actually heard the skin crack on S'aid's face as he grinned from ear to ear on this one.

So to KK, BB, and another, may you're shorts never be left behind again.

Damm, that was a long summer and my last as a returning student.

ADVENTURES IN ARABIA

My adventures in Saudi Arabia began when I was in first grade. The thirteen years that followed were some of the most memorable times of my Life. However, there is one memory that stands out from the others.

My parents loved to get away and go camping in the desert. As chance may have it, we stumbled upon this extraordinary Turkish fort halfway between Udhailiyah and Riyadh. With my three siblings, we let our imaginations guide us thorough the different rooms of the abandoned fort. The mysteries hiding in the shadows of the fort faded as we were embraced by the impressive blackness of the night skies. To this day, I have never witnessed such brilliant stars as those that night. It seemed as if you could reach out and grab a handful.

It was morning as our trek across the desert continued. We left the main road, turning right at the old pile of tires, and followed the trail. We'd driven about fifteen minutes when steam began pouring out of the hood of our car and we sputtered to a stop. The vastness of the desert slowly became evident. It was my younger brother, who saw it first. It appeared to be a lone white Toyota pickup truck. Through the heat of the sands it inched forward, and there, pacing behind, with no chain or rope attached, was a camel frantically trying to keep up. As the truck neared, it became evident why this camel was following the Toyota; there was a baby camel sitting in the back! As the truck made its way towards us we could see the smiling faces in the cab. The weathered face of a seventy year old man sat calmly in the passenger seat, as his younger driving companion pulled the truck next to ours...to our surprise she was a woman!

My father had tinkered with the suburban for an hour before it began working again. In our broken Arabic we had exchanged small talk and extended an offering of ice-cold Miranda's to our visitors. The old man insisted on returning the favor, inviting us all back to their home for tea. We assumed they lived near Riyadh since that was the closest city. But to our confusion he kept using the word for "tent". We followed them a few kilometers and sure enough, they were Bedouins. Their desert home consisted of a huge tent with one side drawn up—goats and children all around. They offered us sweet tea, dates and some sort of a hardened goat milk curd. Their hospitality was unsurpassed. They even allowed us to take many pictures. The moment was magical.

As we were preparing to leave, the father's forty year old son arrived. It seemed like a jovial conversation between my father and the other two men, with hand gestures and broken Arabic proving to be an amusing sight. However, when the hand gestures included fingers pointing at me, then some camels, then to me, then to my father...I realized...at sweet sixteen, I was being bartered for two camels and a goat! With a nervous grin, my father assured me nothing would come of it. Although our new friends invited us to join them for a kapsa, the sun was beginning to set and we needed to be on our way. It's a memory that sticks close at heart though. Cultural bridges were crossed that day in a way that few will ever experience themselves. What an honor to have been there.

A CHRISTMAS TALE OVER THE YEARS

Reading some experiences made me want to tell a little tale. I was sitting at the computer, wonder if the AA guns would get Santa as he flew under radar to give us all a little cheer. When I read a Brats posting about the beauty of her flowers and Christmas..

The next thing I knew a huge, effervescent drop from on my cheek and in the reflection of the computer monitor I saw many things. Santa riding up a dusty dirt path on a huge camel. His "Ho Ho Ho's" heard like thunderous bells in my little mind at the age of five. He sat on a chair and called us one by one. A present you see was there by his side. The glee of each was evident that night. The image shifted, a few years and I saw Santa stepping from a USAF helicopter to deliver toys, "why Mom did he arrive this way". Well, said the wise woman, his sled was stuck in the sand and out Air Force came to the rescue.

Again with the presents, boxes of sweets.

The joy of the youth, the touch of the magic. Santa had arrived and once again all was well. I saw a movement in the tear as it slowly worked its way down my cheek. There was Santa, riding a donkey. This was great fun and as now I was 11 and knew he was one of the mighty men of Aramco. He had been to a few stops to refuel his donkey and had a great time staying on board, but with great determination and spirit he gave us each from his horn of plenty. It was really a shame he had glued on his beard, I heard later he had it for awhile.

Then on through the years, Christmas was for cheers. We gather from around the globe to visit our house and see the tree and the many gifts galore. I remember as a boy getting socks wrapped up and a toy train that ran around the tree. Years later, I saw once again how much this had meant.

The centerpiece of our home was at Christmas time alone. We had all grown and gone with the wind, but I must say, Mom made us come on that day. The paper would fly the cries of surprise, for what you would know, at forty two, I got the other sock.

This Christmas is different, but the spirit is there. I know that my family has put up the tree and they will gather for some cheer. My Father will smile and remember with glee, for he once had all of us, sitting on his knee.

I will look at a small tree, made of ceramic and dark green. Its lights glowing like the past, present and future and through the tear drop will light up with warmth and feeling. The little tree has survived over thirty years. I got it when I was little and going away to school. Mom thought that at Christmas, it would remind me of all that is good. She got a matching one, all in white. I got a message that was addressed to me, I put it under the tree and I know it will make this a really nice day. The gift is from God and the feeling is good, my Mom is visiting and I am glad she's near. I hope she get to the house with cheer, for the thoughts of her have made this a time of good cheer. I remember the donkey, the camel the way it was once and I know in my heart that this time of year is for all of you to share in the cheer.

I had thought the images within the teardrop were going to be of pain, but they were a trip down memory lane. The trip never tends and those who have gone are celebrating with us and in us and remember that single tear? Well, it finally fell and as it did, the lights from the little tree gleamed brighter it seemed. The tear was a pleasure, and the thought of good cheer, so to all of you and to the world in whole, I really do wish a warm and safe Merry Christmas and Happy New Year and my Mom and Dad. No matter where they are, they share this day with me and the rest. May God Bless and eggnogs in the air. Be happy, be free, for in the my little tree, that's what I see....

There is an interesting story about the little porcelain tree. Aramco had a bunch brought in to the toy sale for bachelors, but by the time they got their numbers to get in all were gone. I am sure people got them else where also, and I have a green one and my Mom had a white one. She fell broke her hip and broke her little tree. Knowing I am a sentimental fool she picked up every piece and over a year rebuilt the entire tree. It was our thing. Now my little tree gets out of a strong box, wrapped in Aramco airline blankets and I screw in the light. When the light goes out, Mom has said Christmas is over now. Her tree was destroyed later. I didn't get a chance to get it. You can get replacement lights at Hobby Lobby and I think they sell a much newer version of the little tree, but mine is smooth and branches are more rounded then this one, still, 35 years ago…Merry Christmas Mom. I'll bring my little tree with me for you.

A LITTLE HISTORY
OF THE LIFE OF
SAUDI ARABIA

The next area of interest I'd like to share is Tarut Island which lies in the sheltered bay of the same name. The island is now approached by a dirt, perhaps paved now, causeway. Formerly trips had to be made by Dhow. The island is somewhat circular in shape and had four villages located on it. On the southern end is Darin, on the northern coast is Zor, a mile or two south was Sanabis while a mile or so inland was Tarut.

The most prominent landmark is the old Portuguese fort situated on the jebal overlooking the village. The rounded towers are particularly interesting. On the side of the jebal was an artisan spring that was restricted to women only. Fencing and young men on the outside discouraged any other visitors. The spring is free flowing and deep enough for swimming if you care to jump the five to eight feet down to the water level. About 8 feet under the surface of the water large blocks of quarried stone are in place, apparently to form a retaining wall. Due to the spring men are not allowed to climb the Jubal. There has been only one attempt, an archaeological excavation of the site and that took place when Dr. Geoffrey Bibby of the Danish Exploratory Team was allowed to dig a trench 6'x3'x3' at the base of the jebal not far from the spring. He was limited to two hours but found Neolithic flints and shards of Ibid pottery. As of 1973 he considered this to be the oldest site in Saudi Arabia and contemporaneous with Dilmun on Bahrain.

Tarut Pirates, Part II The donkey water wash is a popular attraction where they are washed in drainage water from the Women's Spring.

Darin is the most interesting. The Islamic poets waxed lyrical over the "masks of Darin" which indicated it's extensive trade with India. Tarut has indications of thousands of years of habitation and certainly it flourished as much as what Dilmun found to be so on Bahrain when that extinct city was trading with the Hellenic world.

The island was once a stronghold of the Persian Zoroastrian religion whose devotees worshipped fire. In the 7th Century AD the inhabitants were converted to Islam, but soon reverted back. This situation was soon corrected by Abu Bakr, the successor of Mohammed, who forcibly reconverted them and this time the job stuck.

In 1915 Darin was the site of the signing of the Treaty of Darin, by England's Sir Percy Scott and Ab'dul Al-Azziz Al- Sa'ud, in recognition of Al-Sa'ud's sovereignty over the Al-Hassa and Najd tribal areas. This was when Ab'dul Al-Azziz Al- Sa'ud completed his consolidation of the scattered warring tribes and founded the Kingdom of Saudi Arabia.

A colorful character of the time was Rahman ibn Jabir who was a member of the prestigious Utaybah tribe from which the rulers of Kuwait and Bahrain claim descent. He sailed forth from the fort of Darin and a second fort at Dammam and can be, without a doubt, called a pirate. He loved to tweak the British noses as they were trying to get rulers to protect the supply routes to India and the British were constantly getting leaders to sign treaties. This wily brigand played a game with the British, not attacking them, but not signing anything, thus causing great consternation among the "proper" British.

Rahman, a truly ugly man, as accounts of his physique are that he had only one eye, face covered with saber scars, claw like hands, and one arm that hung limp. As true to piracy and it's own code of honor, he died in 1826 when fighting a Bahrain adversary he elected to blow up his ship, himself and his son, and crew rather than surrender. An authentic case of putting your money where your mouth is.

The other truly great Darin personage is Abdal-Wahhab, whose ruined home still stands, overlooking the gulf. It is interesting to go into the ruins and the windows seem low but if you kneel, as in you would expect to do in the majalis, you get a perfect view of the gulf and Darin.

Addal-Wahhab was one of those romantic types who pined and sighed after his lost love instead of the old "other fish in the sea" philosophy. Having lost his great love to another(A pirate perhaps) he retired to his majalis bewailing his cruel blow, such as "my love is like a precious pearl, a lost soul, a bride of the sea..."But, had he been different, many tales and lore from his writings would never have happened and history would never know.

The causeway is from Qatif near directly south of Rahimah...and for those of you there, the Saudi Coast guard now keeps a large air flotation, propeller driven armed vessel stationed there to watch for unscrupulous Brat Scuba divers looking for some of the finest spear fishing in the world......
That's it for History 101.

Incidentally, for those of you who have not recognized these historical works, "The Jawaan Tomb, Jebal Shimali, and now Tarut Island" they were published in 1973 and were written by selected members of the ninth grade of 1965 on field trips with Mr. Bill Goellner....Those of you who were there with me, remember as I do....this was living history.

We were bright once, were we not ?

"BAHRAIN OR DEATH!"

Seemingly bright young lads, well educated, allegedly brought up knowing right from wrong. Protected from the world by a sense of security and never having even the faintest idea of risk should perhaps have known better. However, for the RT Pirates of Penance, as we became known, none of the above could be applied.

In a period of time, long, long ago, in another galaxy called Aramco, there was another planet that needed attention. It was a mystical land that was known only from the wonders we had heard from our Mom's and Dad's at parties. It was called "Bahrain" and the only way there was to sail the mighty seven seas to reach it. And this should seem so improbable for three bold men of this bygone time?

Sailors three, we were not, but with a strong will, weak minds and wayyy too much time on our hands we got the idea of making a raft and sailing to this land of Oz.

After all, we knew from tales that the water wasn't deep and hadn't we just heard that a secretary, Ms. Florance Chadwick from Aramco had successfully swam the English channel? Well, with puffed out chests, like banty roosters, we just knew if some girl could swim like that, we three, taught by the master of the sea, Captain Ed, would not have a problem.

So managing to gather as much wood, and learning to dance like wild Indians on the hot sand as we tried to drag the massive timbers, most likely equivalent to a two by four, to the waters edge, we used rope and our scouting knot tying skills to tie together our Queen Mary. This was a really great time as one of us would accidently tie the other to the raft, or worse untie the rope and the wood would pull apart spilling us in the depths of the two foot sea.

With great design skills, several thousand feet of Aramco's bailing string we finally managed to get a raft with sail. Now, no one told us that Bahrain was off the coast near Dhahran, for crying out loud. Here we are setting sail from RT.

Interesting enough was that fact that we set out around noon. Now unbeknownst to us, the tide went out about that time and here were are, about twenty feet from shore with great expectations of seeing "Bahrain" in a few minutes and we hit bottom. Whatttt? Well, the tide was a lot faster then we were. So we are stuck, twenty feet from shore, madder than wet jellyfish and thoroughly disgusted.

Ohhh, did I mention we were so bright we had used our t-shirts to make the sail and managed to sunburn all the way from the hairline to the toe line? The only part not burned was the butt line and that was fixing to be corrected at home when I, with the anger of Captain Ahab broke out in a sailors mouth at dinner about my horrible day of exploits. Which earned me a smack or two, a bar of soap in the mouth and a VERY through cease and desist order from Admiral Mom and a look that would have sunk our raft from Dad. "Don't you have a brain?" "Did God forget and give some donkey your brain and you his?" were a few of the more relatable sage advice comments. My brothers simply sat there waiting for the thunder to pass and to enjoy the storm.

Needless to say, the next day, back at the beach we can not find our "Clipper ship" Did she sink? We wandered out and found no trace. Of course, does the saying "Time and tide wait for no brain dead boys" have any significance here?

Well, about four thirty, sitting at home, dreaming of the land of honey and spice, a dark cloud rolled over RT. Thunder and sirens went bananas. Three boys running up and down the walls of the house looking for escape, although at the time not knowing we had just managed to cause a major alert. By sheer good luck, our raft had floated down to the salt water intake of the refinery, about half sunk and been sucked into the intake of one of the cooling pumps. No serious damage, as I tried later to explain at my final meal, but enough to cause the pressure valves to close off and shut a few things down.

At this point, the refinery guys just pulled out the wood and all would have been fine, until some real eagle eyed night foremen saw what he later described with a gleam in his one eye, a marking, as if the cloth had some sort of lettering. How many remember when Mom's took great pains to put your name in everything. Alas it was so. And of course, the only still readable was some Crocker or some such.. "Why Me?", I yelled in question, It must have been Chris (My brother). Mom only grinned, a look that had been known in the past to take paint off moving cars, and said, so nicely. "Pack, you are moving to the Rub Al-Kahli and being placed for adoption with a wandering Bedouin tribe."

At dinner, all was quiet, and here I could have got out of it all just by eating. But NOOO!! My Dad was one of these tough guys, and he knew that I could not eat spicy food, as was proven a few years later on PIA. So he had Mom bring out the bottle of Jalapeno's that he had been saving for, ohhh, at least 300 years. And ate one and said with a charming smile, "Want one Mr. Tough Guy?" Well, I knew I had to act fast, he was challenging Marco Polo here. A boy of bravery that would have sailed away, but I also knew to eat one would most likely kill me, so I said, "Well, if you're so tough, eat that black one on the bottom of the jar first!" He dug it out and looked at it and popped it into his mouth. Well, most Texans can tell you, that Jalapenos that are sealed for many years will soak into the mother of all Jalapeno's and be one HOT sucker. So Dad begins sweat, much to my glee. Soon his eyes are beginning to bulge and pop, the sweat is rolling down his face and he is red as a beet. I am by now uncontrollable, laughing and gasping for breath, on the floor and practically paralyzed, not thinking this could become a permanent position. Worse, each brother has their heads hung in prayer for my passing which they felt was imminent.

Mom walks in with the boiling fondue pot, thinks Dad is having a heart attack, knows I'm dead already and screams, my brother Kenny stands up, Mom spills boiling oil on him, he screams like a banshee, I am almost passed out and will never be able to take a deep breath again my sides hurt so bad, and Dad is now looking to me like the devil with flames pouring from his ears, steam form his nose and a maniacal laughter as he says, with a voice of total doom that turned all there into ice, "YOUR TURN BOY!".

You could have heard the proverbial tree in the forest fall, with no one to hear as all the stunned silence settled over the frozen tableau of my life as it ended in a flash.

Needless to say, I will be applying for parole again this year, having been turned down for forty years of being grounded, but I might as well. God, it was good to watch Krakatoa ieee Dad go off.

T' WAS THE NIGHT BEFORE CHRISTMAS, QUIET AS A MOUSE

All through the house, not a normal creature caroused. From out of the window, I did hear a sound, tiny feet trampling Mom's flowers into the ground.

I screamed out a warning, away Steve, away Ron, be gone Tom and be away Jeff, But to no hope, the had awoke Mrs. Claus .Her fury knew no end, for she had helped Santa assemble the bike, instructions all in Japanese, and her comments were worthy of a sailor at sea…I Dashed to the door, trying to out dance her but quick as a wink, she hit me with the sink. I knew it then, Christmas was about to begin.

She had hit like a Blitzer and I moved like a Comet making my escape to the outside. I passed by the tree, caught my foot on a string of lights, and fell on my face. The train that ran around the base, shot at me as Mom grinned and gunned the transformer. A scary thought of my days at an end. Hit by an HO freight rounding the bend. I thought for a moment that I was on top of Donner Pass and she was about to make mincemeat of me. I was so tangled up, I couldn't out prance her. The tree was trembling and I thought it would fall, but with a wink, I was out and shot down the hall.

When all of a sudden, I froze in the cold, for there at the end was Santa of old, who looked more like a bear. He had no wink and I tried to think. The only way out was run for the door. My brother was awake and had found his gift, A bow and arrow set, makes a lot of sense. He aimed at me as I flashed before his eyes, but his arrow of Cupid went wide and believe me it was a sight for sore eyes. Mom with an arrow struck on her nose so red, I thought, what the hell, she can pull my sled.

bellow. The camp was awake and full of cheer as she chased me with the vigor of a ten year old, and much to my dismay, she was passing Syeed in his truck, and did he have a look. Security could not catch me for I was gone in a flash, but Mom's are different, they breathe fire and the steam from their ears is from a boiler made to last.

My friends had all fled, home in bed, making snoring sounds that would waken the dead. I know of this because I knew if caught, I would be vinison for the table with bread.

I hit Christmas Tree Circle and found to my horror it was a dead end. I raced around as a thousand camel race, but I knew if I didn't hide quick, a stick and coal would become ornaments of prominence, and not under the tree, but stuck in various parts of me.

And then up above, with a star so bright, I thought for a moment, "It's alright". The quiet was great and I hid under a crate, but peace on earth was only a phrase in a song, as Mom smacked my head and it rang like a gong.

She grabbed an ear, and I felt true fear, but as we approached the house there seemed to be a moment of reverence, as I pleaded, "Hey Mom, it's Christmas you know!" From out of the mist, it looked as if the three wise men had arrived and would save me from a fall. However when they got a lot closer, I knew them all. Easter may never arrive. For in front of my eyes, wide with surprise was Mr. Dickerson, Mr. Kieswetter, and Mr. Crampton, three men that had crossed swords with me often. I knew it couldn't be, for they said they were the spirits of Christmas Past, Present and Future, which was all rolled into one. They confirmed a rumor I had heard at school, If I was caught, they would show me my errors and I would look like a fool.

Imagine my great surprise and I looked into their eyes. For each had been over to the house and it was such a shock, for they were there, not to punish, but to share the greatness of this time of year.

I woke with a start, and most likely a fart, but off like a raging saluki I went, to the tree for gifts to get. It was a Christmas of wonders, the tree so bright. The gifts were galore as each sock was wrapped tight. I was there before the rest, as I knew it should be, for I had to count, double for me. I found a small gift and thought "why not, so I opened it up and found with delight, a Swiss army knife, with all it's delights.

The knife has a tale, and it may well be the "Tales of the twelve days of Christmas" that I may sing, however the knife is another story and Christmas was in being.

My brothers awoke, found gifts all around. A wondrous time was held, while Mr. and Mrs. Santa stood silently in the bright light from above that seemed to glow about them. The greatest Christmas, we were all one.

So I start off the season, I guess for a reason. It is close to the magic and memories must relight, snow babes and Nativities are stories I will write to delight. To one and all and to all in one, I wish you all Merry Christmas, and a season of delight.

THE POOL
HAS WATER!

Well, after burning my rear on the steps leading to the patio snack bar, all due to a very good friend I had little to say to Sebastian, the lifeguard. I have always believed he knew little English and that was.. "You, out, thirty minutes!" I do know that I was visible impressed that steam was coming from my backside as the baggy suit dried out. Ever notice how the alleged "tie" strings stretched when they got wet.. Well, thus an adventure.

I was back as a returning stud, err, student. Working for Polly Robinson in Student Recreation and taught swimming in the late afternoons. By the way. several peoples remarks about Capt. Ed are fairly accurate.

My learning experience with Captain Ed, years before was on the RT beach and the waves were tsunami height and he grabs a chubby arm, flings me airborne and I splash down like Apollo and promptly head for the bottom going "Auuuuuga, Auuuuga, as the submarine I had become. The waves slapped my tail on the sand and I had my first experience of wave "bashing" a favorite sport of retarded older students I thought at the time. You lay there and "body surf" to the shore, waves smacking the fire out of you and talk about pounding sand up your a—. Well I learned very quickly that when

Capt. Ed said, "One over the other and kick" that was the extent of class. I was to reach the ability to not only crawl toward shore, from the depth of about ten feet, but to hold my breath extraordinarily long. I did finally get the hang of it after he had shot putted me out to sea repeatedly.

However I digress. So here I am in my outasite all black swim trunks with the damnest mesh netting inside. Let me tell you about wrapping up things in fish nets, and that was all inside my suit. Later found out that what Jock Straps were for, but not until Charlie Armstrong caused me much anguish. My God, was there ever a more deserving person for an Olympic Medal than Charlie. In his red speedo suit, which I always thought a Band-Aid covered more, however the rows of girls lined up to watch him and his unbelievable dives indicated that one of two things was happening. He was one hell of a diver, or they were all praying mighty hard on that suit coming off. I personally think he had it glued on.

Now how hard can it be to dive. So off I go to show my skill. I get on the board start bouncing. Hey, I like this, and suddenly I am way up there and on the way down, the board returning from its depressed position and my butt made a tremendous impact, which flung me straight up and out. The problem was that the stupid tie string was loose, the impact dam near tore off my suit and as I shot upwards, the resounding smack of my butt and the all metal board was heard in Udaliyiha. If not the wonderful scream from me. However worse yet to come, of course. I flew out and stated to tumble, not a one and a half, more like a cannon shot that failed. I grabbed my suit with both hands, now at the ankle level and completely somersaulting over with legs askew and pure horror and embarrassment managed a 9.0 belly flop, sans suit right in front of Wendy Cyr who was sitting on the edge sunbathing. Well, to say the least my language was spectacular and Sebastian made me "Time out" on the steps.

I had a swimming class of some 40 cub scouts that I was teaching that afternoon, so after a lot of face saving hiding in the shower room, I skulk back out to the pool and there I had a couple of little ones side kicking when Chip's Mom came along. Now I do believe her exact words were, "Here, drown this" but perhaps it was to teach him to swim. I want to say something here that many of you may not have ever known. "Chip Nobles" is one of the finest Brathood ever turned out. His family came to Arabia as Aramco's first Black family and a lot of people treated them poorly. For this I apologize, but until I met Chip and his Mom, I had never seen a Black person, along with snow so maybe it wasn't so unusual.

However Chip and his family were wonderful to me. I called him "Chocolate Chip", and I say that with a very deep warmth in my heart. At the time such a comment was never a slur. He was my special guy in swimming because his mother had told me that she knew I could teach him. He also today, stands head and shoulders above a lot of other friends of all sizes, shapes and colors I know. Anyhow, the little turd learned to swim. Like a fish I might add. I used to walk him home and his Mom always had cookies and such.

Back to the day of disaster, unusual for me I know. That night Aramco had a major value break and the pool drained almost completely. However Peter Pestoni, Me, Tom Painter, Debbie Dirr and a few others decided to go pool hopping and skinny dipping. Well we snuck over the fence by the canteen and Peter dashes to the board, buck naked, does a magnificent one and a half and we hear an almighty smack and scream from hell. He had hit in less than four feet of water. I thought he had been killed. We called the emergency number and he ended up with a few broken bones, but I still remember that magnificent dive in the dark and the unearthly quiet after he hit. Then the scream. I ran all the way home naked as a jaybird so scared. Forgot clothes and all. Remember Mom's sewing names in everything? Well, Naji, Recreation Supervisor was able to read quite well. Two weeks, no recreation.

But...and as you might guess, there had to be. Here comes the Tri-D swim meet. I am swimming against Kevin Colgan and a couple of others. I thought, no big deal, Kevin is a matchstick and I'll power swim away. It was a three lap race and we all had the racing dive down pat. Many a red chest on that one. So "Bang" goes the pistol, I slip and fall in, Kevin does a perfect racing dive, went too deep and scrapped his chin on the bottom and we both stand up, see each other and take off like banshees to the other end.

What a sight that must have been. I know we passed RT and Abqaiq was still waiting on the edge for the signal to go, being deaf and all. The water was churning like a feeding frenzy of sharks and we blasted our way to the deep end, somersaulted around, kicked off and shot to the other end. Our wrists must have hit the pool edge within microseconds of each other. The water looked as if two destroyers had plowed to shore and I won't say who won, but that race went down in swim meet lore. The record set that day has yet to ever be broken and is or was still recorded at recreation. What a glorious day. The sun was out, the crowd cheered, the mighty had swum and all due to a small man, named Captain Ed. may he forever be teaching little Angels to swim.

One last thought. Captain Ed was a real hero, Not many people know that a tanker caught fire and he made repeated trips out there in little more than a canoe and brought back in badly burnt crew members and a few years later was hauling TNT to shore and the load exploded blowing the back end of his boat off, yet he still got his crew to shore. That boat was the one that laid on the shore on the left side (ocean) on the way to Sandy Hook in RT for many, many years. I personally played inside it and I still feel the magic of this man.

After seeing "Jaws" I now check under the bubble bath in the tub before getting in, but there was a day.......

"WALK LIKE AN ANGEL, TALK LIKE AN ANGEL".. MY PRINCESS

While it may seem there is a message here, the real point of my tale below is for each and everyone of you to come to the ARAMCOBRATS,INC. 1999 ATLANTA REUNION. The story below is an example of why I will always go and if not for the story, I would still go because all of you, each and every individual contributes in some way to the memories of a common bond. Our life in Saudi Arabia. See YOU there!

LOVE

Elvis's music still touches me in a way that I can only remember the blazing furnace of true love, puppy love, first love did. I would like to invite you on a trip. A trip of love and loss and hope and despair…So for those of you that are burdened by a hardened heart, or a cold soul, please forgive me as I lay out my "Rose of Arabia" saga. She "Walked like an Angel, Talked like an Angel, and in my eyes, she was my Princess in disguise."

Let me take you back in time, through the mist of life and the patterns of choice and let us once again stand on the heated sands and star blanketed skies of our youth, in a land of magic and passion like the desert movements.

Singing and whispering through the eons of the loves it has seen come and go, forever touching the depths of the dunes, and breaking with the crests of the sea as the two meet together, sand and water. Then separate, as I did with my Princess, in the nights of Arabia, only to find and lose again centuries of life later.

For it was the middle of February, the month of love, in the year of 1962, a year blessed by Allah that I first saw her standing there. Her eyes were like saucers and the intensity was unfathomable. You could read her heart, and hear it beat all in the flash of her eyes, which made the moons blaze off of Half Moon Bay pale by comparison. I know, for I never again recovered from the Depth of her.

We were but youngsters, and talked throughout the late evening and pass dinner and on into the opening of God's eyes in the form of a trillion stars, a million points of love developing as two small figures, took one another's hand and the squeeze was felt throughout the land. Even the mighty sands quivered, for it knew. A love was born and a new star rose. My Arabian Rose, My Princess.

What did we know about passion, we were so young? We knew our hands turned sweaty and then, as if a light from afar called our lips together, the lightest brush, for we knew not fully what a kiss was. Yet I do remember the thirst in my heart and the drink of her kiss. Never again was I to feel the heat and coolness, the rush and the excitement, all at once and forever. I don't think either of us knew what had happened.

We didn't have a chance as things were against us, or so it now seems. A childish prank by some of our young friends, they built a "church" and as we walked in they said "Now you have to get married, for you can never be apart again". We quickly parted and said, "Stop", for this is not how we wanted. The others got mad and told their parents and their Father, being a so-called "good man" called her house and told her Dad. Then called my Dad and the world came asunder for my Princess and I. She was told never to see me and I was told I was placing my Father's job at risk. We never even had a chance as May was upon us and she was away for school the next two years. I stayed on and finished the ninth grade, then away to Military School having never heard again. Others came and went, but the intensity was always short of the eventful night, when the earth and heavens shook." Catch a falling star and put in your pocket…"

One last time, in the waning days of summer in 1968. An opportunity came and went again. We walked home from the bowling alley and spoke for hours in her yard. Once again that magic called Arabia worked its spell and her kiss made me feel as if I had fallen into a well of crashing passion and warmth.

For some unknown reason, we were too late; we were separated once again by fate. I traveled far, met the elephant and looked him in the eye, while she walked another road, one less daring than mine. Her life was not perfect, nor but not knowing where to look.

I then found all of you, Houston 1995. I once again came alive and I knew I Was home. She wasn't there, but I heard of where. So later that year, when Santa was near I sent a card, but was not to hear. For I did not know it, but she had tried, the call was lost. As this time it was I who was back in my beloved Arabia, and had not looked back into her eyes. Upon my return, the Aramco Brats to form and order to come from chaos. For this chaos was what brought me back and as such, brought me to my Princess once again.

I got in touch through another and found out she was there and we saw one other. Life has its tricks and can deliver mighty hard kicks, and this was one. I was able to talk, and for many months, the marvel of electronics made us as one. Her honor intact, for we never crossed the line, for my Princess's is married and happily, and that's fine.

Chandler's reunion was a land of Oz. Many remember the land of sand. When the desert of Arizona became the desert of Arabia and one had become the other, we knew. Thus we talked and the events of what happened in our life became clear. Until the Reunion, we both never knew the story. Each thought the other had done something wrong. I can now shed my tears, because she was still so dear. However Honor and Duty, Integrity and Fidelity remained the order of the day. For she is happy and that was always our way.

Her Knight will always ride hard, his Princess knows he will always be there. Then the sands of Arabia and the boundaries of life are but a prelude to the future, where all things may come true. I tell this tale, not looking for anything, yet perhaps to wish each and everyone the chance to experience what I did and the magic of what the ARAMCOBRAT REUNION and the desert song did for me.

This is my reason for all of us, for the Brats to remain alive and the Memories to flow, for without this, I feel like I have no soul. So I thank each and everyone of you, for you have given me back what I had lost, and now the beast within me may rest, for it knows it's worth. So come to the reunion, one and all.. It is the place of marvels for although life has moved on, for a short while, we may once again be alive in the shadows of our youth and the agelessness of our time. To my dear Princess, as I said eons ago, our friendship will always be there, just as you know.

DEATH OF
MY PRINCESS

To the people I know and to those that were there in the land of the whispering dunes, the singing sand and the stars that came to the earth at night so bright and the best welcome any of us ever got upon arriving home from school, the flares from the air.

The Black Camel has visited us once again and this one is too much for me. I have to say that in the summer of 1968 I found a love that blossomed for the summer and disappeared as I went blindly and boldly into a world and life that was like a Spain's Galleon without a rudder. To run ashore with a tearing crash and a horrifying loss on the rocks of the death of love. That wreckage today floats ashore on the Ras Tanura beach, part by part, mostly of my heart.

Can you remember the soft lips of a young kiss, the exquisite touch of a soft caress, the beating of two hearts that knew not what was really happening and the immortal touch of lying and holding one another on the side slope of Hamilton House hill? Well, I do and the memory is what the shell of what I have left will lose any form of feeling of sanity and only live in the the memories of swatches of life in a movie like fashion where I never got to edit and therefore lost most of the movie.

I so vividly remember the smell of Lilacs and Jasmine and the softness of the ground and in particular, the aura of the glow of the softness of her hair, the sweet honey of a kiss and the sweaty grip of life in holding hands, One time in forty years did I see my Princess and I wrote about it in my Memories of the Chander 1997

Reunion. Those words will be engraved on the crumbling ruins of my heart and soul. At that time we were once again back on Hamilton Hill and the world was alive again. Unfortunately her honor was so very important for both of us that we held hands and softly danced at the reunion, but never was the soul of my dear Princess or her Knight ever compromised.

The last I got was a sweet note telling me that I would always ride the roads of this earthly plain as her Knight in shining Armor and she signed the small scrap of paper, forever in my heart as "Your Princess"

Tonight the tears that flow are a path for the Black camel, bathed in gold and diamonds to follow to her place with our brothers sister and friends who have carved a spot in God's acres called Aramco Heaven. My Mom and Dad, brother and friends will all be there, The Black camel shall walk with pride for he carries the greatest of a man's existence. His love.

She once again is wearing the jeans and tennis shoes along with a golden Abayiah that shrouds her in blazing brilliance as the candle of love in a living heart slowly flickering and dies, leaving only the smell of a wisp of the past.

I, on my knees do not know how to call for the strength to stand. The pool of tears is a lake of sorrow and the depth has torn me apart. I once, in 1997 on a trip to home buried a small jar with two gold Arabic name rings intertwined into the face of the great North Dune at the old Half Moon bay. Someday, they will be found and considered the heart of Arabia. So maybe some will understand the foolishness of a broken heart and the why some suffered so much. All I can say now is that I will place a Golden heart with two names by the Kaaba in Mekka and hope that Allah will see the love under His will. I will say good bye now to my Princess, Martha and hope that her life as she choose was a beautiful experience and that she was happy.

For all the rest of you, touch your loves heart once again and remind yourselves, of what you have and will have again if your heart is alive. For in this Princess passing, I did too in my spirit.

She had a good husband and good family and instead of being a speck of desert, she will always be a full blown desert sand rose of love.

"WHOAAAAA DONKEY"

A white tee shirt, tan shorts, white socks and tennis shoes. This was the only way to survive in Ras Tanura during the hot summer days. There seemed to be a lack of enthusiasm for anything except to pass by the mail center and look for that damn green flag. I think it was so hot that even the flag had bleached itself white. I remember the boards laid across Persian Gulf Blvd. (How many remember that name?) They laid the boards because the tar road surface was bubbling in spots and was very soft

So for the Fourth of July Aramco had a Donkey Softball game. They had planned a night game and before the game, they let the kids play a game. Thus the beginning of the end and all because the adults wanted to warm up the donkeys. At least that's how I thought. The general idea was that we were on donkeys and play softball...Soooooooooo, pitcher up!

The first batter was Dick Burgess and he had on his safety hat and was sitting on a weather beaten old hag of a red henna colored mare. The ball came dropping from a high angle of pitch and "smack" right between the donkeys ears. Well, this startled the mare and Dick had taken a mighty "Casey at the bat" swing and missed, in the process throwing his bat out into the infield and throwing himself forward to where he swung completely over the head of the donkey and is hanging upside down with his legs around the donkeys neck and worse, he is holding her ears as a bridle. This mare gives him a real meaningful eye and the next thing you know, a scream from hell is let loose, parents are running to the home plate to help and the donkey is grinning from having bit ole Dick on the shoulder, which caused him to let go and the donkey simply walked over him.

To make matters worse, Susan Maloney is on a grey stud out in the infield and the thrown bat smacks the donkey she is on in the tail and off he goes. Straight out into the road way and bucks poor Susan off into the gooey, yet warm, not hot tar. As might be expected, she now has a head of tar and steam. Into the field she comes and Dick takes a mighty kick to his behind and goes somersaulting into his parents who all fall in to a crowd. Right where the mare had left a large souvenir pile for them. Manure everywhere. This off course, caused several others to topple off of their donkeys in full gut busting laughter and no one can quite get a grip.

I now know what donkey nonchalance is. They all seemed to just sit back and bray. After all, this had to be a memorable donkey event for them too.

OK, so we are all back in place. Ross Tyler is up to bat, in comes the high toss and Ross smacks one out into left field. Now all he has to do is get his donkey going and get to fist base. HA!, no such luck. This sucker ain't going anywhere. Ross is kicking it's sides with windmill like movement and the donkey promptly sits on it's haunches. This just tears it with Ross who see's the others have not got their donkeys out to the ball yet, so he slides of and grabs the tail of the donkey, throws it over his shoulder and pulls mightily.

The donkey looks around at him, makes a partial stand and "POW" both hooves planted firmly on Ross's tail end, there is a great woosh of air and Ross goes airborne into the crowd of adults with his tennis shoes still where he was standing, looking a little forlorn. Ross sits up and is yelling beyond belief and in his hand is a thick amount of donkey tail. The donkey starts running and a bunch of the others all start off too. Kids are falling off, under, over and behind . Various donkeys and Arab herders are running everywhere with canes smacking donkeys and kids, adults are either scared to death for their kids or having seizures from laughter and spilling all kinds of liquid on the ground.

Then come the final coup d'crap.... While all of these kids are running to their parents and people are yelling at the Arabs from the announcers both, the one really ugly, rather heavy lady, and I won't say who's Mom she was, starts yelling at the kids that they are all at fault. She is about as mean as a wild camel and smelled like one with her forty seven kinds of perfume.

So it seemed to an innocent young man. Remarkably looking a lot like me, who took a large handful of donkey pile and unceremoniously high balled into a beautiful arc right on to her. To say the noon day siren was loud is to say a mouse breaking wind in a hurricane was loud.

Did she ever go off…I must have run twenty miles that night. I still don't believe she cleared the ball field five foot chicken wire fence, but not only did she clear it, but with room to spare. Talk about fleet of foot. I was off like "The Flash" and she was a "Flashette". I made it up to the row houses above the open field, and was not even slowing down when I hit the first row of hedges. She came through them like a tank at Normandy storming ashore. I think along the way she had picked up a palm frond and had stripped all the leaves off it and was teaching it new tricks on how to whistle. I heard that sound as clear as if I had run into a one way tunnel with the Orient Express train coming the other way.

Seeing the perimeter fence and hearing the high pitched whistle behind me I made for the wire of the stalag like a gazelle. She must have developed the winged feet of Mercury as she was able to connect just as I was leaning over the top wire to flip over. Well, the slap of that rod spoiled the hell out of this child let me tell you. There was no mercy given and none taken.

Death to my butt was the word of the day.

So hanging upside down, shorts hung on the top wire and looking at her upside down, my tail a fiery volcano and smoke still pouring off my tail from the one good lick, I got to see a sight that will live in my infamy forever.

She was standing, perhaps all 300 pounds of her when this seemingly huge head comes out of nowhere and butts her square in the oversized Volkswagen of a tail and I hear the outstanding "HEEE HAWWWW". She is flat on the ground, I am hanging upside down and this old mangy hena covered donkey has just made her the butt of the day. Thank God my Mom and Dad showed up before she got worked up again. However, Mom made sure that I did plenty of penance for the act of throwing a certain substance, but you have to have been there. I still remember being walked/carried home by two fast walking parents and the very quiet, but not quite muffled bursts of laughter from both sides of me over what all had happened.

By the way, we ended up 1-0……….

ROYAL BRATS TRIP # 1

I think that it was the expression of the group. They were sitting in the Saudia first class lounge in New York and talking, rather raucously as if they weren't sure of where they were or what was happening to them.

Reminded me of my trip over as a youngster. I was scared and excited at the same time. I think reality came home as each member of the party entered the door to the 747 and it became real. They were going home, to a promised land that most never thought there would ever be a chance at doing. Some had been gone from the land of sand for 40 or more years.

As I lay my head back, and looked out the window, I felt the massive engines come to life and my mind danced back 40 years ago. I saw the guy in the white shirt and black pants standing there with the red fire extinguisher on big wheels and the nozzle in his hand. Slowly the propeller began to spin, then with a loud cough and a snort, the bluish spit of cloud by the engine and the propeller was spinning like a magical wheel. The sunlight blazed off of the blade as the DC-3, The Flying Camel, rolled out of the New York airport.

Allah Akbar!, Allah Akbar! droned from the speaker above my head as I came back to the giant 747 as she lifted off. The traveler's prayer on the long flight back to a Kingdom never forgotten and never left behind. The others were now quiet. I think each feeling the depth of what was happening. The doubt that this would ever come about from a project of almost three years in the making.

It started with a simple request of mine. Please write a story for publication about your life in Arabia. In particular your feelings and emotions and comments if you ever met the King. What is ironic, is that at the time, I had to pull teeth to get responses. I finally got seventy stories and sent them to Arabia. They became the core of the only Aramco Brat book by us, for us and of us. "Forever-Friends" had come full circle. We were now returning with the first group to the home we cried over and thought was lost forever.

The night overtook many of us, after the traditional coffee, tea and dates, a full seven course meal served on bone china and real cloth napkins. No bistro bags here. Had to get the silverware back from Chip Noble and Larry Ives had a problem seeing the individual TV sets each chair had..he needed a pillow, but all in all, we fell into a fantasy of what and where we were headed.

Sunlight poured in through the cracks of pulled down shades and as we looked out and had a hot large breakfast, we saw in the distance what looked like sand.. could it be? Over Jeddah and you could cut the emotion with a butter knife...heading into Riyadh, each person must have felt the twist of the wonderful feeling in their gut.. We were HOME.....

ROYAL BRATS TRIP 2

As the landing gear rumbled down and the 747 lined up for the runway, the Saudi next to me, who hadn't said a word the whole trip, turned and said "Welcome Home". I was astonished and asked how he knew. He said he had overheard the others talking amongst themselves and, while I was asleep had looked at the book "Forever-Friends" that I had put in the chair back in front of me. He asked if that was ok, as he had seen King Abdul Aziz on the front and was curious. I told him to consider it a gift from all of us Brats. I didn't have to explain the name. He kinda got the impression from the activity of the Brats on board.

We thundered down to the ground and when the wheels touched down, I swear I heard the desert dunes singing in their whispering way, "Damm, it's good to see you all again."

Met at the airport and things started happening. No customs, no passport control, they even took all our luggage tabs and moved us thru the VIP area for a welcoming chi and gowa. Out the front, and the first sight of these lost ones returning home was a rare privilege to see. Their eyes seem to glaze over as the hot, humid air struck us full force. They took deep breaths and the transformation was unbelievable. All the ladies were once again pig tailed 10th graders. The boys were once again in jeans and white t-shirts and all were milling about as if in a daze of wonder. As they in. The gleaming armor plated black Mercedes with the gold crossed swords and palm tree on each side just stood there, with a thought in my mind that they, with the doors open also looked as if they were saying." Aslaimilikim ya sidiqqui's".

I knew ahead of time what was next, but we hadn't told the group. They all thought we were going to the Intercontinental Hotel. Some had even told people they would be there. Instead we went through Riyadh with a sirens blaring, lights flashing Saudi Police car in front and rear. We went into a part of Riyadh with high walls and guards with sub-machine guns, Suddenly we pulled up to a barricade. The Saudi soldier smartly saluted and the barrier was raised. We were at the Royal Palace used for guests of the King. The huge waterfall and the shining brass and the entry guarded by a soldier met us. Once past the bomb detectors, and it was fun watching our hosts struggle with all the luggage and clear it all for us. For in this palace were other guests, including a Prime Minister and another Royal member from another country.

We went to the centerpiece and sat in a lounge area. "This will be your home for a day or so as we visit with some people here in Riyadh," our hosts explained. Nothing was said about who these people would be.. perhaps just some local shwarma stand vendors?

Fruit drinks and all we could possibly want was at our fingertips. Here we were met in person by Dr. Fahd A. Al-Semmari, the Director General of the King Abdul Aziz Foundation and a man I call "Brother." He welcomed us with great warmth, as is his custom and the people of Saudi Arabia's way. I could see the brilliant stars of the desert night in the eyes of the group as they looked around and saw the four story chandelier of gold and the lobby waterfall. Each was handed their key with the tag marked with the Royal Logo, off we went to find our rooms and to see the beauty of this palace.

Dawn Lawson, a wonderful person, made the best remark I heard all night, "This doesn't look like the Intercontinental..."

ROYAL BRATS TRIP # 3

It seemed as if I had just drifted off in the biggest softest bed I had seen, with 17th Century furnishings and a bathroom that was bigger than my apartment when the ghostly sound of the morning call to prayer waffled into my room. I had set the alarm as we had to leave early. The alarm was a sophisticated system, which is why I figure most of us didn't get it to work. You had to set the hour hand and push in a button marked "Wake up Alarm". Very complicated for the massed Educational Degree's on this trip. Worse yet, standing in a marble tub and really enjoying the hot water you hear this loud "Whoop, Whooop, Whooop" sound and dashing, soap and wet body flying into the bedroom looking for the attacking whooping cranes (sorry about that) and it is the wake up alarm.

So, with a bite of humble pie from the fruit bowl in my room I headed out to the restaurant type dining room and had beef sausage with an egg that looked back at me and cried over the bloodshot eye that looked at it. It was a long night. The mystical air of Arabia and the excitement had made this old bedu feel so many emotions that I didn't know if I was coming or going. Several of the group sarcastically suggested I go, but I held on.

The crew was there having chi and gowa and heatedly discussing who had to ride with Reed Brooks, but they flipped a Halala and Saad, (one of our helpers who figures into this a lot more when we met some of his family near Ab'ha) got the all days rights to Reed. Hey, I have to pick on someone and Reed was great about me picking on him.. I suspect the web site will hold a few surprises for me later, but he is ok with me...ok, almost ok... He does know computers, I can say that. So can all the rest but the sneaky scorpions of the group won't speak up. ;->

(Warning-I am using some slight poetic license here for those of you who haven't guessed.. I'll pick on everybody fair and square before this epic reaches an conclusion...)

The grand motorcade ran its way through morning rush hour in Dallas, or so it looked and the drivers had all trained in Aramco as taxi drivers. For they flew in and out of traffic with not even an inch to spare. Out of respect for the motley crew, a horn was rarely touched. Reminded me of taxi # 21 in Dhahran.. From the airport as a returning student he always asked "You go Dhahran?" and when you said "Yes" he went straight past and headed to Ras Tanura. If you happened to fall asleep or be suffering from another ailment after a long returning student flight, you might wake up in RT and really raise Cain. The it was only 50 riyals to go back.. yeah, worked on me several times.

So we approach a historical site, the famous Muk Mask Fortress in which historians all agree that in 1902 Prince Abdul Aziz and seven men waited the night and with some additional troops overwhelmed the Al-Rashid and his men and history was born in a blaze of flashing swords and spears, punctured by the sound of musketry. The Prince, Abdul Aziz ibn Saud was on his way to the great adventure, the Kingdom of Saudi Arabia. So who should they bring to the most famous site? Why, a group of Brats....

As we entered and started taking photos, forbidden inside, but they allowed us, we soon had the Saudi's wondering if the fortress was under siege again. You could feel the coolness of the mud walls and looking at the short film we all once saw, part of "Island of Allah," produced by Aramco, you could feel the bullets wizzzing by and the screams of Allah Akbar as a Saudi Alamo was being created. The feeling of the fierce fighting that took place within these walls touched even the oldest and youngest of the trip... for here it all started, the grand adventure our parents joined in later years.

It has been completely reconstructed, using the original mud building materials and techniques. One extremely bright youngster, must have been ten or so, pointed out that the double barreled rifle on display had only one barrel. After all, he knew what he was talking about. So as I was escorted out of the weapons room and into the main hall, amid shouts of "Stick him!, Where's a gun?" and such from what I thought was the curator, I suddenly realized it was my fellow Brats. Well, I and a rather delicate young lady that was a little ill stepped in the only air conditioned part of the fort, had great tea and were quite well off, as the others ran rivers of sweat and learned something. We old geezers know when to step inside...

ROYAL BRATS TRIP 4

"Suddenly, the Saudi crew is dashing like a shamal.." hurry, hurry, Dr. Mike, please you put back artifacts in museum.(Always collecting you see…) Quick we need to run Hammi, Hammi". Well, we went to our awaiting vehicles and siren blaring, roared off like a bare rear ended pool hopping dipper in Dhahran. (With Sai'd of Security in hot pursuit.)

We had been told to wear dressy clothes, and everybody was dressed really nice. Ok, so John Myers was still in his 1960 Tri-D Dance suit, but he looked good…

We flew downtown towards the Royal Palace Offices and all I could get out of Khalid, our Saudi group leader was, "He is waiting, and he wants YOU!"

(I knew I hadn't got caught keeping the Palace guest house Royal Logo keys, as some others did, Thank you so very much, as I sheepishly got them back. you know…He just sadly shook his head, counted the pens on his desk and checked the wall to make sure his photographic collection of King Abdul Aziz was still there and I heard him muttering something that sounded a lot like, "I know your Father, I know your Mother, You no good, What your name?" I had heard this often from Aramco Security for some reason.

Back to a large building and we all piled out and walked in. Stopped dead in our tracks, not even noticing the Saudi soldiers with machine guns all over and looked at the magnificent wall hanging and art work in the lobby. Gold on green backing swords, dancing with their shimmer, Tall marble columns and gold trim. We passed into a room with a large wall hanging of young King Abdul Aziz, his stern visage making sure we stayed on the carpet and we followed the escort to a private elevator. In we went and up like a shot. We entered a formal gathering room and sat comfortably. In comes Dr. Fahd, the Director General and his able associate, Khalid Al-Nasser and dressed in black Bishit's with gleaming gold trim. They got with me and said "We meet with His Royal Highness Prince Salman bin Abdul Aziz ibn Saud and you need to introduce everyone. Blank as a stone wall my mind went. Introduce who?

We walked into the Prince's office and the hush was tremendous. However, the Prince got up, came around his desk and had a large smile that lit the room up with warmth. He looked so much like his Father that I was sure Sheri Ayers was calling him "Your Majesty." Learned later it was a four letter word for the regal settings and awe, but Sheri made all of us proud all through the trip. She never quit talking and calling all of the Saudi's "such pretty little boys", which after I explained what she was really calling them, she blushed like a sunburst and with great dignity said "I meant that they are soooo cute". Well, trying to explain that to Khalid, I think I managed to get something in there about his family tree, but he took it well. Back to the main stage.

The Prince was introduced and I only forgot one person's name. I never forgot it again after the look I got tho.... He sat in his chair and had all the ladies sit next to him.. poor guy, he was being nice but little did he know these ladies were ahead of him. They were going to ask questions. I have to admit my chest swelled out like a she-camel with small ones at the way all of these fine Brats handled their, I'm sure, first taste of Royalty. Not just Royalty, but the very highest levels. No one even spilled their gowa or chi...

The Prince then pulled a chair over next to him and told me, in plain English, "Sit here". I was somewhat shocked, although I had met Prince Salman several times before. He put me next to him and then did what I consider a very high honor. He welcomed the group and reached over and patted me on the knee and called me "His Friend". Well, I was just about knocked from my seat, I saw Dr. Fahd's eyes widen and Khalid just passed out.

He talked with us all and I thought it was like sitting around the campfire behind the third street school in the old campsite by the perimeter fence.

There was such friendliness and you could see by his eyes he was very pleased at our group. Some of the group expressed their thoughts and emotions and I could hardly see as I felt the mist of time pulled across my eyes and I saw them here, talking to their Father's friends son, The son of King Abdul Aziz. Just as their fathers had done 50 years before.

When we had talked and it was time to leave, I know each Brat there knew what a "Majilis" was. You know, I think it is a rather interesting form of Monarchy that allows anyone, at any level to meet with any of the ruling Royal Family during two open periods a day to present anything they wish to their leaders. No questions barred and all welcome no matter what status you have or don't have.

His Royal Highness took a group photo of us all and he wanted the "beautiful ladies" right next to him. An interesting point. Although we had planned on Abyiah's, (Just the scarf) somehow they weren't there all thru the trip. I'll bring this up later again. I think we all left there a little wiser and better from the example of grace and friendship we had been shown.

ROYAL BRATS TRIP # 5

Our next stop was a slow down in pace. We went to the ancestral home of the Saud family. Ancient Dirayiah, once the thriving capital of Arabia and home of the Abdul Aziz family. The ruins of two Saud dynasties are located a ways out of Riyadh. So off we went. The ruins are spectacular. We walked past thousand year old buildings and rooms. Saw one of the oldest Mosques in Arabia. Walked around on the upper and lower decks of the Mosque and heard from a distant past the evening call to prayer as if the old Mosque once again felt the beat of hearts. Remember, this was once a thriving city, and not just a building. The old wall around most of the city had been rebuilt and as we walked on the top, we stepped into the past and looked down at the attacking Rashidi's and Turks from eons ago. The breeze of history carried us from one part of the city to another. At one point, in one of the reconstructed buildings that was three stories high, several of the brave souls went to the top and had a wondrous view of the this worldly city of ruins. I think they could see the many men in white thobes and the women following in the black Abyiah's. I know I saw them and as they faded back into the era of the first Saud's it was like watching a modern day Saudi walk into a force five shamal and slowly disappear as from light to dark. These figures were there, if only in our minds, and you could almost feel the presence of children running through the old mud homes and playing their form of kick ball. They heard the chatter of laughter and surely they may have had for just a fleeting moment thought they heard Abdul Aziz as a child from below. When upon looking in the center of the building, they saw once again, the children of Arabia, now grown in the Brats of today.

You could see the donkey cart with the ageless Bedu bringing in the chaff and you most assuredly felt the emptiness, yet the fullness of the old city and the place it stands in history. From the ruins we could see the skyscrapers of Riyadh, and as the old fortress city looked towards Riyadh, the new Capital of Arabia, it's wall stood just a little straighter and the parapets were a little bolder in their pride with what has become, the jewel of the Kingdom.

We walked in the dust of thousands of sandals and talked long about history that as children we may never have know. We were returning to the land of our growth and learning more that ever before. The Saudi's have maintained the degree of sophistication, along with the reality of the past. Combing the two into a meld of war, fortune, loss and victory. All a story told as the ageless and mystical Darayiah looked and locked eyes with Riyadh. Two entities, founded by the Family that gave a Kingdom a name. The House of Saud and The Kingdom of Saudi Arabia.

The ladies had to leave for they had a Royal call. They were off to an amazing night of meeting with a very progressive and meaningful, as I will tell, experience with the Nahdah Woman's Group. A Princess or two awaited our Princesses.

ROYAL BRATS TRIP # 6

Not having been invited to the woman's group, although I did have an Abyiah ready, I have asked for this part of the trip to be done by some of the wonderful ladies on the trip. Due to rude commentary about me, I have had to change and modify some of this, but the basic beauty of what took place is here. I will say that at the King Abdul Aziz Foundation Board of Directors Meeting, which took place our last night there, a major decision was made by HRH Prince Salman bin Abdul Aziz Ibn Saud in that he has instructed the Foundation to start doing a Woman's Studies and Research section of the Center. This, and what you read below are major steps for our friends, the Saudi's and they should be complimented.

PART ONE

The head of the Women's Society is Princess Moody (sounds like that but have no idea how to spell it). She is the daughter of the late King Khalid. The women for the most part spoke beautiful English and are wealthy, well educated women from Riyadh. The organization provides social services to other women in need. Classes are taught there in computers, languages, cosmetics, art, pottery, etc. They also provide child care to those who need it and transportation if necessary. They fully support about 400 families (if I recall correctly). These are women who have been widowed or who cannot work or whose husband's cannot work for one reason or another. They also have a heritage center in the society where they are trying to preserve traditional work like stichery designs. They design and make modern outfits based on traditional Arab clothing from different regions. These are for sale but, unfortunately, are not yet produced in great enough quantity for export or advertising to the outside. We saw some women putting stitched designs on chiffon scarfs which were beautiful. All the designs are based on traditional tribal designs and faithfully executed. The pattern is printed on the fabric by hand with old wood block stamps and then stitched over. They had in the recent past also taught some women in gold jewelry work since their smaller hands could do the fine work better than men. They don't work in the same factories as the men for cultural reasons so they can do the work at home or in separate factories.

We had dinner with about 30-40 women and had a great time with them. They had prepared (pot luck style) a traditional Arab dinner and brought it to their cafeteria to share with us. These were professional women who enjoyed their lives as they were. They weren't the least bit repressed or downtrodden but active business people in their own rights. Some were business owners and others just did volunteer work. They really were fabulous.

We all spent time with a different group of women so I'm sure the other ladies could tell you different things about them. Those of us who went were given a gift of 2 books, one on Arab cooking and one on Arab antiquities, and a box with 2 hand made Arab coffee cups. Really cute ones.

PART TWO

We were really late and the whole organization had been waiting for us. Including all the young women in the offices. We got out of our Royal limo at the gate and we went through it and a young woman collected us. The place—in the dark—seemed to be several buildings done in that modern Arab style. Two story I'd say. There was a permanent "tent" over at one side where they do outdoor events—fund raising, crafts fairs etc.

The place inside was modern and cheery, done in Italian furniture, black, gray and touches of red with lots of art on the walls—stuff done by children as well as professionals. It was charming and somehow familiar. The

Princess took charge of us—what a powerhouse she is—lovely and competent. Short dark hair. Was she in a pants suit? All of the women were in western clothing—suits and dresses. The only difference in a similar group of American women was their jewelry!

They sat us down for the usual tea/coffee and we talked a little. We apologized about being late and they of course were charming and warm about it. But we were embarrassed especially as they took us through the center and we realized how many people were waiting around for us.

The Princess handed us off to the young woman who is the administrator of the place. She was about 30 in a pant suit, short hair—very business like and warm.

I liked the fact that as she took us through the buildings, introducing us to the heads of the departments—who were all salaried employees and all looked to be about 20, we would get into these conversations and stand in the hall talking about everything. Just like women do. Frankly, it was more relaxed than the visits with men. I really had a sense of letting my guard down. Not completely, because we were strangers to each other.

IT DEFINITELY WOULDN'T TAKE LONG BEFORE WE WERE FRIENDS

I was very impressed with the operation and their plans for more day care, more computer classes, English language, etc. But I loved the dress design plans the best. I had read Costumes of the Arabian Peninsula and was saddened by the Princesses description of how the old Saudi textile arts were dying out. And here was a whole room of beautiful dresses made in non-traditional fabrics using all those old techniques. And the workroom where the girls were doing the embroidery. The young woman who was the designer described how they do the research, collecting actual pieces as well as stuff from books and photos and then she works out the design and the young women who are studying the techniques actually do the sewing. The dresses were beautiful and exotic and very sensual. We all were drooling.

We each sat with a group at supper. Most of my ladies didn't speak English. One was from Khobar and we talked about the changes there. She had had a chance to go to a crafts fair, I think it was, or come meet us and she came to meet us! At one point a woman sat down and someone asked her something and she said a fairly long description. They were all laughing and finally someone took pity on me and told me she was telling them about an episode of a favorite tv show!

Like our friend, Khalid, they all had cell phones which were ringing constantly. I sat with Dane and the Princess and a woman who had lived in New York and spoke perfect American. She heard how Dane organized her life and shook her head: Of course, she said, it's so hard for you. You have no help.

So don't forget these were wealthy, high class women. But the younger women, the employees didn't seem particularly down-trodden either. And they were so professional. Bright. Energetic. Really no difference from visiting such an organization in the States. Except it was all women. Run, organized, staffed by women.

They brought an incense burner out for us as we were finally preparing to leave. There were only a few left—the Princess I remember. They were getting their abiyahs from a closet and suiting up. The Princess sent one of the staff for the cook books for us and we waited out on the steps for them. It was very, very dark and I knew she was tired and ready to go home but she stood chatting with us as though she had all the time in the world. Another woman walked with us to the gate, to be sure our car was there. Right before she went through it, she whipped her face veil over her head. I have never talked to anyone who was veiled and it was a daunting, rather disturbing thing. She just disappeared. Very strange. The image, after seeing all those ladies, was profound.

I know you don't want to say this but I think women's rights is as big an issue/problem to the KSA as racism is to the US. I just hope the changes come sooner than later. Maybe our being there and western tourists will help bring them. Saudi women are so prepared to take a bigger role. And, of course, the exciting news of the Woman's Studies Center at the Foundation is great news. If you thought you had tasted a fine meal, well, this was a true example of all of the tasteful dishes you'd remember. Hamour that was to wrap up and put in a museum it was so good. Spice butter and cheese dips, and I could go on forever, but I have to go to lunch. Wendy's is calling me. No wonder I'm cranky. To go from the exquisite dining we had back to my local…well! The only real problem was getting Jerry out of the kitchen to leave. Seems he offered to help clean up and they thought he was offering to do dishes…LOL…;-)

ROYAL BRAT TRIP # 7

While the ladies were at the Woman's Group, the men were called to the main English language newspaper in Arabia and had a very interesting tour of the facilities. They are quite modern, using a lot of advanced computer techniques.

The Riyadh Daily is the largest English language newspaper in the Kingdom. After a tour we got to sit and discuss many issues with the Editor in Chief Mr. Talaat F. Wafa. He has a strong vision of friendship and education in the Saudi press for both countries. Even got conned into sending copies daily to members of our group.

One aspect of the meeting was that there are many ex pats in the Kingdom that are not Saudi Aramco affiliated. This was the reason he felt the need for a very fast growing newspaper in English and that they have subscriptions from around the world.

At one time, the only printed news was the "Oily Rag", a mimeographed, on the old hand crank machine, paper of the Abqiaq Drillers. Circa 1945. I have two copies of separate ones and they not only talk about local gossip, but also about what is happening in the Kingdom and quite openly. You might guess the Kingdom is rightfully proud of the media it now has. I personally like the old "Sun and Flare" and the "Aramco World" because they directly related to what was going on inside Aramco and also covered areas of interest within the Kingdom. I felt that the "Aramco World" of today has left the origins it once had and is now a interesting, yet not exactly relevant to the Kingdom slick magazine. Award winning, yes, but you ought to see the earlier issues such as 1953 when King Abdul Aziz died and the Aramco communities comments and thoughts.

The next morning, once again awakened by the "whooping crane" in my bedroom, I rushed downstairs as everyone else was ahead, as usual. I had another project to do, but the group left to go to the King Abdul Aziz City for Science and Technology. This my friends is the kingpin of Saudi Technology.

The group was to meet the Director, also a Prince of the facility but due to being a little late they missed out on the meeting. However I believe they saw amazing evidence of the Saudi advancement in Technology. They were surely shown the computer labs, the media center and the various areas of experimental progress.

The display of modern technology and the development by the Saudi's show that as a society, they are very much technologically advanced and yet, have traditional values.

Quickly, as soon as we got back we were hurriedly taken by our crew back to the Royal Office complex. To the Governors Palace. Seems ass if we had been summoned back. Why?, well were weren't sure. Might have been some comment made before at HRH Prince Salman's meeting. Into the elevator again and upstairs. In to the waiting room and quickly into a long office of beautiful thick carpet and marble walls. A man arose from behind the desk in a really pretty off shade of pale yellow/gold thobe and Bisht. Turns out to be an old friend, HRH Prince Settam bin Abdul Aziz ibn Saud, the Vice -Governor of Riyadh. A very warm and friendly Prince. The whole group was introduced and he soon had the whole group mesmerized by his perfect command of English and that he was a "California" person. He has a home in California and showed us US College degree's he had from California schools.

He was very proud of his US connections. He talked to the whole group and had us all gather around him. He has always been a most enjoyable person and a man of much honor and friendship.

I think we all felt very comfortable with this gentleman. His nature is truly a friendly one and he expressed the significance of the trip and of our group. I can say that I feel we all felt as if we had a close friend here and we would all welcome him here in the US anytime. His magnetic personality was just that. Magnetic.

I invited him to be the one to come to the reunion for the drawing of the "Forever-Friends" book contest drawing. He is seriously considering stopping by for a short while at the reunion if he can.

We all got to have our photographs taken with him and amid much openness and friendship we left to tour the Palace Offices.

Now, here is where Chip Noble goes into Brat legacy. We are taken into the Royal Chambers of the Crown Prince and look at the massive meeting room and the really nice furniture arrangement and the Royal symbol on the wall. Tall graceful columns and marble everywhere. They then take us in a really fancy, high class large meeting room which they tell us is King Fahd's majilis room. While we are all looking at the marble and gold walls, Chip goes up, and to the astonishment of the Saudi's with us, sits in the King's throne and get's his photograph taken. Bayonets were being fixed to rifles, pistol holsters unsnapping and Saudi's jaws hitting the floor. Chip jumps up and we are herded in to an ante chamber which is the Kings resting room. Has beautiful wood chests and a bed and very comfortable looking chairs. Chip is given the look of death and doesn't lay on the bed, where I have no doubt he would be today, stuck there with sharp objects.

As we leave the Kings rooms, I see the Saudi soldiers removing the complete chair and cushions and f fixtures of the Kings seat. Was later told they were afraid the King might feel the change in the shape due to Chip's larger rear end and might question who was in the throne. So a Bratty legend is born. "Chip of the Royal Highneeee."

ROYAL BRAT TRIP #8

We left the Royal Office Palace and managed to save Chip by hiding him in the trunk of one of the cars. We went next to a place I can only preface by saying, "My heart moved and my emotions caused tears of joy and sadness."

A few years ago, the very traditional, yet progressive HRH Prince Salman bin Abdul Aziz Ibn Saud opened a unique place in the Kingdom. The Center for care of Disabled Children. Since the time of opening the first center, I believe he has opened two others. These are not government funded and it is something that is truly worthwhile.

The Center has facilities that are very advanced. Nurses, Doctors, aides and specialists from around the world. All there to care for the unfortunate Saudi children that have birth defects or handicaps. I saw grown men and women cry and laugh with these little ones and they all smiled and loved on us. We, the tall healthy American's who became putty in the little boys and girls hands. I knelt with one little girl that had a bumble bee, and she laughed the whole time she was "buzzzzing" me. She was a happy little girl and I think I left a large portion of my heart right there. The Center has housing for the children, I think fifty bungalows and the main thing I saw that really woke me up was that the parents were there with the kids learning how to cope with the handicaps. This was terrific and I think although we have many such places in the US, one has to understand the Saudi Arabia has never done this before. So the effect and the time that went into the development of the facility is staggering.

The most important fact of the center is simple. I didn't see one unhappy or sad face. They all had sunshine in their smiles and stars in their eyes. Their bodies may have hurt and their efforts long, but their hearts pumped pure love and happiness out to all of us. We, the strangers in their world.

So much care and love from the care givers there. I knew those children were children of Allah, for they had been blessed by the care of real love.

I get quite choked up about this particular center. I see the future and see the betterment that the Prince has given the children. There is no cost to the children or their families. The Center survives on support from others, like you and I. Chip Noble is heading up a fund raiser for the Center. He tells me he has received three checks. Right now I will issue a challenge. I will match whatever total that we as Brats donate. Dollar for Dollar. Chip's address is John "Chip" Noble, 2750 Old St. Augustine Road, Z-259, Tallahassee, Florida 32301.

I'm not being a noble person here, I just think how lucky I was to have Aramco medical facilities when I was a child and wonder how I could have been so callous when the little beggar boy with one leg approached me in AL-Kohbar so many years ago with a crutch made from a palm tree branch, and all I could do was say, "Yellah, emsheeee". I'm older now and think I'll do something about that little boy...

So we left the Center and there were a few dry eyes, but I think it was part of the transformation of we, who knew mostly Aramco, were learning "Arabia".

ROYAL BRAT TRIP # 9

Well, you know it had to be. The group, who were now on the verge of sneaking off to collect sand got their chance. The group went out past Riyadh and off into the desert to a Bedu camp that is maintained by a friend of the Foundation for desert excursions. We arrived about an hour before dusk and the Saudi crew built a fire and we had an original Bedu black tent there, carpets spread out in front of chairs, a satellite TV and coolers with sodas. The group wandered off to look at some camels, and found several albino camels. The white camels are always reserved for the King and it is a great honor to present him one. The group found several. The camp site had firewood, a sheep pen full, of which several got photos playing with the lambs.

Once again, a Brat Legend may have been born. Roger Ison was caught on camera rubbing a beautiful camels belly and a few moments later, got a kiss from that camel. I'm not saying much else. I just wonder if they are happy? Roger has been waiting for this story, not sure how far I was going, but I'll tell you this much...when we left, that camel followed him for miles across the desert. ;-)

We drank gowa and chi for a long time as the sun went to sleep and the Saudi's even started to make a lamb for us. They went thru the tradition kill and skinning and preparation, but we finally had to give it to the family that stays at the camp year round as we ran out of time. We had seats and the sky and the electric lights. We were getting comfortable. The Saudi crew was playing cards and watching the World Cup match on TV. The Brats were just quietly talking and looking at the desert. I had the lights turned off and we all laid back. Even with the cloudy sky, soon we saw the blazing moon and stars slipped out from hiding and blazed at us then hid again. I felt the earth move and knew I had once again slipped back in time to Half Moon Bay when I lay there and the stars were just a few feet above me and bright as the exploding nova in my heart from the Princess next to me. I had to shake off the memory and let a single tear just drift down the side of my Arabian/American facade.

We got into our vehicles and dashed back into Riyadh. I was in the Suburban and the limos were behind and we were doing a good 100 KPM when the tire exploded and the truck went side to side and we almost totaled out. We finally stop and fall out of the truck with the hair on our butts still stuck to the seats of the truck. The cars come screaming up and stop and while we are standing there, shaking and nerves completely gone, up comes Sheri Romine Ayers. "Mike, where are our Abayiah's?" I looked at her and I think I said some to the effect, "I just had a near death experience and you want %$#*^ Abyiahs?" Part of the tire had actually hit the car behind us.

So the traditional problem solving situation arose. Larry Ives, ten Saudi's, eight driver's and Roger's camel are all deciding how to change the tire. After about fifteen minutes of heated debate and many rude suggestions, the tire was finally actually approached. Larry took off the nuts I think. Unlike most experiences I have had, this time we had a spare.

All in all, I liked this part of the trip a lot. I was at home with the elements. Fire, Water, Air and my beloved desert sand...

ROYAL BRAT TRIP # 10

Ok, so the group was back at the Palace residence and they are all skulking about..Khalid, our crew chief called me to come aside a moment to discuss urgent matters, all in the meantime telling the other helpers in Arabic to get everyone into the guest room on the floor we were on.

I knew they were up to something, but figured it was just someone wanting to get out and try to shop. I had a running gunfight with the women every day because they could smell the gold market and we hadn't been there yet. In fact, I think they tried to tie towels(Those they didn't load up to bring home) to escape the Palace and get to the suq.

That wasn't it. I walked around the corner and to my great pleasure they had a huge table full of goodies and candy and a big cake with a sign." Happy Birthday Muk" It was my 51st birthday. I know I was as red as the sunset, I embarrass easily. It was a little eerie as my Mom and Dad met in 1949 when he was in the States on a leave from Aramco and even though I was little (Back then babies were on their Mothers passports) I got my own passport in 1951 in Dhahran at the old US Consulate. So in Arabia, officially in '51, and turned 51 on this trip many moons later. Scary, ehhh?

The next morning I heard the sound of dreaded fear arise from the outside. I think that the merchants had a universal vision all at once. I went downstairs and was having a smart breakfast when the walls seemed to push out as if there was sudden pressure released into a bag. The ladies were there. "WE SHOP TODAY!" Ok, I mumbled, we will take the morning and go to the Suq. Well, I know that I had just raised my cup of coffee and I was lifting my head to say something when I heard the cars honking. They had moved like lightening and were loaded, ready and not willing to wait. We took off, and the drivers seeing the gold lust drove like fire trucks to a ten alarm fire. We made it and I had all of the Saudi crew and the group standing there and I pointed to the clock tower and said "We all need to meet back here at 1:00 pm as the suq will close until 4pm. As I turned to repeat and the Saudi's turned with me, we could have been on the moon. Not a soul, male or female in sight.

Suddenly screams were heard from the gold market, merchants were heard to weep openly, gold flew like pennies and the stores tried to make a hahla, but this was a bunch of Aramco Brat trained buyers. Kill and take no prisoners. I took the group to a merchant who once was a good friend. I had bought a lot of gold there over the trips. He and his family are now homeless and broke according to him, and it is all my fault for I led these women to his stall and he lost millions on the gold trade that day. How do you out bargain a lady with the eye of a hunting Falcon, the teeth visa sharp and the ability to outguess even the extremely rigid scale by a percentage of an ounce, all in 10 seconds? You don't.

The men and the Saudi's went to a shop and we all got a really fine Bisht in Black, White or Brown with the fine gold embroidery. This was to go with the thobe, guttra's and agals the Saudi's were giving us. While they were sizing the men, I went down the row to the old suq, where history lies in huge piles and plastic bags packed with mysterious things are hidden under counters and I saw my old suq friends. A couple of the Brats came with me and soon were doing their share of barter with these old Bedu's who were ready. I sat with Ahmed, an old friend and we had tea and lots of water while the guys looked at things. He showed me a magnificent pistol, over 100 years old, French that had gold leaf Arabic writing and told me it was carried by an Englishman named Shakespear. A name that means much in Saudi history as Capt. Shakespear and King Abdul Aziz's brother both died in a battle against the Turks to unite Arabia. This was quite a find and we haggled for a while and then he and I agreed. Another artifact of history, right in the backyard of Abdul Aziz.

It seemed to be a little quieter now in the gold suq, so we men went back and bought what scrapings of gold and shavings that we were able to find. Back to the Palace and an afternoon to relax. Tonight we went to the King Abdul Aziz Foundation and a traditional major Saudi meal, meet with TV media and after the meal, which was unbelievable we prepare for the next day.

As an interesting historical note, we sat in the open area of the old Maraballa Palace that King Abdul Aziz Ibn Saud built and the only remaining buildings of this huge Palace are contained within the Foundations building and grounds. We actually ate the huge Saudi meal in a room the King himself once ate in.

Called the Mud building, which was attached to the King's majilis and two story building it is one of only four buildings still standing.

However, for now we were going to the Saudi Radio Tower and restaurant. It is like the "spike" at the world's fair or one of the tower restaurants in the states, except this one is normally closed, It was opened for us and at the top we could walk around and see Riyadh and Di'yriah and miles and miles away. We had an excellent meal here and a really big meal so that we needed the rest. The elevators were small but mirrors everywhere so things looked a lot bigger. Well, maybe not one that is a little smaller than me, Mr. Van West, but close.

What a view... The new and the old laid out before us.

Tomorrow we will board the Royal 737 assigned to us by the Royal Family, Yes, we had our own 737 that took us everywhere. We are destined to fly to Dhahran and Al-Kohbar.....

ROYAL BRAT TRIP # 11

The 737 lifted gently into the clear sky and as we flew towards our destiny with our past, the conversation slowly dwindled away. I knew what they were thinking. The same I had felt five years earlier when I had made this trip to memory lane. You knew there was a lot of apprehension in the air and even a bit of trepidation, but always a swelling you could feel as people begin to feel the magic drumbeat in their hearts of home, our Aramco world was coming up fast. We landed at the all new airport between Al-Kohbar and Damman.

As we stepped in the blast of hot, humid air, I immediately went to stepping out of the Flying Gazelle and looking for my Mom and Dad in the crowd at the old mud customs shed. Suddenly a big ugly person shoved me aside, flew down the stairway to the ground and placed a full blown lip lock on the ground an we all felt the wave of emotion as we all imagined ourselves kissing the ground of home again. The oldest Brat on the trip had not been back in over 40 years…I think that the smile on his face was the answer to a dream.. he couldn't stop grinning. My God, it was a tremendous feeling to see and be moved almost to tears by the expressions as each person stepped to the ground and touched the land they never thought would ever be under their feet again. It was a true "love" moment.

There were nervous cries and little giggles and even a tear or two, but this moment shall forever be imbedded in my heart. I think even the nearby desert was struck with awe and admiration for these children returning home and stepping off the plane in bodies of adults. I doubted I would feel this kind or emotion and feeling surge through my body ever again. Our Saudi friends seemed to absorb the moment and stood quietly, as if reflecting on their own childhood and their homes they may not have seen in awhile.

On to the bus and off to the Gulf Meridian Hotel in Al-Kohbar, built where the old dhows used to tie up for unloading fish. We passed Dhahran and the cries of "Look, the cutoff", "Look at the tree's!", "Hey, that's the old US Consulate, is it still used?" "My God, That's where Bargers used to be", "The Hospital, it's still there, I gave blood in "C" Clinic 35 years ago!." echoed around the bus.

My eyes and ears took it all in, and the sudden silence as we passed allowed me to look at each person.. They were there, on the hill going up to where the Barger's old house was, and they were kid's scrambling on all fours and running and sliding down the sand, reaching out from a distant past. It seemed that Dhahran was leaning towards them, as in "welcome.. you are us and we are you!".

We reached the hotel after the "Ohhhs and Ahhhs" of the new Kohbar passed us. Many saw the old traffic circle and were flat amazed that it seemed to be so far from the outskirts, where as in my day, it was the start of Khobar. The view from the Hotel was majestic. It overlooked the cornice and the Arabian Gulf. You could almost see Bahrain and you could reach out and touch Arabia.

ROYAL BRAT TRIP # 12

We were so close yet so far away. Dhahran beckoned like the brightest star in the heavens and yet we knew it would be the next day before we would visit our beloved homes. We went to a really fantastic restaurant in Kohbar called the Heritage Village. What a place. We had history living around us. The food was extraordinary and the gulf shrimp swam right up from the gulf to our plates. Humas to die for and of course, all the traditional dishes, served with all the warmth of tradition Saudi hospitality. The building itself was designed to reflect various tribes in Arabia and each room was a mini- museum. We went into one of the main rooms for after dinner chi and gowa and a man who had been with the military for many years gave us a display of rifle handling that reminded me of a drill team. A proud warrior. The restaurant had old photos on the walls which several people recognized and a lot of artifacts of the ageless Arabia were on display. I highly recommend any and all of the Saudi Aramco Brats, if they haven't been there to go. It has a five star rating in my belly.

We left early the next day to Abqaiq. "The Friendly City" and they mean it. As we approached there were comments such as, "they moved the main gate", "Wow, look at those pipes", "Hey, look, there the commissary." We were met by a public relations gentleman who along with the Saudi Aramco representative, Jassim, who was excellent took us to the recreation center. The lump in Danee's throat was about to burst. She was home, and I swear as she stepped off the last step of the bus her feet didn't touch ground. I saw the cloud of emotion that she slowly floated by on. This woman was in heaven and deserved it. Her glazed look was one of a child at Christmas and it was a humbling moment for me.

I want to follow her and then will return to the group. We ended up looking for some old homes that people had lived in and we found Danee's. It was empty and with the aid of the Saudi Aramco guides, we went in. Danee was contained and doing well until the moment of truth. The swell of emotion was so intense, that even the Saudi's had tears rolling down their faces as she was in her old bedroom and looking at a bed that was there, fully in tears and tremendous pleasure and pain at the same time. I fell in love with her and her past so many times that very instant that my own heart was in tears. There was so much emotion that her tears were a reflection of all of ours. Not a dry eye there and all we could do was hold each other. Our knees had to be weak and I know that for a moment, Danee was lost to this world and once again heard the call of her Mother, "Time for school, get up". I will always treasure what happened to Danee as she had come full circle. She was home and at long last, it was all ok...I will always cherish that moment until my death for I saw the true heart of all of us right there. She actually reached out from the year 2000 back to her childhood and touched the face of herself through the mist of time. She was now and then together. She was and is whole...and forever a friend So, the old Bedu has a thought...The Foundation is very much looking into the part women have in the history and culture of Saudi Arabia. I have a small collection of photographs of women from all parts of Arabia. I have donated a complete set of Saudi/ American cookbooks from the 1940's to the 1960's of Arab recipes and some kitchen style utensils I have run across. What say ye Ladies look through your resources and anyone that has photos or film or other materials about women in Saudi Arabia, let us copy or donate them to our collect

STORY OF
THE REAL
BABA HATAB

As far as Baba Hatbib went the story at the time was that he was directing the Palestinians youth and some UPM students as to which house to attack. However the real fact was that he was trying to drive down the hill from Bargers to warn many of the American's of the rioters who had come in thru the perimeter fence by the hospital. They did penetrate the fences in several sections, but the vast majority came via the hospital tunnel..

I have a lot of photos of overturned vehicles that were turned over at the admin. building and the hospital parking lot. Only one or two were burned. A lot of windows were broken, including my house. However many house-boys also showed great courage and yelled and carried on by standing in front of the homes and yelling that there were children present and that this riot as wrong, etc. Many Arab families had marked their houses with sign's claiming that they were Moslem. Not all did, just a few.

Ben J'awli's office was contacted immediately by Aramco and Saudi Bedu Army (The barefoot Army) was sent from Damman and with a very short time had things under control.

As to what caused the riot, not only are those of you who stated Gamel Nasir made inflammatory remarks correct, but Egyptian TV showed tanks and armored vehicles with Israeli troops, only the vehicles had American ID, such as US stars and insignia. This was due to the fact that the Israeli Military had used up so much equipment and so much had been destroyed by the Egyptian 3rd army, later to surrender, that the US pulled armor and other equipment out of Germany and other Nato countries and they were sent to the front without even being painted over. A stunt US State Department officials later claimed was an overt act by the Israelis to antagonize the Arab League forces.

This deliberate act by the Israeli TV and media was then picked up world wide was shown over and over. Thus a lot of the statements of Gamel Nasir seemed supported by visual images. Some US units in Germany were stripped to within 50% of their combat readiness capability to shore up Israeli loses.

I think as far as the USS Liberty that US Politics caused the death of most of the American servicemen and that Israel lied about the attack and that even to this day, as Joe Meadors can tell you, there is much heated debate as to the US Govt. cover up of the Israeli attack on the Liberty. For more on the Liberty, go to :http://www.ussliberty.org/jim/ussliberty/

Yes, many of the Saudi gardeners and others knew about the impending riots and many warned Americans they knew and were fond of. Many others just crept away. There are many stories about this, I personally was descending into Dhahran Airport when the Captain said over the intercom that we had been ordered away and to Rome. His comment, immortalized in my young ears was, "Ladies and Gentlemen, This is the Captain speaking. We have just been informed that Israeli tanks have crossed in Jordan and Egypt and that all flights are canceled." He did not say Arab tanks had rolled into Israel as Israel had taken the initiative and attacked first. They later said the Arabs were planning an attack anyway, but who knows and history, a long time from now will have to decide this.

As an aside to this, the US Embassy was also attacked and the American Flag torn down. The young Palestinian who did this fell and when the barefoot army reached the compound, he was beheaded where he fell. The US Marine Embassy Guards had been ordered to keep the rioters from the building interiors but not to fire unless they tried to enter, which they did not.

Baba Hatab got a bad rap from all this and many still believe he was guiding the rioters, but many more heard him very clearly yelling at the rioters to stop in the name of Allah, for they were wrong and this was not right.

He was cleared by Aramco and was actually jailed by the Saudi's until American's, several of them women spoke up on his behalf. He was Jordanian and was expelled anyway. Not sure if he ever came back.

I did get home, but not until several weeks later and after we, boys and girls caught in Rome were put up in the "Hotel Love" by the Aramco rep. I shared a room with seven ladies.. They were great people and we had a blast. However Aramco found out and soon boys were sent to stay at Notre Dame and the girls to Marymount. SO ends that "Love" affair.

That summer we had very little activity in the districts and no dhow trips, but we did have tri-d dances,

911 THOUGHTS

DEDICATED TO THE ONES WE LOVE:

It is with a proud yet heavy heart I write these words. I hear the screams and the thunderous crash, feel the massive fireball and the impact as my mind and soul are torn to shreds with you, although I am thousands of miles away. May God never bring again such pain and torture of the heart and soul to the innocents. I am the office worker...

I run to the stairs my heart pounding, the massive stream of flashing faces as I try to reach the trapped. my oxygen tank sounds like the rush of a train in a dark tunnel as I climb. Suddenly there is a brilliant white. I see and feel the floating of myself. I hear no noise but sense the presence of my dear God. I have come to help and feel the earth fall away beneath me. Others are so close, yet I feel only the warmth and intense love coming from the brilliant white light. God has my hand. I am home. My last look back lets me see the last of my mortal remains. Crumbled beneath the ruins of the 78th floor. S weet Lord, I thank you for bringing me home. I am the Fireman...

I dash to the stairs, I am covered in dust, the people are following my instructions as I yell for them to run and I head into the stairway. More and more I pass as I try to help and protect those that I am here to serve and protect. I feel the tearing of the earth, feel the sway of the mountain and feel the crush of the world. I see the path and I am at peace. I see that a person has picked up something from a huge pile of what looks to be debris. It is shiny, it is mine. Badge number 5570. I am the Police officer...

My life is startled. The news is clear. We have been hurt. I sway to one side. I feel a terrible burning, I hear the horrendous scream of my bones. I sense the ripping of my flesh. I tremble as my legs are burned out beneath me. I know I am falling, I know I will hurt my insides and the living parts of myself as I drop in final pain. I see my brother fall, I hear his anguish as he calls to me. I am the Towers...

I am at the house. John will be home in an hour or so. He made a great stock deal. He has promised me and our little boy that we will get the long awaited vacation together. It makes me so happy that we are together and a family. I love him and he loves us both so much...what do I hear? The news. OH MY GOD!!! I am the family...

I am in an airplane. I feel that I am doing what my God has told me. I shall have the ever lasting life of Paradise, for Os'sama promised me. These infidels shall die for the glorious Jihad. I await the awaking of Gods blessing and the promises of Paradise. What is this? I awake in the flames of hellfire. My soul screaming in pain, I am on fire. I am burning, I am dying, I have no heart. God has denied me. I am in such pain. I am in HELL. I am the terrorist...

I am above, I look down and see the ruins. I feel the tear as it winds down my face. I see something here. what is it? Three men raising something. Red, White and Blue. It is mine, It is our flag and I am proud. I am the life of America and I shall carry the razors of my talons to the far off places and put the steel of my heart into the bodies of those that have hurt me. I am the United States of America. I am the American Eagle...

A DAY, LIKE
ALL DAYS
BUT......................

Running like a dervish across fine grained sand in a cool morning because Mom yelled "Mike Crocker, get home now for breakfast... you'll be late for school again!!!

Thanks Mom.

Stumbling through the rough school of arithmetic when you had to count on your hands, and some used their sandals feet, It was explained to me that on my one hand I was better than all the rest because I has disproportionate sized finger and Mom said, "Well, you have the advantage because you already have fractions down. Whole, half, third and eighth. As far as your other hand you have five there too.

Just two are hidden numbers".

Thanks Mom.

Tying one of my Dads huge ties around my neck and wearing a suit that was for church only, but for the 9th grade prom dance and my first date I got to wear it. The corsage made of paper and string. She told me I was so handsome and my date was beautiful.

Thanks Mom.

For when Sa'id of Security brought me home at 3:00 in the morning as a grown up returning student, hardly able to walk after a night of brown and white, and Mom making me eggs and toast quietly so Dad wouldn't hear us.

Thanks Mom.

For the terrible tears that racked my body when a friend had died on MEA 444 and asking "How come, Mom?" with her response that God needed then and one day I'd see them again.

Thanks Mom.

For being so proud when finally, after what seemed like years of school and mishaps, graduating from San Marcos and the hundreds of times she helped me with difficult summers and for believing in me in school.

Thanks Mom.

For the smacks, thumps, bumps and butt pops I had justly deserved which made an impression on why and why not. Even if I didn't know, or at least told her I did know it was wrong to chunk eggs at passing cars.

Thanks Mom.

For the pain and for the reassurance I got when the love of my life broke up with me. cried for days, she spoke softly and held me. She knew it would happen again and again as I grew up. Although she always reassured me there was someone for me too.

Thanks Mom.

For the times I lost a job, or was hurt on duty as a police officer or just plain needed to talk, always there and always ready to help.

Thanks Mom.

For making sure my life was filled with adventure by taking the chance in 1951 of going to Bahrain to marry a man she had met and start my life of great and glorious adventures.

Thanks Mom.

For smacking me or hugging me and loving me no matter what stupid thing I did, all the way into my 50's and still.

Thanks Mom

For the Christmas as a child where two packages were one sock each and special after shave in later years and always the required underwear under the tree when we had little.

Thanks Mom.

For waiting for me to get to you, to hold you for hours, to say "I love you" and for fighting until I held you, with tears falling as rain on you from a giant of a man, I knew you were there.

Thanks Mom.

For being a Guardian Angel riding on my shoulder now and whispering now and again, "I love you, son".

Thanks Mom.

So for all you did and the wonderful life you gave me and for so many others I want to say, with out reservation. You did it always.

HAPPY MOTHERS DAY TO ALL MOTHERS WHO ARE ALL HERE AND THEY ARE ALL WITH US TODAY. A MOTHER'S LOVE IS ETERNAL.

A P...AH FOOL
TO
REMEMBER!!!

When I was a returning student in 1968 there was an incident that I have thought of for years. I have often wondered how I managed to get in so deep by doing nothing, as all know I would never attempt confrontation with Aramco Security.

Seems as if five or six of us decided to do a pool hopping race around Dhahran. Now there weren't a lot of private pools, but we managed to take a phone book and mark the ones we knew about. The idea was to jump the fence, strip down, skinny dip across the pool, dress and dash on to the next pool.

We were going to end up at the main pool at recreation. Well, as one, might expect, bright lad and lassies that we were, no one bothered to actually check and see what, or if these people actually had pools. So off we go and we hit the Lupiens house first, HA!!!!A pool about 20 feet in diameter and five naked Olympic medalists trying to swim it across it and getting all tangled up. With all the confusion of getting dressed a shoe or such got left behind. Tom who was fastest took off up the hill and jumped the next yard hedge. We all followed suit and here was a real pool. Dashing like stalled

Dolphins we went across it and lights came on and here we are jumping and dancing for our lives, butt's a bare and all and off we go.

By now, someone has called Security and S'aid was hot behind us. We hit two more pools on the hill and started towards 6th street. We knew Polly Robinson had a pool and her house was next. The problem with Polly's pool was that it was tile and slippery. Talk about a ruckus, I do understand that a pair of delicates was found the next day and perhaps we should have realized that we were telling on ourselves as we went around to the drag leading to recreation. One more pool we thought of and over the brick wall down by the Goellners house and the screams of agony were heard in Bahrain like you would not believe. A damn WADING pool??? I am still amazed that no one broke the backs or arms or legs. But we tore it up, that was for sure.

So off we head, now with the lights of Security all around and we are into the game of "starlight, star bright, try to catch us tonight".

Many people never knew that there was a small pool right next door to the Reed girls and we hit it with a vengeance knowing that we were within sight of the big pool at recreation. This pool was about ten feet long and was designed for a person to use as a single lane training pool. What we did know, naked and one after the other we swam it, that the boys were winning. Think a pair of drawers was found at the bottom of the pool the next day.

Suddenly and without warning as we are hopping and jumping around dressing to hit the main pool trucks come from several sides with lights ablaze. We mighty mice caught in the brilliance of their spot lights and bright beams. ZOWIE, we were gone. The girls, being much wiser stayed behind the last fence and snuck home.

We three men of orient bare, headed into the trap of there…ok, so no poet, but we knew no matter what the main pool had to be hit. Over the fence, knocking over the guard house at the gate and whooping like crazed Indians into the pool.

The first shark hit about two minutes later and soon the swarm of feeding frenzy of parents, mad pool owners and Security were upon us. The pool overhead lights are on and here were three are. Rather shamefully in an exposed position and to the merriment of all, many a rude comment on young boys was made. We crawled like a sea turtle on hot sand to the shower room, and there met with Mr. Kieswetter and a few imposing people. We thought we might deny it, but what fools we were to not remember that Mom's always sewed name tags into everything. The evidence was overwhelming and we faced the news of recreation being so far off limits for us for the rest of the summer that we might as well have gone to RT and swam in the gulf.

Best of all, the girls had got home, and when awaked, they looked so innocent and in unison, "Those boys must have stole our things to get us in trouble". I actually heard the skin crack on S'aid's face as he grinned from ear to ear on this one.

So to KK, BB, and another, may you're shorts never be left behind again.

Damm, that was a long summer and my last as a returning student.

ANNUITANTS REUNION

I just returned from a fantastic Annuitant Reunion. Saudi Aramco and the Reunion Committee did a first class and professionally run program. The food was fantastic, San Diego is absolutely beautiful and there were quite a few Brats that showed up.

Many of the Annuitants were quite pleased with the turn out and many commented on the number of Brats that were there. Have to admit, while talking with Wendy Cyr (Brat) we realized there was the possibility some of the retiree's were possibly younger that we are. Now that's a blast. We had a terrific meal provided by Aramco Services and a top notch speaker from Saudi Aramco and so many more showed up that Barbara Bowler-Predmore (DH65) had to have extra tables. Brats, Barbara doesn't like a lot of light shown on her, but many, many people will tell you, that is one top of the line operation that our fellow Brat co-chairs. She handled one issue after another and with amazing grace. Kudos to her from all of us that were there.

I was pleased and proud to see that our Aramco Brat, Inc. President and Treasurer were both there and made all Brats look good. I know many people enjoyed talked to Diana and I heard from several people that anything they wanted to know about the Brats, they could get answers from

Diana and Kathy Montgomery right away. I think, ABI might be able to let us know who all was there, that we must have had forty or so. We were well represented by our elected officers and all of the Brats there appreciated the ABI had a sign in sheet for us there so we could see who was there. Many thanks to you both. We did have a Brat Group photo taken right before the Bar-B-Que and there was at least one Brat older than me.. Sorry Bill, had to do it. Self defense you know.

My old comrade in night stalking, Jeff Yeager, (DH51) tried to sneak in for free food, but his Mom and Dad caught him and he has been grounded for a week.

The display room had Aramco Services and the Saudi Aramcos "Heritage House" people there and they had dates, and Gowa ready each morning. I was able to collect an additional 3,750 photos and many more coming which I will get up on my website for all to enjoy as soon as I can.

Many of the people there had stories to tell me about my beloved Mother and that made a wonderful experience for me. Many knew my Dad and spoke about him and told many tales. This made the difficulties getting there all worthwhile.

A massive "Shukran" to Barbara and the Annuitants organization. They made us all young again.

DADS DARN
RADIO

I walked outside, first time since school let out for the month of June and headed by habit right for the bus stop to go to school. I remember thinking that I had so many things to do that I better go to the pool and layout and think about what to do first. I was wearing a neat set of tan shorts and white tee shirt, most likely from some guy named Tavy. I had been to RT the week before you see. My sandals were the delight of Arabia, Michelin made. They, unlike my non tagged sears sneakers would get at least 50,000 miles, although tended to flap a lot. The unmistakable sound of a sandal, the slap of the flat part against your foot. In particular if they happened to be your brothers sandals, the brother called "Bigfoot", was a sound you could try to get in sequence.

Today however I had major serious worries. It was deemed by my Mom that I develop a sense for the world and so I had my Dad's safety award battery operated radio and was tuned into the Aramco Public Radio station for some tomfoolerly about just how much pain the radio station operator was in. The news came on promptly as always and I was by then a remarkable red from lying by the pool making big decisions after catting around for awhile. Charlie Armstrong was, as usual taking all the glory from us dolphins as the girls were all watching him make spectactacular dives from the diving board. I always wonder what held that suit on. There was more material in a hand towel but he always came up to a hand of applause as he was fantastic and most certainly a work of art.

However I digress, the radio was talking about some earth shattering opinion and the talk around the pool immediately turned into a blazing debate about nothing and so after piles of spears were left armoring around we moved to the main conference room, the baby pool. This was the life of the world. My little radio was now bashing the world with the far right sound of elevator music and the debate was really getting nasty. Someone said it was Miller time and so we surly bastards all got up, politically exhausted and went to the teen canteen window and immediately demanded that Mohammad Al- Canteena being us our square burgers in a large size on round bread. Once called Arab bread but in the small bushes we had for decoration, the ridge made it almost impossible to let our dreams fly, so we had to be politically correct and not call it Arab brad in an Arab land. We all knew that wasn't democratic.

Suddenly there was a shriek from the ladies room. A huge Hakuuuu had been heard and the first and to my knowledge the only Mag pie bird was seen doing dives and pearling around in a great show of air power when the life guard ran in to help the young lady in distress. We mighty men of the T-makers Society had already got our duck rolls in a row and were on our way in to placate her trauma from too much bird of prey. Unfortunately for us, the joint was full and we weren't allowed in. Who was this guy that stopped us heroes? Ohhh, thirty minutes out of the pool you say? Now I remember, Sabastian the lifeguard, once known in his home of Pakistan as Mr. Ramorse Ali Gatea. Moved to Aramco for security sake and had elevated the blood pressure of us young men to an elevated level of bright red.

Now the radio took on urgent meaning, there was an interruption. In the gulf of baby pool, a breaking news story was in process. We scurried to the pool, burgers and bebsi's in hand. What was the urgency...dammit, some one had sat on the raft we had the radio on and it, raft and all were compressed to the pool bottom. The lady in black weighed in at several hundred pounds and was patrolling the baby pool for suspected troubled youths that may have had plans upon her young children.

The rush was fast and furious to save the radio. we needed our daily too long dose of the ever intrusive news commentary made by the minute.

Someone offered to use push pull tactics and we arms inspectors grabbed one each and tried to get her up. Sad dammit we found that the Al-Samsung had been destroyed. I had to report this to the security council at home and there, Mom had Turkey cooking, Greece was spilling, and I made a comment that she should be careful not to burn her Ankra when Dad darkened the door. "Where is my radio and your brothers shoes, you are in violation of rule number 10,5441 and have been for eleven hours." "You are hereby ordered to self destruct in one week or I alone, without your Mothers vote will make you pay for the disrespect you showed in taking your brothers shoes and my radio." Wasn't life so much better before....chatters, I have had fun with this and if I offended anyone, tough. For those that need a term paper of this, citations listed below. Ahhh, those bygone days of simplicity..... I think I am going home and take off my shoes and socks and wade in the Persian Gulf one more time. On a serious note, I will be in Riyadh and Dhahran at the end of March and first week of April.

AWOL AND
A FEW OTHER
COMMENTS ;->

A s far as going AWOL or pulling pranks, I think San Marcos Baptist Academy had a large percentage of such stories. Mayhap because so many Brats went there. Kevin Colgan was my roommate and we lived in the "fishbowl" dorm called Crook Hall. I always wondered about the name. One of the stories that I well remember was when the Commandant, Col. Archie Buckner came out when we were at morning roll call and parade and announced that someone had stolen underwear from another Cadet and we were going to do a spot check right there. The parade ground was between and in front of several dorms and a lot of females students passed by on their way to breakfast. We normally marched to the mess hall.

So without much ado, we were ordered to drop our pants and the Company Commander was to inspect the labels as we all had our names sewn in. The best part of this was the fact that many didn't have time to get properly dressed and so there were many a shiny hinney showing to the great amusement of the girls and others. The culprit was not found and I always thought it was due to a different escape over Christmas which I'll tell later. I also left the school without permission and was expelled in my Senior year. I actually graduated from San Marcos High School and even tho I have financially supported SMA I did not finish there.

As far as fitting in, in 1968 Aramco Security, where I spent my last summer student job in tried to put together a plan to explain the conversion from Aramco to Stateside, Mr. Hank Brentari and I worked on this but at the time Aramco never got it off the ground. Hank was a great Security man and a friend over the years.

I followed the exploits of many of us for years and there was a very obvious thread of not fitting in and although we, or many did adapt, most seemed to be loners or dropped away from their Aramco heritage and became as the locals.

I have always felt that by not having finished High School in Arabia, many of us never got closure, I found that in the previous reunions, much closure was achieved by being able to once again touch a dear ones face, or shake the hand of a best friend.

On the note of the reunion, I would encourage all of you to go, although I will wait until the next one as I want to see more of you and hopefully it will be like before in a Mid West or Eastern area so we can have even more fun. I have had many Brats ask about a smaller gathering in Texas, but think that we need to support the ABI and not have separate reunions, although gatherings are always great. I would like to plan a small gathering in San Antonio or Austin for the near future.

One thing about reunions, the group is so diverse that many have various feelings about facing the past or seeing a person that was once so special. Most reunions and in particular Chandler were and are magic. The next reunion will be such I think. I have heard many are concerned about money and cost. Let me tell you, there is no cost or sacrifice that is not worth suffering through in order to once again see the ones we held dear.

The unemployment issue has been brought up and the points of comment are interesting, but I also lost my business and employment, but turned other things to my advantage and although not as happy as I was once, will live just fine in the world of employment, even if it is tenuous at best. I find the extensive reporting about "conditions" in the employment field to be an excuse. I'll put up with a lot to have some security. I can always fuss later. Too many of us are out of work and many of us were close to retiring and many have had to adjust. So we adjust and maybe not make the "standards" a major point.

Iraq seems to be a diversion by the Bushies, he will have his way or as his Dad, go back to hiding. He did the same tactics in Texas, "His way or the Highway" and when the time came, it was the highway, although I feel that we have pushed him out of Texas to the Presidency for which some of us feel may have not been prudent.

All of the above is my own personal opinion, not wanting the typical twenty day debate on words or lines of words, but the most important thing of all is to remember that we are all Americans and we grew up in Arabia and a lot of what happens affects us somewhat deeper than it might a local person.

I think that many Brats have chose to let go of things that were negative in Aramco, and there was a lot more then the few we have heard about. However we, and I am as guilty as others, have made our time there seem to be a fantasy, and in reality it wasn't. Our education may have been the best thing to come from Aramco, but there was also a sense of safety and freedom that we and Saudi Aramco kids today no longer have. Ladies and Gentlemen, the world has changed and we are parting the veils of history to look at a past that seemed much brighter and free, however the dark side was there also. The Aramco I knew is not the Aramco of today, but that is a good thing for Saudi Aramco has achieved many great things and progress always starts small and in this case, grew up fast and furious.

This soapbox is really shaking so I'm stepping down.

BRAT CHAT

I joined Brat Chat many moons ago. I had a great time and enjoyed writing many a story, mixing and matching and remembering gentlier times. We have traversed the great dunes and walked the sandy beaches and rode a schmal of politics'.

It is time now to wander off and check my camels, for they still bellow for attention and the sheep need gathering. My black tent I will fold and the tales for around the fireplace I shall share with the time honored Bedu's I have met and enjoyed.

My stories of the 1000 days and nights of Arabia I shall continue, but alas I no longer have the desire to live in the present climate of Brat Chat and the dominance of those who seem to be most vocal, for they do not recall the unbelievable spearfishing at the old Half Moon Bay and many never even heard of Sandy Hook or Imhof or that at one point Abqaiq had 18 families and Dhahran was under a square mile, or that tar roads melted and bare feet ran across RT main boulevard on planks of wood. Or that Santa came by B-24, DC-3, Helo, camel, donkey, horse and on staggered foot.

But most of all, the smell of jasmine and the honey suckle…the trillion eyes of God staring down at night and the multiple shooting stars, sometimes so many you couldn't make a wish they came so fast. Or the all night Tri-D's, the unbelievable swim meets where whales and sharks and tuna and guppies all played as one.

The hero's of youth, Mr. Fairlie, Mr. Quick in Scouting, Bob Long, Mr. Sprietsma, Mr.Goellner, Ms. Crow, Ms. Fry and so many more to even include the ever present Mr. Riley at the Senior Staff School. Larry Barnes, a noted and worthy bedu, Mohammed at the Teen Canteen next to the Hobby Shop that so many hobbies were done at. Naji of Security, Mr. Kieswetter, Mr.Hank Brentari, and the early night forman, Hank, Bob, Brock and the many taxi's that knew your house and had the savy to drop you off half a block away so you could crawl if possible to the house. The white and brown, which was our heaviest substance abuse, perhaps because other than that we had little else. Now it is chic to talk of dark horrors that many of us knew, but I choose to forget or at least try to know that with all good there is some bad.

In Arabic, the traditional, almost total goodbye is more serious than Mas'allama so many use. I use the formal, Fi'Atmata'La. Fi'Atmata'la ya siddiq's e ya binta ay bints ay ibn's.

DRIVING 1966

It was a typical Saudi summer evening. Flies were stopping at rest stops for salt tablets and water and I was a returning student for the first time, My family didn't own a car. My Father thought that it was lazy to walk five blocks to work. I thought differently, for how do you achieve fame and fortune if you can't drive. My Uncle John, John Reagan, Nora and Mike's Dad, decided to help.

He had a 1959 huge armored vehicle called a Dodge. We got in and when the door shut, I felt a vault door had shut. He gave me the key and told me that the funny sticks with little round pads on the floor was the brake and the clutch. Clutch? I thought that was my grip on the knuckled black steering wheel.

We lived at House 639 at the top of sixth street and so the logical way is proceed down sixth and then back up. Right? This car had a rather steep slope to the back and the rear window wasn't all that large, and the side view mirror, yes, mirror was on the drivers side only. My Uncle had told me all about the hand out the window in various poses for signaling turns and stops, but he forgot to tell the Arab drivers that these hand signals meant something. Not that I had a clue, but the air felt good on the bare arm casually waving all around. I did learn the certain unintentional hand signals are very offensive to some adults. Guess they felt I had made a statement about their intelligence.

After about fifty feet of driving and over one hundred jerky stops and starts my Uncle was speaking in tongues. He had explained with great clarity what a "H" pattern was on this funny stick that came off the side of the steering column, but there was also a second stick like thing that had a handle on it with like a clasp. Yes, it is called a parking brake and it does have a purpose. Not used to shift gears, but impressive when you hit the curb in a fabulous parallel parking stunt. Course with a door on the passenger side stuck to the curb with a very neat line dent and the door sealed shut, pulling the parking brake and grinning like a chimp is not the way you impress a man that drove heavy equipment. He taught me a new hand signal, commonly called a left hand slap to the head. Signaling a complete lack of respect for such skilled driving.

The "H" pattern is rather amazing and to find reverse took some contortions I only wish I could do today I understand that Aramco later requested my Uncle pay for a multitude a scrapes, dents, dings and out right smashed parked cars.

I finally made it back up sixth street and nosed into the curb in front of my house. My Uncle, no longer capable of speech got out and the large bottle of third run he found seemed to drop dramatically. He made the remark I needed to take Aramco's Defensive Driving class…repeatedly. However, while unsticking my sweaty butt from the nalgahyde car seat I stepped out with a grin that was a bright as the Arabian noon sun. I thought all of those people coming up the hill were shouting words of great praise, and that was all I heard, although later I found out that I almost became a motor vehicle fatality.

However I DID DRIVE. I did take Defensive Driving later, and have a fine certificate signed by our very own Bill Cohea.

For the rest of you, have faith in your children. You raised them and I know all of you are good solid people that would have passed on their cares and concerns about driving. Incidentally, I do not teach Drivers Ed. In'sh'Allah.

May God ride on their shoulders as they enter the world of endless experiences, the driving experience.

DHOOOOOOOW,
THAT HURT

So it's hot. Something new about this, in Dhahran, August 1967? I had secured the plumb of summer jobs, I was in Student Recreation. We had it made. Planning dances, tri-d swim meets, trips, and Dhow trips to Bird island, Taurut Island and a strange sand spit in the middle of the Persian Gulf that only four Dhow captains in the known world knew about. Course we proceeded to hire these guys right away for their vast seafaring knowledge. You would think that with past experiences we would have at least run down to the pier in Al-Khobar and look at these magnificent floating palaces before hand, but nooooooo, we were able to leap tall buildings, outrun a speeding train, fall under a tall donkey and many such wonders. So, we booked the great Dhow trip of the year. Forever to be known as "That idiot Crockers idea".

Now as many know, Dhows will stay afloat with just the Captain and the engine running. No need for a boat, if just a few planks get back, it is considered a successful sailing. The ones we had rented were fine examples. We loaded up at the Dhahran theater with about 60 fine and true returning students, with all the anticipation of a dazed camel in the desert. We get on the mighty Kenworths and with a magnificent roar, we head to the pier. We were riding in an open trailer behind the truck and it was great fun. Just 9:00 am and already we are in the process of obtaining a outstanding sun tan. We had water cans, igloo's of course. Always thought that was an oxymoron for Arabia, but we also had a hundred cases of Bepsi and about three hundred pounds of ice. Which we had got chitties for from recreation and then promptly forged the amount to twice what we needed. "Be Prepared", Mr. Fairlie had told us as Boy Scouts.

We reached the pier and after clearing customs, a small trick of one person arguing with the official, waving all kinds of papers and the rest just proceeding to the wondrous yacht looking Dhow .Suddenly there is much milling about, confusion and questions from half opened eyes, I make it to the front and the ships guard is saying something in a high pitched voice, which from the night before was not going over well. This is not our ship, but there, he points. I thought the sun had affected me and no doubt many felt the same. There were four Dhows. Looked to me like four canoes with a sail. One looked a little down at the bow, but what the heck. Onward. We split the group up, all girls on mine and everybody else on the others. Ha, didn't I wish, although later this was a real dangerous thing to have done.

We had a ship to shore hand carried radio and plenty of box lunches from the Dining Hall, so we started off. Might have got a hint that things weren't right when the first Dhow backing out promptly settled in about ten feet of water and sat. Really an interesting sight. I think the sea floor was all that had held it up to start with. So we are now down to three Dhows and we set sail. We had agreed with the Captains that we would all go to Bird Island. Their interpretation of that was any island that had birds on it I guess. After about two hours and some absolutely breathtaking sights, the sunbathers you see....we arrive. How do I know this? Well I am playing Christopher Columbus at the very front and I see this little speck of island and suddenly with a great crunch I am thrown about fifteen feet off the front of the Dhow and land on my butt in two feet of water. The fool had sailed right into a sandbar and I wasn't holding on. Oh, one other point of brilliance was that I forgot the rope ladder so we end up using a plank and a roe to lower everybody and get to the shore. Remember this plank, It becomes important.

Now, you had to be there to understand the yelling and raising hell when everybody found out that "Bird Island" was about twenty feet wide and fifty feet long and that's that. Hell, I'm not Magellan, I don't navigate. So we are all soon sunbathing and spear fishing, having a great time. Mike Mandis is spear fishing and catches a sea turtle and we get several people to ride him as he swims around. The water is azure blue and the sky nothing but a huge yellow ball hanging there. The weather seems to be getting a little windy so we all start back to the Dhows, which are now at high tide and the island is fast disappearing. We start climbing on board and pushing and shoving some of the ladies to the deck. This created a lot of rude comments from the ladies, but I was innocent I promise.

Finally we start back, still extremely hot, everybody seems to be turning bright red and the wind starts picking up. The water is getting choppy and I notice that boards seem to be floating away from the Dhow. As all or most of you may remember, the Dhows had a little enclosed hamman on the back that hung over the water. Highly sophisticated toilets. So in goes Tom Masso, and suddenly there is a large swell and we hear a very vulgar comment and the entire hamman cabinet falls off the deck. If words could only express the thoughts and the tremendous amount of gut wrenching laughter that took place as Tom is working his way out of the fast sinking hamman. He swims to the Dhow and we pull him on board, all the while translating in about twenty languages what he is calling us. The little Dhow Captain is almost unconscious with laughter and we are going in circles as he has the tiller hard over and he can't calm down enough to straighten out.

Well, we finally start back and we are considerably lower in the water, the other Dhows are out of sight and we seem to be sinking. The Captain is puffing on his Hubbly Bubbly and has no concerns. I am on the Aramco radio screaming for help and then the rain starts. Figures. I still hear the little "Putt, putt, putt, putt, putt" of the small engine and no, I am not thinking "I know we can, I know we can, I know we can". Instead I'm thinking about how this will look in the "ASH" student newspaper with commentary from 30 badly burned and mad returning students.

Suddenly the motor quits and we start to sink. Panic everywhere, and most amazing was Tom and some girl using a little hand crank pump about the size of an oversized flashlight trying to save us.

Well, after settling in about fifteen feet of water we stop sinking. We are on the bottom. Soon an Aramco tug comes blazing across and what a sight. They had heard us and came after us.

We get back to the pier, the others there already, and they are being transported to the Dhahran Health Clinic. Massive sunburns and bruises.

Over twenty spent the night in the clinic due to almost third degree sunburns and worse, once again parents are everywhere.

Now to make the day, I am stopped by two Saudi police who want to
know if I plan to pay for the sunk Dhow. "What" I screamed, that fool tried
to kill us all. They calmly explained that the Captain told them I had taken
the plank that held that floating pile of scrap together and never put it back,
and thus we sank. I see Mom out picking up the plank, and I know it is not a
good sign and I also know what "walking the plank" meant. I think she meant
to "walk" me all the way home with it. Smack by smack. Anyhow, remember
the ice? Well it was still solid and full of Bepsi, so I traded the Captain the
whole lot for sinking his ocean liner. He thought that was great and I heard
later that he hired a bunch of donkeys and some pearl divers and they fixed
it and towed it in and he made a handsome profit off of the Bepsi.

Needless to say, I was somewhat shunned for weeks after that until the
last Tri-D dance held by Student Recreation where due to unforeseen circumstances some major embarrassments came about and sealed my fate as a
summer student recreation leader for all time. That's a story for a later date.

DIARY

Mike—My name is Christi Baumann Lillesand. My mom, Lois Baumann was a teacher in Abqaiq and Dhahran from 1963-1986. I wanted to let you know that I enjoyed your journal so very much. I went home for the last time in December 1981, only I didn't know it was my last trip. Sort of felt like there was no closure because of that. Your journal entries and details really brought things back for me and I was so nostalgic! the only portion that threw me for a loop was the cemetery entry. I never knew there was a cemetery in Dhahran, although if I had thought about it I would have figured. I do remember going on Girl Scout hikes back by the incinerator?? and my mom said that's where the cemetery is.

DOES ANYONE
KNOW WHY?
PERHAPS POETRY?

A small boy walks about the sandy ground. his eyes twinkle and his thoughts are of mischief. There are few others and he seems in a daze, but what is happening is the beginning of a great part of his life's phase. He knows he will travel the land alone but his heart knows he must do it. His mission, to find a friend. His skills, not too finely honed for he is alone. You can tell that he knows but won't accept that dark cloud in a scorching bright day, for its a young adventurer, alone and that way to say.

His Mom is at home, no grass to water, no water to waste. His Dad is working, an office somewhere. He knows not where. His little heart seems surrounded by doubt, but he boldly goes and looks about. There is activity as he looks and the wind is blowing. The sand stings his face and his cherub like features wrinkle from the heavy thought he understands not. He know he is alone, for he sees his tracks. A single pair that run nowhere. What does one do when one has run, and now looks around and sees that he is now fifty three. His tired eyes look around once again. The grass is green and the place is a maze. He walks the path where he trod as a boy, but where did he come from and where does he go. He feels the pain of a thousand alone, yet knows he walks the path of many others before and after his vigil began. He knew as a child he would stand tall, but he knows as a man that he has fallen down and maybe it was that day so long ago...when he looked down the sandy road and felt for the first time, the emptiness and loneliness inside. He knew back then that friends would not come, a loner perhaps without any fun. He grew in his life, but doing not well, his mind accepting he had no one to tell. What did the boy say at the age of one? What does the man do as he passes fifty two?

His mom and his dad, his family and more, he feels the heat but his heart is sore. He doesn't know why, and he starts to cry. But perhaps its best, for young he may be he knows he must die.

Many years later, passing this way, he looks around where he used to play. The ground is now hard, the sand is gone and concrete is the name of the land. His playground of dunes has become the well of progress and his friends all gone, or where they ever there to start with? He looks with eyes that see many a day and his heart hurts as he surly did pay. And now as he sits, in the land of his life, and looks at the people, he knows it is not right. The place has changed and the people have gone, what happen to them and why did he forget. He loved this place, the home of his start. A leap of faith and a thought of his fate, but then he remembers, he loved this place. The taste of the sand, the smell of oil, the water lashing the beach of his youth. He walks the roads and paths of a child, his mind lost in the days of his youth, but where does he go and how does it seem, that fifty years later, the boy still has his dream?

As you have guessed, he is really a mess, but he finds that if he goes back in his mind, his heart does lift, a little as time drains away as the sand from his tilted hand, yet he also knows there is only so much land. His mind is numb from all of the fun, but his heart is cold for it is in a dark place. Someone shut the door to it a long time ago, he never opened it again and now he must go.

However fear not my dears for he shall return, he will do it all again and again. He loves the air, the night above and although much older, he wanders that sandy road and always looks as if he knows, but in reality, the boy is lost. He will one day see this and decide to change, but change is hard and friends are not there, so many are gone and he wonders if it is fair?

At the best he can only say, It is another day and the way is more clear. Yet the pain of the life that lost so much makes him struggle and then shake like a bear. The sand flies off of the storm about his soul and he feels the weather change and knows he must go. He looks around and glances down, the sand is there he has but to touch it and become once more aware. God gave him his life to enjoy as best, but he might have missed it if not for the rest.

Perhaps he thinks this jumble of words has a goal but he knows not what. Just some thoughts from awaking from a dream of the sand. A single tear rips from his eye and thunders down his face and flies into the sky. It strikes the ground and shatters, yet in a way, it is all that matters. His youth is there, in the sand of his soul, but the life he has, he made by his will, now let him start, for he knows he must. He has awakened and lost his touch. But the boy who walked into the sun, shall once again make a rule of fun.

DUNE RACING

I'm sure that many of you went sand dune racing in company trucks at one time or another…well, here's my version of why desert seduction doesn't always work..

Late one night in 1967 I was involved with a young(Now geezer)lady and thought that I would impress her with my fantastic ability to run the dunes, so off we went to the beach and into the dunes. Well, on top of the ridge we were doing just fine. The stars were crystal clear and the mood was fantastic for love.

From atop this one dune we could see the flares and light of Dhahran, so we stopped. Being a sophisticated seducer I had brought along the necessary supplies…bottle of brown, blanket and summer love.

Well we sat there for about an hour, walked to the water and went skinny dipping, I remember how she was all lit up in the water with phosphorus luminescence and this just made her more beautiful. The brown certainly wasn't hurting either at this point

So back to the truck and I'll be dammed it the thing wasn't sunk to the bottom frame in sand….Seems as if you can drive at speed over the sand, BUT you never stop to smell the roses, or in my case Kiss a camel.

Aramco had the foresight to have had a piece of plywood in the back and for over four hours I dug and worked and sweated and believe insulted every living, dead and past desert creature. She, of course, seemed to have lost the mood.. never did figure that out...

So after hours of work, I got the damm thing on the boards and we got in and I told her.. "I'm smarter that this dammed desert, I'm going to get a running start and we will be out of here". I think that due to a mixture of sweat, sand and temper her response is best lost to history.

So after gunning the engine I shifted and took off like a rocket, straight down the dune and into about six feet of water. This of course made her night and she was soon stomping merrily on her way home, while I was considering suicide, after all, the truck had been borrowed, and having always been the brassy devil I thought I was, it was Mr. Crampton's personal company truck.. He was the Dhahran District Manager.(As an aside and not that she was involved, Barbara Crampton is a classmate.)For you youngsters, that made him the mayor of Dhahran...The end result was that for the remaining time I was there for that summer, I had to report to his office at least three times a week for "light duty assignments" that he could think of...Thank God there weren't that many pets in Arabia then or I know what I would have been doing with a spoon....

I do drive better now...stuck Camel and no Camelette

EXECUTION OF A BRAT

TRUE STORY

It was humid, and the night was so, so long...I knew that some reflections might help, but the thought of the dawn and the method of execution was overwhelming.

Yes, I had done the crime, but they tried me as an adult, although I was only 17. It was a sentence of death and I knew in my heart I would never look at the sunlight this way again. My appeals fell of deaf ears. Rejected by all and pleas of mercy were to no avail.

The Warden was female and even though I thought she took pity, there was a sternness in her eyes which told me she would carry out her job. She told me that the pain was brief, and that I would be released into a new life.

They had made me get a haircut and I had even gone to Mass where the Priest heard my confession. I told him all I had done that I could remember. The hurt and the pain I had caused so many. I tried to justify the bad with the good I might have done and asked repeatedly for a reprieve. All I wanted was one last chance. The ruling came down, an hour before sunrise. The final plea had been rejected.

Tears whelmed up in my eyes, I had been allowed to see my so sweet love just for a fleeting moment, knowing I was seeing her for the last time. Our lips had brushed, but there was no time left.

The Warden brought my last meal, eggs, and sausage and a glass of orange juice. She told me to be brave, but the ache in my heart and the weakness of my knee's told another story. I had to go to the bathroom and yet, I didn't. Fear was rampant thought out the room. Worse, just a hint of sunlight was starting to creep over the top of the brick wall and I knew it was close.

I was led out, they even packed up my pitiful belongings and carried them out. Down the hall out the door and into the vehicle, with the warden and her staff to be taken to the place of execution. Another building away from all the rest. We passed by barbed wire fences and eerie silence. Suddenly we were there. I was passed on to others, who weren't so caring. Quickly they led me into a room that could be pressurized and sat me down. The strapped me in and within minutes I felt the floor tremble as the generators turned over. The lights blinked once and as I looked around, fear, panic and terrible loneliness drowned me. I looked thru the glass and could see the members of my family who had come to say goodbye. There was my Mother, tears running down her face. My Father, stoic as ever, and many others I did not know.

Suddenly there was an eerie silence, I felt my straps tighten against my body. The light was blazing in from the window and the pressure was almost pushing me back into the seat. The tears in my eyes were blurring all sight and the crushing pain in my heart told me it was almost over.

I looked one last time, feeling the bursts of emotion surging thru me and causing me pain, and out the glass I saw, for the last time before my vision failed, all the people and places I had loved so very dearly disappearing behind me. I could barley blurt out "Goodbye" when I was gone.....

I will never be able to explain it any other way, This was my last trip to my home and as the plane arose from the desert floor, I lost my heart knowing I was leaving my beloved Arabia for the last time as a returning student. Truly an execution.......

EYE OF THE BEHOLDER

" An eye for an eye" was the expression used by my mother as we went out of the Main gate to the Amir Jawuli's Palace. "So help me, if you even think of embarrassing your Father tonight, I will show you what Saudi justice is all about!" This from my own mother, who as far as I knew had no reason to deliver such a sermon. I mean what could happen at some old Arabs house where I was being forced to go and eat.

I knew all about the fact that a camel feast was some kind of special winding, but after all, I felt it was way out of line to make me put on a suit that was way too small and made my butt stick way out and high water pant legs that might have covered my knees, but I doubt it. And worse, a BOLO tie? Where did that come from. I later found out that a mother, using both hands may strangle a first born with ease with one of these. A fact she denies to this day as not being why she made me wear it..I, however wanted to appeal to the Supreme Court on the issue and demanded she prove she was my Mom, to which she simply said. "I'm not, we found you among some camel droppings and felt sorry. So shut up and sit !"

The Amir, one big sucker I thought when I saw him, was being introduced to a bunch of Aramco big wigs and when it was Dad's turn, he introduced me as his "sway wahed walid fe maufy muk"The Big Arab had on a black thobe and black robe with gold trim. I found this interesting and

175

grabbed part of it to see i f I could get some of this gold. He looked down at me, from about forty feet high I thought and with a simple gesture froze my blood. He smiled.. He then told the story about defending his cousin King Abdulazziz Ibn Saud and how a spear was thrown clean through his body, to which I in total disbelief said something to the effect, "HA !" Well the room dropped about forty degree's, I saw Mr. Barger, My Dad, Mr. Zadorkin and others all looking for tent flaps as we were all seated around this large area that was covered with rugs. The Amir, with what looked like the crack of doom on his face called me over. So what else, Mom pushed me to him and he did something which I heard later was common and he had a lot of fun with it, but you can imagine the shock effect on a 12 year old. He pulled up his shirt and there was this terrible long scar and he showed us all where it had another on his back. He then told me, "See that door. STAND THERE AND WE SHALL SEE." Well, as I peed down my leg the Amir and many others doubled up with laughter. All except Mom. I think she actually wanted the spear thrown... So now here comes the food. great trays full and three large ones with baby camels on them. Heads and all. This one fool kept filling my little cup with the most awful drink. Later found out that was coffee and if I had not pointed it at the server each time, I thought to get rid of it, he thought to fill it, I could have stopped drinking this stuff. I had already poured five or six cups into Mom's purse, How would she know? I thought it was neat that they had cooked a baby camel and wondered if it was real. Without a thought I lifted the leg and tail part of one, why? Who knows, and it came off in my hand. I yelled and the Amir almost died with tears streaking down his face. I thought I had torn off a leg and didn't really know what I was doing. Mom's first smack of the evening was heard by guards in the desert who rushed to the tent. The Amir waved them away almost unable to control himself.

So I dig in, hey, this is great. Fruit, rice all kinds of stuff. The came the big moment. The Amir was going to award the eyes of the three camels to the honored guests. I was flat out amazed and my eyes were as big as saucers as they carved out the eyes and the Amir passed them to Mr. Barger and two other big shots. Little to my knowledge the Amir was having the time of his life with my antics. He saw what I had done with the coffee and had ordered one of the servers to get a small tray and put two black olives in some milk. This he then proceed to tell all was a "special" set of eyes for the young man of so many questions. I damn near died. I was going to eat an eyeball.. Not me, no way, Fi A'mana' La, adios, goodbye baby. Mom being her normal self, gave me a look that stuck my butt to the floor as if I had been glued down. The Amir sent over this tray and my stomach is heaving.

The damn things were looking at me for crying out loud. The room became as still as the desert night and I knew my stomach, by now full of camel and fruit and rice was not staying where it was supposed t o. However, knowing that Mom had plans far beyond those camel eyes if I caused any more trouble, I took one and gamely popped it into my mouth. I never even tasted it, for as I bit down my whole meal came up and into Mom's purse and lap. That blew the top off of Mom and the Amir was shaking uncontrollably and I distinctly remember Tom Barger grinning like an old Bedu. They were all in on it and when Mom got done with me, I think I had a camel eyeball where the sun doesn't shine and I should be allowed home sometime around the millennium.

Yet, let this not end on this note. I also have eaten of the eye and done so several times. It is indeed a little hard to do and the best method I have found is to swallow whole and fast and then rice in a hurry.

The Amir Jawuli was as good a friend as we Americans ever had in Arabia. Many of you may not know this, but for many years, in the early days, when ever there was an outing of scouts or whatever, out in the dark of the desert about forty feet apart we were always surrounded by Bedu warriors charged with our safety. The King had ordered it and Ibn Jawuli carried it out. It was many years before even Aramco knew about this.

I got to know the Amir over a period of time, and his passing to be with his King was a sad day. Aramco and America had lost a friend.

I'LL TRY TO ANSWER BOTH YOUR QUESTIONS ABOUT FR. ROMAN AND MR. EARL GRAVES

Fr. Roman left Arabia at the request of Aramco and the Local Catholic Dioceses. He was assigned to the Gila Indian Tribe, Gila Reservation right next to Guadalupe, Arizona. That's a small unincorporated town of mostly Indian and Hispanic descendants. There is a really nice Catholic church on the reservation and Fr. Roman is buried there I believe.

FR. ROMAN DIED OF NOSE CANCER IN 1978/79.

He was well liked by the tribe and has been given credit for a lot of modernization of the facilities on the reservation.

***************** Mr. Greaves**********************

Mr. Greaves was here to see me in 1985. He had been to South Arabia as a Missionary passing out Bibles and had entered the country from Yemen illegally. He was shot in the leg by Saudi border patrol and was treated in a Yemeni Hospital and deported to the USA. The US Govt. rescinded his passport and he decided to leave the US. He was last heard from in South America, Bolivia doing Missionary work. He had developed a bad drug habit of pain medicine due to improper treatment of his wounds and I last heard from him via post card from Paraguay in 1988.

His family had no contact and wanted none with him. I have several of his art works and a sculpture he did for me while he stayed here with me in 1985.

FATHER ROMAN
AND MY CRUSADE

Ahhh, it's Friday, and although not Sunday, it is Sunday Service in Dahahran. But, before I relate the end of the story, perhaps a short trip as to how Fr. Roman and I developed a particular meaning to the word "Altar Boy".

As a good Catholic boy who never had much to confess, (AND you can stop laughing right now, Doral), I think because this was done on a weekly basis, I decided that I wanted to become an Altar Boy for the Church. My Father was very devout and I attended Mass wether I wanted to or not. Most times kicking and screaming after a night of skinny dipping in a pool run, or an exhilarating run across Dhahran, with the dogs of Security snapping at my heals. So, as one might imagine, going to Mass at 8:00 am wasn't real popular around me.

However having met Father Roman in Catechism and taking class at his house, which had the small chapel and class room, I decided that to calm the mounting danger from Dad I would proudly announce that I was going to follow his footsteps and become an Altar Boy. I mean, how hard can it be, plus I actually thought that there was real wine in the back.

First, you had to learn Latin as the whole Mass was in Latin then.. What a job, I had to write cheat notes on the sleeve of the Church vestments/garments we wore so that I could say the right thing at the right time. Now imagine trying to read these while Fr. Roman is glaring at you and the Church/theater is full of adults, AND the front row is full of your peers, who were, of course very supportive.

I actually did ok until one terrible Christmas High Mass where I set new standards among the Church for patience. Fr. Roman had given me the easiest task, and I thought most demeaning of jobs, to simply stay to the left of the Altar and swing the incense burner and keep it lit for the service.

First, I am most likely the only person alive who could fall asleep on my knees, but worse, let the incense burner fall on the floor and catch the rug on fire. So now, in the middle of Mass Fr. Roman boots me with his scandal, sets his robe on fire and spills out the incense which also catches fire. Nothing major, just horrendous silence from the packed theater as I believe most thought Fr. Roman, known for his calm composure, was going to revert to a pagan ritual and sacrifice me right then and there. Well he stomped out the little fire and me and then we relit the burner and in plain english, no latin, he told me that if it went out, so did I.

Well, after my heart got back in my chest I realized that he was serious and so I started swinging the little burner back and forth as fast as I could in little motions. This caused great hilarity in the crowd as I soon had the stage smoked up and you could hardly see. From nowhere a scandal got me again and, caught by surprise I was in a swing and let go of the incense burner and it went over the stage into the front row of my, by now, advid fans and caused great delight.

Now Fr. Roman, known for his stopping Mass and lecturing, did a little "spin doctor" something to effect that I would be doing penance for a long, long time, but that God would understand the punishment. I was sent back stage and the Mass proceeded.

I didn't agree and so started the saga of Fr. Roman and Mike Crocker. I would go into confession and do my best to shock him with some kind of sin, just short of Mortal Sin as I still wasn't really sure about some of this. I would tell him things like I needed a little cash for a date, so "borrowed" it from the poor box at his house, at which he would go into a fit behind the confessional screen. Luckily for me, Aramco had let us use the right down front exit of the theater to hold the confessions in and the screen kept us apart. One drawback, I forgot he had the power to issue penance. I did so many "Hail Mary's" and "Our Fathers" that I developed callouses on my knees. It really got bad when he would pass out the host and place it on our tongues, I tried to bite his finger and he held a flat gold mirror shaped plate under your chin to catch the excess, and guess what, without so much as a blink, slap, and on to the next person. he was really good with that thing.

As to the wine. Well, Fr. Roman got wind of what I was attempting and filled a whole big bottle with prune juice right before Mass one day. I snuck in and drank a huge amount of the bottle, and thought "Man, that's bad wine". As most of you know, Fr. Roman's Masses go on for days if wanted to talk, and I developed a very serious problem about an hour into service, and kept wondering what his evil little grin was about every time he looked at me. As might be expected, I paid for that little liberty also.

One last thing..Fr, Roman never started Mass on time and, if worked up, went on and on. Well, one time and only once, I was in the crowd with my Dad and Mass started on time.. My Dad looked at his watch, shook it and tapped it to make sure it was running right. Exactly fifty minutes later, by this time the Mass was in English and we were all supposed to answer the end when Fr. Roman would say, "Go, in God's name and Peace" and we were supposed to answer "Thanks be to God." But, to this day, and my Dad vehemently denies this, I swear I heard my Dad say "Thank God!".....Mass ended.

I still have the Altar Boy pin I got from Fr. Roman, and have a deep belief in God to this day. Fr. Roman ended up being a dear friend and confidant in later years, although many a time he told me he knew I was his "test" from God. He just wished it wasn't daily.....

Rest in God's Peace my dear friend, Father Roman...

FINAL WORD

Hey, this "old Feller" has something to say about the litney of intelligent discussion on "Balls".

I think we are all "Balls up "as the English say..

Just to set it straight, I was referring to a colloquialism the "They are hiding, they have NO———s"...no reference to what women go thru or men.. AN American slang expression for someone who wants to take pot shots but doesn't want to go face to face...

However, I can relate a little incident....STORY TIME....that happened in 8 th grade. Where I learned the true meaning of pain...any hint here ? How many of you remember gymnastics and the side saddle horse or whatever the damn thing was called. All I know was that we were to run, jump up, grab the handles and throw ourselves forward. On this momentous occasion I did close to that, but hung up on the tail end, and kind a rocked forward on to the floor.

So after that smashing Mr. Goellner has us on the trampoline, and as many will remember there was a rope with a sling that we could use, but being brave and bold, and a little tender, I thought that I could just jump and twist and twirl with the grace of an elephant. This I did and higher and higher I went until I decided to really go for it and heaved up as high as I could go, came down near the edge and threw flung myself out onto the gym floor. Anybody remember gym floor burn ? Well that stunt got me a set to be proud of.

However as my luck runs, it wasn't over yet.. I was walking home, or rather limping and waddling home when I saw Barbra Crampton up ahead and made some smart rude remark about her tennis playing ability.

I then learned that you can actually serve a——from a standing position without being on a court....I forgot or ignored that she had a racquet in her hand, so I feel that I may be somewhat of an expert on——s.

I also know that a horse can teach a man a very healthy respect for riding properly, but that's another odd ball story for later.

This Old Feller is going up to his seltzer water bath and put the heating pad on and dream of eternal youth....))))

Incidentally, I have a lamp made of a Camel——that was inflated and shellacked...any one else remember those ?

Seems like that reminds me of a bowling ball story, but perhaps another time;>

FIRE DRILL
AND SCOUTS

It all seemed very reasonable to me…and even now I still don't think the punishment fit the crime. It was just one of those days.

Wednesday Morning and the school is out for a fire drill on the black-top behind the gym.. It is Fire Prevention week and the Fire Department was there with several trucks and Mr. Fairlie had us Boy Scouts there to give a demonstration of semaphore message sending. Well, I was at the far end and was signaling to Bill Cohea I believe, and nobody was paying any attention so I sent him a message remarking about the ancestral history of the donkey and Mr. Riley, school principal. Something to the effect that there was a definite relationship, perhaps physical.. Unfortunately, the Girl Scouts had also been learning this flag message system and had a US Navy Officer, from one of the visiting destroyers in Rt. showing them.

Well, without me seeing it, several bright and very helpful young ladies read the message, went to the Officer and he went to Bill Cohea and had Mr. Riley and Bob Long and Mr. Fairlie watch.. They made Bill ask for a repeat and so I sent it, with some colorful elaborations and some very physical embellishments.

I understand the Officer was translating aloud and evidently Mrs. Riley was close by and passed out....I still say it was the heat.. I heard later that Bob Long and Mr. Fairlie were planning some real evil for me and that in my after life I would still be talking about it. I, blissfully unaware of all this started signaling a few choice thoughts about Debbie Dirr and certain physical characteristics that I greatly admired. By now I had the attention of most of the school and some unhappy adults. This officer was a lot of help by making sure even my mis-sent words were written down for Judge, Jury and execution.

Bill signaled that we could stop. My next position was to be at one of the fire trucks and assist, for a merit badge I might add. They had this hose which we connected to the fire hydrant and then to the truck. On this particular truck they had two huge wheels with hose, like a garden hose reel. Well, I thought it would help to pull out a length and did so.. In the meantime Mr. Riley, already having written my epitaph, Bob Long, Mr. Fairlie and the Fire Chief and the Naval Officer are all coming for me, without my knowledge. I was on the back side of the truck.

The Fire Dept. started a small fire and what I didn't know was that if you pulled the hose, it would trigger the pump and start the water. So I had the vicious end of a hose that suddenly came to life with 500 pounds of pressure, a hose I later learned was supposed to be held by three full grown men.

As is my fate, around the truck comes this group of killers and I flat out bowled them down with the water stream.. I was airborne from the pressure and wasn't aiming, but managed to get all of them. It was like being on a huge Cobra. Whipped the hell out of me.. They cut the water and I'm standing there, the adults are soaked and getting up off the ground, I see what has happened, still unaware my death was already a certainty from the messages, and run for the nearest truck. Right at that moment the Fire Department decides to put out this gas fire they had started and used the foam cannon on top of one of the trucks.. I ran right thru the stream and to the crowds delight the fireman turned the foam away from me and caught Mr. Riley and Mr. Fairlie, Mr. Long all over again, as they were in hot pursuit of me. Only this time with heavy foam. Down they went.

I ran to the school, and down into the locker room to change, out the front and was negotiating with a Dhow to go to Bahrain when Aramco Security got me...

I'm not sure how long I spent in various offices around town the next few days, but punishment upon punishment was the norm.. I had to paint fire hydrants, wash commodes at school, was restricted from recreation for life and came close to getting run over by Mrs. Riley later on. Did make friends with Debbie tho...So all's well that ends well, or in my case, looking up from the bottom of a well.

FISH STORY

One of the many fun things about Arabia was the scuba diving.. I remember Half Moon Bay and the sunked boats, one of which several of us put a goat skull on and called it the Holy Grail.

But the most fun I ever had, and almost drowned from laughter was the day that Chris Mohlman, super diver, and a bunch of us were out in the bay and poking around...remember how you had to dive below forty feet to get under the layer of jelly fish....seems as if the had found a level they liked. Anyhow there was this huge sea turtle and Chris decided to spear it.. Than thing probably weighed over a hundred pounds, (And I did see the one that washed up on the beach in RT that they said weighed over 300 pounds).

Anyhow, Chris managed to hit the turtle, but not fatally and the turtle got mad..I think he actually hit the tail...So this turtle starts spinning and Chris has a wrist strap on his spear gun and can't get loose...Pretty soon this turtle and Chris are flying thru the water, fifty feet down and the dammed thing takes him up and down thru the jelly fish at least ten times and drags him, it seemed like miles, before Mr. Goellner caught up with them and cut Chris free, Chris had welts like you wouldn't believe, But to top it all off, James Goellner was still at the bottom and the rest of us were heading up when he sees a big fish and spears it.. turns out to be a small, four foot shark and it turns on him and us. I learned to walk on water with swim fins that day, and I know the rest made it to shore faster than you could believe. I almost gave up diving after that, but now the stories are fun to tell.

Well, that's Fish for thought...

FLIES

Once year, I guess in 1977, I was moving with an armored column along the pipeline while on a training mission with the Saudi National Guard. We received a call from an Aramco spotter plane, you known the ones that flew up and down the pipe looking for stray Bedu's who might shoot the pipe. Anyhow they reported seeing an Aramco truck about three miles ahead of us. Upside down.

We moved out and investigated and found that a Saudi inspector had somehow passed away at the wheel and crashed. This was beyond description, but to >even get to the vehicle we had to fire several round of WP (White Phosphorous)near it to drive off the millions of flies. To this day I hate flies and can still hear the tremendous buzzing around that truck.

FLORIDA 1990

In May of 1990 I was in Florida at my main office, which was located in a seventeen story Hi-rise apartment building we owned. It was our headquarters for the firm and I had the whole East coast to travel over as VP of the company.

Anyway, in this building we had a security gate, guards and underground parking. All fenced and well lit. It was mostly retired New York Jewish people who lived there, all over 65 and we went to great lengths to make sure they were protected.

As I guess you figured, I have been licensed to carry a weapon for most of my life and on this particular day the manager, a very close elderly friend of mine had to make a bank deposit and asked if I wanted to go to Denny's for coffee. So we went to the elevators and down to the underground parking.

There was a little area off the elevators that had coke machines, etc. and the door way leading into the garage. I stopped to get a coke and she went out to get the car. Well, this property also had a boat dock and slips for boats that came up to the garage and two Haitian boat people had slipped over the dock and into the garage. I heard Pat scream and I went out the door. There she was leaning against the wall with blood pouring from her side and stomach. The Haitian was yelling for her to give him money, but didn't give her a chance to do it before he stabbed her again. About that time I came up and warned him to drop the knife, that I was armed and if he moved towards her I would stop him.

His friend only had a stick and the guy with the knife yelled again and I repeated it in Spanish. He understood and made a lunge to grab Pat and stab her again and I shot him in the head. The other guy fell to the floor and the shot drew Security who called for the Police and ambulance. The first officer to arrive took my weapon and got a statement from all concerned. Pat had over forty stitches and was hospitalized for two weeks. They weren't sure she would make it.

The Police department called me down the next day and returned my weapon and the Captain said they would have to put it to the Grand Jury, even though he had never heard of anyone being allowed to carry a weapon "anywhere" before, but he had been informed to turn the weapon over to me and ask no questions.

The Grand Jury returned a "no Bill" was only upset because when they asked me why I didn't just wound the man, I replied, in what they described as "very cold blooded", that I wasn't wasting a good bullet on nothing. The local papers ate it up and I became somewhat of a folk hero to the elderly of Miami Beach. Turns out the man had killed two teenagers two days before and the Police were still investigating that incident. He had robbed them and stabbed both. His partner confessed to it all. Incidentally, I have no regrets...

FOOTBALL

A while back someone asked about football in Arabia. We played flag football in the 60's but I don't remember any equipment, although based on my most memorable event, we probably should have.

I think it was 8th grade when I joined the team. I was a big kid, but basically didn't have the aggressive drive that is so needed in playing the game. I was on the T-Maker team, and although I was a bench warmer most of the time, I did actively participate in the scrimmages. I forget who the coach was at the time, but he had devised a number of interesting plays, and one of them was to be used against an overaggressive lineman, and was supposed to dampen his enthusiasm. It worked like this, the offensive line would allow the lineman to penetrate and as he did the two backs would come running directly at him, not quite shoulder to shoulder, but with enough space to catch the lineman on each of his shoulders.

I knew about the play but forgot but about it in the heat of the moment, and I couldn't believe my luck when the line opened up and I was able to penetrate-until I looked up to see Mike Crocker and Bill Cohea heading right for me. There are a number of expressions that come to mind-being hit by a train, ringing my clock, being hit by a pile driver, etc (none of them come close). Needless to say I was knocked silly by these two grinning behemoths. Perhaps helmets and pads would have been useful at that point but I doubt it.

Soon after that, I ended my football career, and took up the sport as a spectator. Chris Miller

GOOD CATHOLIC

S peaking of religion brings to mind that I was once a good little boy. The day of the Confirmation Dinner, I not sure how old I was, but under ten.

My best friend, who later went on to become a golf semi-pro was Douglas Burke. He was a good Catholic boy also, but we used to fight like cats and dogs over Catholic dogma, for example on the day of our Confirmation, living in Abq. several things happened that caused the questioning of faith.

To start Mom and Dad's day off right I had gotten one of the little girls who lived behind us on 13th street in Abq. to go for a ride on the Camp bus, which for us old timers, know it went around the camp all day. I saw nothing wrong with us riding the bus, but her Mom, mine and most of Abq. was out looking for these two little kids, because a Shamal had blown in and they thought we had got out of the fence, which I guess I might have been guilty of, and got lost in the desert. Well Aramco sent out over fifty search vehicles, A Saudi tracker was brought in and they started looking at the fruit market which used to adjoin Abqaiq. In the meantime we went by this activity at least twenty five times and enjoyed the excitement...never guessing we caused it. Nonetheless, about four thirty, knowing I had to be at Confirmation at 6:30 that night we got off the bus and started home. I got my bike and Doug showed up, and we got into a fight about if God was dead or not.. This fight got real physical real fast. The argument was that if He wasn't dead, how could He be in Heaven...By now I was real mad, dirty from fighting with Doug and riding home by the school as fast as I could, my bike hit some sand and over the handlebars I went. I know my hand hurt, but now my face was scratched up and Doug had put a lump on my head to start with. So home I go..no one there so I get dressed for the dinner.

As an aside, The Catholic Church had a Bishop from Aden, His Holiness Bishop Magleni, who was to be at the Confirmation dinner was in town, and a band made up of houseboys followed him around all day while he met with people and played "Never on a Sunday"...My Dad, a devout Catholic to this day, has never gotten over the fact that the Bishop liked the tune so much, he kept asking for it. The only problem was that the American's all knew the song refereed to a prostitute not working on a Sunday.. a day of rest. No one had the courage, until later, to stop the band.

Well, I got Doug, who looked pretty much as I did and we wanted to see what the excitement was all about, but didn't want to go all the way to the market, so we though "Why not climb something and we can see from there."

There was a 150' high communications tower in Abqaiq to talk with the exploration teams and was heavily fenced and had a guard. Once again, the guard messed up and up the tower Doug and I went. Evidently someone from the market saw us and the camel manure really hit the fan.. Seems to me that by the time we were brought down, the town was there...I thought I saw a rope or two, but most likely my imagination. Mom still claims our argument about God being dead or alive was the cause for the tower climbing, as we thought it went to heaven being so tall, so we wanted to find out for ourselves...We did find out what "spare the rod, spoil the child meant" however.....

At the dinner I was seated close to the Bishop and had trouble eating as I was having two problems, one my butt hurt like hell and my hand was swollen to almost twice the size. The Bishop noticed and cut my fish for me and mentioned to Mr. John McQuillen, my sponsor that it looked as if I had hurt myself somehow.. I had broken my wrist, or actually fractured it in three places.

Off to the Clinic, and the day ended. Some rather lengthy conversation about little boys and girls took place, but I don't recall all of the evils I was told about, except one...you go straight to Hell if you are naughty with girls.. and some comment, off the wall remark from Dad, about warts.....

There is a story about later visiting Jesureluem and dropping my Dad's Lieca camera into the cell Christ had been held in, but another time...

MY DAD AND
HIS STILL

My dad was one of many that had a device that seemed to take up much of the kitchen many days of t he month. I was always somewhat interested, but when I asked, it was always a very short communication between he and I. "Leave!"... very simple and direct. Usually meant with a conviction that spoke volumes without the blink of an eye. In fact, to this day his eyelashes seem to have a permanent twist which has always given him the appearance of a devilish sort. Something that a bright young man should, cue word here, "should" have realized they didn't curl like that due to an immeasurable sense of humor. Not when the kitchen was 300 degree's and he seemed stuck to the plastic of the kitchen table chair.

Well, I had heard a discussion between my mom and dad and another friend of theirs and it seems they were planning a large reception. They decided to put two of the devices on the stove and run them in tandem. Now this would have intrigued anyone, much less a very bright young lad with the brain pan of a mouse, as was stated later. My dad had let me see a little of what he was doing, as I was being forced marched out the back door and to impress me, he opened this little spigot and put just a few drops of this, what appeared to me to be water, in a spoon. Holding it out he took a match lit it and "Woof!" the spoon ignited and there was a flash and a little fireball. The point he said was that this stuff was very tricky and I should go out and play dodge the traffic on sixth street. That way I would stay out of the forbidden zone. "What if I get hungry?" I yelled, "Eat Grass" was the rude retort...This comment was a direct reflection on the fact that the day before I had taken the challenge from someone like Tom Painter to eat one of the green caterpillars that were in the hedges. I did and proved that projectile exporting is not just a scientific term. Course Tom wasn't at all happy and his mom had called my mom, thus the smart remark when I said I might get hungry. Now Locust, that was a different story. Not bad when fried by the gardeners...course one has to realize that you don't go up to your mom and, with the back end and feet of a locust in your mouth, ask her opinion. The smack jarred teeth and the locust loose. Didn't do to much for my ego to hear the howls of laughter from the Saudi gardeners who were frying more in the yard.

So after sitting for about an hour, on the curb in front of my house watching the massive New York style traffic flow, I think one donkey cart passed by with shrimp for sale, I was really bored. Now a bored rapscallion is similar to turning a water buffalo loose at a chess match, sponsored no doubt by the local church having a pie sale. Just to make sure I covered the bases here.

Having played with my toy soldiers from the giant Civil War, Blue and Grey set I had for Christmas, I got to thinking that I could most likely build a cannon and play for real. After all, I had the toy one...Inside the hedges were pipes every so many feet. It took several hours to dig one loose, get the wires off it and set it on the ground. Course I was scratched to the hilt from the hedge, but when one is intent on evil ways, you don't notice you look like a neighbors Manchurian tiger pet cat had had you for lunch. Now I needed to mount this pipe and the Cohea's that lived across the alley had some old car springs that were loose on the side of their house. Try dragging that ton of scrap across the alley and into the yard. All of the time with the wailing and tearing of clothes from the hysterical mirth of the Arab gardeners, who by now have called friends over to watch this crazed American sway wahlid.

I finally got the spring upside down to form an arch, used mom's clothes line, just cut a section, she'll never notice, and spend some time tying the pipe to the spring. I actually had a pretty good looking field piece. About a

155 Howitzer compared to me, but still…I had blocked the one end by digging a small hole and setting the pipe in it and now needed to find something to fire. I had a cap pistol and knew the l ittle red caps would go "Bang" when struck, so I put about a years supply down this pipe. At this point one of the Arabs crawled over, stopping to gather his wits ever so often and told me I need to pack it in and find a way to light the caps, which would then make a "bang". So digging up the buried end I put one of mom's dish cloths from the now useless umbrella revolving type clothes line. I mean, come on, who knew all those dumb strings stretched tight made the thing stand out. Not now, but in better days.

I added in a bunch of rocks in the pipe for cannon balls and lit the fuse. Nothing..It just went out. So did several of the Arabs, now about ten, who could no longer stand the laughter and whose sides must have really hurt. No fear, the dauntless one is here. I had a stroke of genius, one which mom has for years refereed to as a complete black out of electrical signals in my brain and I headed inside to the kitchen…Yes, you got it. I remembered the small spoon and ball of fire.

Dad must have gone to the bathroom and I saw a bowl in the sink and so I filled it withe the water from the little spigot tap and grabbed some more Aramco safety matches, a true misnomer if ever there was one according to mom a short while later at Clinic "C". I poured this water down the pipe and put some on the cloth and with a might swipe of the red and blue tipped match, caused Aramco to shudder and I am sure indirectly brought about the near death of ten Arabs who were now semi conscious and almost paralyzed with laughter.

The blast wasn't so bad, but the pipe end that was supposed to be blocked except for the so called fuse, had done what the Doctor later told me, jumped up and "back flashed a huge ball of fire" that got me. It only lasted a second, but I had very little hair left, no eyebrows and a tee shirt that looked as if someone had heaved a pile of camel dung right on me. I think I was almost completely black and still smoldering when mom came out the door like a rocket. The Arabs are by now lying down and uncontrollable and mom must have thought I killed them all. The pipe was about twenty feet down the alley and I was flat, spread out and smoking still.

Well, to say the least, once home from the clinic the sympathy stopped flat dead. Mostly because mom saw her clothes line. To say I was soon smoking again might be an understatement.

AFTER ARABIA AND
A POLICE OFFICER

Well, I know it may not sit right with some, but having been a Police Officer and ex Military, I have to say that I prefer the chance to protect myself. I wish we had the technology to make weapons safer, but until we do, tragedies are still going to happen. I have only told the below story to a very few close friends, but it shows a choice of using a weapon or not.

THIS IS TRUE, NO EMBELLISHMENTS, BUT BE WARNED!! EXTREMELY GRAPHIC !!!!

The winters in North Texas can be brutal. It was a very cold night. With the wind chill factor it must have been about 35 below zero. The highway at the city limits made a sharp turn south right at a blind corner and on one side was an embankment about six feet deep.

We had a full blown blizzard out and the roads were so icy that I had spun in a circle several times when trying to come to a stop in the road. Even with chains on the police car I had trouble. Wondered why the devil I was out in this weather, but the Department of Public Safety had advised all local police that people might get stuck in drifts and freeze to death, so I had coffee and blankets in the car.

The other cities had set up road blocks to advise people not to head on, but this one gentleman and his wife were in a station wagon and pulling one of the single wheel round trailers, like you see on construction sites. Just big enough for a couch, very small stove and small bed. No bathroom or anything else. Probably only four feet wide by about ten feet long. Now these old trailers had a door and only a 8" wide window that was only 4 "high. Very small and only good so that a person could look out the back of the trailer if necessary. Could not open the little window.

Well, they were in a hurry to get to New Mexico and ignored all the warnings and as they came thru my town the missed the curve, but got back up on the road, however started spinning and whip lashing the trailer. Like most small border towns we had a volunteer fire and ambulance department. You had to go to the f ire station and push a big red button to sound the siren and then pick up the telephone and all the volunteers would answer and you could tell them where the problem was.

I happened to be coming down the road and saw the station wagon on it's side and the trailer twisted and turned on to it's side also. I called in to the police office and got one of the coffee makers to sound the alarm and get some help out to me. In a small town, the Mayor, Judge, Doctor and Preachers were all also volunteers, so I knew we could get some people out to assist.

I ran and slipped and slid up to the station wagon, but there was no driver. I did however find his head on the floor board. His body was lying on the road so I placed his head next to him and went back to the car. The woman was still alive and I got her out of the car, which was still running, I couldn't get to the key.

I dragged her out by the leg and found she had lost an arm, but even while I was applying a tourniquet, she kept screaming and pointing to the little trailer. I finally slapped her hard and got her to focus and I could hear the sirens of the other emergency vehicles coming down the road. We were about fifteen feet from the car and she was trying to talk and not go into shock when the car exploded. The blast blew me and her over the embankment and burned off part of my heavy winter uniform. She then said the words which are still engraved in my heart with ice..." My baby's in the trailer... you've got to help her... Please, Please, Please." I asked her how old and she said three. I covered her in a blanket and ran to the trailer, which by now was also burning.

The fire department truck had spun off the road about two hundred yards away and they were trying to get it free and the ambulance had made it to me and they had the lady in it. The trailer had flipped onto the side with the door so I could not get in. I ran around to the back and there is this little window. Can just barely get my arm in the window. The fire is now in the trailer and I have my hand in the little window, my body actually freezing to the ground and I'm shining my flashlight around. Suddenly this little hand, with such tiny fingers grabs my hand and I hear the terrified wail and scream of the little girl. She has crawled as close to the little window as she can get. I can just see her face. I yell for the Doctor and the Judge who were there and we all tried to pull open the trailer. There were no "jaws of life" back then. Even using fire axes, we were slipping and sliding on the ice covered road and couldn't get a sturdy enough stance to chop a hole. The firemen were there and we had no water as the pumper had frozen up while stuck off the road. They were frantically throwing snow on the blaze, but the gas from the car had everything burning. Several firemen jumped on the top side of the overturned trailer to try to chop in, but they themselves caught fire and had to jump into snow.

We can see that she is now on fire and screaming badly. The heat has burned off the hair on my arm and my eyebrows and I am actually smoldering myself, along with the Judge. The Doctor and Judge and I look at one another and the baby hand comes out the little window and the terrible screams and then the real horror, we see her face pressed to the window and her face is on fire. She is screaming beyond belief, I am screaming and suddenly I knew what my decision had to be.

I pulled my service revolver out and looked at both the Judge and Doctor... Tears freezing on our faces in that split second of decision making. They both nodded and her screaming is echoing in our heads. She no longer has a face as it has melted from the fire. Her little arm that had gripped my hand was no longer attached, it had burned through and was just a twisted, burned item. I very carefully placed the gun barrel against her tiny head and even as the weapon got hotter and hotter, there will never be a worse heat then the last look at her faceless head as I pulled the trigger....

We rolled away from the trailer, which by now was completely burned and the fire truck was still stuck. I was shaking badly and had second and third degree burns on my hand and arm. My weapon had actually had the blueing burned off the barrel. The Judge was crying like a child himself. The Medical Examiner got there and had an attitude because he hadn't been called right away and asked me where the driver was. I told him "He's up there on the roadside, dead." The Medical Examiner yelled at me that I wasn't qualified to judge a person dead or not, so I grabbed his arm and shoved him to the man's body and handed the Medical Examiners the mans head...

I guess in retrospect, after it was all over I shouldn't have done that, but the rest was so much that I didn't care. The Doctor did the autopsy and stated the little girl was dead medically before my shot, but we all knew, including the Judge who ruled her death "by burning" that we had ended her little life.

The only thing worse was when I had to tell the Mother her child was dead......

God has that little baby girl...and I know deep within my heart she knows and in my own way, I know that she says "It's ok, God has me"...

HALF MOON/MOTORCYCLE

I guess most of you remember how we used to have picnic's sponsored by Student Rec. etc. at the old Half Moon Bay. Anyhow, this was also the first summer that ARAMCO had allowed motorcycles in camp, actually only Honda 50's with the big front shield. Anyhow, if you remember Half Moon Bay you remember the pier that went out into the water and at the end it formed a "T" with the main walkway to the "T" being anchored and the front or top bar of the whole "T" floated up and down with the waves and was hooked on to poles so it could go up and down with the tide also.

Well, there was this little ramp that you walked up or down to get on the "T" top and a this time the water was pretty choppy and was making the floating Top go up and down. Debbie Dirr was sitting there if I recall right.. She's a special person. Anyway, Tom Masso, I believe, came roaring down the walkway on his Honda and was planning on scaring the people off the end into the water. Well, he hit the little ramp just as the floating T rose up and that propelled him into the air.

Amazingly enough, I can still hear him changing gears as he went over us and into the bay, about ten feet from the edge. The language used at the time was record setting and I hurt so hard laughing that I was in tears. Anyhow, we finally dove down, got it out and spent a good part of the day drying everything off…and you know, that tuff little machine came to life and was ridden back to Dhahran. Harley's, hurmph !

I do apologize to Tom Masso if it wasn't him, it might have been Peter Pestoni, but the humor of the day has made my senile mind go blank.

HALF MOOOOON BAY

You know, it is not always smart to take on a teacher in a dare. I found this out when I brazenly smarted off to Mr. Goellner that as far as I could see, he was all talk about his scuba diving. Needless to say the challenge was met with a stare that froze the hair on my butt. Yet even worse was the calm, detached voice of impending doom. Which said, "Have you and your buddies at Half Moon Bay at 9:30 Thursday morning and we dive on the old yacht wreck. 60 feet. Got it?"

Having dived many times on the wreck, we called it the "Holy Grail", as someone in the past had struck a sheep skull on the bow and it was eerie coming up on it. Anyway, I knew it well and thought "HA!" the old geezer is in for it now. So bright and early, Tom Campion, Chris Mohlman, James Goellner and Myself were there and preparing for battle. Knives were finely honed, triple rubber "arbelete's" were armed and made ready. Warheads attached and aqualungs bled and swim shorts adjusted. Just never could get the hang of the nylon net inside of swim suits. Was there a purpose other than to put you in a strangle hold at 40 feet and hopelessly twist and turn as you buddies died laughing. I don't think you will ever see such a sight as five divers with massive air bubbles heading up as they literally blew up with laughter. Hell, get rid of the shorts, it was easier and who was there but us men…so as you can imagine, here are us mighty men of the deep, two with suits. Real Olympians I'd say.

Down at the wreck Tom see's the mother of all hammour's. Quickly he goes for the kill and Chris takes a long angled shot. Both hit this massive monster and by tugging managed to fill the water with fish parts and, yes, you guessed it, blood.

Now these two are engaged in a death struggle with each other and James Goellner sees something on the bottom and goes over and sticks it with his spear gun. Chris later claimed someone shot at him as he had a spear thru one of his fins. Never was able to prove anything tho.…

Suddenly the sand explodes and the menacing shape of what I saw as a fifty foot grey shark darts away and moves around. Mr. Goellner is giving everyone the signal to head up and this shark rips the hammour right in half. Now this pissed both Chris and Tom off to no end. I am more concerned about what may be in the water the sharp might decide is tasty and ignoring all diving rules, went to the top, and allegedly beat Mr. Goellner and James to shore only because I was able to run on the water like a bat out of hell, flippers, gun and all going in every which direction.

The visual on this is the group of people under the canopies and the sight they must have seen. Two naked boys, masks and tanks, and moving like enraged camels to the kill trying to get to shore and all the time coming close to drowning by yelling, "Sharkkkkkkkkk" Salt water in the mouth and throat tends to distort words.

Meanwhile Chris and Tom have attacked the shark with twin spear shots.. While we are on the road to Dharan, flippers, butt's and masks running at a heady pace, they are calmly pulling this thing out of the water and hanging it on the old hook scale by the flag pole. I guess it was more like 3 feet, but it looked like "Jaws" to me.

A large crowd is gathered by now, and of course, what does the unflappable Mr. Goellner do, "Hey Crocker, come over here and lets get a picture of this". Yeah, sure, naked glory and a shark about half the size of a Hamoour. He laughed for days and made many points in gym class about our daring "exposure" with the shark. Claimed the shark preyed on shrimp, what ever that was supposed to mean. Yet I do remember a lot of snickering.

What made this event so memorable was that I believe it was the first recorded case of "Mooooning" Aramco employees in the beginning of a long and fine standing tradition carried on bravely by younger Brats in later years.

In particular on the Kenworth buses going to and from the other districts. Must have really done a lot for public relations.

Can you imagine where all the sand went?

By the way, for you that don't know it, Chris and Tom had their photo in the Sun and Flare a little later for spearing a Hammour or Sea Bass that weighed in at over 300 pounds. At the time, the largest ever caught. Speared off the old water injection plant by the massive North dune.

Another fine mess my mouth got me into.

HALLOWEEN THOUGHTS

Just had to jump in here a tad. One Halloween we (me, Jay Johansen, and Barry Knott) egged an outside party at the Cramptons. Just tossed 'em over a big hedge, ran like hell. Caused quite a ruckus, I believe.

Later, we encountered a large dark figure apparently leading a few smaller ones in the conduct of nefarious deeds.

Through yelled coversation, we learned that they had big blocks of wax and were writing neat things on the front windows of houses backwards so they could be read by the owner from inside. Well, we'd never heard of this activity and thought it was darn cool...we wanted to do it too!

I yelled a request for the large kid to toss me part of a block of wax so we could partake of the same type of mischief. He tossed it alright. He sent it over like a major league pitcher. It being a bit dark, I missed catching it, and it hit me square between the eyes; nearly knocking me out.

Who was the "pitcher"? Mike Crocker, of course.

Michael R. Grimler

HAPPY BIRTHDAY
MY FRIEND...

I remember the fact that my feet burned, and that my Arab friend laughed with a barking sound, for which I called him "Jackal". He in turn called me "Tezick", meaning female camel. The sand was hot and sank up to my ankles and running down the dune and into the Bay we would push each other and try our dammdest to drown each other.

The old salt water injection plant stood guard at the entrances to Half Moon Bay and he and I decided to join the "Hamoor Club", for which you had to climb a towering pipe and go out over the water and dive in. The pipe was actually an old crane unit and the leading edge stuck out about fifteen feet from the base of the platform below. At low tide it was said that the drop was ninety feet, perhaps to us, at our young age it seemed as high.

Under the water was the old grating that had come partially loose and floated on tides up and down, from two feet under the water to ten feet. The water was crystal clear for thirty feet down and you had to jump when the mesh was low or you might hit it.

Several of us were there, and all jumped. Very successful dives by all, except for my friend Jamal. He managed the worlds greatest belly flop known to man. The smack was heard in Dhahran and I'm sure fish for miles out convulsed from the impact and shock waves, and then died in droves from laughter at the foolishness of this thing called man. We thought his body would surely break into parts and float away, and I know he had knocked the air out of his lungs, but after we pulled him ashore he seemed fine.

Jamal was a typical Saudi, his Dad worked for the Saudi Government and he lived in Arab style. I had been to his house several times in Dammam and never knew what his father did. Just that he was important because of all the attention the house got. His family were the ones that taught me to ride the Arabia stallion like the wind, and he always won in our races..

Jamal liked to go with us on trips and things we did. He was a real clown in Al-Khobar when he would pretend to speak pidgin Arabic as a lot of us did, but he would get his greatest joy from giving Taxi drivers, with twenty passengers in their little yellow Toyotas, pure hell in fluent Arabic and when the driver would get out and chase us and try to switch us, Jamal would show his identity paper and the Saudi driver would always run with sandals flapping and thobe flying. What a hoot..

He was two years younger than I and when I left for school I would hear from classmates what he was up to. His favorite Aramcon was also my teacher, Mr. Goellner. Although he never attended an Aramco Senior Staff school, he did get to go on a lot of field trips for he spoke Arabic and he seemed to work magic with the Saudi's whenever there seemed to be a problem.

I returned in 1969 as a returning student for my last summer there and he was no where to be found. I found Mr. Goellner and he told me where my friend was. I went out into the desert, about five miles from Jebal Shmal and on a barren part of desert, where there was no evidence man had ever been, I could not find him. He was a Bedu at heart and his Family also. So in that tradition I knew I would never find him again.

He would be 45 today. This would be his birthday, but my friend Jamal Al-Turki, son of Prince Khlid Al- Turki, The Ambassador to the United States. However Jamal will not share today with me.

On a trip to Al-Hasa with a group of 8th graders with Mr. Goellner, he had dived to the bottom of the Al- Hasa well and never came up. He was one of two who met their God in that well. I had dived in it in ninth grade and seen the many palm tree sections at the bottom, but Jamal never learned to use diving gear and could hold his breath for a long time, but unknown to those above, he fought a desperate battle sixty feet down with a palm tree log jam, his foot caught and lost...

They had buried him in the traditional Arab fashion of Kings...no marker, a simple white thobe and beneath his beloved desert. I had not found his resting place although I had looked. I only wanted to share this story, because today I miss him and as I look around, I feel the hot desertsand and wind and her the words "Tezick"

HAPPY EASTER AND WATERMELONS

HAPPY EASTER TO ALL..

How many geezzzers and gezzzeretts remember the patio at the deep end of the Dhahran pool. Before it was fenced off. It had a half clamshell type of stage and a smooth rock floor, which was great for skating.

For you youngsters, this was in the time of the fifteen meter and ten meter high diving platform...How many knew that one...and the rules and regulations of the pool were printed, in stencil, of course on a 4x 8 high sign, one rule which was no diving...with the high dive board go figure... After 1963 I believe the little board with the adjustable tension wheel was put in.

Every July 4th the company would put on a picnic on the patio and serve ice cold watermelon from fifty-five gallon oil cans filled with melons and ice. I can only vaguely recall who might have been responsible but on one such occasion there was a tremendous watermelon fight..it was every where.

Bob Gollan, Brent Cleaver, myself, Bill Cohea were fixing hamburgers and hot dogs on a long grill by the little snack shed and I suspect our cooking might have had something to do with it all..

All I know was that there was watermelon every where.

What this has to do with Easter is that at Easter Sunrise Church this morning, I wasn't looking at the Texas sky...I was once again in Dhahran for Easter Service at Dawn...

Not to offend anyone, but may I take the time to thank God for our youthful lives and the impressions it made on us this day.....

HELLS ANGELS-HONDA 50 STYLE

A ramco in it's infinite wisdom had banned all motorcycles within the compounds around 1957. By 1963 they had relented and thus was born the Hells Angels, Aramco Chapter, Born to Lose "biker gang....Course they restricted us to Honda 50's with a two liter engine and automatic shift...not the "Hawg" we wanted, but close enough.

The fact is it was August and 120 degrees and the leather jackets were about 200 pounds heavy and we were most likely the laughing stock of the known world, we knew we were truly lost rebels...Motorcycle boots, nah, coolie boots were all we could bear. So starts the adventure.

To show how impressive we thought we were..here is the mental image. Ten roaring motorcycles, with black leather jackets, chain swinging from every pocket, roaring up to the stop sign on 3rd street going to Recreation.. imagine "Bringgggg-ding-ding-ding, Brinnnng-Ding-Ding", the sound of ferocious motors revving up and the tough, albeit clean shaven faces of the toughest eight and ninth graders in town. Not really tough business and you could take that to the bank...

The fun part was roaring past Security and getting them chase us. At 30 mph top speed we were real threats to the peace of the camp, but Security felt obligated to chase us. Might have had something to do with the water-melons we threw at Sayid, but that's just a guess. So off we dash, it's getting dark and several cut down a hedge lined sidewalk on the Hill. Unbeknownst to them, some fool had added a room extension to their house and the end stuck across the sidewalk, allowing for a very skinny person to get by. Well, you can imagine the cal'am that took place when three devils from hell shot down the sidewalk, no lights and shouting remarks such as, "Moonlight, Star bright, Security couldn't catch a tur-le to night. "HA ! the resulting pile up set records for abusive language and commentary. Sayid almost passed out with laughter and owner of the house came out with a garden house and started spraying the guys for their language.

Their ride to fame was short and in great humiliation, they had their Honda's confiscated and were sent home as Sayid roared out loud, and was heard for miles with such soothing words as "Lost, neede ride, wantee go home you toughee guys." Nothing like walking down the road, 200 pound jackets, dragging butts and chains and trying to act like nothing happened. Plus I personally think Sayid threw watermelon at them every fifty feet or so, but I can't prove it.

I, and five others on the other hand had gone home without knowing of this terrible defeat to our collective egos, but the next day, we beat them by far.

A glorious Wednesday and school is out and we roar up to Recreation, hitting the gravel right by the library and piling up. Seems we did a lot of that. Quickly jumping up and making sure no one saw us, we decided that we would head out the Half Moon Bay and camp overnight. The ride was one where the sand was blowing and we were hot as all get out and worse, a donkey cart and Arab passed us.. no power at all against a strong wind, but onward we went. Getting there and drinking all the fresh water and even the shower drinking water we finally cooled down. The next day was the Forth of July party and we were all tough as nails and strutting around in out swim shorts and black jackets. We were so bright we had painted on the back of the jackets our club name. I never was good with spelling and somehow came out with "Hells Angles". I just knew the rest were wrong.

Once back in town I took Sissy Quick and her sister and I all on the mean machine and started towards their house. That poor little machine had what looked like sand tires on it and I believe a speed bump thru Debbie off and onto a padded, I hope, backside.

I broke the rules for Honda's one last time. We weren't supposed to leave the camps with them.. License, what license ? But I drove it to RT from Dahahran. I must have lost fifty pounds of sweat and ended up in the clinic in RT with Mom and Dad coming to get me. I think my Honda went into the Gulf, but was a little delirious from the ride, the yelling and the amazing amount of times a small woman can smack a butt while on the run......

WAS ASKED TO WRITE A POEM, AND I AM NO POET BUT I MADE THIS EFFORT. DO YOU ALL THINK I FELL OFF A VERY LARGE CAMEL WHILE QUITE YOUNG?

Remember, in poetry, grammar doesn't count..please!!!!

"The Great North Dune sings it's song of love to the Desert"

The Great North dune slowly puff's it's way across the blazing desert floor, the sand whispers to its neighbor as it crawls to its end the great desert will reach the gulf and the life shall expire.

However my heart listens and as the wind blows the wisp's from the top, the dune sings it's mournful song of life and loss, for buried in its heart is the love of two, two who may never touch, two who shall always be entwined as the dune and the desert are.

For their love may not consummate and heads for the end, to fail as the great dune fails to stop the rush to it's death at the hands of the water.

The sand stings and whirls, but to no avail the dune sings in a whispering way, It's call, a call to love, but the end is near and the dune has no cheer. The warmth of the dune and the blazing sun of its heart will slowly like life, extinguish in a blaze, or whimper into the night air.

But as the stars reach down, brilliant lights of God, the dune feels the tremor and knows the love will live, for the spirit of the desert may not be put to sleep. It will sing and sing, of love, life and God.

Michael R. Crocker Copyright 2001 Michael Crocker

HISTORICAL PERSPECTIVE
(FENCING)

Acclording to the 1947 issue of : "Aramco and World Oil", under "Safety and Identification," the first use of fencing was to protect building sites from materials being misappropriated by other Americans using the materials to build the complex and varied projects throughout the field of operations. This led to individual groupings of fencing and in 1953 when three oil company vehicles were recovered from Yemen, where they had mysteriously appeared, the oil company started protecting it's assets. Until 1950 many facilities had no fencing whatsoever.

Many facilities were located outside of any fencing until 1955 when Aramco, from California ordered all residential areas to be fenced in order to prevent disease infestation from wild donkeys, sheep and wild dog packs. Also the fencing was erected because several personnel had wandered out into the desert during storms and had been lost.

This also was the introduction of "Fish fly traps" in order to prevent infection from flies and mosquitos that abounded within the tribal groups who came to the American facilities to see what was happening. They "are to welcomed and referred to the Safety Department should any employee come into contact with them."

In 1953 the first complete fencing was done around Abqaiq and a set of gates established to protect materials and residential areas. Thus the materials handling gates and the Main gates to the camp facilities.

Incidentally, and I quote here "The availability of alcoholic beverages is a privilege of all Americans, but it could be lost to all through serious abuses on the part of a very few......A second condition was that whenever any individual might imbibe too freely, he should remain in his quarters and not pass without or out of the camp into any Arab community." Sounds as if the fence had multiple purpose.

However, nowhere have I found any mention in the 1948, 1950, 1955 Govt. Relations Handbook, or anywhere that any "Official" reason of separating the two cultures is mentioned. In fact 1949, 1950, and 1955 publications all seem to lean towards mixing the groups as much as possible," with the exception of weekends in which all the local personnel were sent to their homes and Americans lived in seclusion."

This last statement is not found in 1960 or other "Aramco and it's world" publications I have.

There is more, but I'm fenced in right now.

HOW "LOON" WEEN STORY

Well, you knew there had to be…right ? So it's October and everyone is deciding what to go out trick or treating as, guess this was about 1964. I seem to recall this night and the coconspirators I will have to leave nameless, as they may come back with another story later that I really don't want to be reminded of. Although since they live in California I'm probably safe.

Many of you will remember "H" street had at the bottom of the hill, two areas of plantings that separated the road. "H" was connected to Recreation by 11th street up from the circle splitting "H" where the AC tower was. Now we knew that the was a all girl sleep over at house 1026(Almost sure of this) and we also knew that since it was Holloween we ought to really give these girls a fright and scare them out of their sleeping bags.. Yes, I know, such perverts….

So we decided to paint ourselves all black with a white skull face and therefore all you could see would be the skull. That idiot T. decided that we needed something to paint ourselves with and so he was in charge of getting the paint. He went to the art class and got several large bottles of black paint. This was going to be great. We got rags and painted our faces black, we had on black shorts and t-shirts so all we had to cover was our arms and legs. The using white paint we drew the skull on our faces. P. decides that we ought to take advantage of this and hide in the planted area and jump out at little kids and demand candy or we would devour them. A little early on life of crime I guess. Real Hi-way men. We knew we could get away clean as all we had to do was jump into the cooling tower and wash off the paint and be home free.

Somehow, great plans of mice and boys go astray. We did get a lot of candy, but soon heard a commotion and here comes several parents with flashlights and rather a bad frame of mind. So we run for the ac tower, planning on hiding behind the concrete wall till they go off and then go over to the sleep over and wiggle our heads thru the hedges and scare the devil out of these girls.

Several of you have talked about Kit Simon, well she figures into this in a minute. Seems as if the parents of this house had a few friends over while the girls were camping out. So we manage to get our heads thru the hedge, and that hurt let me tell you. The bad part was we let T. pick a spot, and so our heads, painted black with white skull like markings pop out looking right into a group of about twenty adults, with Mrs. Simon, costumed as a witch AND with broom being head butted by one of us as we struggled to push thru the hedge. Needless to say, she managed to use our heads and do a clean sweep of all three and her cackle was heard all over and the hollering and girls screaming and parents cussing, One hell of a pickle. Now we can't get out of the damn hedge and, as you may recall there were wires in these hedges and we are hung up. Mrs. Simon is getting ready for a home run on our heads with the broom, several parents over in the planted area with flashlights hear this commotion and start over to see three butts squirming like fish on a boat floor trying to get loose and suddenly the earth opens up and here is Danny Noskys' Dad with a branch behind us. (We had got his little sisters candy.)

Finally we break free, T. into the yard and P. and I out of the hedge and away like Saluki's we did go. I swear to this day Mrs. Simon was coming behind us like a banshee on her broom, but undoubtedly this is part of my fear syndrome of witches. We managed to end up over at one of our house's and we know they still don't know for sure who we were, but our butts are sore and we all have headaches and visions of the broom coming round like the mighty Casey at the bat. So we start to scrub of the paint and we are doing fine, beginning to think we are too "cool" when we made a major discovery. That fool had got two bottles of India Ink.

Well, school the next day was a major illness time at home, but to no avail. Mom said just because I had turned Black overnight was no reason not to go to school. I argue this point with her today and still lose. Mom already knew it all as Kit had recognized us, had a field day and told our parents and so we all went to school. Talk about social outcasts. Perhaps the worse part...several of the little kids had told their parents they had twice as much candy as they did and we had to make it all up to them. I'm sure the Golding brothers did well on Mars bars....No, I haven't forgotten Martin...

Holloween just hasn't been the same since those days. Ohh and for the curious, Lava soap does not do well in removing India Ink. The only think that saved us was the fact we had healthy skin and kerosene did get a lot of it off. But I think even today I seem to have a slightly darker complexion than I had looking at baby photographs........

SUBJECT: HUMOS

After exhaustive research, days across the burning sands, no myya and wajid Brown, I have achieved a near utophian answer..To hell with Tibetan Monks and their search for truth, I as an ARAMCO BRAT shall leave not one pebble of sand unturned for the truth of life.....and here it is.... straight from the most impeccable sources known to mankind....OUR MOTHERS....

"The Abqaiq Cookbook", compiled by Syble Allen, Areej Atallah, B. Baily, Cindy Baily, Lyslie Baily, Marguerite Baker, Opal Ball, Jackie Baxter, Elizabet Bishop, Barbara Blanchard, Dorthey Bradley, Jean Boccagna, Norma Branch, Ann Burgess, Lucy Casswell, Mariam Cuthbert, Chris DeSantis, Majorie DeSantis, Ann Ruth Duke, Judi Elkins, Cindy Ellison, Gerry Ellison, John Fermendzin, Vicki Fermendzin, Karl Fitzgibbons, Peggy Foster, Anne Gadberry, Beth Gibson, T.V. Gibson, D-J Gorthus, Nancy Hahn, Jennifer Harbert, Midge Harbert, Faye Harris, Jean Heard, Diane Hefferman, Pam Hermannsson, Mary Lynn Hicks, Lou Hollis, Brigitta Hoss, Kathy Hunter, Marge Johansson, Doris Kent, Jeanne Kellum, Joyce Kirkpatrick, Ikbal Khalil, Laverne Krapp, Sharon Kulchisky, Eileen Kurtz, Charlotte LeTellier, Tina Light, Zada Kaye Lindquist, Lynne Malarkey, Joyce May, Ida McCloskey, R.C.McFatridge, Joyce MvLemore, Stephannie McNochols, Linda Medros, Brenda Miller, Sharon Morris, Rose Mowbray, Latifah Naji, L.D. Nicholson, Betty Nix, M.A.Norton, Mary Parks, Alice Rector, Jean Richards, June Ritter, Judy Roth, Roberta Rothelle, Najia Salamah, Brenda Schnell, Mary Schultz,

Helen Shields, Mary Sprietsma, Linda Snapp, Evee Stanaland, Helen Streker, Etta Sutton, Sharon Thompson, Ruth Walkden, Janice Walker, Ruth Watson, Phulis Zercoe, Riad Zarka.....

ABQAIQ 1953

HUMOS
1 can pureed chick peas pinch of salt
1 lemon 1/3 cup of water
1/4 cup oil 3 gloves garlic, crushed
3 heaping tbsps. tahina
Mix tahina with juice from lemon, water,crushed garlic and salt. Mix until very smooth. Puree chick peas; add and blend well. Sprinkle with oil. Refrigerate. Keeps 2 or 3 days. Serve with Arab bread.
ADDITIONAL recipes available
Baba Ghannouj
Sepeha
Samboosuk
Sambosia
Arabic Bread
Kabsa Hijaziah
ALL time favorite TUNA Casserole or, and I like the instructions on this one,
HERBAL MUSTARD COATING FOR ROAST LAMB
1/2 Dijon-styled prepared mustard 2 tbsps. soy sauce
1 garlic clove, mashed 1/4 tsp. ginger
1 tsp. ground rosemary or thyme 2 tbsps. olive oil

Blend all ingredients except the oil together in a bowl. Beat in the olive oil by droplets to make mayonnaise like cream. PAINT the lamb with the mixture and set it on the rack of the roasting pan. The meat will pick up more flavor if coated several hours before roasting.(OR if you let it wander in the yard a few days...)For a 6 pound leg of lamb,(One leg at a time here, don't want to waste a perfectly good Lamb), roast in a 350 degree oven for 1 ti 11/4 hours for medium rare;or 11/2 for well done. The Dijon style mustard may be purchased in Al-Khobar. (Where you purchase the lamb was left out).

The () are mine.. just poking fun at the recipe..all the rest is as in the book.
ALSO......
>From the Dhahran Womans Group, of 1971 we have available for your request, by personal invitation, (Over two hundred names, sorry no list) recipes for:

Barzac

Basboussa

Ghuraybee

Ka-ta-yif

Ma'amoul

Mint tea

Sambousik

AND...we can provide the ratios of feeding from one to 100.....

SPECIAL NOTE: Cooking class by Elloner Goellner has "Survival Rations", "Good for one or two days or until help arrives "- not sure why, but it is there.

Mike, the Galloping Camel Gourmet, Crocker

After all the religion discussion I thought I'd throw another perspective on the fire...

ISLAM AND JESUS

Muslims respects and revere Jesus and await his Second Coming. They consider Him one of the greatest of God's messengers to mankind. A Muslim never refers to Him simply a "Jesus", but always add the phrase "Upon Him be peace". The Quran confirms His virgin birth (a chapter of the Q'uran is entitled "Mary"), and Mary is considered the purest woman in all creation.

The Q'uran describes the Annunciation as follows: "Behold!"The Angel said, "God has chosen you, and purified you and chosen you above the women of all nations. O Mary, God gives you good news of a word from Him, whose name shall be the Messiah, Jesus, son of Mary honored in this world and the Hereafter, and one of those brought near to God. He shall speak to the people from his cradle, and in maturity, and shall be of the righteous."

She said "O my Lord! How shall I have a son when no man has touched me?" He said "Even so, God creates what He will. When He decrees a thing. He says to it, "Be!" and it is. (Quran, 3:42-7)

Jesus was born miraculously through which the same power which had brought Adam into being without a father: "Truly, the likeness of Jesus with God is as the likeness of Adam. He created him of dust, and then said to him "Be!" and he was. (Quran, 3:49)

Jesus performed many miracles. The Quran tells us that he said: "I have come to you with a sign from you Lord: I make you out of clay, as it were, the figure of a bird, and breathe into it and it becomes a bird by God's leave. And I heal the blind and the lepers and I raise the dead by God's leave" (Quran 3:49)

Neither Muhammad nor Jesus came to change the basic doctrine of the belief in one God. In the Quran, Jesus is quoted as saying, "To attest the law which was before me. And to make lawful to you part of what was forbidden you; I have come to you with a sign from your Lord, so fear God and obey Me." (Quran 3:50)

The Prophet Muhammad said "Whoever believes there is no god but God alone without partner, that Muhammad is His messenger, that Jesus is the servant and messenger of God, His word breathed into Mary and a spirit emanating from Him, and that Paradise and Hell are true, shall be received by God into Heaven." (Hadith from Bukhari, Quran)

According to Islam, man is not born into original sin. He is God's vice-gerent on earth. Every child is born with the "fitra" an innate disposition towards virtue, knowledge,and beauty. Islam considers itself to be the "primordial religion" (din-al-hanif); it seeks to return man to his original,true nature in which he is in harmony with creation, inspired to do good, and confirming the Oneness of God. Another issue commonly brought to my attention and many questions asked is about women's equality in the Islamic world and in the Qu'ran.. So here is the next in series of articles I am sending.

WOMAN IN ISLAM

A lot of people have misconceptions about the role and presence of women in the Islamic, or Muslim world. This is due to two major factors. One is the lack of knowledge by others of her responsibility to her family and society. The other is the failure of most western peoples to understand what Allah and the Prophet stated about the women's rights as an active member of society.

Allah presented in the Holy Q'uran a holistic approach that clearly defines the responsibilities and rights and roles of both men and women.

In the Q'uran, Allah clearly states the equality between man and woman. "He created you from a single person; then created, of like nature, his mate." (Qur'an 40.6)

Allah also mentions in the writings given to the Prophet Mohammed that men and women are equal in His sight.

"And their Lord hath accepted of them: Never will I suffer to be lost the work of any of you, be he male or female. "(Q'uran 3:195)

However people are different in their responsibilities and duties. To protect the strong family and moral value, Allah has addressed the issue with great detail. "O Prophet! Tell thy wives and thy daughters, and the believing women, that they should cast their outer garments over their persons (when they are out). That is most convenient that they be known and not be molested. (Q'uran 33:59)

The main cause of this covering is to protect the women from the illness that may lie in some peoples hearts. This prevents sexual harassment and shows that the ladies are believers. This will also prevent the spread of gossip which denigrates the family and social value. This action elevated women to the point of their honor and respect would be guaranteed. It also set the correct approach that no man should desire another man's wife and thus by the cover, the male weakness would not become evident and thus giving the woman more right to privacy and quality.

In the sense of a male making false accusations or gossip about a woman, Allah has even decreed the punishment. "And those who launch a charge against chaste women and produce not four witnesses (to support their allegations), flog them with eight stripes; and reject their evidence ever after: for such men are wicked transgressors." (Q'uran 24:4)

Allah also stated that men and women, upon meeting in common areas should lower their eyes. This also assists women from being seen a sexual object. When society allows for a women to become nearly naked, the woman loses some humility. They become exploited and a target for men with evil in their hearts. It opens the door for harassment and un-pure thoughts.

A woman is a mother, which is the source for man's knowledge of kindness, affection and love. The Prophet said "Heaven is at the feet of the Mother's." A woman is also a school. She is the base for education in Islam. Her moral and family value is passed on to her family and children and if you multiply this a hundred thousand times, you see the purity of the character.

When people take matters into their own hands, and leave out the teachings of Islam the result is what we witness today. The loneliness and alienation between the sexes, thus the mistrust in interpersonal relationships. This has resulted in the loss of moral and family value and caused the breakup of families and also the collapse of civility between races and people. This result has also caused many women to look for personal security, and this is not bad as long as we remember that the woman is equal in all respects to man and although we have different family duties, we all work together in the following of the path of righteous and clarity

SMALL HISTORY LESSON

Many of you, as scouts or just bedus visited the site I'm about to tell about, but many of the folks from the 1980's on never even knew about it, so...

The Ain Jawaan Tomb, located off the Dhahran—Ras Tanura road about six kilometers from the Sufwa turnoff. The road to the site is sand, and at first Aramco kept it well packed, but in later years it went back to the desert.

The Jawaan Tomb was discovered accidently on March 22nd, 1952, by a bulldozer operator who was clearing the overburden of sand to get to the limestone beneath the sand. The edge of the blade nicked a hard surface and broke open a wall that was buried and a passageway was seen. Dr. F. Vidol of Aramco was called as he was a trained archeologist. On the same day he made a preliminary investigation. Three days later President Tom Barger reported to HRC Amir Salad ibm Jiliwi about the tomb as it was within the Aramco lease area. Aramco was asked to undertake an examination and report to the Government.

Basically the building is a large chamber tomb with a long central passageway entered from the west. From the center five alcoves open, one to the east, and two each to the north and south. Only one burial pit is located in each of the north and south alcoves, but the eastern one has two pits, one behind the other.

Four burial boxes were built against the exterior of the tomb on the outside of the northeast, southeast and south and southwest. The construction material is limestone, cut into blocks and fitted together with mortar. On entering the tomb it was evident that the tomb had been entered a long time ago as many items were strewn about. During the time of the research local villagers also got in and looked for supposed hidden treasure.

The four Americans who had found the tomb, quietly quit and left Arabia within a week. One, who is passed away now, named Bill Arnold gave my mother a small candy style silver dish, which I still have, Beautiful peacocks and design and very intricate. The others live in luxury here in the US.

The whole search took 22 months and they first dug a trench around the tomb. Thus they discovered the four outside boxes which had never been opened. All four people in the outside boxes had been interned in palm wood boxes along with their personal possessions. Three of the boxes were occupied by male skeletons in age from 21 to 50 years old. The northeast box held the remains of a girl of about six. The skulls of all of these had been crushed and one male had a stab wound to the head. This is assumed to have been done at the time of burial of the people inside the tomb. The tomb was of major construction and the outside boxes imply the family slaves.

The only artifact found in the southwest tomb pit was a small gold hair ring. The south tomb pit contained two gold hair rings and the remains of an iron short broad blade sword on the left side of the skeleton and a handle of ivory.

The southeast tomb had a badly damaged skeleton in it. A long narrow iron sword broken into eight pieces was found with it. The northwest tomb, holding the remains of the small girl had suffered from water. She, too, had been murdered and buried with her possessions, but because of the clay seeping in, more was found. Two statuettes, one of alabaster and one of gypsum were found. Also a bronze bowl, a bronze mirror, and a small ivory figurine. The girl had been wearing a garment fastened at the right shoulder with two gold rings, Her hair had been fixed with two gold rings also. She had also been buried with a gold neck ring from which a garnet inlaid pendent had been suspended. Also an elaborate earring set with earrings and a dangling pendant of gold and pearls fastened by a gold chain to the other earring passed underneath her chin. Chemical analysis showed she also had been wearing silver across her chest.

It is assumed that the tomb contained the Lords of the Jawaan settlement. The tomb may have been used to bury the royals as they died and when the last died, the tomb was closed. As was the custom, the four outside boxes were to accompany the Lords into the afterlife. Thus the two males with swords may have been bodyguards and the other non-armed male a slave/servant.

The little girl, also ritually murdered may have been a favorite slave or a playmate of the Lord's daughter. By the burial and the objects contained it is obvious she was treated with dignity.

The area around the tomb was once a thriving settlement of a seafaring type of people. Most people assume that because of the shape of the tomb, almost a cross, but with one cross bar high and one low that this may indicate some for signs of early Christianity, but dating has proven this not to be. They were most likely pagans.

All evidence points to the tomb being built in the second century AD or roughly about 500 years before Islam.

The tomb was surrounded by a wire fence and locked and the keys given to the Saudi Government. They ignored it and in 1965 only about twenty feet of the tomb was accessible.

The interior was famous amongst scouts for the camping out around and the late night, once a year story telling of the vampire story "The Sarah Tomb". This was also one camp out night that the scoutmasters had no problem with roaming scouts.

All items, that were given to the Saudis are in their Antiquities Department, and due to the nature of the alleged religion of the burials, are forbidden to the public. I will bring the dish to the reunion along with the original report on the tomb.

Anyone else remember this ?

JEBAL SHIMALI-HISTORY

Jebal Shimali is the most prominent landmark on the Ras Tanura-Dhahran road. The 409' peak is an erosional remnant of the Dammam Dome as are the other jebals and remnants in the area. As one approaches it, you will notice it is tilted in a Northerly direction. The slanting rock strata give it the appearance of an up tilted shield. Hence it is officially known as "Mirda Shimaili", which translates into "Northern Shield".

The Jebal area was very popular with Aramco scouts and for three decades was used by all. Then the Saudi military sealed it off to make a radar scanning site.(Interesting note, when the Hilton was building it's thirteen story hotel in Al-Khobar, the Saudi Military told them no more than ten stories as their radar would be blocked and enemy jets could sneak in and get to the Jebal.. The fact that the jets would have to fly right thru the hotel never occurred to the Saudi Military, but Hilton shortened it's building. interesting to me, while I was there is that the "Hawk" anti-aircraft missile batteries that were controlled by the dome on top of the Jebal were all aimed towards Dhahran. Since this is all old news and everybody knew about it, they latter hid the batteries better....)

The North side has a tramway now and there is a set of steps to the top also. There are 317 steps to the top. The Saudi Govt. blew off the top to level it for their military site.

Dotted along the sides of the Jebal are a fair number of small stone tumuli, or primitive grave mounds. Originally there were about 150 of these sites. There were also several slit type burial vaults cut directly into the Jebal also. These have now all been destroyed. Partially all of the timuli have been opened by treasure/souvenir hunters.

Anything that might have remained was weathered away many years before western influence came about. Archaeological fields being studied on the island of Bahrain are often be struck immediately by the similarity of the mounds, by the archaeological experts.

Many small items were buried with the bodies, but mostly non-precious materials. Several small caves were thought to lead into caverns, but to date, and due to the military, no further exploration was allowed.

Most of these burials are indicative of after Islam became they are unmarked and very simply done, as is the custom of Islam. King Sa'ud, King Faisel were buried this way, washed, wrapped in a clean thobe and buried without ceremony.

There are more of these burial sites in the Rub-Al-Khali desert.

Many a Boy Scout camping trip was held on the Jebal and "Capture the Flag "was fought hard and heavy with the winner posting thief flag on top of the Jebal. That's about all I can remember as I grow older daily and memory fades.

I was going to tell the Pirate tale today, but be assured, I will tell it tomorrow and it is full of interesting details about pillage, forts, raids, and treasure. Tune in to HZ 22 TV Educational Hour tomorrow.

JELLO FISH

I had to do a little checking, but I had remembered something about Jelly fish and RT. Seems as if on July 4th of 1959 off of the RT beach by the Surf House, My brother Kenny Crocker, my Dad and some fifty other Aramcons and families were having a 4th of July bar b que and picnic. I know the surf house patio was making burgers and hot dogs.

Mr. Ira Costad was the first to dive in the water and then my brother and the rest. They and most else dove into a large gathering of Portuguese Man-of-war jelly fish, which have long tendrils that are multi colored. They have an acid base and stung the heck out of everybody. My brother was allergic and My Dad and several others rushed him and some twenty two other people to the RT clinic, where they were treated. My brother was given a shot and kept over night as was Mr. Constad.

The Portuguese Man-of-war was not a common jelly fish in the area, but I later saw some off of Azzia Beach in diving. As the construction in the gulf increased they seemed to come in less and less, I don't know why.

Some of you may have been there that July 4th. Some 22 people had to be treated and Aramco closed the beach. These jelly fish have a large sac and are considered poisonous and have a sail like structure on top which moves them.

I do remember diving and cutting jellyfish in half and so on, doubt I ever cut one of these suckers. I do recall a story about a jellyfish sandwich..... ohhh well another day perhaps...

JUMPIN'JACK
FLASHER
(R RATED)

In 1968 it was a mean summer. The heat blazed off our rears like when the paddle Mom kept behind the door was arbitrarily applied. It didn't matter whose kid you were...get caught and "Wham!", "take me out of the ballllllpark"(sung in a high falsetto voice with flaming butts)...However I digress.

This was a summer of mounted forays against the enemy, the fiendish "security men" and their devious and sneaky ways. None of those ways we had by the way. Our furious steeds, of massive horsepower, roared into the night. All 50cc's of them. I was always suspicious when a car passed and the driver was hardly able to stay on 6th street from laughter at the "Hells Angels in leather coats, anchor chains and our mighty motors going", "Rinnnng dinnng, dinnng, dinnng." Not the full roar of the throttle of savage engines of 2000 cc's that danced in our empty heads. I think we really impressed them that it was August, 190 degree's and 100% humidity. Or so it seemed. Might have been the clown with the garden hose and we just thought it was humid.

So there were three of us tough guys who decided that we were going to go by Ned Scardino's house, rev up our mighty engines, honk our massive air horns, (Anybody remember the beeep, beeeep of the mighty Honda's and still not question my insanity?) Then with mighty daring do, stand on the seats of the Harley Honda's and do a full moon at his window and roar away.

Well, with all good plans, there is usually a serious fault. Mine was in letting my good friend and ingenious planner, TM, plot our escape. We pulled off the "full Monty" with great aplomb, roared down the street, tremendous "G" forces leaning us almost to the ground, we flew like avengers from the dark side of the moon straight into the next alley and down towards the new construction going on behind the 3rd street school. In order to set this up, anybody remember "Portapottys"

Well, laughing like wild Jackels, streaking down third street, flashing by history with very large shit eating grins we shot off into the night. No street lights back here and so, who would have guessed that the workers had lined up about six of the massive obstacles, green in color with very ugly blue water and horrendous smells across the street.

Well, to say that we tore ourselves a place in history would be mild. TM actually went through two of the wonder "pots" and I slammed head on and toppled head over heels, hit the ground and heard a sound which shall remain in my poor mind forever. A huge wave of rushing water, A tsunami of shit you might say…which drenched me and turned me into the doughboy of the worst smell and completely dyed blue. I won't even look down at the ocean when flying over it. Talk about traumatic. Then comes the grand finale. BCB hits the entire mess, running behind TM and I and knocks over the remaining sloshing honey pots all over us. He, of course is dry and clean. I am again doused and by this time am beyond rage. Now, try chasing a motorcycle with two pounds of manure and soaked to the skin, in a leather jacket and a damn chain. To say the least, I never did catch him, but heard his rancorous laughter all the way to the 3rd street playground and fading away like the Lone Ranger.

Unable to even stand in the slippery mess and unable to even right our massive machines, now painted brown, we give up and just flat out cried.

Comes the grand finale…Security had watched the whole thing and were so sick from laughter that they weren't able to even stop us as we walked up the street going home. I, to a waiting Mother, by now, called by Scardino, and the fearsome killer of butts. Yet, not to make it seem as if the fun is over, here come Scardino and to make matters worse, he gets behind us and puts his lights on us and as we walk along, he is honking the horn to advise people of a "Alert"- smell problem coming by....

The end result? Well, guess who got to spend Saturday washing and shoveling behind the school in the new construction.

Imhoff Gardens would have moved it's location to avoid me that night. And as many a geezer knows, Imhoff was a mighty hard place to take in the hot sun.

I learned a moral that evening, and it's a quote of the day..."The world can be a shitty place sometimes."

Mike Crocker (DH65) Affectionately called by his father for years to come as the "King of the Shithouses".

JUWAN TOMB

I remembered my Uncle Collins telling me stories about Juwan Tomb and forwarded him yours. Here is his response. Yours, Curt Hern

I am more familiar with the Juwan tomb than most people. I was inside it before it was excavated. I arrived in Ras Tanura in September 1949 and by the spring of1952, I was a foreman in the Utilities Division. As a 27 year old bachelor, I was living in three bedroom apartment 16J in the sheep-sheds. A friend had an uncle in Government Affairs who had told him about the tomb and plans to excavate it. One Friday we decided to go out there on his motorcycle to>see>what we could see. We enlisted a well endowed single girl named Olive>McDonald who lived a couple of doors down whose mission was to beguile the soldier we knew to be guarding the tomb. Her boy friend also had a motorcycle. The four of us drove directly up a gentle slope to a flat place where we saw a soldier standing. As the Arabic speaker, I asked about the tomb. He pointed to rectangular hole in the ground. We went over and looked down into Juwan tomb. About the only thing we could see was that the floor appeared to be about four or five feet below.

We decided that we wanted to go inside and had Olive make motions to the guard that she wanted to do so. He willingly agreed. Olive's friend stayed outside to pull us out while three of us dropped into the tomb. The only light inside was coming through the top entry hole but it was adequate to see that the entire floor area was covered with what appeared to be very old human bones in a very advanced state of disintergration. The only parts I recognized were parts of large leg bones and parts of skulls.

There were lots of jaw bones with teeth still intact. All of the teeth That I looked at were ground down flat and were only about half normal length. I still wonder what could account for those teeth. A few years later I spent several weeks in Arabic language school in Hofuf and saw dates being packed in the date market. Some of them had a lot of sand in them. I wonder if the teeth ground down from sandy food. Aside from bones, the only other thing I saw was a few spent flash bulbs. The shape of the tomb was visible. There was no way of telling how deep the bone layer was except by digging. We didn't dig. My friend was overwhelmed by all the human the bones and didn't Tarry long. I had war time experience which prepared me for the situation. Olive and I stayed inside for about five minutes. For her to get out, I bent Down on hands and knees and she stepped on my back to reach high enough to Be pulled out. I then followed. The whole round trip from Ras Tanura took perhaps an hour. At the time, there was no way of guessing what the outside of the Tomb might look like except for its inside shape. The existence of the Outside crypts was unkown. I never heard of anyone else who entered the tomb before it was excavated. We didn't talk about it thinking that the authorities would take a dim view of what we did. The next time I saw the tomb, it was fully excavated and had a good fence around it.

A year or so later, Vidal was the main speaker at a monthly management dinner in the old RT dining hall. Foremen and above attended these affairs. I had a strong interest and listened closely. Vidal described excavation of the tomb and what was found. My memory of what he said generally corresponds to Crocker's account except Crocker doesn't mention all those bones in the main bomb. My memory includes these additional or differing points:

The tomb was thought to have dated from about 50 to 100 AD. The contents of the outside crypts appeared to have some Greek influence. The tomb appeared to have been entered (and probably robbed) within a hundred or so years after it was built. (At the time I wondered how they could determine this with all those bones in there.)

Some time about 500 years before modern times, the tomb had been Used for mass burial of several hundred human bodies under undetermined circumstances. (I still wonder what they did with all those bones.)

My memory of Vidal's speech put the age of the young man in one outside crypt at about 20 years and the girl in her teens.

I was always under the impression that the tomb had been Discovered several years earlier that 1952 during working of the Juwan quarry and Then covered up until the decision to excavate was made. The rumor at the Time was that one man had removed articles from the tomb and had left with a couple of footlockers shortly thereafter. After seeing that thick layer of bones covering the entire bottom of the tomb, I never gave much credence to the likelihood of anyone finding much in modern times. Maybe they did. I would have thought something would have been overlooked for Vidal to find in the main tomb. I never heard of anything being found in the main tomb during excavation. In later years, I saw quite a few well made individual empty crypts in the area of the main tomb as well as in an area near the bend of the road around Sufwa. Possibly one or more of these had escaped the ancients Some of the artifacts from the outside crypts were on display in glass cases in the basement floor of the old Dhahran Ad building for several years. I particularly remember the girl's choker consisting of several gold discs.

LAST CHANCE
MUSIC CAREER

Well, It all started out fine.. I was in class in Miss Carters art class and we were in the process of learning water color. It was raining really bad out side and water was everywhere. Outside of the windows of the art class room you could see the open area that faced the library. Right under the windows was a flower bed, made of concrete and mortar, new about forty feet long and empty.

Well, the flowerbed were full of water and it was beginning to soak into the concrete block wall. They sent for some maintenance help. This little guy, about 4'6"" shows up and says he will need to make a hole to let out the water. Being the ever valiant Knight, I told him to get a sledge hammer and I'd make the hole for him...he DIDN'T say which wall, so when he came back dragging this hammer I took it inside the art class room, which by now was empty and with a few mighty bangs busted the wall to let the water pressure out of the flower box..

I didn't understand the little guys look of pure terror until I suddenly got a message as if from above, "Flower bed wall, you Idiot! ".and there was Mr. Dickerson. I, by then had enlarged the hole and water was pouring into the class room.

He and I and the little Saudi all fell and pulled over paint pots, edsels and all kinds of stuff, making a rather handsome suit for Mr. Dickerson and water now gushing from a forty foot long flower bed, that was full into the classroom and into the hall.

It didn't really matter what Mr. Dickerson had to say, I was long gone when I realized they wanted a small hole in the end of the flower bed wall, not the classroom.

BUT, that was only the beginning of a day that has lived in infamy, and as late as last night I was reminded of it by a Brat.

Seems as if it was the Tri-D Music Festival night. I, along with all other press ganged students had to take band from Mr. Danielson in the portable. If I ever hear "OHHHHHH Dannnnny Boy" again it will be too soon. He sang it, hummed it, whistled it and I think Far—d it in class. He had decided that I was to use the slide trombone, which was great in marching and good for lifting dresses, all by accident of course, but was a real pain to use. Slide out, pull back, and actually make the proper noise.

Well, here comes the big night. All the stands are in place and instruments are there and I and another brat decide that we need to have some brown on hand to get thru all this, so we wrap a bottle in a towel and put it in the tuba. Now Harry Ellis was the tuba player and I always wanted to smash the cymbals together so I arranged to sneak back there and trade places for this one part where I would follow the tuba and bang the cymbals. Suddenly there is "Ole Danny Boy" again, I'm getting that familiar homicidal urge and decide I need a shot, but no such luck. Danielson wants a quick practice and everybody takes their places. Parents are filling the gym and so we start.

SO into the Sousa March and I hear Harry back there really giving it hell, but no sound, He is turning blue and red as hell and I was afraid he was going to explode. Danielson is looking at him, the music is playing and all of a sudden Harry goes ballistic. Seems as if the lid had come off the Brown, soaked thru the towel and when he sucked in a great breath to try to blow out he took on about a gallon…well, that dammed near killed him. I jumped up and grabbed the cymbals and smashed them together, trying to draw attention away from Harry, managed to smash the hell out of my finger and let out a string of non-musical vocabulary. Danielson by now has entered the area known as insane rage and is climbing over people and after me. I run towards the back of the stage and he did get in one really good whap with the Baton, which I always thought of as his personal riding croup.

I made it to the boys locker room and hid in the shower. Bedlam was going on upstairs and my only thought was "escape"…but how…so I decide to get into gym clothes and pretend that I'm not involved at all and just out jogging around the black top. Half into a jockstrap and the door blows of the hinges…Blood pouring from their eyes, it is Mr. Dickerson, and Mr. Danielson. They start for me and I jump in the shower and turn on the hot water, which burned the shi- out of me, here I was really thinking "no way they'll get wet", but I guess it had been too much for them. I was dragged, jockstrap and all into the gym and they are yelling for my parents..

I was no longer in Band, and Harry did live, although never thought really right after that. My parents wanted to leave the country and I appreciated the many comments on the outstanding jock at school. Took a long time for that one to die down.

I never did get along well with Mr. Dickerson..I think it started when I got on the school announcing system, behind the main desk and paged "Would the Bald guy come to the office where he is supposed to be"…… but that's for another time I think.

Speaking of sneaking out and doing nefarious things, while still a returning student in Dhahran this little tale occurred.

Bill Cohea, Tom Mestrezat, Myself, and David Mestrezat snuck out and decided to go the school to do a little "late night" football on the grass field.

Now for you youngsters, that used to be behind, or I should say where the handball courts or building look to be today. Behind the tennis courts behind the school.. There, finally got to where I was going..

Well Aramco had these water hoses running and the grass was really soaked, with a running start you threw yourself on to the ground and slid at least fifty feet or more on your stomach, or in todays terms "break danced" across the field. The idea of course was to out do each other, and thus the original "total carpet burn". Seems as if in the dark we didn't see the area where they had dug up the ground and put down pebbles for a Tri-D sports and field day…As you might guess Bill out did the rest and hit the gravel, I'd say doing about twenty miles an hour.

The scream was heard in Abqaiq and lights started coming on in the houses across from the field.

To make the day even better, or night, the exit we had parked the Honda 50 at was at the other end of the track that ran around the outside of the field for track and marathons.

So while we ran for the exit, we saw another Honda coming from the far end and we thought "Hey, great, an extra set of wheels".

It was Paul Simon on a Honda and he had also snuck out and was coming to join in…as we watched him coming around the track, he flat out disappeared and the silence was deafening.

We got on the other Honda, ALL four of us and actually, to this day I think we really pushed that thing around the track, because I don't see how we rode it, but we got to where we had seen Paul disappear, and lo and behold, Aramco had dug a large hole to replace a water line and he had driven right smack into it and was sitting at the bottom of this pit with the damndest look I have ever seen.

Well, that did it, we tore off home, and as I was sneaking back in, my Mom say's to me…Have a nice time ? Just a slight touch of sarcasm, but to make her point, the next day she had our houseboy nail my window shut.

I did, however get the last laugh, she nailed the wrong side shut. The side with the little winder to open the window was not nailed….When she hears this I'll get hurt, but it's worth it now..

Don't, to this day, know how Paul got out of that pit or how Bill explained the burns on his chest.

Anyone else do the grass thing ?

LOVE IN THEATER

WARNING...THIS STORY MAY BE OFFENSIVE TO THOSE WHO ARE OFFENDED BY NUDITY, SEXUAL CONTENT, OR WEAK BLADDERS..

Growing up in a land where we were so protected, it left us protected from all except ourselves.. THUS....

It all started out innocently, this you can believe... but innocence may be best judged by the eye of the camel.

I was seeing a lady (L) who was well endowed, for a Senior in college, yet only a 11th grader and we went to the movies and decided to sit in "lovers corner". Right rear of Dhahran Theater.. The movie was something very popular, most likely "Oil exploration in the Rub Al-Kahali".

Well I started to mess around and she was responding well and since we were alone AND mature adults we decided that taking off her top was no big deal... So, as your minds can now imagine, we are both disheveled and getting hot and heavy when out of nowhere this big adult sits down two seats away. Smoking a large cigar... I'm shocked and so is L and we suddenly realize what I'm holding onto, but before we can even move, he turns and says' polite as can be.."don't let me stop you kids..."

Moving so fast that Superman couldn't keep up with us we jumped up, still topless and ran out the side door by the little wall in front of that corner of the movie house. We took off for the area behind the woman exchange in order to ensure a little privacy and around back of the exchange was the photolab. Remember ? So pick the lock and in we go. Got it made now. Once again in the grip of passion, only this time a telephone which was there, (Perhaps a hint for whom the bell tolls ?), rang and scared the daylights out of us.

We decided we would really be romantic, and L if you're reading this, you can stop laughing right now....we climbed up a date tree in front of the Womens exchange. >

Anyway the tree is so thick and we find a branch to sit on and began kissing again...mind you all of this time topless...however we still hadn't got the flame of passion down enough to realize that we had left the two shirts, or one shirt, one blouse and bra, in the theater...

Suddenly she pushes me back and scoots up a little, but in so doing pushed me right out of the tree. Down I went like a sack of potatoes and hit like a ton of bricks.

That did it, and to make it better the sprinkler was on.. So we left and sunk over to my house to get her a t-shirt and call it a night..it wasn't worth it anymore...and we get in and she says...I'm hungry, like there had been anything to work up an appetite over, right...So I look in the refrigerator and she see's some cheese and starts munching on it. I having worked too dammed hard for all this, see a plastic container with what looks like a piece of roast. So I grab it, wondering why Mom would have put in milk, and tear off a chucks the size of a small loaf of bread. To this day I absolutely hate liver. Raw liver waiting to be cooked the next day..so after gagging and heaving all over us, it's time to call it quits.

Of course, that never happens, so while we now have on t-shirts and getting ready to go back out to take her home, the phone rings, and I without a brain in the world answer it...Aramco recreation had found our clothing and if you remember, Mom's used to sew or write our names in everything back then, and Aramco recreation, innocently I'm sure, had called her house first, told them what they had found in the theater and also told them about my shirt.

So I'm on the phone, and here is her Dad on the other end. I told him that my name was Chris Crocker, not Mike and that my parents were out but I'd have them call him and ran like the wind, probably around the camp perimeter fence several times looking for the first ride out of town..She goes home to face the music and I am trying to bribe an Arab to take to the Jordanian Border...

Spent a good part of that summer grounded....Always wonder if maybe that encounter just wasn't meant to be. L, I did miss you and still do....

Youth and pubescence, both possibly fatal.

LURKER STORY

I had almost faded away when I heard the call of the Bain of Canada....a story is born....The Lurker event, cicra 1964. A very serious group of three young, but adventurous boy's who would be men, gathered at the witching hour and started out to a certain woman's house. She was known to do exercises, delicately put, dressed rather skimpily. We knew about the time she would be working out, and so...off we went. We decided to leave our bikes at recreation earlier so that our parents would not hear us riding away.

On the way to Rec we decided that it would be best to stay out of sight of security and so played "Star light, Star Bright" (any memories here ?). On passing the Lupiens house, across from Hamilton Hill, we saw a car approaching and threw ourselves over the hedge. I heard a great splash, some vulgar comments and a muffled scream...Much to my surprise I got up and looked back to where Tom Painter had gone over the fence and I see his feet straight up in the air, and Mr. and Mrs. Lupien in their round pool skinny dipping. I still remember the look of shock on Mrs. lupien, look of murder on Mr. Lupien and the one most impressive was Tom's look of stupidity and admiration...for Mrs. Lupien I guess. Bill Cohea and I were up and gone like a flash to the Hill and Tom followed, sloshing like a wet bag of clothes.

We made it to Rec and got our bikes...Now the serious hunt began... we knew we couldn't use our bike lights and so we convoyed in the dark. Suddenly we see Security coming and we whip down a walkway, with tall hedges, which twisted and turned like a snake. Bad enough that we had no lights but street lights, but on top of that the adrenalin was running high. A loud smash, a scream, another crash, foul language and then me into the pile up, with only gentle words escaping my mouth. Some fool had built on to their house and the extra room had extended across the walkway, effectively blocking it except for about a foot and Bill being first had tried to get his bike past that, hung up and flipped and then Tom and finally, with great dignity, I too added to a really neat pile of wreckage and bodily damage.

Now we are up and running, left behind the bikes and finally get to the house, but alas, we had messed around so much, all the light's were out.

Unbeknownst to us, Security had been following, stopping every few minutes to roll around on the ground and stifle their laughter at the three fools ahead of their truck. We made so much noise being stealthy that we never heard them, in a truck no less.

So suddenly, with our faces pressed to the glass of the house they turn on their lights, honk and the house lights come on and manure was flying everywhere as we tried to run. Unfortunately the portable next door had been moved and only the foundation remained, and so, badly skinning our legs we went over the edge and into what seemed like a bottomless pit. Of course full of brackish water, CamelPee no doubt.

Well, when Security stopped laughing long enough to get us into the truck, where our bikes were and took us to the main gate. Then the thirteen steps up the gallows to Mr. Kieswetter's office and the seemingly 300 hour, but really 15 minute wait for Mom's and Dad's. Leaving with our heads down, much was to be said for the sensitivity of Security who were heard to be laughing for days.

The final blow was the next day when said Lady asked for three volunteers to come to the front of a certain classroom and write a story about late night adventures, One hundred times each on the blackboard...

CES'T LA VIE !

Subject: MEA 444 1964- some memories. It was a day of pure tragedy. Many of us were found in many places with our red rimmed eyes and the horror of our loss evident everywhere. There was just so little we could do or think of. MEA 444 had just been found and all aboard the Beirut to Dhahran flight were gone. The pilot had been coming in low and one of the worst schmals of our times was upon us. The pilot had made one pass and out over azziza beach he went and turned, banking sharply. I'm sure many looked out and could see nothing for it was so dark and sand was blowing and even if they had seen, would they have comprehended as the wing tip buried itself into the Arabian Gulf and the plane began to somersault? The nose and main fuselage broke apart near the nose as the nose buried itself into a sand bar some 600 yards from shore. The tide came in and all but a small section of the tail disappeared from sight.

The plane itself was fairly intact and most of the cabin settled onto the sandy bottom and the depth was just at 20-30 feet down. Due to the storm, and even with over 100 Aramco vehicles out searching the desert, it was three days before an incoming KLM flight saw the tail section and told Aramco. Saudi and American alike rushed to the scene. Their bond, one of fear and love for their families made them one person in their hearts and souls, no matter their position or place in the Aramco world. Islam and Christian offered their thoughts.

This was a day of pure horror for me and several others. This was the day we became men and our youth died some, for this day, six very young boys 14-16, were called upon to dive down and bring up materials, items, and long wrapped objects that were scattered around the plane. The water was clear as the Al Hasa oasis well and springs, but I know we didn't see what we thought we saw. It was eerie and scary. There were two US Marines from the Consulate that were trained divers that handed objects to us, who were also using our own diving gear. We were constantly going up and down. The Marines had a chopper above the site and Aramco had a massive floating crane on site and we were sent ashore.

What I personally remember the most was the silence and the medical team that took each body and examined them. Each one was said to have a broken neck, yet some had bandages around their heads and upper bodies. Who had done that we all wondered? The theory was that some were still alive and someone aboard the plane had treated those that had breath, Yet the worse was to come in the enclosed section of the plane above water. The tide came in and there were at least six that autopsy later showed had drowned…a watery death and most likely horrifying as the plane filled and no way out.

I was standing, leaning against the wire in an exposed part of the hedge, near the school, holding Vicki Muzika in my arms when we were told about the crash. I did not know I would be involved, I was way too young, but the family needed us all. I never touched a body, but did help bring the nose wheel up. They kept us away, but as you can see, not far enough away.

Many friends and family were on this ill fated flight. Several of us had classmates there and some of our teachers were on board. I still have a small section of silver bracelet, the kind we used to buy and give our girl friends to wear, or they gave us. The one I have, just the plate and part of the silver chain has Janie Baumgartners name on it. It is locked away in a safe and secret place, and my next trip to Arabia, when I bury some of Bob Quicks, Sissy and Debbie Quicks Dad's hair in the open desert, I plan to return this piece of my life long pain and sadness to the depths of Azzia.

I tell this short historical story now for it is fast coming up on thirty-five years ago…..Lest we forget, I want to remind all of us, these, both our beloved Saudi and American's friends were together.

Here was my original post about this, back in 1996……..

Flight 444 was a regularly scheduled flight from Beirut to Dhahran. She was a French built SE 210 Caravelle jet airliner. She was carrying 49 Aramcons, 6 crew and 13 other nationalities. I'm including the Saudi's with the Aramco group as most were kids.

There had been a really bad Shamal for two days and the flight had been postponed once, but finally left and came to Dhahran. The pilot swung out over the water at Azziza Beach to turn to make his final instrument approach to Dhahran. The air was sandy and he relied on the French Altimeter. Unfortunately for him, the altimeter was rather crude and had not been calibrated fro some time and was off by 158 feet from actual measurement.

So as he made his turn to the approach lineup, he banked to the right and as he did, the wing tip, about six feet hit the water surface. This caused the plane to cartwheel several times and finally settling in the water. As fate would have it, the plane ended up on a submerged sandbar and the back twenty feet, including the tail were above water. Both wings had been torn off and the cabin separated.

Aramco was notified and sent out over 100 search vehicles into the desert in all directions as at first no one knew where she had gone done. The

Shamal was still bad and USAF helicopters could not get up to help. Two days later the Shamal stopped and one of the USAF helicopters saw the tail end of the wreckage. (This was how I originally thought it was found)

There were complications with the Saudi Government over how to go about the rescue operation and it ended up that Chris Mohlman, Tom Campion, Myself and I believe Bob Gollan were the only ones with SCUBA gear in the area. The water was too shallow for the Aramco barges and crane boats so we were asked to go out and see what it looked like underwater. The water was very clear and the plane was broken into several parts, but I do remember two US Marines, also divers, going down with us and helping us. I got very sick and threw up in my face mask, as did all the rest, but in the end we were able to help remove over seventy bodies.(They had been wrapped by the Marines, but we must have known, I just can't remember, but I do remember getting sick) You couldn't tell that anything had happened to them as they all looked as if the were asleep. Which is how I choose to remember it. You couldn't make out features, being under water and the Marines did most of the un strapping seat belts and handing out the bodies to us and we took them up.

Aramco finally got a dive boat in and several divers from Udahliyah went down and we were told to just bring up debris or locate stuff and put markers that popped to the surface to mark the spot and Aramco divers lifted the wreckage on to a floating barge and towed it all to shore where the wreckage was taken to hanger 8-1. The aircraft was reassembled there and for many years, until 1968 it was still in that hanger. I last paid my respects in 1968.

The Aramco autopsies all showed that everyone of the people on board had a broken neck…the only question unanswered was why did some of the bodies have water in their lungs (drowned) and why did we and they find several bodies with bloody bandages around their heads. These questions have never been answered.

Every single body except Mr. Ralph Devenney was recovered. Some had floated as far away as seventeen miles and washed ashore. Mr. Al-Dossary, a Saudi National lost all five of his sons and attended every single memorial service, be it Catholic, Protestant of other that was held. Arabia may not be as it was, but honor like Mr. Al- Dossary showed will always be my Arabia.

I lost several very good friends, Janie Baumgartner, Thelma Carter, Keith Sounders and Dad, and to make this worse, the other Sounders child was killed a year later in a car wreck in Arabia and three generations of one family were buried in that little plot of land called the Aramco cemetery. There are a lot more, but I don't think I can go on much more today.

We were the only ones there with SCUBA gear and the Saudi Govt. wanted proof that the people who would be diving were certified and we all were by Aramco. The fire station would not fill our tanks unless we had the proper PADI certification, which we all did. My parents had to agree and sign a waiver for the Saudi Government and the water was shallow so we weren't diving deep. The US Marine's used our equipment and did most of the bad work. We mainly floated bags to the surface…Aramco had divers, but most of their stuff was for deep water diving, hardhat equipment and the water was too shallow. Eventually divers who were certified were brought in by Aramco from Operations offshore by Udahliyah, but the first day of the find we were there because the authorities thought that there might still be living people as a good portion of the wreck was above water.

KLM/USAF CRASHES

First I'll tell the story of the USAF crashes. They are not too bad and even a touch of humor.

The USAF was transferring six Lockheed Shooting Star twin-jet fighter jets to Dhahran Air Force Base in 1953. They were en route from Cypress and had bad weather along the route, resulting in one by one they ran out of fuel.

The first two went down and both pilots ejected to safety. The third flew on a little further and tried to belly land in the sand dunes and upon crashing the pilot pulled the ejection seat which fired off and blasted him into the air, but not high enough and when the chair came down, it landed with his head exposed and broke his neck. The fourth went down two miles from the road between RT and Dhahran. The fifth actually landed on the road between RT and Dhahran, and Mr. Al Garing from RT, an Engineer was driving to Dhahran and pulled up to the jet and the pilot opened the cockpit and climbed down and told Mr. Garing "This is for the ****** birds." This quote was famous in Aramco for a long time after this. Mr. Garing gave him a ride to the USAF base at Dhahran and the last jet touched down at the airfield, bone dry on fuel and glided in to the runway.

All of the aircraft were recovered by Aramco for the USAF and all but two were repaired and flew on to Tripoli. One of the aircraft was in Hanger 8-1 for several years. May still be there. This hanger is important as I'll explain later.

KLM, flying a Vickers Viscount four engine propeller passenger plane on a routine flight from Amsterdam to Dhahran ran out of fuel also and belly landed in the sand dunes south of the airport. This was in 1951. All crew and passengers were fine and no one hurt. Aramco got a crane and a flatbed and went out and picked up the plane, loaded it and took it to Dhahran Air field also. Mechanics flew in from KLM and in three weeks had the plane repaired and it was flown back to Amsterdam. Incidentally, the pilot had tried to land with his wheels down on a hard stretch of desert and missed hitting the dunes. The USAF said, at the time that had he hit the hard surface, with no engines, essentially a "dead stick" landing he most likely would have broken the nose gear and caused a major crash. The dune was soft and absorbed the impact.

MESSERSCHMITT'S
AND RECLAMATION

How we discovered Reclamations must have been on one of our frequent escapes from the wrath of 1. Mom, or 2. Aramco Security. Somehow we discovered that if you went on the other side of the incinerators, you could enter the ultimate fantasy land. Disneyland was for the tooth fairy after we found this place. Out past the driving range and around behind the small Jebal....wow, what a adventure. We were all in the ninth grade and it was during break in our ninth grade year.

So, It soon became a place of magic, however as with magic there is both white and black. I still think Mom practiced the dark arts as she always seemed to know....Think she still does.

Well, once again the intrepid Bratateers decided to explore.. Tom found this huge boat, looked like a yacht and only had a small hole in the side. We got to thinking, that if was out here and nobody wanted it....well why not. We could easily fix it up, load it on a flatbed, there were many lined up out there, and off to launch in Half Moon Bay. Using a fork lift we put two dentist chairs we found on the deck and, needing a cannon of some sort we took two of the exhaust pipes off of a kenworth, which looked like 40 MM cannons to use and finally enlisted the help of Chris Mohlman, who was knowledgeable about welding to weld on a cap that we could lock on the back of these pipes. We now had our whaling gun, two rear seats for lounging and catching the King of Hamoors and had patched the hole with, and who would have known, we used concrete we found in bags. I guess never realizing that Aramco must have had a reason for putting it in Reclamations to start with.

The inside had sets of theater seats and two hospital beds, which we could imagine all kinds of nefarious schemes with the way they folded.... We had a stove which we had hooked up to what Chris told us was Gas cylinders, and having full belief in our elder, didn't test it. The cylinder was green.. get a clue here ? The shower we fixed easy. We found a gas tank off of some BIG truck, put it on deck and ran a hose with a regular water tap for a valve.

Found plenty of weird paint and ended up with a dazzling camouflage scheme, although not intentional. We were also painted, but with the help of a paint sprayer on a portable compressor we found, it was easy to paint the inside. I think back now and wonder if the Prison green color wasn't a harbinger of things to come. Well, we made drapes and lots of goodies. This whole event taking almost the whole break.

Finally the big day. Chris drives around a flatbed and we use the fork lifts, we by now had three and using a fire hose section as a belt under the boat, we managed to get it on the truck bed sideways. Chris blocked it with huge wood blocks and it sat in place, sideways on the trailer. I was getting a little concerned as we were ready, so we thought to head to the beach, and Chris say's, well we can't go down the road this way, so we will cut across the desert. Chris said that Aramco always had an escorts, so we went into Dhahran and got two of the little three wheeled Messerschmitt cars, just borrowed of course, and made up our convoy. As most of you know, the desert was very hard and after knocking down part of the perimeter fence, off we headed.

Needless to say, we lost one Messerschmitt in soft sand, and it started to sink out of sight, scared the hell out of all of us, but on we went. We made it to water and thought we were at the beach. By now it was dark and we had only headlights. So Chris backs the trailer into the water and this boat starts to float. We are ecstatic.

We can't get the trailer out, but Chris say's ARAMCO will find it and we will have sailed off to a secret cove. So on to the boat we all go, Chris fires up what must have been diesels and we move about fifty feet forward and slam into something. Dead in the water, but can't see anything.

So we decide we have hit a sandbar and will wait for high tide. Dinner to be made and most likely a touch of brown was involved. Tom goes down, lights the stove and our first disaster hits...The entire back end of the boat disappears in a huge blast. Were we had stored the cylinders of gas. Turns out later we find out they were oxygen. I had been knocked of the side of the boat and Tom out the side, right thru the cement, which had dissolved and we were already sinking and didn't know it. SO in desperation Chris say's we need to fire a "rescue signal" so that ARAMCO fire department can get to us. He goes to our home made cannon, and to this day I never put gas in anything except my car, he pours gas in the barrel, and lights the fuse at the cap. I know ARAMCO saw the flash, I was blackened and blind for about twenty minutes on my back again, and the front of our luxury liner is gone.

It is time to make our escape, so with little or no clothing left, dirty, blind, and black, our ship afire we jump in and on the remaining Messerschmitt and run like hell as far as we can get, back to the fence and we decide it would be best to climb over, so we bury the car, I still know where it used to be, but from Rodney's tape believe I'm safe.

I knew we all smelled bad, but didn't know until the next day when ARAMCO was all talking about a ship that had exploded in one of the big sewage ponds beyond the camp. Also that somehow an ARAMCO Kenworth was sunk almost to the cab and they were trying to dig it out.

Somehow, someone found out and Chris got named...I saw him years later in Saigon and he told me that they deported him the next day, but that he never told. He said he never went back to Arabia after that and had moved to Australia and was hunting Kangaroo's for the Aussie govt. I always admired him for that. He took our blame and never got to graduate with us. In the ninth grade graduation photo I have, his seat is empty. He deserved to be with us, and is in my mind, forever a hero and fellow brat...

Incidentally his Dad was the undertaker for ARAMCO and always used to wear a chain with a skull that had rubies for eyes and carried a tape measure that he would use at parties, measure you and say, see you soon as he wandered off. Measured me many a time. I miss Chris and wish him well. He was truly a young "Indiana Jones" way before his time....

MIKE'S ESCAPADES

I just read the note on Mike & his escapades. Nope, over in RT we were just like Mike! For years, they kept a bulldozer down at the beach in RT. Needless to say, it took a lot of unscheduled trips. Heck, we used to start the thing every Teen Canteen dance (once a month) just to bug Security! Fortunately, both for ARAMCO and us brats, we tended to be very nondestructive. The aim was not to destroy things, but just to have a little fun. Of course, every once in a while things got out of hand. When that happened, the community was so small that the "culprits" usually got caught and punished one way or another. Looking back, I realize that a lot more was "noticed" than I realized at the time. When I was in 6th grade ('67 or '68), Duncan Smith, Phillip Nelson, and I decided it would be a good idea to make a little nitroglycerin. We had the recipe, we had the lab equipment, so all we needed were the acids. Fortunately for us, when we raided the Science Room for them, we took whole bottles, and of course, their disappearance was immediately noticed. The excitement began when they added up what could be made with that particular combination of chemicals. Just before lunch they called an Assembly, and it was announced that if all materials were returned there would be no consequences. On the other hand, if they were not returned, those responsible, once caught, would be kicked out of

Arabia! We had a conference, and Duncan volunteered to be the sacrificial goat. It turned out that wasn't good enough. He came back and told us he had been told we all had to come in for the deal to work. Man, I still remember that afternoon quite clearly! What impresses me in hindsight is that a few months later Mr. Smith and few other men took us down to the swing sets on the beach (halfway between Rec and the North Fence) and demonstrated dynamite to us. I still remember a 2 ft thick and 5 ft by 5 ft slab of asphalt road flying 50 feet up in the air. I lost my enthusiasm for reckless explosives after that. Our parents were smart people

MIKE'S TRIP TO ARABIA

At 01:40 PM 3/21/97 -0500, JEFF94172@aol.com wrote: If after reading about Crocker's trip the people from AAAA don't give it up they are really spitting in the wind. In their invite they said they were concerned about hostile takeovers—I would think that at this point anyone can see that the deed is done—there's nothing left to take over except the money I guess. I mean, I don't know where he gets the time but what Crocker has done with this Chat thing is way beyond good. Not to mention the internet thing too. On top of that, this trip to Arabia to get us the recognition and possible benefits from the Saudi Gov.—well all's I can say is AAAA, what have you done that remotely compares to this? I'm not being nasty here—I'm saying he who does the work should get the benefit of it and if Crocker wants to be King of the Brats the pleasure be all mine!! Because he sure has brought me a lot of pleasure with this thing. I suppose now he'll want me to kiss his butt when I see him in AZ and although there is alot to kiss I guess he probably deserves it. To you guys in AAAA, forget about this San Antonio thing, come to AZ prepared to eat a meager portion of poo-poo and then hang with your old friends again—just like when we were kids. Jeff Yaeger dh64

Jeff comments have always been the goal of all of us..to be family and friends. This has been my goal since day one and it is people like the brat-hood that make it all worthwhile... PS, Jeff, have reserved spot on ample tail for well planted respect.

MIRANDA

While I appreciate the homage to my short career lifestyle in Arabia, I always found that Miranda was nothing to mix brown or white with. I usually preference the product, fresh from the still tap, siphoned off, before Dad knew, AND therein lies Mondays tales from the past....

Oh, one other point, Miranda was bottled in Egypt,(eventually bottled in Dammam) shipped to Arabia and was the drink of choice before bepsi came along..The real mixer for those of us who loved the effect of bubbles of white up our nose was White and Ginger Ale.

WELL SHAKEN AND.....WELL, I'LL TELL HOW THAT ALL WORKED OUT LATER

Monster Slide Aramco took care of us kids, but I always felt there was a touch of malicious thought, most likely by parents who had kids who always caused them grief. I, not having any knowledge of that sort of thing, will still plead innocent to all charges. However, the 3rd street playground was being set up and as a jolly young, verrry young pirate, I saw nothing but opportunity.

The main feat was for Aramco to build a dreamland, then surround it with terrible dangers we had to brave to play on the various kill-machines that they bought from some kid hating person. First they build this wonderful playground, then surround it with a foot kill zone of desert sand about thirty feet deep to the first playground equipment. My feet were like that of a Camel after three months of the playground. Flat, ugly and shod. I learned to start running at the top of the street, kick off my flip flops and do a dancing bear leap to the nearest toy. Which happen to be a series of wooden horses which were mounted on a single large spring and would rock back and forth and side to side and up and down…whew, getting a little dizzy all over again. Anyhow, leaping from about the fourth third degree burn to my poor little piglets, I managed to leap onto the saddle, blister my butt on the really hot wood, and putting my little feet on the wood pegs I rocked forward with the sped of a Gazzelle and found out the first devious plan of the evil empire parents. The darn things were only meant for kids that were slightly less my size, so that in going forward, I smacked my face right into the blazing sand. Left a cute imprint and a string of invectives that stood the hair up on my Mom, who was at home three blocks away. To make it worse, the recoil then sent my tail off of the little horse and a really neat back flop onto the sand. Trying to catch my breath I suddenly realize an interesting fact. The darn sand is HOT.

Well, now we all know about the large "A" frame swing sets. At my age, they stood about 100 feet into the air and the seats were a sandpaper leather with chains going into the sky. What a plan. I'll bet that if you swing hard enough and try, you might be able to loop the loop and completely go over the top bar. You know why they refer to the horizontal bars, across more blazing sand "Monkey Bars"? Most of you thought it was because as you cross, you look like monkeys. I am here to tell you that it comes from swinging so high that you get dizzy, the chains are actually whipping a little and suddenly you are airborne, and then engage a set of bars that resemble a latter and like a monkey falling from a tree, you and it become one. Spent two weeks with my hand in a huge bandage and needing a bigger one on my rear end after Mom got me home from the emergency room.

BUT, was I one to quit..ohhhh nooo. Not this mighty adventurer. There was still this funny round machine with a spoke wheel in the center and what parents tried convincingly to call a "Merry go Round." Even the name sounded fishy to me. Why would Mary want to go round?

Well, a bunch of us got on this beast, and one of the huge guys from a much older age started turning the wheel. Grab on, the beast is awake and we are going round and round. Faster too and slowly we start to slide off the metal railing and no matter what kind of offerings to the older brat nothing works. I even offered my brother into eternal servitude. No avail, this guy intended to make us all seasick or off by centrifugal force. So while once again airborne and reflecting on life in flight, I hit well and only bruised every body part possible. Add to that the ever popular third degree sand burns and my day was just about made. EXCEPT, with a quick run I found this amazing monster. The GIANT slide. Took almost a week to climb the steps, they were even in two levels. One to rest on I guess.

Now many people would say, doesn't he ever learn? Well, nobody told me that metal slides, and bare legs don't work. You STICK, and cook about halfway down. So with a mighty yell and very foul weather language I tried to crawl back up the thing to the top. Only here comes a good friend, sitting on wax paper, he the wise one, and we have a multiple person crash rivaling a downtown Los Angeles freeway wreck. The next person piles into us and of course, who goes over the side, drops like a large stone and smack face down into..yeah, once again with the sand bit. This time the trip home was even more interesting from the emergency room. Me with a hairline crack in my leg and a cast on my foot. Mom's foot having no cast and very little trouble reaching the only unaffected part of me and I'm out of the playground for two months.

Years later I looked at the that playground, now fenced and guarded. I saw the monster and it seemed so small. I saw the wild ride and the little ponies. Yet deep in my heart, I saw me, and the beast once again jousting for mastership of the playground.

Incidentally, at the ripe old age of 49 on my last visit, one thing you still don't do even after thirty five years, you DO NOT take off your shoes and socks and walk in a dream like state to the slide. The darn sand is still blazing HOT!!!

Made the guards day tho........

MOTHERS DAY

Running like a dervish across fine grained sand in a cool morning because Mom yelled "Mike Crocker, get home now for breakfast... you'll be late for school again!!! Thanks Mom.

Stumbling through the rough school of arithmetic when you had to count on your hands, and some used their sandals feet, It was explained to me that on my one hand I was better than all the rest because I has disproportionate sized finger and Mom said, "Well, you have the advantage because you already have fractions down. Whole, half, third and eighth. As far as your other hand you have five there too. Just two are hidden numbers". Thanks Mom.

Tying one of my Dads huge ties around my neck and wearing a suit that was for church only, but for the 9th grade prom dance and my first date I got to wear it. The corsage made of paper and string. She told me I was so handsome and my date was beautiful. Thanks Mom.

For when Sa'id of Security brought me home at 3:00 in the morning as a grown up returning student, hardly able to walk after a night of brown and white, and Mom making me eggs and toast quietly so Dad wouldn't hear us. Thanks Mom.

For the terrible tears that racked my body when a friend had died on MEA 444 and asking "How come, Mom?" with her response that God needed then and one day I'd see them again. Thanks Mom.

For being so proud when finally, after what seemed like years of school and mishaps, graduating from San Marcos and the hundreds of times she helped me with difficult summers and for believing in me in school. Thanks Mom.

For the smacks, thumps, bumps and butt pops I had justly deserved which made an impression on why and why not. Even if I didn't know, or at least told her I did know it was wrong to chunk eggs at passing cars. Thanks Mom.

For the pain and for the reassurance I got when the love of my life broke up with me. cried for days, she spoke softly and held me. She knew it would happen again and again as I grew up. Although she always reassured me there was someone for me too. Thanks Mom.

For the times I lost a job, or was hurt on duty as a police officer or just plain needed to talk, always there and always ready to help. Thanks Mom.

For making sure my life was filled with adventure by taking the chance in 1951 of going to Bahrain to marry a man she had met and start my life of great and glorious adventures. Thanks Mom.

For smacking me or hugging me and loving me no matter what stupid thing I did, all the way into my 50's and still. Thanks Mom

For the Christmas as a child where two packages were one sock each and special after shave in later years and always the required underwear under the tree when we had little. Thanks Mom.

For waiting for me to get to you, to hold you for hours, to say "I love you" and for fighting until I held you, with tears falling as rain on you from a giant of a man, I knew you were there. Thanks Mom.

For being a Guardian Angel riding on my shoulder now and whispering now and again, "I love you, son". Thanks Mom.

So for all you did and the wonderful life you gave me and for so many others I want to say, with out reservation. You did it always.

HAPPY MOTHERS DAY TO ALL MOTHERS WHO ARE ALL HERE AND THEY ARE ALL WITH US TODAY. A MOTHER'S LOVE IS ETERNAL

Mike Crocker (DH65) Spending the day with my Mom. It has been a lifetime and my birthday and my Mother's death day, one and the same, is fast approaching. Along with never saying "Happy Mother's day" I had this really unusual vision or dream and my soul has quit screaming as much. So I'll tell the story and you can delete but this is my dream and I chose to share with friends. Call in the morning of my birthday, "Come quick, the hospital has called your brothers to the ICU" I booked my flight as I went out the door for a two hour drive to the airport. Now starts my vision: I was standing on the right side of my beloved Mother as the steady pumping of the respirator went on and on. I cradled her as she must have at one time cuddled her newborn. She held my hand and the medical staff proclaimed that there was brain activity. I called to her in heart screaming pain and put my forehead to hers and tried to take her pain and let me die. She moved her body on the bed and her eyelids fluttered as she fought with the heart of Gen. Patton and the strength of a super woman. My tears must have made an impression as she seemed to finally hear me and she seemed to relax. She had "coded" seven times until I took her in my arms, and for six hours I held her and drenched her heart with my bulbous tears.

Suddenly I heard a slow plumping down of a massive foot. There at the door was the most beautiful shiny black haired camel, regal in all it's bearing. The sterling silver camel bells around it's proud neck were ringing with a glorious melody which was soundless except to Mom and I. The great beast stuck his head down and a tear, in which the glow of the brightest star was reflected slowly fell on to my Mother. She seemed to completely relax and I heard her smile.

I picked up my Mother and slid her gently onto the solid gold camel saddle with reins in her hand that were woven silver with diamonds. The beast looked directly into my eyes and bowed his massive head as he slowly turned and stepped out in the hall. I followed and to my great amazement there was nothing but miles of whites dunes and blazing stars right over my head. The camel started very slowly and my Mother started changing into a thirty year old beauty in a bright summer dress of blue and yellow. As the camel moved into the dunes I fell to my knee's in stunned awe. My dear

Mother stopped the great massive and turned. I saw her smile and the words came like a hurricane but surrounded me so gently I felt I was in a bed of pure cotton. "I love you son, and always will."

With that she turned and way off in the background I saw thousands of glittering shiny spots of light and a small group detach itself from the thousands with the reddish Arabia sky burning behind them ride down the greatest dune I had ever seen and join my Mom. Her family and my brother I saw clear as my watered puffed eyes could see. Slowly they gained speed and a long flow of desert lilies flowed back. They reached the top of the dune and I seemed to snap awake. Kneeling there in the hospital floor with the purest white desert sand running from my outstretched hands through my fingers and into nothingness. A bright flash and Mom was with God.

Mom, Happy Mothers Day and I will always love you.

Your son, Michael

MICHAEL

I know you must be busy. I've been reading your posts about your trip, crying for the last 2 hours until I was numb, and then crying some more. And now I finally know what I've been so sad about for so many years. Your words were so clear, and so moving, I could taste, smell, hear, touch and feel what happened to you there. (and I really hope this isn't too presumptuous) I was transported back to Jasmine Street in RT, I was in Dhahran by the rec center, I sat at the deep end of the pool, and on the Big Dune with you. I revisited the stables, the tower, the university—and you never knew it.

Because of you, I've cried more and laughed more than ever before in my entire life, all in this last year—I am finally free to see that what I grieve most and constantly is the loss of my beautiful precious family, my dearest friends, my homeland, my future, and especially my truest soul, which has been in hiding, scared for her life for the last 20 years. I want to transform my best memories into something beautiful and encouraging for others who may be in the same pain or confusion. It helps me ease my own somehow— by helping others. It is the only way I know how.

Although I've said it so many times, and you must have grown tired of my ramblings, thank you again from the deepest part of my heart for what you have done. You are loved and honored by many—the kind of person I've always dreamt of knowing, skeptical when I finally met you. So, Thank you again, Michael, for all the brats who may not understand the depth of your love for them or our country, and for those that already do, and especially for me. I wish I could say this better—my words are very inadequate today. I have accepted already that I will always be lost.. but perhaps that is the "brat-way".

Patty

ASSALAMU ALAIKUM WA RAHMATU ALLAH

As I stood on the sands of the desert once again recently, I felt a tremor go throughout my body. It was a warmth that can only be described as a sensation of pleasure mixed with deep sorrow. The Brat life blood which pounds like the Ras Tanura surf in my veins was matched only by the Flare in Abqaiq that lit the depth of my soul in my eyes as the way home as we flew the dark skies. Arriving at the main gate at Dhahran the flood of emotions of being safe from the world was once again forming an aura about me. For as the Crown Prince said to me at a meeting in Riyadh, "You are not here Amerike Bedu, you are sailing the Rub Al'Kahli with your spirit. You seem to ride with our father and yours from so long ago. Are you happy?"

The answer must be one that can only come from the spray of fine golden sand from my fingers as it piles on the third street playground. Yes, I whisper, for I have touched the face of my youth and found it to be me. The Great North dune will always sing it's words of sensuality in my heart, if I travel a million miles away. I will always feel the touch of my Arabian Princess who's love can never die, and forever in my mind is the haunting Call to Prayer of the faithful. The touch of the beach, the smell of the shops in Al-Khobar, the sweet taste of the honeysuckle from the hedge. How can one measure all of the feelings and emotions. It is really easy. It is love. For each Brat that I know and each that I may never meet, but will always know, the sands of our youth have touched me.

I am moving on from being your President for the past six years. I am told it is time and as a wise Bedu once said.."Man and the flow of the dune must always move." So be it. For I am alive as I have never been. I have found the Brats and they and I have played the alleys of time once again. We have touched Christmas past and been present for the future. We have grieved for the loss of so many of us, but most of all, I have found, in each of you, a place of heart that may never die.

The greatest gift that God has given me, and He has been generous with me, is you. All 4800 we have brought together. A Brathood of many, with a feeling of one. We have done a lot my friends. For that is our thread of humility..the friendship that life gave us all from a common bond. Let us not forget that we have a purpose, a goal, a responsibility. One of friendship that will last lifetimes.

I wish to thank each and every Brat alive, whether I know you or you know me, for you have given a lost dhow a port of call..The port of friendship.

I hope to be able to see each and every one of you at the reunion, for it shall be my last as your President and I hope we will have pleased you with the efforts of the many that have formed the Aramco Brats, Inc. group. For they truly have fought many a battle and passing the torch of one to another is always hard.

But judge not us hard, for we came from the past and fought through the shifting sands to find a place of magic. A place we can all call our youth for a few days. In Tucson at the Reunion, I will once again be safe and feel the emotions of the past, present and future from you.

I will always be there for my beloved Brats, and I hope that in the future you look kindly at the man who wanders the reunion with the glazed look of a bemused and content camel, for that shall be me seeing each and every time the beauty of you all. My Brats.

Ma'sallam'a siddiqui's
Michael Crocker (DH65)
Dr. Ahmed bin Saifuddin,

The below is one of the articles that I have published in the local media. You asked about what I had written and therefore I have put it here.

Thank you for your call. It was if there was an added blessing to my day that I give praise to Allah for.

Mike Crocker

"ISLAMIC BELIEF IN JESUS AND OTHER QUESTIONS"

There is a question that I am asked many times by a lot of people here in town, so I thought I would take this time to address in the newspaper a few thoughts I have learned from my studies and acceptance of Islam as my true path to enlightenment. I have already stated part of this in the book, but it bears a great deal of weight to understanding both Christainty and Islam, so I will repeat.

I profess my faith in Arabic here and in English for you to understand.

ash-hadu an laa ilaahah allallah, Ash-hadu anna muhammad-ar-rasool ullaah

(I bear witness and attest that there is no god worthy of worship but the One God Allah! I bear witness and attest that Muhammad is the messenger of Allah)

Now then, to explain as best I can some questions you have asked of me. Praise be to Allah that I am able to answer with His guidance.

Islamic peoples respect and revere Jesus and await his Second Coming as prophesized. They consider Him one of the greatest of God's messengers to mankind. A Muslim never refers to Him simply as "Jesus", but always add the phrase "Upon Him be peace".

The Quran confirms His virgin birth (in fact a chapter of the Quran is entitled "Mary"), and Mary is considered the purest woman in all creation. Many people ask, Why is it that only Jesus shall return? My answer to this is very simple. Only Allah is aware and knows the wisdom of what He does and why. It is written the when the Angel Gabriel (Quran 3:46) announced to Mary about her son, Jesus, he spoke that Jesus would come and speak as a child and again at maturity. Allah alone knows all and shall decide all.

The Quran relates the Annunciation as follows: "Behold!" The Angel said, "God has chosen you, and purified you and chosen you above the women of all nations. O Mary, God gives you good news of a word from Him, whose name shall be the Messiah, Jesus, son of Mary honored in this world and the Hereafter, and one of those brought near to God. He shall speak to the people from his cradle, and in maturity, and shall be of the righteous."

She said "O my Lord! How shall I have a son when no man has touched me?" He said, "Even so, God creates what He will. When He decrees a thing. He says to it, "Be!" and it is. (Quran, 3:42-7)

Jesus was born by the same power which had brought Adam into being without a father: "Truly, the likeness of Jesus with God is as the likeness of Adam. God created him of dust, and then said to him "Be!" and he was. (Quran, 3:49)

There is the evidence that Jesus performed many miracles. The Quran (3:49) tells us that he made the statement: "I have come to you with a sign from your Lord: I make you out of clay, as it were, the figure of a bird, and breathe into it and it becomes a bird by God's leave. And I heal the blind and the lepers and I raise the dead by God's leave" However, the miracle of Muhammad is most great because the miracle is the word of Allah, direct and without distortion and has never been distorted or rewritten. It was written at the time of Mohammad and not over a period of centuries, with many revisions, as was the Christian Bible. The Holy Book, the Quran is the final miracle as it is original. What more of a miracle, that can be witnessed today stands true and without versions than Gods word to the Prophet. The most amazing aspect is the fact that the prior prophets made miracles happen that were only short lived or even supernatural. Modern science can make wine from water, but no man has ever been able to write the Holy Book, the Quran. This is the true miracle of Allah. Via his messenger and

Prophet Muhammad. It is my humble opinion that Allah created the miracle that would convince all people, everywhere and for all time. Thus Allah did pass to Muhammad the Holy book, the Quran, which addresses mans need and disciplines with great light and direction. Never changing and centuries later, a book of revelation and guidance as it was in the beginning and is today. This is the miracle of the true path, leading to the enlightenment of man by his devotion and love and belief in the one God, Allah.

Muhammad, and not even the Christian Jesus were upon the land to make revision or change the one true path of belief that is the belief in one God. In the Quran, (Quran 3:50) Jesus is directly quoted as speaking "To attest the law which was before me. And to make lawful to you part of what was forbidden you; I have come to you with a sign from your Lord, so fear God and obey Me." Thus we have full support of the one God and the true path of Allah. The comment by Jesus so fear God and obey me is a direct reference back to the one God and not to fear me being to fear Jesus. For Jesus was a prophet and messenger also.

Prophet Muhammad spoke "Whoever believes there is no god but God alone without partner, that Muhammad is His messenger, that Jesus is the servant and messenger of God, His word breathed into Mary and a spirit emanating from Him, and that Paradise and Hell are true, shall be received by God into Heaven

According to the beliefs of Islam, man is not born into original sin. He is God's vicegerent on earth. Every child born has the "fitra", an innate predisposition towards virtue, knowledge, and beauty. Islam considers itself to be the "primordial religion" It seeks to return man to his original, true nature in which he is in harmony with creation, inspired to do good, and confirming the Oneness of God. To accept the Angels and to believe in the fact that there is life after death. In Islam, death is but a gate to the life after death. There is a paradise awaiting the believer and the fires for those who chose to follow a path not of oneness with God.

I hope I have cleared up some misconceptions about Islam, I am not an expert on anything, but I am a true believer and my belief brings the light of Allah into my heart and lightens the weight from me whenever I speak of the one God.

Allah Akbar.

Michael Crocker

OFF WITH A BANG

Seemed to me that the sand was unusually tart about the time I left school. It was one of those wind swept hot summer days and the whirlwinds of sand followed you like an avenging mom. I had worn the usual, shorts, tee shirt and sneakers. Yeah, the old white sidewalls with strings that I always felt the maker of sneakers deliberately made a foot too long so that no matter how you tied them, they still managed to get loose and try to trip you. I always wanted to ask them why they waxed the strings. I must have tied mine a thousand times a day and always at the wrong time. You know, stop suddenly, bend over to tie shoe and Mr. Riley the Principal walks around the corner with his arms full and falls over you. Great way to start the day. In his office before the first bell. Not that that wasn't a usual stop over for me on a normal class day, but this weekend was different. It was the Fourth of July. So I was being extra careful that no dreaded phone call went to my house. I had plans!!

Now I've told the woeful tale of watermelons before but what I haven't spoke about was the Aramco Fire Department and the fireworks display put on by the AEA. As usual, this was planned for the area near the King's Road ball park and Aramco had put out a lot of folding chairs. This was great fun to ride your bike through and knock over and watch the recreation guys go off the deep end. I mean, why would any adult heave a folding chair at a cherub that was innocently passing by, along with a string of invectives I didn't know. I did take notes of the words for future testing on Mom, which usually was a tragedy right up there with wetting your pants in class…

Well as you might guess, we, and the guilty parties are now respectable men of means so I'll save them having to explain to their kids why they say "Don't play with matches", but lurking in their dark corners of the mind is the awful story I'll tell.

In Khobar there were several stores that sold "Black Cat" fireworks in red plastic wrapped packages or you could get just plain handfuls of small "Bangers". While watching the firemen set up the truck and after getting told to ride my damn bike off a cliff by several verbose men, I began to see a way to have a great laugh on all of them. Never one to do anything that might offend Father Roman in confession, I hurriedly gathered up the gang and off we went. We made stops at places along the perimeter fence and at Imhoff gardens and in Khobar. Quick trip to the commissary and we were about ready.

Now back then, Aramco used to turn over 55 gallon oil drums and use them for putting a cloth over and a lamp or smudge pot all around the chairs. For light and for the extra touch of the "Tiki" flare effects. It was the Fourth you know. Now many of you know, a smudge pot is something that only fifty gallons of water, and burying it twenty feet down under sand it might just go out. Chances are there are buried pots still smouldering today. They just wouldn't go out.

Mentioning Father Roman is because I kinda considered him a bank. I would stop by, borrow a little cash loan from this small wooden box, something about "Donations" and then always return it on allowance day. So we hit the jackpot and found about 100 riyals. Well, I knew it would take several allowances to make this up, so I simply signed a IOU with my brother's name. Security blanket you know. This was to be a black day around my house once all the facts were into the kangaroo court Mom held. I mean what idiot misspells his own name on an IOU. Obviously the hanging judge felt it could only have been someone in the family that knew he had brothers but had long since forgot that they were not there for his convenience.

All day long there had been a parade and a carnival and a lot of fun. We, in the dark alleys and hedgerows were planning and plotting. We had picked up the material I mentioned, about two hundred packages of the Black Cats and from the fence we got some of the two week older rotten fish from the fly killer traps and we had come across some really great beauties of camel and horse, ahhh, spillage at Imhoff. Begin to see light here?

All of this we placed in a bag, after unwrapping hundreds of firecrackers and pouring all this massive firepower into a bag. We then filled the top of the small box with a mixture of the fish and "chips". The fuse was a long string from where? Yup, a well rubbed in powder sneaker string. They did have a use. One small oversight is that to run like a drunken stallion on a desert of soft sand and flash by the world on asphalt that took rubber off tires from the heat was not bright..Why? you say with a slight curl of the lips..well lets say that for lack of a string, there was lack of a sure foot and for lack of a sure foot that was no lack of a sore butt.

Another mistake, one is never enough when dealing with Mom, was to go home and pointedly gripe about smelling like a dead fish and camel sh— and wondering what happened to the high price help around the house not doing anything and where were my clean clothes and so on and so on until the house grew deadly quiet and a cold front blew in and the sky opened and the smack of the fly swatter and resulting scream was undoubted considered by many in the camp to be a familiar sound from the Crockers house and just went about the daily routine with a smirk, knowing full well I had got caught at something.

Now it was a matter of revenge. After all, what right did the Fire Chief have telling Mom I had been helpful all day at Recreation and suggesting that I be tied to my bike and dropped off a Dhow near Bahrain?

We went to recreation and set up our massive, what felt like two hundred pounds of "stink bomb", yeah, you all remember the jokers that got some of those and stomped on them during a movie or once, a poor soul did it during one of Father Romans Mass services and almost met his maker right there, but that's another story .

What we didn't figure on was the fact that we had no real container, just this cardboard box and so that to get any effect, it would have to be against something solid so that the, what we thought, smell would be blown over the group. So we placed it inside the drivers section of the pumper truck that was parked behind the display area and facing the crowd. We knew the wind would spray perfume over all of them. The fuse was laid out ever so careful and we hid behind the truck. The crowd gathered, and to our delight, the front row was filling nicely with big shots, Mr. Kieswetter, Mr. Scardino,

Mr. Riley, Mr. Dickerson and all the wives in really nice dresses and a lot of parents. Then the band from school played the National Anthem and the flag was paraded up front by the Boy Scouts and set off to one side in stands and the fire chief begin to light all of the sky rockets, which we always just used a coke bottle, but he was a lot smarter. So we lit our fuse and skulked back out of harms way we thought, and gleefully waited. That darn fuse kept going out and I had to keep running up, slowly relight it and run back. Well, as might be expected, the best laid plans of mice and boys...

SO I open the door, madder then a wet Dhub, and go to re-light this monster and what do I see. The flame disappears into the box.. Well, next. BANG!!!!

I know the truck must have rocked and I was ten feet back, flat out, smoldering and covered in ten pounds of dead fish and camel manure. From head to toe and almost completely black. The white of eyes and the size of them must have been beyond belief and I was on fire I'm sure. Of course some of this wondrous mixture went out the windows and managed to spray just a few in the front row. I didn't know the Fire Chief was manning the foam sprayer on top and to this day I still think he took great delight in foaming me under about forty feet of foam. This of course made the mixture worse and as I said...run? Ha! Lucky to just stumble. Even without hearing I felt the earth tremble as the mass on the other side of the truck realized what was sprayed on them and the ground shook from a thousand high heeled hooves that stampeded to be the first to be in on the kill.

Now history was made that bright starry night as some say a small figure, chunky, maybe, was seen running with a frenzied mob of humanity following, some say with a stout rope, others say a lot of beltless pants were seen as whips cracked the air, but the nomads and bedus still speak with awe at the wails that arose that night from the house at the top of 6th street. The applause was heard in other districts I'm sure and I think the company took the next day off in celebration knowing full well it would be years before I sat down again.

One side note. At the last annuitants reunion, a woman approached me, and with what I saw as a great tenderness gave me a shiny small silver object. It said, "Fire Dept", Aramco logo and the word "Chief". It is in my Aramco collection and when you see it at the next reunion, imagine the aroma of the story....

GO HERE FOR 4,500 PHOTOS OF THESE TIMES http://arabian-camelot.com

OKAY MIKE! HERE'S MINE.

After reading Mike's story of his valentine experience, I had to tell you about my valentine story that happened a few years after I left Dhahran.

In 1960 I was twenty two, and had just gotten out of the Air Force. I was working in Jacksonville, Florida as a X-Ray Technican at St. Vincents Hospital. I met a cute student there named Kathy King. We started dating, and when her parents came back from Europe on a vaction and found out that we were seeing each other, they tried to do everything possible to break us up. Determined me, I wasn't going to put up with that, so I told her that we were going to elope on February 12th. I would met her at her back door anytime after midnight, and we would drive to Alabama and get married. Well I was there, and about twelve thirty she came to the back door, and told me that her mother caught her packing. I told her to go back to bed, and wait until they went to sleep. After the mosquitos kept on attacking me, and I had waited a couple of hours, I decided I would be creative. Kathy's house was a large two story brick house on a very secluded lot of the St. Johns River. I went into their garage, and got and aluminum ladder off the wall, and went to her bedroom window and placed it against the house. The problem was, it was about three feet to short. So I proceeded to get a lawn table and chair, placing the chair on top of the table and the ladder on the chair. Great! it worked, I was able to reach her window sill. I tapped on her window, and she undid the screen, and I removed it, and started receiving her luggage, after making two trip up and down the ladder, her parents light went on in their bedroom. I just lowered my head, and held on to the window sill. Suddenly the table and chair fell over, and left me suspended, hanging from the window sill. About this time I said to myself "Why Me Dear Lord". The mother came into Kathy's room and asked what the loud noise was, and Kathy told her that she fell out of bed, she went back go bed. To my surprise, I looked down, and the ladder had not fallen all the way to the ground, it was just in the reach of my foot. I tried to reach it, and when I did, it fell very loudly, the rest of the way down to the ground.. Damn, what do I do now. Mrs. King came to the window this time, looking down at me, screaming in the loudest manner possible. I looked up at her, and in a timed way and said "Mrs. King, its me Don, let me in". Where upon Mrs. King proceeded to beat my hands, in order to make me let go of the window sill. I was thinking to myself, what the hell, and I let go of the window, and fell two stories to the ground. I guess I was so frighten that I didn't hurt myself at all, but started running like hell down their long drive way, knowing as the outside lights came on, that I would be shot in the back by her father. Didn't happen! The next day February 13, we spoke on the phone, and decided that when her parents had their big party that night, celebrating their return from their trip to Europe, she would sneak out of the house, and meet me at the end of her long driveway. About ten that night she did, with only a fur coat on a very pretty party dress on. We drove all night to Ozark Alabama. It was a Sunday, on February 14th 1960, but we did find a judge Adams that met us at the courthouse, and married us at 4PM that day. That was a wild one, if I do say so myself, and all of it really happened…Her parents disowned her, and the marriage only last four years.. That's the way it goes, but there were no children. I learned a lot from that experience, and have been married for twenty nine years now to my second, with three beautiful children.. But I always chuckle when I think of my youth and the things I have done over my sixty one years.. Hope you enjoyed that one! See Ya. Don Raposo dh-51

PARTLY NON
ARABIA -RATED
"R"

Thought before I go quietly into the night, albeit perhaps screaming back with a vengeance I would relate two non-Arabia or at least post Arabia stories. I must warn that these are real stories and graphic. People ask what happend to a lot of us after Arabia, and so I thought I leave with these. I have written a lot more that I have been sending only to a very dear, to me, lady and since I have been asked a lot about my brother KC from many who knew him, I'll tell them what happened.

STORY ONE: After returning from the war zone I knew I had to go back to college. I didn't fit in. First I was older and the free love, peace ideology was still around and I didn't understand it. Some amazing encounters with female undergraduates took place as they all seemed to want to prove they could "take down" this "Baby Killer" from the war and wanted to do it sexually. Never worked, but I had a great couple of years. I was proud of my service so never backed down even with Professors or others who spent a lot of time talking, but with very little substance about the war. I was not in the Army per se, but a civilian agency attached to the Army.

I didn't know what to do with my life, so while at school I started a long tradition that has continued right up to now. I overloaded my system with work and play and made it all put terrible strain on myself. I joined the University Police Department and had the 11:00pm shift till 8:00 am and then class from 8:30am till 3:30pm. Used to go to class wearing our uniform which consisted of a blazer with police badge and under the coat a gun belt with weapon and all. This was a turn on for the girls but uncomfortable for me.

I remember one girl named Pam who wanted to become a police officer, and as it was late and no one was around I thought, well, I'll take her to the firing range and teach her how to shoot. She had a damn near perfect body and face, but that of course, never entered my mind. So we went to the ROTC indoor range and I taught her how to fire a service revolver. I also taught her how to shoot nude and as a result was lying on the floor of the ROTC building, totally nude with her, spent cartridges all over, sound asleep, and in comes the class for the first ROTC lesson of the day. Well, needless to say, the Chief of Police and I had a serious conversation and I ended up checking doors for about two months, which led to this next adventure.

I was checking the interior of the oldest building on campus when I noticed a small door at the end of the hall open. It was just a janitorial closet, but I got to being nosey and behind the desk found what looked like a top section of a door frame with about three feet of door sticking up from the floor. This intrigued me as I could not for the life of me figure out why anyone would have such a partial door there. So I moved the desk and forced the door part open about three feet and climbed down in this black hole like area. Using my flashlight I crawled along what seemed like a tunnel with one side being the foundation of the school building and the other side rough brick. Suddenly I fell forward and down about three feet and hit hard. I rolled about ten feet further down and laid still. I found my flashlight and noticed that the sides of what I had fallen into was all tiles. I shined my light around and saw something at the other end of this pit. I walked down to the other end and saw a bronze fish and a plaque. The plaque read "This pool was donated by Chas. Watson on this date 1912". The bronze fish was the water flow to fill a pool. I suddenly realized I was in a swimming pool underground. About two feet above the pool was a solid concrete floor. I didn't realize it right away, but I was looking at the parking lot bottom that was outside the school building. The school building had been built in 1913 and I couldn't even began to think where the hell I was.

I went back to the shallow end and found the tunnel I had been in. I proceeded down the tunnel in which I could now stand. I found what looked like a doorway and forced my way in. There was a room that had what looked like science lab tables and I collected several glass breakers and found some human bones. Evidently I was in what had once been a classroom, but I was at least twenty feet under the school building and it had no basement. So where was I and what the hell had happened.

I continued my movement down this two to three foot wide tunnel and suddenly found myself in a fairly good sized room that had an old Coleman lantern. I lit it and found myself in a Civil Defense storage bunker, There was food, water barrels, several old rifles and a very old radio. All of the stuff was marked 1917 and 1918. There was a table by the lamp with papers and they all proved to be about defense of the Academic building of West Texas State Teachers College for Women. I couldn't figure out what school that was as I was attending West Texas State University. Plus I had never heard of an Academic Building.

So back I went, thru the pool and finally out the, what I discovered was the top part of an old door that had been hidden behind the janitors desk all those years.

Then I went and talked with the Dean and all kinds of commotion broke out. The glass flask was dated 1911 and had a school seal on it.

Turns out that West Texas State University had been originally built in 1910 and had only one building, called the Academic Building which was four stories high and had a basement. It had been called West Texas State Teachers College for Women and in 1912 had caught fire and burnt down with the top floors caving in and covering the basement which housed the library(which I did not find) and the pool and the science lab. Two students had died and their bodies never recovered. After the fire the school rebuilt over the old foundation in 1913 and evidently was a little smaller by about fifteen feet than the original building. At one point someone knew about it because the had put in the civil defense center from WW I. However, by 1972 there was no history of the old school and no one alive to tell about it. They did a search of old newspapers and found a photograph of the old school on fire and thus the mystery was solved. The bones were recovered and buried and a lot of the items from the lab and the Civil Defense group are now on display in the University museum.

This saved me from the nude gun toting, hot coed incident and made me a hero until this next event.

Late at night while on patrol I got a radio call that there were strange noises coming from the old Fine Arts building. Well, for about a week the local police and others had been telling stories about how a police officer had been killed in this building and me being a rookie and all they thought they would scare me. What they failed to think about was that I had been to Nam and was ready for almost anything. So I entered this old building and I do hear a noise from down the hallway. I went into a corridor and opened a door and found myself on the stage. I walked onto the stage, and the whole place was in the dark and some outside light was filtering in, which gave the whole place an eerie shadowy movement. Suddenly a figure comes out of the dark, dressed in black and pointing what looked like a weapon at me. Well, the other officers had pulled a joke, so they thought, and had pushed a manikin dressed in black with it's arm outstretched towards me and as I was standing near the middle of the stage I simply backed away from the oncoming figure, drew my weapon and shot it six times, completely destroying the manikin and while I was backing up fell into the band pit, about five feet down and broke my leg. Well, to say the least all hell broke loose. I was treated and on leave with pay to recover, two officers were slightly wounded who were behind the figure and all of us got reprimanded.

I also was a Frat Brat of Sigma Nu and we were a Social so we partied a lot and we came up with the perfect "little sisters, Chi Omega" program. Each of the Sority girls had to interact with each of us and then write a report on abilities. For iniation we had one guy who wasn't really wanted by us so we stripped him, taped his entire body with duck tape except for his eyes and mouth and left his male part hanging out and dropped him off at the Dean's Welcome to the Faculty party. Needless to say our Fraternity was banned from the campus and our charter pulled after they found out about these two incidents. Ohhh just as a momento, Sigma Nu is still alive and ell.

KC- MY LITTLE BROTHER.

Finishing my undergraduate degree I was recruited by the US Govt. to go back to Saudi Arabia as a advisor to the National Guard. I did get breaks where upon I went to Amsterdam and stayed in a house of loose morals for weeks at a time. This was part of my life where my education in the finer arts was greatly enhanced.

Unfortunately, being with an armored column of Saudi tanks day in and out was really trying. We lost vehicle after vehicle because they wouldn't stay in column and the vehicles would sink into soft wadi's and we'd lose vehicle and crew. Some we managed to save, but in one month I lost two tanks and twenty two soldiers plus some tracked vehicles.

One year, In 1977, I was moving with an armored column along the pipeline while on a training mission with the Saudi National Guard. We received a call from an Aramco spotter plane, you known the ones that flew up and down the pipe looking for stray Bedu's who might shoot the pipe. Anyhow they reported seeing an Aramco truck about three miles ahead of us. Upside down.

We moved out and investigated and found that a Saudi inspector had somehow passed away at the wheel and crashed. This was beyond description, but to even get to the vehicle we had to fire several round of WP (White Phosphorous)near it to drive off the millions of flies.

To this day I hate flies and can still hear the tremendous buzzing around that truck.

There isn't much to this period except that Mom and Dad were still working for Aramco and living in Dhahran. I had hired all of my brothers thru Saudi friends to get them jobs in Arabia. However my brother KC was very active in trying to get a business started. He went out and recruited constantly. Mom and Dad left for Long Vacation right about Nov. 1st and two weeks later KC called me via radiophone and asked if I was going to be at their house for dinner. I told him yes and I'd see him then.

We were doing some practice firing of blank charges to save money and ammo from the tank main guns and I saw one of the most amazing things I have ever seen. We had stopped for Noon prayer and lunch and a short nap. One Saudi gunner used to lay on top of the tank and sleep. Well, somehow he had got out along the barrel of the main gun, about the size of a eight inch pipe and had managed to fall asleep with arms and legs hanging over the side of the barrel. Looked just like a cat on a limb. His crew officer thought this was embarrassing and ordered the other gunner to fire a blank charge. Well the resulting blast blew this Saudi about fifteen feet into the air from the main gun recoil and he came down on the barrel spread eagled. Really was something you had to see as he slowly rolled off the gun and dropped to the ground. I laughed so hard I wet the front of my uniform, but at least I wasn't alone.

About an hour later I got an urgent radio message from Aramco that my brother had been in a very serious car wreck and I was needed at the Dhahran Hospital immediately. I ordered the crews to button up and we took off across the sand and all towards Dhahran. We were about fifteen kilometers out and got there fairly quick, I didn't even slow down as we rolled right thru the Aramco fence and up to the front parking lot of the hospital. I ordered the tankers to form a ring around the command units and they must have scared the living hell out of Aramco as they all turned their guns out to face the buildings and such in order to provide protection for our command vehicles which were now in a solid circle of steel. The Saudi troops had no idea what was happening and were ready for a fight. For all of you who were there and your parents who were in the Admin. building, I apologize for the scare. I heard later some woman actually had a slight heart attack as she thought there was going to be a uprising.

I ran inside with an escort of about fifteen troopers with heavy weapons at the ready and the Dr's. and Nurse's all hid behind the counters. I yelled out that I was there because of KC Crocker and one of the Nurse's came and took me to the emergency room. They had just put him in a small room and left me alone with him. He had just died and was still warm. I held him and slowly said goodbye. About ten minutes later I come out of the room and the Saudi officer with me had lined up the entire medical emergency room staff and had a squad of men ready to execute the lot on my order. Typical reaction, but I told him it was my personal family and to move the units back out and across the Kohbar road and put the fence back up. I'd join them soon. I asked the Doctors what happened. The Doctor told me that KC had cut in front of a truck and got hit on the passenger side. He was in a Toyota and the other truck was a big Mercedes. The Yemenite with him had been torn apart and KC had broken his neck. He was still alive when they got him to the hospital and they told me he kept screaming for me. The Doctor told me they tried to restrain him but he kept trying to sit up and finally his neck went all the way and it was over.

Since Aramco had no mortician anymore I had to take him to the old undertakers room near the Dhahran fire station and with a Saudi friend, I helped embalm him so I could bring him home. Aramco finally got hold of Mom and Dad and told them. They called me at the house and Mom said, "Mike, when are you bringing my baby home ". That almost killed me so I told her in three days. She told me that Aramco had said it might be ten to fifteen days and I told her I wasn't Aramco and would deal with it. I cried in the shower the one and only time over my little brother.

With the help of Amir J'Awli I was able to get the paperwork and Aramco provided a plane to take him to Bahrain where the Bahraini Military met us and moved him with Military Honors, I guess for respect of my rank and being Military to a 747 and I brought him home. I resigned my commission and about three days later we buried him in Arizona where I have gone to see him and take him gifts every Christmas since.

I had not been back to Arabia until this recent trip.

I think now I'll go into the world of lurkers. Those that will, enjoy the above, those that won't, well, as a most famous Bedu once said "Ko'lawahad" Shukran, masala'ma,

PELLET GUNS

A fondness for weapons has lasted most of my life. After the war, I no longer cared to actually shoot anything, except perhaps my cat if he doesn't knock off ordering Domino's without me knowing.

Anyway, I digress. I thought I had told this story, but may have done so while talking with someone on the phone, so…

1963 and we had discovered that a shop, Green Flag or Baloki's in Al-Khobar had started carrying "Diana" pellet rifles. These were the type that you had to pull down the barrel to cock it, insert the pellet and then hunt street lights.

As is usual, a couple of good buddies, Peter Pestoni, and Tom Painter and I decided to go to Imhoff for two good reasons. One, the hobby farm and we knew Heidi Knott would be out riding, such a beauty, both horse and Heidi. Two, no one knew we had these weapons of mass destruction.

Now being great white hunters and stalking lizards and scorpions was just fine with me, but Peter decided to hunt a Camel. This seemed fine to us, but after finding two of them just moseying around, we found that our huge cannons were just bouncing off the thick hide of the beasts and that they weren't even aware of our Herculean efforts. This just pissed off Peter, but Tom and I had given up. The sand was really soft and Peter goes out to the

Camel, and using some form of logic, picks out the big one to hunt. Once again he just wastes his time and is getting madder because he is down to a few pellets and we won't share. So while we are sitting about 200 feet from all this, that fool goes around behind the Camel, Lifts it's tail and shoots it in a tender area.

The look on that camels face wasn't one of delight, but not of pain, more like "NOW, I'm really pissed off". It turns and see's Peter and he see's it. The pellet had no effect except that now it's a mad camel and Peter is running like a madman in the soft sand going nowhere. The effect on us was catastrophic as we couldn't move from laughter and then the Camel caught him and did it's best to make him a part of the desert.

I'm not sure how we got him free of the mess he was in, but he was black and blue and I believe we had to go to the hospital because he had been bitten. Told the Doctor that a stray Camel, had for no good reason, attacked him.

I went home and without thinking was telling my Mom, who immediately told me that Dad would die if he knew I had such a weapon. I told her that it couldn't hurt anyone and about the Camel. She didn't believe me, so without further ado, she was about forty feet from me, I shot her in the leg to show how they just bounced off..

Her look had a strong resemblance to the look on that camels face. She looked down and there was a trickle of blood on her calf. Off we went to the hospital and the Doctor dug out the pellet, which was in about a half inch... She broke my pellet gun, and I won't say on what, and told me that if I ever, for the next 100 years did anything wrong, she would tell Dad... I was fully aware of what that meant.

So ended the Great Hunt..

PIA AND CURRY

One of my favorite stunts as a returning student was to take the tickets Dad had sent from, and who else, Kanoo, and turn them into an adventure. Dad, being all wise and knowing that I was a foolish lad, would try his best to make the trip from Texas to Dhahran straight as an arrow. I, would try to get as many stops, where the plane arrived late and the airline had to put me up at their expense at hotels, feed me and then off to see the sights I would go.

My best trip was a record for me and caused some anxiety as I didn't arrive for a week after I was due in Dhahran. Although Mom and Dad had got used to me by now and figured if they hadn't heard of a Foreign Govt. executing a child, I was most like country hopping and would get there eventually. Of course, when I did arrive, the penalty phase would commence.

One trip they had me going to NY then to Amsterdam and then on to Dhahran…boooring…and I already was well known along Prince Albert Strassee, behind the red wall in Amsterdam…the walkway with the windows ? For window shopping….That to is a story of true love found in a gutter, but later perhaps.

So I decided to go the other way, Japan, to India to Dhahran. Somehow, I managed to screw up and only got a twelve hour layover in Japan, in Kowloon. But, I did go sightseeing and bought a Aqualalung and regulator there to take to Arabia..Plus, what a city..I like to never made it back to the hotel and loved the excitement. Rode a rickshaw for hours with a very delighlightful companion, speaking a common language.

The real trouble started at the the airport next day. Seems as if the only flight to New Dehli was via Pakistani International Airlines...well why not. The was a flight from hell.. We had goats, chickens and bedrolls the size of houses laying over chairs, people in fifty languages yelling and talking, and three hundred heads bobbing every time they said anything. I got dizzy watching them talk.

On top of this, I was sitting in a aisle seat and they put this mountain of a lady, who proved beyond a doubt that she was allergic to water and soap and had to lift the arms of the seats to get her in. I was waiting for the portable crane to help her. She was in the window seat, and there was no middle seat, although there were three across.. Get the picture. So finally the Captain takes off, I think losing one goat that someone had tied to the nose wheel waiting to load it and before we are even fully airborne, and I had my doubts we were getting off the ground, and it did seem as if the plane was struggling to get altitude, this crazy woman decides it is hamman time..She gets up and instead of giving me a chance to jump and run to let her out, tries to get over me. Well the plane angled up and I swear to this day I know the meaning of "G" forces.. She sat right down on me, and I, as big a guy as I was, completely disappeared. Talk about a ton of————. Anyway, the Stewardess is yelling at her to get back in her seat and the woman is wailing, I am slowly passing out from being crushed and suffocating and can not move, when the lady reaches the point of no return and suffers an internal accident. Guess who was the portable potty at that point ?

My screams of agony and true horror must have made an impact because they got her off of me and I was ripping off my shirt and trying to get out of my pants, in the middle of bedlam and the Stewardess is trying to find me a blanket and I am using language in seventy different tongues and with a calm voice the pilot says "Hope you are all enjoying the flight, we will be serving dinner soon". Never in all my life did I want to kill as badly as I did that Captain, although a little later he saved my life again.

We are back to normal, I'm wrapped in a blanket, the Stewardess is cleaning up my shirt and pants and the heifer is asleep. No doubt exhausted from the liberal tongued lashing I gave her and all aboard. So here comes the food cart...

Now on PIA they offer several forms of curry. Western and Pakistani. I, who have a very strong problem with spice and can not even drink V8 juice as it is too spicy, thought, well why not just eat the western stuff. What the hell else can go wrong. I got the plate and took a huge spoonful of curry and started chewing. Within seconds I was on fire, I spewed out the remains on a bald guy in front of me and was screaming for help, trying to tear out my tongue and actually running it up and down the cloth seat in front of me to get this curry spice off. I had the blanket halfway down my throat and am standing there, in shoes, socks, underwear and a t-shirt screaming for the fire department. I actually ran my tongue on the floor carpet, or so I was told. I have my lips around the Air condition valve above the seat and I'm drinking everything in sight. Including some hot tea, which set me off again...

The Captain comes back and gets ice to put on my tongue and literally froze the damn thing. I had broke into a sweat and tears were running down my face from the intensity of the curry. The stewardess had given me the Pakistani bowl by mistake instead of the western bowl. On top of this, the lady wants to go to the bathroom, caused by massive uncontrollable laughter at my fate, which by now is a sewer of unimaginable mess from all the fouled up food and people on the flight. That did it. I finished the flight in the jump seat behind the Captain. Who was British, on the flight deck.

I landed in Dhahran, and had no room for irritation left, and I get Dhahran Taxi number 21...How many remember this clown, "you want me take you to RT ????" "NO, Dhahran".."Ohh you like Abqaiq", "NO, Dhahran.. D>H>A>H>A>R>A>N".."Oh, Dhahran, OK, we go"..and straight off and pass the main gate and on to the road to RT.. Finally made it home, walk in and Mom says, About time! Your Father wants to speak to you about you're wandering and plan on not doing a lot this next two weeks...OHH, never saw my bag again, it most likely is the talk of some Pakistani Lady who still laughs constantly.

POLICE BABY- AN INCIDENT WHEN I WAS A POLICE OFFICER

Summers in North Texas are as bad as the winters. With the ac on high, the inside of a car might get to 85 degree's. So the best way to provide police protection, and not dehydrate is to park along the highway in the shade and not move…Just let people think you are doing something.

So I'm calmly sitting off the side of the road, back in with the tail end just slightly over the embankment so that the nose of the police car is pointing up just a little..so I could get back under a shade tree. I'm soaked to the bone from sweat and really working my deordorant overtime, supposedly watching old Route 66 for speeders, although I think the radar was off..too noisy…

Well I see this old Chevrolet coming down the road and it is moving in spurts, like a jack rabbit that's overheated and there is a plume of oil smoke that would do honors to any self respecting oil spill burn off and the driver is wide eyed as can be. He sees me and heads straight towards me. I meantime am getting a little ansey as I don't know what this fool is doing. Well about twenty feet from my car, his car just quits. I could almost hear it say "enough already". The driver, a very skinny Black gentleman, about five foot three jumps out and is running circles around the smoking car. I started thinking of the old "Sambo"s Restaurants" where the tiger chases the little boy around the tree. So I, with a great deal of disgust, get out of the police car and grab this character. This was long before Crack cocaine so I just thought he was drunk.

Turns out he is all excited..his wife, in the back seat is pregnant and in process of having the baby. Well, my border town is twelve miles from the nearest hospital and I don't have time to call for help so I open the back door and almost passed out.

Here the back seat of the car is not visible. This woman must have weighed in around 400 pounds easy. How she ever got in the car I don't know, and I ask the dumbest question of my life. "Can I help"…"Well of course you fool, I'm having a baby and I need to get to a hospital." So I asked the driver to follow me and I'll use the red lights and get her there quickly…No such luck. His car was deader that a doornail. So we started trying to get her out of the car and there was just no way to pull her up. I'm a big guy and I couldn't move her, and "Shorty" is about useless. Well he gets the bright idea to open the other side door, that she is against and I swear to this day that when she fell out that side I thought he had been killed as he completely disappeared under her. I started laughing so hard I almost died trying to roll her off of him. I could see his hands and feet were moving slower by the minute and I just knew he was suffocating. So I finally roll her off and get him up. He was almost flat.

So between he and I, and believe me a forklift would have been greatly appreciated, we get her into the back seat of the police car..Now, quickly we jump in and I put the car in gear and turn the wheel and we go no where. Remember the little embankment I was on, well, this lady had lifted the front end of my car off the ground, swear to God, and I had to work the car like the devil to get all the wheels to ground to get enough traction to get going. All the time she is yelling and carrying on, "Shorty" is fidgeting all over the front seat and before I can radio ahead for an ambulance to start my way, the fool kicks the police radio and we are now cut off, six miles out in the middle of nowhere. So OK, we'll make the run all the way, when BANG, out goes a back tire and we sway from side to side as I fight for our lives to get the car stopped.

I jump out and yell at "Shorty" to try and stop a trucker or car or some- one. He manages to get a eighteen wheeler to stop and the driver uses his

CB radio to call ahead and patch in to the Police department and they say they'll send an ambulance. Well, too late....I am almost deafened by the screams from my car..I run over and open the back door and here is this lady, or at least what I could see, about to have a baby. I look for "Shorty" and he is passed out. The trucker is staring at this mass in open mouth amazement and I'm yelling at her to hold on. I yell at the trucker to get me a blanket or something and the fool hands me a greasy covered cloth. Well, by now I'm considering burning my car as the smell from sweat and other matters has turned the inside of my car in what I thought was an elephant bathroom. Suddenly she screams and I'm standing there and here is this little tiny head looking at me. I immediately reverted to my training and start helping her deliver. I get the baby out, and hear the ambulance coming and "Shorty" is standing next to me and I ask for a knife or something. He flips out this blade that looked like a small sword to me, and sheepishly hands it to me, knowing full well I'm going to shoot him when this is all over. I cut the cord and tied it off, wrapped the baby in the cloth and here comes the ambulance. Well, it took the driver of the truck, me and two attendants to get this unconscious lady from my car on to a gurney and then they couldn't lift her into the ambulance. We are all sweating like pigs, and suddenly, it rains.. Just long enough to turn everything into a steam bath. But that was such a cute little baby. The ambulance takes off and I lean back and suddenly realize I'm alone, a flat tire and a car that has to be hosed out with a fire hose, and, six miles from town. To complete the day, my spare was flat..But I was still grinning several days later when the hospital sent me over a photograph of Momma, on two beds, baby and "Shorty" who looked like he was swelled up to twice his size.

I'm standing in the bathroom thinking about all this and using the little boys urinal and in comes my boss, who yells at me "Why aren't you out writing tickets instead of standing grinning like a fool", and without thinking I turned towards him...I was on the late shift for a long time after that, but it was cooler....

Michael Crocker (DH65)Still slightly crazy.

SUBJECT: POLICE STORY

Chatters....I have been asked by a couple of people that if I did live thru Arabia, what happened next..So this story actually happened after Arabia, but because of the circumstances, I see WHY it happened and Blame Arabia....

I was working as a police officer in a small border town in West Texas. A brand new rookie, not long out of the Police Academy, but of course, knew it all.

I had seen snow, but in the Panhandle of Texas, snow is snow..So we had a wee blizzard. Snow drifts were five and six feet high, and being new boy on the block I had the 11-7 am shift.

There was this crossed eyed Deputy Sheriff, old timer, who handled the county while I was on in the city. We had talked all night on the radio and got a report from the Dept. of Public Safety (Hiway Patrol) that a robber was hitting the 7-11 stores and they were following him, but that due to the storm, visibility was now down to about 100 feet, they thought he might try to hit ours.

So the Deputy pulled rank and said that he would go inside the store, hide in the back and I was to park my car behind a fence, across an open field from the store where I could watch and be able to get there right away.. Our signal was to be a double click on the radio so that the robber wouldn't hear the radios.

After what seemed like hours I heard the clicking on the radio, jumped out of the police car, grabbed the riot shotgun, pumped a round into the chamber and took off running towards the store, across the field. The snow was really blowing so I could hardly see.. Unknown to this intrepid Keeper of the Law, the city had a broken sewer line about halfway across the field and I ran across this little hump, tripped and fell headfirst in the four foot ditch of raw sewerage.. This wouldn't have been too bad, as I was stopping myself from actually falling into this smelly mess, except I then proceeded to fire the shotgun directly into the pool..This caused me great discomfort as I was now covered in shit. I got up anyhow and ran on to the store, to find the Deputy drinking a cup of hot coffee and had one for me.. He says "I called you because I thought it might be getting cold out there", as I stand there dripping excrement on the floor. "OH, by the way, the patrol got him in Amarillo about ten minutes ago." I started to shoot him, but the smell was killing me.. I stomped out and went home to change.

Back on patrol and mad as I could be, I was really looking for a criminal now by Golly...The storm was upgraded to a full blown blizzard and I couldn't see more than two or three feet in front of the car. I was on the road that led past the dump and past some large open fields so I was really going slow.

I radioed the deputy that I had to take a pee call and he replied," do not get away from your car...I'm coming along behind you, so turn on your red and blue police lights so I can see you when I get close and stay very close to your car because if you get ten feet away you'll get disoriented in the swirling snow and I'll never find you in the drifts"....That made me real comfortable.

So after getting out of the car I walked to the front and standing two feet from the headlights I let the call of nature go. I saw a red light out in front of me, or so I thought, but figured well it's just a reflection from my lights on top of my car...At this point, I'll finish the story as the deputy related it for years later...He said, "I was about fifteen feet away when I saw Mike's car lights, so I was slowing down when I saw a tremendous blast of white, looked like lightening had hit his car...I got out and walked up to Mike's car and there in front of the car, officer Crocker was lying on the ground, actually smoking..He looked as if he had been blown up and he was still holding on to the.....part that goes wee wee, and it too was smoking...I was able to get him up and he pointed out into the dark..That crazy officer had seen a red light and while turning to look at peed right on a electric fence transformer"....Well, as I remember it blew me completely off my feet and dumped me in front of my car. Standing in wet snow didn't help the shock and where it took it was rally bent out of shape so to speak. I threatened to kill the Deputy on the spot if he didn't get up off the ground and stop crying with laughter over this and swore him to the highest secrecy I could.

The next day at the coffee shop I heard all about burnt items and for years the story has been told in Law enforcement circles to new rookies... NOW, how the hell was I supposed to know about electric cattle fences... Learn that one in Arabia ?

I still get a slight tingle whenever I pass a cow pasture and see cattle....

POOL STORY-DORAL

I liked the pool, it, on occasion liked me..At one point in my youth I taught swimming, and did so for the entire Cub Scouts group as daily class. Had about fifty at one time holding on to the edge and kicking. Had fun with the whistle.

But, there were times when fate had other things in mind for me.

WARNING————-FOR PERSONS OFFEND BY NUDITY OR COMMENTARY————DELETE NOW————

One year, while attempting to roughhouse with Doral, as we all know she was and is a beautiful woman, and as a young lassie, caught many an eye, including this old geezer, youngbrat then. So in the ensuing roughhousing, never allowed in the pool as you know, she dunked me a few times and then attempted to climb out of the pool at the shallow end, down by the baby pool. Well, not to let this go I jumped up to grab her and caught her suit, a nicely done red one piece.

Much to her shock, I managed to pull down the entire top, which garnered the applause of many there, and would have just been a simple error, with great potential, EXCEPT....sitting within about fifteen feet from the pool, under the canopy was her Dad. I think He ate his cigar and I'm sure that most likely I ate several..but Doral was wonderful and kept him from getting his gun and I had gone underwater, planning on drowning as being preferable to having to deal with her Dad.

Four years, attending parties at Dorals house, where we would play walk the egg, or or such, her Dad followed me from room to room, making sure Doral was at the other end..He never really said anything, but there was that certain look in his eye that told volumes of what he'd like to see happen.

Doral denies this all vigorously, but I warned her I would tell and now I'm thinking who else do I remember stories about......any volunteer out there to remind me ????

Incidently, over the years Doral has become one of my closest friends and I'm sure her Dad, even now, knows what a wonderful daughter he had...

October was always a fun time. The weather was fairly reasonable, Mom was sedated, err, calm and I had the honor of leading my brothers on a trick or treat excursion. Now in my opinion, trick or treat meant that. No treat, well......tricks were planned with meticulous thought and foresight.

First stop was always on the Hill in Dhahran as we all knew the candy was better on the hill. My brothers were only required to pay a toll of 1/2 of what ever they got so I thought things were just fine. The Goldings were out of town so I knew I had no competition for Mars Bars, but I was looking around small bushes with a Falcon's eye in case they had come back from long leave early.

I also knew that my bag of tricks was to be used for those special people. Teachers, Security, and about 80% of the camp that I had small run ins with over the year. Aramco had gone out of their way, much to their regret the next day, but at the time I am sure that someone in management thought bringing in pumpkins was a great idea. I do believe they were from the local market, but don't know. I do know that people had carved these suckers in all sorts of ways. My personal favorite was one that Mrs. Simon had made and looked a lot like her. Looked just like a witch, and her costume was always that of a really authentic witch. Mayhap not a costume I wondered. This was to cost me a little later but for the time being all you could see where flashlights and groups heading all around camp going door to door. All of my brothers were in costume and I had a Royal Mounted Police costume, rather ironic.

I knocked with great authority on Mr. Kieswetter's, head of Aramco Security's,door and thought it rather rude of him to actually sit down and cry with laughter at seeing me in a police type costume. I think he laughed for days and I know I was outraged. I still hear the laughter when the moon is full and goblins are on the loose.

Down sixth street to Mr. Goellner's house, and of course Mrs. Goellner always had popcorn balls. Now these animals were a real beast to eat. I always was of the impression that she put extra caramel into them so that once you took a big bite, you spent what seemed like days to get your mouth open again. So here I am with my mouth carmelled together and along comes Mrs. Simon and a whole bunch of kids. She is wearing her witch outfit and her ever present broom and the devil stepped into me and before I had the slightest idea of what was happening, I swear, I had taken the big pumpkin by the door of a house and hid by the hedge and when they passed by I, using both hands and heaving it like a basketball backwards catapulted it over the hedge and heard it hit the ground right in the middle of the group. The stunned silence was unbelievable. The the scream's and yells of indignation. How was I to know the Mr. Dickerson, the Vice-Principal was with them?

Around the fence and banshee's a wailing they came. I told my brothers, "run, and make a lot of noise". Thus I thought I could slink off to a quiet part of Imhoff Gardens and catch the morning tide to Bahrain. My brothers, true to the nature of the beast, immediately pointed out where I was running and made darn sure everyone knew I was responsible.

I had made it to Hamilton Hill and fell over a few unnamed couples there when the first pumpkin came out of the dark and hit a tree not ten feet from me. The Great Pumpkin fight of Aramco's glorious career was about to begin. Sides were drawn up and racing around camp many a pumpkin gave it's short life in the cause of justice, depending on who happened to be where. All this time Jeff Yeager and others are marking windows with dirty words using soap and of course, signing my name I believe.

I did not think it was possible to get pumpkin seed where I did, but once I managed to get home, there was Mrs. Simon, Mom, Mr. Dickerson, the chief executioner of Aramco and a few others all calmly waiting. My brothers having given sworn affidavits I'm sure, are all gleefully counting piles of goodies and to this day, and even Mom would verify this, I never knew my Mother could pick up what felt like a 100 pound pumpkin and smack me right on the top of my noodle and all the while to the ringing applause of the gathered adults.

Then to add shame to disgrace, Mrs. Simon got me with the broom and I headed for Hofuf. The next day Aramco had a lot of comments at management levels about the mess the pumpkins had made of the camp. The school had been plastered and some were found to be in the closed pool at recreation. I know nothing of these deeds and my mind has failed after all these years.

One additional note. I did well in grades in school, but for some reason Mr. Dickerson called in my parents and told them that he thought it would be best for me to do the seventh grade over as I needed some "maturing". So I went from Class of '64 to Class of '65, but I am sure that my further adventures caused him to wish he had passed me to the ninth grade and out...

My Dad for years has referred to me as "Pumpkin Q Head" for some strange reason. I think the sight of the pumpkin smashed by Mom on my head was too much for him. I really do think he had to crawl to bed due to the intense pain in his sides from the extremely loud and very obnoxious laughter at my fate.

Thus passed another calm night in the land of sand and the camp of dreams.

HAPPY HALLOWEEN TO ALL

REUNION MEMORY STORY

Houston, 1995 was the first reunion I have ever attended. I arrived to find the lobby empty and no one stirring about. I registered, no room block, but I had only reserved three months before thru the reunion committee, now I know why…but as I walked to the atrium area I saw what looked to be Doug Romaine who had been best friends in Abaqaiq in the third grade.

We talked for a few minute's and he said to me, "You are the only one who knows what happened at the birthday party. My parents never told me the story, do you know ?

Yes, I did know, I was there…He had a lighter, one of those old silver, very heavy type that you had to fill from the bottom with fluid. While trying to fill it, he accidently flicked the striker and set himself on fire. We managed to get out the front door and he was able to roll around until someone in a passing Aramco truck grabbed him and took off to the hospital. He was badly burned over a large part of his body. He never, until forty years later knew what had happened. Incidentally, he and I both still have one of the lighters. There were two on the table that day…

Soon, as I was doing verbal battle with Anil Baretto and letting him know I didn't want to hear about his reasons for not having the reunion on

Memorial day, due to Bill Owens tragic death in Viet Nam and the fact it was Memorial Day.. I finally told him, IF I don't care, and I was there, why should you who weren't there ? He left and I didn't see him for two days.

Soon, I saw a vision of pure beauty and loveliness come into the hotel... A true Lady that I had had very deep feelings about in 1964. She ran into my arms and for just a movement, I was standing on her back porch, holding an Angel...MY God the energy that pulsated in my mind and heart and soul. Her touch was that of God's gift to me...

As I sat in the lounge area, after finding the registration room and getting my packet, I was suddenly rudely jumped on by none other that my ninth grade best friend, Steve Reed. Good Lord, thirty five years and still the tall, energetic friend I had shared so much with..Where do you start...

Every momenent my heart pounded with excitement and anticipation as I saw others, Little Sally, still most beautiful, A brash bellow and Doral is on me...Another wonderful friend and her truly amazing Husband. I'm at the pool, reflecting on the waters of youth and Mo and Sharon McQuade are there..two of the most wonderful people you could ever hope to let your heart touch.

Mary Barger, a truly timeless beauty and bundle of energy, Linda Juszack, a very dignified and admirable lady, Jeannette Rebold, at which this reunion I feel we remade friends, The three sisters, one of which "Fell" into the pool, no fault of mine I'm sure...

Conversations with so many that the heart and mind went numb, dinner with those I loved and do love. At the dance, Candice Riley and her husband, Lexe and Mike Benjamin, and so many more my mind swims in a memory of the past, flowing like the river of love today.

The girls getting even with me for one of them accidently falling into the pool by having the belly dancer drag me out on to the floor and the amazing number of people who came together.

The final event, My most memorable part of the reunion, was the last dance with my sweet and dear friend...Age has not diminished her ageless beauty and her heart pounded against mine, and for one last momement, they beat in synchronization.

Never let it be said you can't go home again...home was there, in the heart and mind and soul of each and every person who touched another and made the spectre of time vanish...

This next reunion, if it does 1/2 of what I found and felt, and I know already it will be ten times better, I will be perfectly happy to lie down and join with the stars and God, for I will truly have found the utopia of my life.

REVISED FOR PUBLICATION-ONE OF MY BEST FRIENDS, WITH DEEP HONOR AND RESPECT.

The morning of May 2nd was like most then, hot humid and miserable. A 12 men Special Forces team was going to be choppered into a dense jungle area near Loc Ninh. The team was inserted and very soon met intense Viet Cong resistance.

A Medical Evac. chopper was called for, casualties were bad. Three separate attempts made by extraction chopper crews were met with withering fire from the VC and the Green Beret team was down to less then four men still combat capable.

A sergeant was at nearby Forward Operating Base at Loc Ninh and heard the calls over the PRC radios for help. the team was being cut to pieces. He jumped into a chopper and they landed, after numerous hits on the aircraft and the sergeant ran about 75 meters to the team. En route he was hit in the right leg, face and head. Despite these injuries he carried and dragged the wounded team members to the chopper. He then provided covering fire for the chopper as it moved to where the team commanders' body was to recover classified documents and the officers body (Green Berets don't leave theirs behind). He was hit again in the stomach and grenade fragments hit him in the back. The helicopters pilot was killed and the chopper was damaged beyond flight. He got the survivors and bodies out and formed a defensive position. Finally got air support and directed the gun ships and gave aid to the wounded. He was again hit in the left leg.

Another chopper landed and he was making trips carrying the wounded and dead when a VC soldier jumped him and clubbed him over the head. He was wounded again twice before being able to kill his opponent. Finally getting the last of the team on the chopper, he fought hand to hand with two VC sappers who were trying to throw a grenade into the chopper to destroy it. He was able to kill them and was dragged into the chopper himself. His efforts saved the life of at least eight men.

This man was later at a ceremony where I received the Silver Star from the President and this nation gave him the Medal of Honor, to my friend Sgt. Roy Benavidez, Special Forces(Green Beret) and after talking to him yesterday, He reminded me why we fight...Some things are just worth all we have.

The moral of this story is not about war or valor, but for belief and friendship. His answer, "Mike, my comrade in arms, we have traveled heavy duty trails, yet why ? Because some things are just worth fighting for".

I believe in the duty and honor and the friendships and the relationships and in the fact that no matter what...we are a unique bunch and I still, to this day extend an open hand to any and all of our family, past present and future, because quite frankly, YOU ARE WORTH FIGHTING FOR.....

"Fighting soldiers from the sky, these are men that jump and die, for these brave men, wear the Green Beret..."

Mike Crocker

HOUSE OF
THE AL-SAUD DYNASTY

Thunayyan-Brother to Muhammad
Abd Al' Aziz(2nd King) 1765-1803
Abd'Allah- Brother to Abd'Aziz
Sa'ud(3rd King) 1803-1814
Abd Allah(4th King)1814-1818
Mishari(5th King) 1820
Turki (6th King, son of Abd-Allah) 1824-1834
Ibrahim- son of Thunayyan
Thunayyan-son of Thunayyan
Abd-Allah- son of Thunayyan
Faysal (7th King) 1834-1838
Khalid (8th King) 1840-1841
Abd Allah(9th King) 1841-1843
Faysal(was 7th and 10th King)1843-1865
Abd Allah (11th King,again) 1865-1871
Sa'ud (12 th King) 1871-1875
Abd-Al Rahman (13th King) 1875
Abd-Allah(14th King, again) 1875-1889

Abd-Al-Rahman (15th King, again) 1889-1891

Abd-Allah son of Abd-Al-Rahman

Abd-Al-Aziz(16th King) 1902-1953- The King we knew (son of Abd Al-Rahman)

Musa'ad- son of Abd Al-Rahman

Sa'ud (17th King)1953-1964(son of Abd Al-Aziz)

Faysal (18th King)1964-1975(son of Abd Al-Aziz)

Khalid (19th King) 1975-1992(son of Abd Al-Aziz)

Fahd (20th King and curent)(son of Abd Al-Aziz)

Abd Allah (next in sucession) (son of Abd Al-Aziz)

This list is very simplified...there are hundreds of Prince's and Princess's who hold most Ministry and Govt. ranking positions.

SA'ID (SECURITY)

I too am deeply distressed to hear about all of these terrible delinquent people who so freely flaunted their indifference to rules and regulations... I, of course, would have never behaved in such as fashion, being an Altar boy and all... I must, with further ado, disavow any and all knowledge of "Security Stumping", "Star Light, Car Lite", "Steal the Security Car and hide it "or any other such frivolity.

Incidently, in honor of Sa'id, he was a Somaili and came from a well known tribe and was even a member of the ruling family of his tribe. This I know from working with him and riding with him many a night.

For all you evil n'er do wells that are confessing, your files in Aramco Security downstairs had copious notes...Sa'id and Rash'an (Another chaser) kept excellent notes which were reviewed daily by Mr. Kieswetter.

SAD note: Sa'id passed away in 1987, after retirement in Northern Somalia.

I understand from Mohammed Su'Bey, Head of Saudi Aramco Security that he was buried with full Military Honors as he had served with the British Army, which I did not know.

ally wanted a story for those alone on Christmas and I was saving this one, but if it will bring a smile, then I'll send it now and call it a Christmas smile story.

MIKE

Being a young man, adventurous and willing to try most anything, and as such always need a few extra riyals, the perfect solution hit me one hot day in 1964.

The shrimp guy was coming down the alley with his donkey pulled wagon and had fresh gulf shrimp the size of baby whales. Well, I though, Hmmmm, opportunity strikes. My brother Kevin, about 3, I guess, blonde hair and all was playing in the yard and after much heated debate and barter I had agreed to sell him to the Arab for the wagon of shrimp. The deal was that he had to wait until I sold the shrimp and then off they would go. Nothing so bad about this deal. I get out of babysitting, can go around to all the neighbors and sell shrimp, make lots of fa loose and deny all knowledge of my brothers whereabouts. Plus, he had pissed me off royally earlier that day.

I had been on the telephone arranging a date for the tri-D that night, last minute expert here, and he had stuck a wind up toy train on my head and turned it on, wrapping my hair in the wheels and even after smacking him with the telephone I couldn't get the damn train to stop. He in return gets Dads hammer and comes back around the corner, where I am trying to get the train loose, use normal language with the lady on the phone and pulling out great globs of hair, plotting his demise, and WHAM, I see stars and drop the phone, I look at my dumb brother and he has this hammer trying to break loose his toy train, which by now is fully engaged in my hair. WHAM, again with the damn hammer. I now am on the verge of murder so I get him, lock him in the closet and run for Dads barber kit that he always gave us haircuts with.

Well, I managed to get the train out of my hair and see that I have plowed a nice neat path directly down the center of my head. Imagine if you will the expression I had looking in the mirror. AND I have a date for that night with an angel. After franicaly running up and down the hall screaming what all I 'm going to do to my brother, I decide that I can take one of Mom's wigs, I mean she had several, who would know ? Yea, right. So I cut a big piece off the back of one of her wigs, wondered at the time why it was out in the bedroom and not in a bag in the closet, but ohh well.. Dad had been painting the patio and had told me that he was using and epoxy cement type of adhesive, so I thought, that'll work for glue. Off I dashed to get the epoxy, slap some on the hair, slap it on my head and as soon as I do I decide I can manage this and trim it all up to where it looked somewhat >normal.

Problem was, the damn wig was red and I hadn't noticed. I now have a red streak where shortly before there was no hair.. Damn, I'm getting panicky now and I dash into the kitchen and start throwing things everywhere. Well all I could find was Red Number 4 food coloring. So I applied it to my head. Making a match don't you see.

Match my butt, my whole head, except the wig is now dirt red and streaking my face and the wig part has turned bright orange. The only answer..well I had heard bleach would take out color. No one told me straight bleach was not what they meant so off I go. I soon learn the folly of this fiasco as I know have slightly mangy reddish blonde green egg hair and a patch in the middle that has gone white.

At this point I give up and hope that when Mom comes home She can straighten it out before the tri-D that night. Now to get rid of the main problem, that brother. I let him out into the yard and then comes the Arab..I could swear it was devine intervention, but Mom later called it something I had to look up.

So I go house to house and sell a ton of shrimp. I save about ten pounds and give Kevin to the Arab, with my blessings. The Arab and Kevin had a really good time with my hair, but I knew that milking camels for life would fix his wagon. Mom comes home and I sell her the shrimp I had left, making a tidy profit and although she almost blew a capillary over my hair, thought it could be fixed.

So I'm thinking all's well that ends well when the phone rings. Mom answers and to this day I have never heard a sailor use such language. Plus the look I got caused me to think it might be time to call Fr. Roman and ask for last rites.

Security at the main gate had my brother. Seems as if the Arab thought the whole thing was a terrific joke and he and the Security guard were in hysterics about the dumb Americans when the wrath of God fell upon them. Mom from above. She had to repay the Arab for all the shrimp, none of this I was aware of, blissfully sitting on the barber stool at home waiting for Mom to fix my hair.

She comes in with Kevin, and I thought a rather wicked look in her eye, but figured alls well that ends well. She fixed my hair, and to make a long story short I was the first Aramco kid with Damn near no hair at a Tri-D. Who says Mom's don't have a sense of humor. BUT wait, I have saved the best for last. Mom and Dad were going over the the Aramco AEA big deal dinner and about half way thru the big ceremony, after Mom and Dad have been called up on the stage to receive their awards, some fool yells out, "Irene, what the hell did you do to your hair." Seems as if there was a major swatch missing from the back.

I, in the meantime was dancing and not a care in the world, no hair, but played like I was stylish, and not pulling it off well what with all the rancorously loud laughter..Suddenly there was a voice, sounded like the crack of doom to me, but others said they thought there was much promise of great times in the tone of voice, as my name was called out to please report to the front. YOUR MOTHER IS HERE !

Needless to say, I had to go to all of the neighbors and pay them for their shrimp, which they got to keep and I was dateless for ever. I had to trade off a Scuba lung for a new wig, had to babysit for years, in fact just got off that punishment last week. Yet the worse was to come.

Mom made me go in front of the whole AEA and tell the story and the laughter was heard for miles across the barren waste of the desert, where I wanted to go. I still hear occasionally about the famous wig and shrimp sale. Keven still watches me with a close eye and Mom still talks about I STILL owe her over the embarrassment.

Ohhh well, Merry Christmas

MIKE CROCKER RT LIFE

Unusually cold for Ras Tanura in 1956, but we had just moved there and lived in house 1-G. Across Jasmine street and straight up the hedged death row to the Senior Staff School. Post office was on the corner and there was the bus stop with the telephone in the grey box. Across the street was the recreation area, but no pool then. Now, behind the snack bar was a hallway and out of it was the RT patio that many a fine talent used to entertain us. There was a small stage located to the front left and on one side double doors that opened up into the lounge. The small window for the snack room was by the front doors in a corner and this was SANTA's place. Holy ground for a 7 year old adventurer.

Now the RT woman's group and AEA had done a bang up job of decorations and the huge tree in the lounge was being worked on. I asked a lady there if I could help, since I needed as many brownie points as possible right before Santa got to Mom. The lady suggested, once she saw it was me suggested I go to the main gate, catch a ride on one of the big trucks and bring her back some sand from the middle of the Rub Al-Kahli... quite helpful of her I thought.

So wandering around I found this large pile of lights, all in a big pile. I thought, ok, here's where I really make Santa happy..I'll layout a long glide path of lights. So grabbing the end I tugged the whole group out into the hall and outside. Heard strange "popping" noise, but wasn't worried, couldn't be anything I was doing. Once out front I started untangling this pile. First I nearly strangled my self and looked as if I were a small Christmas tree and then after what seemed like hours of struggles with this deadly "snake" I was able to lay them out in a long row. In fact almost to the school. Yes, in my brilliance I stretched them across the street. So I hear a lot of commotion and see a white car stopped sideways. Who would ever run over a string of lights, get them wrapped around an axle and then think I had anything to do with it? So after my yelling for him to get off my lights the driver he gave me a hard desert sand boot and threats that were very Un-Christmassy I got things lined out again.

Now Mrs. Killingsworth, a family friend comes out the door at recreation, see's the lights and starts hauling them back in. I see the darn thing start to wiggle across the road and back from I just dragged the beast and my eyes were likely wider than a camel in heat as I was astonished this thing was alive. I had tied them together and so grabbed the end I had. Well, to say the least, the comments that my Mom's good friend said when she came like a tornado across the street were even less Holiday spirit and more like what kind of spirits I might be visiting soon if I didn't "get!".

So back to recreation, and by this time Dick Burgess had joined me. Now he tells me that we can find out if lights work because a friend of his told him that all we had to do was stick our finger in our mouth and then touch the little silver part of the light. Now known to be as a light socket. But we learn....So taking his advice and after being told we could straighten out the lights in a pile and test them, without moving one foot near anything else. I decided to test the light set. Well, to say I managed to have hair standing straight up and a scream from the depths of the Persian Gulf is mild. I caused some guy to turn on a step stool and fall, right into the table with a lot of little colored balls and Dick already heading for safe ground. I was sitting there with a look of pure disbelief on my face when Mrs. Killingsworth grabs me and checks me out. I had shocked myself, but these lights, the gezzer days, ran off a little transformer and so I had got the equivalent of a battery charge that I had also once tested by putting my tongue on it, That too was a blast. Anyhow, once she found I wasn't hurt, the Al-Khobar customs office got a call from Bahrain wondering what the loud smack they had just recorded was. I know that my eyes had to go completely around in my head and I think I was dizzy for about an hour. That was just the beginning of the day as she then took me home. They say that the screams and begging were heard with great pleasure all over Ras Tanura. I do believe people actually brought lawn chairs out in front of our house as Mom, embarrassed beyond rage, was showing me the finer aspects of what a Christmas belt could do as we circled the house. And not an belt of eggnog either.....

So sitting in the corner, a butt with the heat of the Arabian sun on it and wrapped in my blankie, I was really ticked off. I didn't mind the clapping and cheers from outside, but the comments from Mom about, "Wait until your Father gets hone, you might as well plan on never sitting again", was a little intimidating. Plus I knew Santa was most likely in the emergency room from histerics over what he had surely seen. Aramco didn't have enough trucks to haul the coal I was getting.

Mom had a really nice tree up and it was all white with red lights. I had got to put my little train set around the base and it was really pretty. I decided to help. Mom was making cookies with occasional comments about "bad seed" and "where the hell did we go wrong" remarks from the kitchen and so I waddled, not quick moves here just yet, too sore, over to the tree. I try to get the little train to go around and it won't. Now I knew it was plugged in and having just learned about electricity the hard way, I wasn't about to touch anything. So I took my Dad's pen from his Christmas card writing list and stuck it into the tree light fixture to wiggle it.

OK, so the whole house went dark, so the kitchen shut down, so the tree was smoking a little, was that any reason for Mom to call Ibn Jawuli? The cookies, several trays were in the oven, Mom flips the electric on, unplugs the tree for fear of fire, calls the hospital and checks to see if they have a bed with restraints and comes looking for me. I thought the dark clouds meant snow, however Mom had other idea's. I think the shot-put of me out the side door was a world record. Then the stern talking too from her was nothing when she smelled the kitchen. Something close to the smell of burning tires. Cookies left in the oven when the lights went out and forgotten while she was determining how to claim the hospital had me mixed up, and soooo, burnt black as camel droppings on the pie tin. Not the smartest time in the world for this youngster to smart off, "Yeah, can tell you are named after Betty Crocker". POW!, the light went out again for me. Never knew you could bend a cookie sheet on a head, but found it can be done.

Banned for life to my bedroom and the back of the house, I found new adventures, which involve hidden presents, a bathtub, Dad's newest golf shoes and my life flashing before me repeatedly in seconds...perhaps before Christmas.

MERRY CHRISTMAS TO BRATS WORLDWIDE
MIKE CROCKER (DH65)

So, locked in the dark passages of the tunnel of the prison, or actually being in the back bedroom. No real chain and ball will ever be effective as a heated up Mothers thrusting rapier of a glare. Yet, I felt that there was treasure afoot. I had heard Mom's instructions to our houseboy, a Pakistani named "Mo". At least that all I could pronounce. She had told him to make sure the wrapped gifts were all hidden in Mom and Dad's room. A place that was so forbidden that the Chinese "Forbidden City" was nothing. Mom had explained that parents rooms were not only off limits, but required an "A" pass from Aramco Security for anyone to ever enter. The door seemed to me to be steel and the lock that of a vault door I had seen at the local merchants shops in Najmah. She even told me of spiny monsters that lurked in the dark closets waiting for a young morsel. This I believed in full, having met some of Mom's demons in person a few times, to the regret of my highly regarded target of opportunity, my butt.

However, knowing the day was going to be very long, I snuck down the hall and just slightly peeped into the bedroom. It didn't look to bad, although the bed had dark areas under it and there did seem to be the hissing of something in there room. Years after this event Mom told me it was a vaporizer for Dad's cold. I experienced a disaster and this infernal machine, I didn't know of, plays a major part. So in I glide, like the proverbial sand viper. All ears and radar going looking for shiny wrapped goodies.

Now Mom and Dad's room had a king bed facing the closet with two of the old Aramco issued metal chest of drawers. I worked my way carefully, seeing the steam breathing monster sitting by a chair and partially hidden. He can't see me, as I can't see him...this from the brain that Mom claims was transplanted from a Hamoor. So in I go, and the room is really dark. I dash behind the chair as I hear Mo going in. He goes to the closet and I see him reach high up and there, lo and behold, the treasure of the Sierra Leone.

Millions of wrapped packages and surely all with my name, but wait, he is leaving and once again the teachings of my religious youth spoke, and in a scream, "Don't do it!!!" At this point, being deaf completely to the noisy Angel, I heed the red robed one with a tail and head into this cavern of Ali Baba.

Up on a chair, in the dark, pulling for the light chain and trying to do this in a vacuum of silence, I suddenly pull lose a large group and I feel the chair shift and down we go. But, without a sound. So here I am. I have about ten packages and they are wrapped. Shake, rattle and roll and I still know nothing. So, just open them and use the Elmers paste to reseal them. I didn't know about scotch tape. Not a single goodie out of the pile..How could Santa be so dumb. A pair of socks? Had he lost his mind? So I climb back up, teetering on the back frame of the chair and "FLASH" on comes the light in the room and Mo yells with glee…M'shaib, Y'allah, sway Muk inta hamman wajid" As he yells I fall and land on Dad's brand new golf shoes with metal spikes. These make a tremendous impression on my already world record sore butt and I throw my self forward, knocking over the vaporizer, and as you geezers remember they had steam with Vicks rub in them. This goes on Mo, he starts tearing off his white shirt and screaming, Mom comes in the door with what looked to be an axe handle, later found it was a rolling pin, and I am spread out in a pile of presents, which have opened and paper is stuck all over me. Some damn glue. The Vicks rub was all over me and what a greasy mess I was. Smelled beyond belief and Mom's says, cool as the glacier ice.."Guess who has Church in ten minutes?" NOWAY," smelling like this I screamed. "Father Roman will knock me out!" Mom's smile said it all…I didn't know that a smile could reach behind a persons ears. Eyes that had a dancing fire in them…Glee, as I found out later.

So into the shower and scrubbing with, what else..Lava soap to be exact. This stuff will take the paint off a moving car. Think I wasn't a bright pink! Well, rushing into my dress clothes, my shoes soaking wet, I decide that Dad's shoes, that are new and shiny and tried to kill me would work. Heck, I knew where to get socks…They were quite large, but no matter. Off and out the door I went. Our Catholic Christmas dinner before Mass was that night and it was also the night a visiting Bishop from Lebanon was in. Well to try and tell you how I managed to step on peoples feet with those spikes, running right out of the shoes and dashing about like a madman, I can tell you today..You never, and I mean never put shoes of any kind with a spike on them on a chair and forget where you put them. As you may find out, certain ladies are very concerned when they sit and get poked by a dozen spikes and the jump up, scream, smack the nearest kid, usually me and yell, for a rope and a tree.

But the best was for last. I had no idea that Mom had bought these special type of shoes, had them flown over in someone's suitcase and hand delivered by the Flying Camel and had hid them around the house for months. How was I to know. I just knew they had to be gone and I ran to the fence close by and heaved them over thinking no one could trace them to me. They had, unbeknownst to me, been marked by Mom with Dad's name.

To say that he was heard in Udaliyiah, before there was a Udaliyiah is an understatement when some sheep herder came to the main gate the next morning and wanted "Backsheesh" for the well chewed up shoes and for one goat that he claimed got sick.

I didn't know there were so many recipes for goat my entire life, but I found out. I think Mo sent to Pakistan for some to help Mom come up with more for me to sample daily. Had to do it standing up of course, but to this day, the thought of those brown topped, lower white bottomed shoes with metal prongs just tends to make me stay as far away from any kind of golf course at all.

MERRY CHRISTMAS

Now, one would think that the young experiences that I had would have taught me that Christmas, Santa and I were words not used by most adults in the same sentence. However, remember, Santa tends to forgive little boys and girls. This does seem to be questionable and was raised on more than one occasion around my house, yet…there is always hope for the condemned at the last sweep of the second hand that Mrs. Claus might intercede. Knowing now who that was tends to make me think that I was dropped repeatedly by the Doctors at birth. In fact, there is some proof that Mrs. Claus aka Mom requested the droppings from the Obstetrician. Something about thirty six hours of labor and fat kid…Don't know the details. This would explain why I thought Mrs. Claus might step in and help. I may have had brain damage.

The problem started with the annual Nativity play at King's Road baseball field in Dhahran and that the adults wanted to use real animals. Seems to me that was just looking for trouble when an rapscallion was loose and perhaps a bit curious.

I will start out by commenting that when I offered to help out, I had no idea that Mr. Fairlie, our scoutmaster and a truly knowledgeable man with first hand knowledge of my escapades in scouting, was helping. So the suggestion that I be assigned to shovel the 12 tons of droppings from various beasts of Biblical reference should have been no surprise. I didn't know that a Camel was capable of completely burying me without warning should the ugly beast so decide, which one huge momma camel did. Think she may have been the one that was hunted at Imhoff Gardens in an earlier adventure. Talk about ripping off clothes. Now wonder if she knew my Mom.

I was fascinated by the line of donkeys, while Jeff Yeager seem awful interested in the sheep....

Anyhow, while trying to shovel behind the donkey's, and they aren't too bad I managed to get a shovel into the old wood handled iron wheel wheelbarrow that they had and was supposed to get fresh straw and set it around. So leaving the wheelbarrow behind this old red henna dyed donkey, I head to the straw pile.

Arms full of straw, passing the camels and sticking my tongue out as I ran for my life, I hear this scream and something to the effect, "THAT DAMN CROCKER KID" I was confused. What had I done now? Seems as if Mr Sitar and several ladies were rehearsing a song or something and the donkey kicked the wheelbarrow and some pellets became airborne, landing amongst this fine group of carollers.

I thought sticking the straw where the donkey doesn't shine might be helpful, but by then I was no longer able to catch my breath after out running several ladies with switches. Now these switches are interesting. The donkey and camel herders seem to take great mirth in giving them to the ladies and watching me do a 440 in new world records.

However, as is the norm, Aramco had what I believe were smudge pots, which were like black balls with a torch top. Drop kicked that sucker right into the straw. Fire department was right there of course and wet it down, but did scare some of the sheep. All over the place as a matter of fact. Now sheep are hard to catch. And the wooly little beasts, when scared, do tend to make little messes and those are well renown for causing slippery spots and soon people were falling all around and I swear I heard the Christmas song,

"You better be good, you better be nice, Santa's coming to kill you tonight" but I'm sure that was a figment of my imagination.

Finally all is well, and calm restored. I'm locked in the baseball score-keepers box sorting out the Christmas music and stapling them together. So I staple twenty or so sheets together..no one told me they were two sheets to a person.

Ousted again and told to go home, I head down Kings Road and arrive at a wondrous sight. Christmas Tree Circle. All lit up and music coming from inside and a bright star on top, just memorized me. The signs said "Merry Christmas and Happy New Year to All" One had to admit, inquisitive minds wanted to see the music and how come this particular tree could sing. So I find a cord leading out the bottom of the tree and follow it to one of the sever row houses near by. Looked inside the window and what a place. Tree and gifts everywhere. This made me know that I needed to get home fast as Santa had obviously been there and was early for some reason and I knew he might actually be talked into not stopping if Mom got to him first, so off I shot.

Unbeknownst to me, the house with the presents was a decoration house and wasn't even occupied. Someone had said a lot of prayers that day, or I may have decided to look inside and check it out.

I get home and Mom, from a long day of decorating tells me.."You're wanted in Safanyiah…hurry, you can catch the last bus out" Real welcome I thought.

I got a new bike for Christmas, a American Flyer called the "Hiway Patrol" bike and I flew like magic all over the camp that day.

I wish I had that bike this Christmas…..

THE OLD
ARAMCO CEMETARY

Many of the plaques are missing and while brushing off many to take photos, I lost my gold Arabic name ring. Perhaps it is best as it will remain with so many of our friends who are there forever. I was given it in 1967 and lost it in 1997. Somewhat poetic, but also perhaps comforting to me to know a part of me was with the Sounders Family, and Janie Baumgartner, and Thelma Crow and 112 others I could find, even if I didn't know them all, they are all part of me.

SCOUTS TAIL

Well, it was about as hot as I had ever seen. Even the local flies were trekking across the sand behind the school as it was just too hot to fly. This was a beautiful clear day in August, about 1964 I would guess. Mr. Farlie, our ever loving Boy Scout Master and Mr. Bill Goellner, famed throughout the land for things he could do in wrestling class, and with one hand. I never thought you could spin a kid of 150 pounds on his head like a top, while hanging onto his jockey strap the whole time, but he proved it one day as I spun round and round. "Pointy head", Mom's only comment was as I proceeded to soak in cold water at the house for about ten days.

But I digress, back to the burning sands of Jebal Shamal. The Scout masters had decided that we would have a "hike", short little walk as I recall the infamous last words. It was about 8:00 am and we were heading out the Main Gate and down the road, which was suspiciously beginning to feel softer to my step. The truck with all our camping supplies had left earlier and we all had canteens full of water, well, most, some bright boy had kool aid, which will be an important part of the great "Lost Patrol" saga shortly. In those days, we wore shorts and knee socks and white t-shirts. All of us had a walking stick, mostly because we knew that a short hike to these two might well be to Safaniyah.

Now at the section of the road, where there was an old gas station, of sorts, you could see the Jebal quite well. It did seem to phase in and out, but our Troop masters told us. "This is an assignment for your compass merit badge." You will go in two groups and make it to the Jebal by different approaches. "Crocker, you'll take the Wolf Pack and go towards Abqaiq and after two kilometers, use your compass and bear striaght North you will find the Jebal. I heard him whisper to Mr. Goellner, "You think this is wise. He can't find his backdoor from the front yard normally" Mr. Goellner's all time reported comment was, "Hell, he can see the Jebal the whole time.. how could he get lost.?"

He told the other pack, the Cobra pack, to head straight out and turn east to the Jebal. The main difference was the way I was going had a few sand dunes between the road and the Jebal and the other way did not.

So, still smarting from the comments, we headed out. I had five guys with me and we all knew we were the top of the line, mean, green sand stomping machines. The sand thought different. One of Mr. Goellner's last comments to me was, "If you lose sight of the Jebal, just follow your footsteps in the sand back to the road." Now, I never knew that they had already had other assistants located to where they could watch us the whole time with binoculars. The old Aramco safety net. So I truly thought we were the out there alone.

About three hundred yards into the little stroll and after climbing what seemed like mountains of sand, no one told me to climb the suckers by walking at an angle. So we dug and clawed our way to the top each time. Rolling backwards and up and down, we finally conquered this massive dune. Later measured at about 8 feet by a mirthful Mr. Goellner. Anyhow, we found on the front face a nice shaded spot so I called for a break. Out come the canteens and it seems as if we had lost one, so I passed mine around. After words, we were commonly refereed to for years as the "Blue Mouth Lost Patrol", but I'm getting to that.

I guess because it was so hot, we got a little drowsy and there is a slight possibility that we dozed off for a few minutes in the warmth of the sun. Anyhow, jumping up with a start, I yelled to everybody, "Hey, we gotta run like the wind or we will never hear the end of this. Compass upside down on rope around my neck, I simply looked at it and off we went. We walked for about forty minutes and one of the guys say's, "why don't we climb this dune and get a compass bearing on the Jebal". Smart kid.

We climbed the dune there and for miles ahead all we could see was desert. My first thought was I had led the whole group into the Rub-Al-Kahli having been told by my Dad about people finding bleached bones of lost people there as it all looked alike. Not knowing he was really talking about camel bones. This is important as we stumbled across what looked like a persons bones, (They were a dog as I was pointedly told later) Sarcastic comments like "You couldn't see the long tail part, or the head jaw?", really didn't raise my confidence level. The other remark that went into legend was "Never thought to look behind you either, Huh?" I had no clue that by walking in the wadi, between the rises of sand, we were about 150 yards from the Scout camp at the base of the Jebal.

Ohhh No, I told the gang we are lost. OK, we follow our tracks back to the road, "WHAT TRACKS?" screamed a much less impressed Scout of my leadership and compass training ability. We had been walking on the hard rock desert surface for awhile and the sand dune was way back. A quick hand to hand combat action with walking sticks followed, with the majestic swordsman backing his way out fighting the Sheriff of Nottingham's men all at once, at least in his feeble mind. Anyhow, I got a pretty good whack, and still think it was that snake in the sand Jeff (DH64) or perhaps Kevin (DH64) that got me. After a sound go around we were really hot and beat. Once again I passed around the canteen, and right at the moment, when we knew it was all over, we with our blue mouth rings from the kool aid, hear this voice from above…"What the @$#^%$@^%@$ are you doing Crocker?"

There was the other troop, Four adults, and Mr. Goellner with that glint in his eye. We were led to the campsite and that night I was still digging the 4,000 foot long latrine trench for the camp.

However, sitting on top of Jebal Shamal, at sunset with Mr. Goellner's arm around me, and him telling me it was ok, even if I did want to run away made it all worth a million stars blazing at me later that night. Until he came around to the pup tent and remarked, "You know Crocker, tomorrow we have wrestling again....."

Incidentally, that night, sitting around the campfire, Bill, (Class of '65) became a legend in his time by sneaking a full large can of baked beans into the fire and the result was rather interesting. That will have to be another story.

SCOUTING

Speaking of Boy Scout's, it was a slightly warm day in 1964 and Scout troop "Cobra" and troop "Jackal" were given the assignment of a five kilo hike to jebal "Shamal". Since we could see the jebal from the main gate, and since Mr. Quick was busy, he left it to us to get there, set up camp at the base and he and Mr. Fairlie would join us.

Now, using the very latest in Boy Scouts compass and azimuth readings, we headed right for the jebal, via Al-Kohbar…seems as if we weren't as good as we thought..Several days later, perhaps 40, wondering around in great circles, we managed to get to the jebal.. By looking at it and walking to it.

Now it was tradition to take the newest member of the troop and do something, so that it would be memorable…We were beat from over, by now 50 kilo hike and set up camp in a wadi at the foot of the Jebal. Course we climbed all over it and went in caves and looked at the tombs on the far slope and put our troop flags at the top. Well, Mr. Quick and Mr. Fairlie got there and made us comply with normal practice, wood and hatchet use, knife procedures, make a fire while rubbing two damn sticks together for hours on end, I rubbed two matches together, got my merit badge qualification and went on to cut myself with the hatchet.

They told us we had to spend the night alone and they would be back in the morning...let the games begin !!!

First we had set up our camp in a depression, to take advantage of the warmth, as we all know it gets cool at nights. Then we played capture the flag, with much unsportsmanlike behaviors, something about flashing other players and rude remarks about family, etc.Seems there was some controversies over how the jackel flag was used as toilet paper, but I know naught of this. We had to dig a slit trench latrine, which with great enthusiasm they guys digging had made about forty feet long and two feet deep.. causing some terrible comments and threats when people, while running to steal the flag fell in...

Anyhow, about two we all crawled into our sleeping bags, boots inside to avoid scorpions, and went to slept. NOW, the real fun started...we, I am geezzering here on names, went to Danny Kemp's sleeping back, which he was in and deep asleep. We zipped it all the way up so just his head was exposed and placed him out in the desert away from the camp. We knew that when he woke up, not be able to get out of the bag and panic...back to camp and to sleep.

Well about four a.m. it started raining bad, we, had no fire and were cold, but suddenly the shi- hit the fan, water came rushing down the wadi, through our depression and swept all before it.. We all managed to get out of our gear and standing around in various stage of undress, wet and looking very bright, we huddled together until morning. Our gear was scattered all over the area, and some probably made it back to camp for all I know. So after the sun was up for about three hours and we had pretty much gathered our wits, BANG, we remembered we had put Danny out in the desert.

Immediately we fanned out..no sign of him anywhere, we began to panic, did we kill him ? We knew the Scoutmasters were due any moment and all of a sudden we hear this scream.. We had found Danny. The rain and gully washer has washed him, bag and all into the latrines trench...And the sun had cooked his face..I guess he lost about five pounds from sweating in the bag, but I know he lost more when he realized what he had slept in..Such unbecoming language for a Scout...

The end result, OH, one other thing, during the big campfire the night before Bill Cohea, snakily put a can of baked beans in the fire and as we all sat around, lying about exploits and smoking, it blew up and covered most of us with beans…I know Bill will remember this because I think the troop planted the flag in his backside, or there about….

Back to the end..The Scoutmasters arrived and, notwithstanding the heat already, raised the temperature several more degree's with commentary…Some of which I still hear today. All merit badges suspended, and we had to hike back to Dhahran, while they went back in a stake truck with Danny.

I'm still looking for a canteen, believe some future archeologist will find it, take a big swig and explode on the spot if he is smoking at the same time….contents were very volatile….

Our troop sign was the three fingers up, with an occasional extension of one….

On top of this, I made Eagle Scout two years later. Later in life I actually acted as a Scoutmaster in Dhahran and took a bunch of Cub Scouts to see a Destroyer tied up in RT…Still have a photo of that trip.

"On my Honor",………………there's more I know, but like all gezzers, I need a nap.

SECURITY AND POLICE

Since I was always in the middle of many things in Arabia, and spent a good amount of time in Aramco's Security office, there is some justification for what happened.

Last summer in Arabia, think '68 or '69 and Aramco had started giving us returning students a ID card, but I found that it was a little too restricting. I think I was allowed to go from the house to the pool and back.....most likely a type of preemptive attempt to prevent past reoccurrence's.

SO, after finding out that the building next to Security was where they processed badge's and ID's I had a brainstorm...Why not just go in, late at night of course, and make my own. No big deal...

So off I went, alone this time, and if not, silence is still golden, because I don't think Aramco has a statute of Limitations on me...I got in the back window, as it was a winding kind that if you shook it enough the little handle would turn. Soon I was in...now, quickly I found the file of passes and not knowing the way everything was coded, decided that the one with the big red stripe and high number had to be good for most things. Over to the ID camera and I had to change the backdrop cloth to the proper color, believe it was blue and by really working at it was able to get several photo's done, all a little close, but everyone knows that no one really looked at the photo's right ?

I put it in the plastic card laminator and attached the little clamp after typing in my name and student ID etc. Had to have some authenticity...

Well, out I went, happy as a lark and ready to travel where even Captain Kirk boldly wouldn't go...because he had sense...

Well, the next day I got royal treatment all over the place..admin building, dining hall, recreation, commissary and even out to the shops area. Decided to push my luck and went to RT to go to Sandy Hook, which by now was off limits being so close to the refinery. Passed thru with no problem...

After diving for about thirty minutes I surfaced and swam to shore to be met by what I thought was the D-Day landing force. I believe Brock Powers was even there, along with some very grim and evil looking gentlemen I seemed to recognize.

I was introduced to Mr. Tom Barger that day...seems as if my pass was one of maybe ten in Aramco..All Senior VPs and President and CEO. Mr. Kieswetter was there, Ned Scardino and a few others, and I knew that the wooden platform the Saudi's were building in Mr. Barger's back yard looked a lot like Clint Eastwood's movie years later...something along the line of "Hang em High".

Amazingly enough, Mr. Barger said, "This fellow has way too much potential, if he can bypass our measure's too not be put to good use." I was stunned...maybe the rope wasn't for me. Then came the crack of doom..." Let's put him to work in Security"....my God, my very nemesis...but Mr. Kieswetter had an evil look and the next day I was given a new pass, from my house, to main gate to bathroom to house.....and thus was the start of my Law Enforcement History. I know more about swirls, loops and palms, and crime scenes and lock picking, etc that most people see on TV. My immediate supervisor, MuHommad Su'bey, now head of ARAMCO security, taught me a lot and when I finally attended the Police academy in West Texas to become a certified peace officer, I was well ahead of my class and ace'd that sucker...

Oh, and incidently, they used to keep an index file an every kid that got in trouble, I had a file several inches thick of cards, well......seems as if they and some others got lost at summer's end. Interesting to read now, I hear, of what they did and didn't know.

Many's the time I wonder if Mr. Barger wasn't wise beyond his time...

Oh, I still have that ID card and all my others...I had made six or seven, and used them with impunity with the magic word. "Security!!!"Never did get called down on those. Will have to put them on display at the reunion.

SEWAGE ET AL

Thanks for the explanation of why the sewage wasn't frozen. And of course, depending on the temperature, the addition of other substances to the water might have lowered the freezing temperature. As near as I can calculate, you must still be grounded for at least another 20 years; how do your weekend flights to DH to continue your community service of cleaning out commodes (which will last for at least another 30 years) affect your budget? (or do you own an airline, too? You seem to be in just about every other kind of business...)

Your cat calls out for pizza? Mine call out for fish and chips. On the other hand, one night last week *I* personally called out for pizza. When it came, I went to the door and the pizza man was standing outside, and about four feet behind him was my neighbor's dog, ears cocked forward alertly, doing everything but drooling, because SHE KNEW what that man was carrying: FOOD! And maybe some of it was for her! (alas...) To add to this, as soon as I had seen Nicky, right at the bottom of my door (Dutch door, I only open top, pizza can come in, our cats can't get out) something said, "MERRROWWWW" which turned out to be a stray cat we had been feeding, who really thought he ought to live in our house. We compromised and convinced a friend of mine to tkae him in a few days later. And poor Nicky didn't get any pizza. HMMM—sometimes we don't bother to eat the crusts and put them out in the back yard for the squirrels. I wonder if Nicky has been coming in and getting them?

I am FINALLY caught up with Brat Chat. Maybe I'll find some time to post again now.

CHRISTINE

Short NL comment

The dunes softly whisper your name. Camels move effortlessly across the red sea of sand, the gulf caresses the white shore. The child within you screams, "I want to feel again."

As your President, through thick and thin, I have attempted to preserve the feeling of the breeze on a scorching night and the fragrance of jasmine as we walked the byways of Aramco and the Kingdom. I hear each one of you and feel every heart pounding as we visit the warm corners of our spirits and souls.

May I say only that the warmth of the land of sand we call home is in each and every one of us and my greatest hope is that all of us, including those who have gone before, never forget why we are who we are and the bond that, like a ribbon of golden sand twisting and swirling, slides through our lives. It is the thread of friendship and Brathood. I thank God every day for each and every one of you.

See you in Tucson and straining at the bit like a racing saluki, I eagerly await seeing all of you.

Al-Humdaliah!

Michael Crocker (DH65)

ABI Founder and President

SIGNS

BRATTERS

I have the one (Stop) sign that has the red hand and the word stop in Arabic, but all of the fingers except one was painted out. This sign was on the corner of "I" street and "10th" in Dhahran. Amazingly, it stood like this for the whole year from September (I saw it in August as returning student)1967 until it found it's way to Texas the next summer, 1968.

I plan on bringing it to the next reunion. I have heard of others, but even after all these years, I can't tell if the fingers were painted over, or if someone in Aramco shops just slipped it in.

I also have a photo of Rise Johanson standing next to the sign.

SIREN AND SUCH

OK

The sirens were mounted on a large pole, there were four large speakers, square shaped on top of each pole. They were originally installed in Dhahran and Ras Tanura because of the attempted bombing by the Italians during 1943/44. The stabilizers was being built above Dahahran at the time so the siren was mounted inside the main gate, to the right as you enter in front of the Heavy Equipment Shop, in the Transportation yard. In Dhahran. In RT it was located at the old refinery, at the end of the long road thru the salt marsh area to the refinery itself. They were painted red.

The one that was placed in Abqaiq later was in the pipe yard and was used for fire and emergency also.

They were controlled in the early years by a push button on the bottom of the pole and Security had the responsibility to set them off.

In the 50's and 60's they were used in the following manner:

6:00 AM wake up (Long)

7:00 AM to be at your work site (short)

11:30 leave for Lunch(Long)

12:15 to be back at your work site(Short)

4:30 to go home(Long)

By long I mean about 15 seconds.

In the middle 60's and mostly due to "Rock Wednesday" they set up a system of Wardens and block areas, and if there was a loud long continuous siren sounding, it meant for the American Block Wardens to get everybody to the school for safety.

It was also use to signal the volunteer fire fighting personnel made up of Americans.

Two shorts warbles and one long meant a fire in one area, two short and two long meant a fire in another are, and three long and three short was fire in the main camp.

The entire system was also connected to Security switchboards that would, upon hearing the siren warnings for danger of one sort or another, call all the top brass of Aramco at one time, and they all had separate telephones for this only. Most of these phones were, appreciatedly enough, red. I'll bring one to the reunion.

This system was phased out around 1975 or maybe a little later I guess. My mind is gezzering now. The telephone system was more reliable and wasn't so obvious.

COMMENT ON A TIME LONG AGO. I THINK THE FIRST PART OF THIS STORY IS HERE. IN THE BOOK

Gotta be quick here but I just want to say that I am not repulsed or horrified or anything like that. I am well aware of the nature of war and I am also well aware that you were in authority in hand to hand combat. That is never a pretty picture. So please know in your heart that this story does not change how I think of you one iota. I already knew this. Have I not told you a thousand times that I know you well?

As for the "small world" portion of it, I thank God that you did not take Robert out. Look how you carry the burden of Donna when you had absolutely nothing to do with her death. I shudder to think of how you might be haunted to this day of the thought that you authorized the killing of a friend. Perhaps it wasn't coincidence?

I will be praying you have a peaceful Christmas. Please try and get some rest. I worry about you so much.

Keep in touch. T.

Teresa Kiersznowski

502-495-6700 X108

SNAKES, TITLES
AND THUGBA..

s far as the current subject of military titles go, in my day a female officer was addressed as "Yes, Ma'am!" and a male officer was "Yes, Sir!" All NCO, (non commissioned officer) ranks were addressed by the position. As in "Yes, Sargent Major", or "Yes, Sergeant" or "No, Corporal" etc.

Later I had heard that the army tried the all inclusive "Sir" applied to all officers regardless of gender. The current trend you will have to ask Christine husband about. Incidently, whenever I go to the VA hospital at Ft. Sam Houston Medical Center I am always addressed, even in my civilian clothing as the rank indicated on my ID after signing in. It is always, Yes, Captain, or "Turn right and cough, Captain" or we're sorry Captain, but you are not allowed in the Nurses quarter's.

On the telephone it depends on the unit. A lot of units are based at Forts where they are in basic training and recruits or troops are used to answer telephones and since they are mostly in shock still, automatically answer with a "sir", using the army logic of "I won't offend anyone I don't know by the universal "Sir". However, after distinguishing the gender, which may not always be possible as in Thugba, they should change to Ma'am or Sir.

As far as the snakes, I can remember a lot of yellow and black striped snakes swimming under the lights of the old wood pier at Half Moon Bay. Playing with them and ignoring then down at 45 feet spear fishing. Only to later find out that ALL snakes in the gulf are poisonous. However, their mouth is so small that they would have to bite between, ohh let's say the thumb and fist finger or somewhere akin to that area.

Eel's on the other hand were famous and legendary for their ability to bite and hold on. I was always told to just let one bite if it was close and stay as still as possible as it would think it could change it's grip and release to bite again, which meant you could pull away. I never saw one, but to this day I don't know why, with the size of the diving knives we macho's all carried,(made most swords seem like letter openers and Rambo's was a toothpick), one didn't just behead the beast. After all, this was the local custom I recall

FLASH FLASH FLASH THUGBA DEVELOPING STORY..THIS JUST IN......

Do Wa do Wa do Watiity Where's the Khan of Nacog o' City....Ohhh, excuse me, you wish to know why the Great Khan is appearing from the depths of HRH Ted's palatial domicile ? Well, seems as if the fleet of foot HRH was busy promoting and demoting, and the urly Duke was pontificating, the Khan was enhancing the future of Thugba. Seems as if Mata Hari reported Macarema music from near the Casbah...well, close..The Great Khan in his magnificence was making sure the next generation, and as Khan, he boldly goes when no man had been before, or so they told me, in the HRH Teds, harem.

Hopefully, as in the neighboring lands, proliferation will allow the gathering of the tribes and the Great Khan will be Khan ibn Sa'nd and future Thugbatites will, of course have a stronger generic makeup.

Off to wells of Aquwa for date and myah to meet with Harun ar-Rashid..., Yel'law emsheeeeeeeeeeeeee...

END FLASH END FLASH END FLASHING, OPPS, END FLASH

SOME OLD
MEMORIES

I was just sitting here and had a call from Helen St. Croix, Class of 1964 RT who thought I had been killed, or was told that, by several Aramcons in a war many years ago. She just got the newsletter and called and was telling me about some of the things she remembers. She and I played together as kids in RT and they lived right behind us. She remembered Ross Tyler and Dick Burgess and we both remembered the twins, one who passed away while we were still there from leukemia, Keith Willamson.

She asked me about the old school play ground and could I remember anything about it. As I can remember it. There was a three foot high concrete maze that we had, a large swing set to the right and a teeter totter next to it, some large rubber tires and a bicycle rack at the front. The maze brought back a lot of memories. I always was a little curious as to why the maze was there. I never saw another...except on shows about white mice... wonder what teacher had that built so we could be studied ? The maze was on the blacktop and the rest was on sand. There were painted games on the blacktop, one being hopscotch or hop something...Painted safety yellow of course. There was also the famous or infamous climbing dome.. Many a head crack from falling off that thing and the ladder walk, where you went up two rungs, and then walked with your hads on rugs to the other end. The swing set had swings with wood seats and chains and at one end was a small slide attached to the swing set. There was also a rope you could climb attached to an extension of the swing set.

We remembered the old Mail Center being in one end of the old row house on the corner of the street by the school and that reminded me of the Nursery up the street and before the old tennis courts, which we used as a skating rink and played "crack the whip" with many an injury. I distinctly remember the large bags of DDT at the Nursery. I remember the small palm trees you could get and plants and the other shurbs.

She is sending me a bunch of early RT photographs, showing the "Surf House" being built and completed and other 1947 onward photo's. Guess this will end up being some kind of video once I get all of these photos in.

How many of you are having trouble with emotions ? Do many of you "feel" the old or is it inconsequential now that life has changed so many of us.

Oh, and before I drift off to the past again, have any others received the reunion newsletter that was sent out, and comments ?

STEAM ROLLER

It seems that in 1957, I was about 8 years old and Doug Romine and I were just looking for something to do." Being curious is all"…this disclaimer is necessary to protect the guilty…

Anyhow, Aramco had just started to put down oil and asphalt roads and there was one which was in progress in front of our house. This was in Abqaiq.

I still think ARAMCO should have been responsible, rather than me getting my butt tore up, but suffice to say, Mom disagreed. The beginning of a legal career for me…trying to win in Mom's Kangaroo Courts…

There was this large steam roller…..get a hint ? Anyhow up and away we went, after all, you only had to push this long stick thing and it moved. So down the road we went and along the way managed to run into a few minor objects, two cars and a truck, but the damn thing wouldn't stop.

So we go over the sidewalk, of course crushing it, and into this bachelors yard and the weight of this beast sinks down and breaks a hot water feed line to the row houses, which then sprays into the air. We got very hot water all over us, and since we were now stopped, Doug, the dog, takes off and I ran home.

Now Mom, as the Supreme Court Justice, wasn't going to buy this, but I thought it was worth a try. So I ran in and yelling at the top of my voice that this Old guy down the street had, without any provocacation from me, sprayed me with hot water and I had been burned and that's why I was wet and looked bad.

With amazing disbelief, She bought it and called ARAMCO security to report this guy...Problem, Now I've got security there, and MOM. They want to go to this guy's house and confront him...Mom is madder than a real wet hen and I am planning my last meal.

At that moment life as I knew changed forever...for down the sidewalk comes an American and two Saudi workers...the crew of the steamroller who had seen the whole thing...and talk about looking unhappy....I kept waiting for the axe to bite into my neck as they all started talking.

Things just got worse as here comes the guy, AND my Dad, whose yard I went in and who I had blamed for spraying me..seems as if Mom had called Dad(I did't know this) and Dad had called the guy.

By the time the long line of people in the yard got done cutting switches off of the Oleanders in out front yard, there were only bare tree's standing there, and in my mind looked like tombstones.

It took weeks to sit properly, but I did learn one valuable lesson...when opportunity strikes, run like hell...don't stand still.

Mike Crocker

Still walking with a limp...

STONE'EM !

Well, let me jump in here. I think Miss Crow was meaner than an old witch, Mrs. Fry was downright vindictive, Mr. Goellner beat me up all the time, Mr. Dickerson was gruff and etc, etc. etc.

Now then, how about the fact the because they were such bad to the bone people, I have the best education I could have ever received. Wonder how that happened?

I played a WHOLE lot meaner tricks than any potato stunt in my day, and I might add, called many a teacher much worse, however I must say..I will now and forever be eternally grateful for every harsh word, thrown eraser, foreign language I know, and geographic site I can pinpoint and every bit of history, science and math I use everyday.

I still am called "incorrigible" by some teachers I had in sixth grade, right Jeff? Yet, they, for all of my devilment and torture, came back the next day and did battle with me again and again.

Thus, did I become a bright boy.

Also, in all seriousness, I feel that all teachers who take the road to teach, do so because of their teachers and the knowledge and education they pass on as their legacy. Mr. Goellner stood me on my head numerous times. Years later, his constant stomping me saved my life when a trick he taught me saved me from a bayonet. I managed to escape the Gendarmes in Gay Paris one night because I was able to stumble through French from the dedicated Mrs. Fry, and although my English and grammar are solely in need of serious repair, my ability to write comes from Miss Crow.

Would I call any of them names. You better believe it, and do so with as deep a feeling of respect and love as any man/woman alive.

Did I hate, despise, play tricks on them...yes indeed. Was I wrong..not at 13 years of age I don't think. After all, how was I to know that one day, I would realize they gave me the world and let me learn.

So am I offended by name calling? Or others defending? NOT IN THE LEAST, for each of us measures our own life by our own ways and means. I think, and still do that Mr. Reily tried to kill me off...yet I owe that man a lot. I may have hated the earth he walked at one time, but now....I still have no love for him. (HA!) And you thought I would play bleeding heart. HOWEVER, I did learn no matter how hard I tested ALL of my teachers.

I will also say that of all my Brat Brothers and Sisters, it has been my greatest pleasure knowing that many of you picked up the torch of education from the hand of those before, and you carry it now.

I never did like Jeff Yeager He had short hair, long nose and always got me in trouble. Would I have wanted him as a teacher? You better believe I would.

So, call them grumpy, hateful, or any other name, but remember, at one time or another, we all benefited from them. HOWEVER, they also benefited from each and everyone of us...

Ohhh, by the way...SALLY ONNEN (RT65)- TEACHER OF THE YEAR IN AUSTIN, TEXAS—way to go classmate and Brat friend forever. (Meaner then an old armadillo tho!)

Now, all together, JUMP on Mike....1, 2, 3...GO!

Mike Crocker (DH65)

Ought to have been (64)

Could darn well have been (67)

HAPPY DAYS
AT THE REFINERY

It was a cold and chilly day, unusual for the furnace that I was usually in, but then that may have been the weather of Mom. Never knew so much hot air could bellow at various small innocuous things. Here's why it was cold. Santa flew by, never stopped, dropped coal all over my house and it was now the New Year. If one could call a cold day New Year in Ras Tanura. No going to the beach, although Mom highly recommended it as the water was freezing and potential sharks all over, but I had other plans.

I went by some friends and several had got bicycles from Santa the snake, and I had a red wagon. Now what fool would give a kid, without a driver license a semi motorized vehicle to try on various places. Talking Dick Burgess into going with Ross Tyler and myself, having worked out a deal that we would hook the wagon to the bikes and ride around.

Now near the refinery, there were two unguarded roads back then that traversed the salt marsh and so we went on the side that had the water injection plant water inlet. I mean after all, that water was supposed, note supposed to be warm. Carcogenic ? Didn't know how to spell the word. The intent was to ride the wagon down the sloping cement path that fed the water to the long stone moat to the Gulf. No fences in those days. The water was only a few feet deep and we were men of action. In fact I am sure that action figures for generations to come came from out exploits.. You should remember, "nah, nah nah, Fatman, err, Batman".

No one has to remember that the refinery shut down several days a year then for steam cleaning and high pressure washing and lots of technical things. Who knew or cared. We just knew that the slope was dry and the water out the injection site was low. Who needs more. Cold as a Bears butt in a polar suit, off we went to ride up and down the slope.

Many people knew that these Red Ryder red wagons had wood sides that could be put on and taken off and a metal handle with rubber wheels. Great for holding on to and going down the slope. Not wanting to get our shoes and rather small sized jeans wet, we got down to our little denim jackets, tee shirts and under wear. The following events was what Mom refereed to as the Last Hurrah of a Palm Tree without a single date for brains. Rather unusual and new comment.

All of a sudden there was this huge crash as the main flush valves were re-opened to allow the wash out and the re flow of the intake. We of course went ten feet underwater and tumbled like a sock in a washer, but managed to make it, darn near the end of the intake stone passage to shore. The force had sent the wagon to sail the seven seas with most of our clothing. I still had a tee shirt, but no jacket or underwear. The others were about the same. For a confused moment thought I was looking at a worm, then realized it was in my mind a huge sea snake. Mom didn't think so when all three of us went screaming back to out houses, much to the grand applause of hundreds of classmates and adults. I still won't eat beanies and weenies.

The worst part is that it really was cold. I thought Mom was going to literally die laughing as car after security car pulled up out front. She was just in convulsions and made a strong point to the Night Foremen (Security then) that were had gone fishing with our worms. I saw no such humor and the door darkened even worse as Dad and Mr. Crampton strode in.

Seems we three kids had breached a "red" zone in Aramco security and all wanted to know how. I demanded compensation for my wagon and got a butt blast that rocked most of the Arabian Peninsula and had a hard time sitting for many years, Still limp to this day I think.

The end result was good. Mom took pity after some hundred Management had come in and the volume of yelling was that of the mid day siren going off in my kitchen, but all's well. I got cookies. Of course I understand there was a lot of screaming down the street and across the road and grounded until 99, but still. A way to start a New Year.

ANOTHER CHRISTMAS TALE

Tis was the night before Christmas and all thru the house, a mother was stalking a small but determined mouse.

Faster than a speeding train, the mouse ran, for the thunder of hoofs followed close behind.

The thought was that Santa and fallen down the chimney, and meant more for the mouse, but the lady of the house a mousse pie for plans, and the mouse would soon be waving goodbye.

But this mouse was friends with a Dancer and a Dasher and some dog with ears and a red nose, so he dashed up the roof and to their side,

The Reindeer were pulling, to loosen Santa stuck in the vent pipe, err, chimney and all their strentgh could not free him for the rest of the mice of Aramco Town.

The mouse was able to get below, the witch had flown into the kitchen and the mouse was able to grab Santa's beard and pull with a mighty heave. Santa popped like a cork and toys galore, an extra one for the mouse as he headed for the door. The lady was shocked to see this fat man in the living room, but her cookies and milk and a beer or two and they were soon swapping lies about the behavior of the mouse.

Who just happened to live in the house.

They say the New Year is the year of the OX. This mouse grew tall and strutted without fear, for the Orientals had made him an ox.

The lady of the house was not so bemused, she whacked him so hard, his tail and nose went round and round to touch, like that dumb dog that chased it's tail. However, soon it was quiet, the Ox now strapped and restrained from future endeavors before and after Christmas, and may yet still be strapped to the gurney in case Mom needed to hook him to the wall socket. Yet all in all the New Year is blooming bright.

A DOCTORS VISIT

Last night I was watching a series that I particularly like, "House" on USA. Anyway this crazed Doctor brought back some penetrating memories of a recent medical experience I survived.

Seems if the TV Dr. House put a thermometer into a Police officers rear end and then, with something akin to my experience, he went home. In his case this was TV and led to a whole series of happenings, while I on the other hand will never understand how I get my rear in strange positions.

So I am at the Doctor's office for a refill of my prescriptions and the regular Doctor is out and in comes this ambling, bent forward, white haired figure. I thought perhaps the houseboy until he says" HI, I'm Dr. Hess and I am here for your yearly physical. I cried, screamed and begged that I didn't need a physical and he seem to have a hearing problem which became very evident shortly. Seems as he was in his late 80's and still allegedly active in practice. Although I should have got a clue when he whispered in my ear on each side to see if I had any hearing loss.

Using a mallet, which had to be 100 years old he tested my reflex's, which brought tears to my eyes, but not as much as the rest of the story. I swear he could hardly pick up this hammer he hit me with, from which I now add a limp to my score of medical failures.

But on to the fun. He tells me to drop my pants and shorts (should have know better and called a Boxer rescue team). So I am here, butt naked, pants around my feet and I see him put on gloves. I offered cash, my car, someone else's first born but to no avail. With deadly accuracy for a half blind man he hit the target and the cold lifted me off my feet. Talk about an experience. Well, while he has this large finger where sunlight doesn't go, in walks this 400 pound Jamaican nurse and he yells at her, "Don't you know how to knock", to which she explained quite loud that she had knocked and so turning back to me, flapping in the wind, nurse still there and he starts wanting me, who is in a bent position, still anchored to the Doctor and starts arguing with me did I hear her. Yeah, I have a lot to say at this time and he and the nurse are still arguing about knock, knock, who's where? The nurse left and with a rather rude and hard jerk we unhooked and I almost started looking for something sharp. He writes up that I have no prostate problems, perhaps a little latex burn, but that will heal..yeah, heal my ass was on my mind.

The worst part was I could tell the nurse was going door to door to other patients reveling in the story. If he had been around much longer, I may have had to consider a new lifestyle. So he finishes and goes to leave and the nurse comes back and tells him I am the wrong patient and that I am there for my medicines that was all, all of the time she is trying with great aplomb to not even crack a smile. He has no clue and goes out. I leave and for some strange reason get the feeling that everyone knows about the whole thing as people are all deep into their magazines, some even being talented enough to read upside down.

Now one would think this was enough and I was sure on fire, but what really capped the week was the next day, I get a call from Dr. Hess and all he wants to know was did he do a prostate exam? My dog had tears in her eyes from the language I used.

Now the final chapter and clincher, no pun intended, Dr. Hess died a week later of an apparent stroke and the records were never updated so my new Doctor greets me on Friday with, "Well it seems you have not had a prostate exam for several years"........

FDR AND KING ABDUL AZIZ IBN AL- SAUD

R oosevelt told his senior advisers after the meeting that Arabs and Jews were on a 'collision course' toward war in Palestine and that he planned to meet with congressional leaders back in Washington to seek some new policy that would head it off."

INFORMATION COURTESY OF THOMAS W. LIPPMAN

Everyone who watched was mesmerized by the spectacle, at once majestic and bizarre. Over the waters of Egypt's Great Bitter Lake, an American destroyer, the USS Murphy, steamed toward a rendezvous with history. On a deck covered with colorful carpets and shaded by an enormous tent of brown canvas, a large black-bearded man in Arab robes, his headdress bound with golden cords, was seated on a gilded throne. Around him stood an entourage of fierce-looking, dark-skinned barefoot men in similar attire, each with a sword or dagger bound to his waist by a gold-encrusted belt. On the Murphy 's fantail, sheep grazed in a makeshift corral. It was, one American witness said, "a spectacle out of the ancient past on the deck of a modern man-of-war." Awaiting the arrival of this exotic delegation aboard another American warship, the cruiser USS Quincy, were three admirals, several high-ranking U.S. diplomats and the president of the United States, Franklin D. Roosevelt. As they watched in fascination, the man in the throne was hoisted aloft in a bosun's chair and transferred from the Murphy to the Quincy, where he shuffled forward and grasped the president's hand in a firm grip. Thus began the improbable meeting between Roosevelt and the desert potentate with whom of all the world's leaders he had the least in common, King Abdul Aziz ibn Saud of Saudi Arabia. In five intense hours they would bind together the destinies of their two countries and shape the course of events in the Middle East for decades to come.

It was February 14, 1945. The end of World War II was finally in sight as Allied forces advanced on Berlin and fought their way toward the Japanese heartland. With victory assured, Roosevelt was looking toward the future and envisioning new security and economic arrangements for the nation he had led through twelve tumultuous years. He ventured to Yalta, in the Soviet Crimea, to negotiate the postwar world order and the creation of the United Nations with Prime Minister Winston Churchill of Britain and the Soviet leader Josef Stalin. Before leaving Washington, he arranged to stop in Egypt after the Yalta conference for brief meetings with three leaders whose role in the war was marginal but whose place in the future might be significant: King Farouk of Egypt, Emperor Haile Selassie of Ethiopia and King Abdul Aziz, then commonly known as Ibn Saud.

That Roosevelt included Abdul Aziz on his list was a dramatic demonstration of how far and how rapidly American strategic thinking about the Gulf region had evolved during the war. Before 1942, the U.S. government had no official interest in Saudi Arabia, even though an American oil company had struck oil there in 1938 and had created a small community of American geologists, drillers and engineers to deliver the oil to global markets. No American official of higher rank than minister in the diplomatic service had ever before encountered the bedouin monarch, and the king, in all his 64 years, had ventured no further out of the Arabian peninsula than Basra, in southern Iraq. His domain was impoverished, isolated and backward; its levels of education, public health and mechanization were among the lowest in the world.

In strategic terms, Saudi Arabia, though never colonized, was in the British sphere of influence; the British were entrenched in Iraq, Bahrain,

Oman and the trucial states on the Arab side of the gulf, as well as in Egypt and Palestine. The U.S. official presence was minimal in the entire Arab world, and so was official U.S. interest. In 1941, Roosevelt rejected State Department advice to provide financial assistance to Saudi Arabia under the Lend-Lease program with the comment, "This is a little far afield for us!" The war changed all that almost overnight.

Roosevelt's military and economic advisers, alarmed by the rate at which the war was consuming U.S. domestic petroleum, began to see the potential long-term value of the Saudi fields, the only ones in the Middle East where an American company held exclusive production rights. At the same time the U.S. Armed Forces, fighting a global war, wanted an air base someplace in the Middle East that was not under British or French control. And Roosevelt, looking past the combat, nursed the hope that Abdul Aziz, who despite his lack of formal education and his country's backwardness was a hero in the Arab world, would somehow be helpful in solving a daunting problem that the president knew was coming: the future of Palestine and the resettlement of Europe's surviving Jews. The Nazi death camp at Auschwitz had been liberated a month before the president left Washington en route to Yalta, and the full scope of the Holocaust was being revealed to the world. The Jews had a claim on the world's conscience, and on Roosevelt's.

The United States established diplomatic relations with Saudi Arabia in 1939, but no American diplomat resided in the kingdom; Saudi Arabia was the responsibility of the U.S. minister to Egypt, who lived in Cairo and rarely ventured into the Arabian peninsula. The Saudi Arabian government, which consisted of the king and handful of his favorite sons and trusted advisers, had no representative in Washington; when Abdul Aziz wanted to conduct business with the United States, he did so through the oil company, Standard Oil Company of California, known in Saudi Arabia as CASOC. (In 1944 the name was changed to Arabian American Oil Co., or Aramco.)

Only in April 1942 did the State Department post its first resident envoy to Jeddah, a career officer named James Moose. At that time Saudi Arabia was paradoxically more isolated and poverty stricken than ever because the outbreak of the war had shut off its oil exports only six months after they began in 1939, and had mostly halted the Mecca pilgrimage traffic that still represented the Kingdom's principal source of revenue. As the war dragged on, Saudi Arabia was experiencing serious food shortages, and CASOC increasingly urged Washington to provide assistance lest the king revoke the concession and give it to the British, who were providing him with financial assistance. British interests had opposed American oil companies' entry into Iran, Kuwait, Iraq, and Bahrain; the British lost out on Saudi Arabia when King Abdul Aziz chose the American firm, but the king could reverse himself at any time. Busy as he was with more urgent issues, Roosevelt was still flexible and perceptive enough to include Saudi Arabia in his long-term thinking.

The entreaties of the oil company paid off in February 1943. At the urging of Harold Ickes, Secretary of the Interior and wartime oil administrator, Roosevelt declared Saudi Arabia vital to the defense of the United States and therefore eligible for financial aid. As the British journalist David Holden wrote in his history of Saudi Arabia, "The great American takeover had begun."

Official contacts between the United States and Saudi Arabia now multiplied quickly, at steadily higher levels. In July, Roosevelt sent Lt. Col. Harold B. Hoskins, an Arabic-speaking intelligence agent, to ask the king if he would meet with Chaim Weizmann or other Zionist leaders to discuss the plight of the Jews and the future of Palestine. Hoskins was well received personally but got nowhere with the king, a committed anti-Zionist, who told him he would not conduct such talks himself nor authorize others to do so. The issue, however, could not be brushed aside or wished away. The stranded, traumatized Jewish survivors in Europe were clamoring for resettlement; their plight had reinforced the determination of Zionists in the United States to create a Jewish state in Palestine.

In August, Secretary of State Cordell Hull instructed Moose to ask the king for permission for the United States to open a consulate in Dhahran, the little American settlement on the oil fields along the Gulf Coast. Permission was granted the following year. At about the same time, the U.S. mission in Jeddah was upgraded to legation and Moose was replaced by a higher-ranking official, a colorful U.S. Marine war hero named William A. Eddy. Col. Eddy, who wore his Marine Corps uniform all the time he was the State Department's representative in Saudi Arabia, was to be a crucial figure in bringing the president and king together for a successful encounter.

In September 1943, two of Abdul Aziz's sons, Princes Faisal and Khalid—both future kings—were invited to Washington and were well-treated. Vice President Harry Truman put on a dinner for them at the White House. They stayed at Blair House, the official government guest house, and were provided with a special train to carry them on a sightseeing trip to the West Coast. Upon their return home, they reported favorably to their father, and also informed him that they had been told President Roosevelt enjoyed collecting stamps. That gave the king an opening to approach the president directly. He sent the president a set of Saudi Arabian stamps, then quite rare in the West.

On February 10, 1944, Roosevelt sent the king a letter thanking him for the stamps. He expressed regret that he had been unable to meet the king during a recent trip to Cairo and Tehran—a trip on which he flew over part of Saudi Arabia and conceived the idea of bringing irrigation and agriculture to the region's vast deserts—and expressed the hope of meeting Abdul Aziz on some future journey. "There are many things I want to talk to you about," the president said.

The king took this as a commitment from the president to visit, and began asking Moose when he could expect Roosevelt's arrival. The president's journey to Yalta was to provide the opportunity. Moose, by then back in Washington, claimed credit for persuading Roosevelt to meet Abdul Aziz on the Yalta journey; the president's cousin, Archie Roosevelt, wrote in his memoirs that Moose had "buttonholed everyone in State concerned with the president's trip" and when the professional diplomats were not responsive "he got someone to send a memo to the White House, and when it reached the president, he jumped at the chance for this exotic encounter." From the historical record, however, it seems that Roosevelt did not need much persuasion. He was genuinely interested in Saudi Arabia.

On February 3, 1945, acting secretary of state Joseph C. Grew cabled Eddy and the U.S. representatives in Cairo and Addis Ababa that the president wanted to see the three leaders "on board a United States man of war at Ismailia about February 10"—that is, only a week or so later. Grew's message sent off a frantic scramble to make arrangements, complicated by the need to maintain secrecy about the president's itinerary.

The president would travel to the Mediterranean aboard the Quincy, fly from Malta to the Crimea for his historic meeting with Churchill and Stalin, then reboard the Quincy in Egyptian waters for his encounters with Farouk, Haile Selassie and Abdul Aziz. The Navy's Destroyer Squadron 17, which had been on convoy duty in the Atlantic, was detached to escort the Quincy. That was the easy part of the arrangements. The hard part was delivering King Abdul Aziz and his entourage, who knew no way of life other than their own and took for granted that their habits, diets and religious practices would travel with them. Roosevelt was a wealthy, educated patrician with a sophisticated knowledge of the world; Abdul Aziz was a semi-literate desert potentate whose people knew nothing of plumbing or electricity. Yet the Saudis assumed—rightly, as it turned out—that the two leaders would meet on equal terms; Abdul Aziz would accept nothing less.

The story of how this amazing feat of diplomacy and cultural accommodation was accomplished is told principally in the accounts of three participants: a brief narrative by Eddy, "F.D.R Meets ibn Saud," published in 1954; "Mission to Mecca: The Cruise of the Murphy," a 1976 magazine article by U.S. Navy Captain John S. Keating, commander of Destroyer Squadron 17, who was aboard the destroyer; and "White House Sailor," a memoir by William M. Rigdon, who was Roosevelt's naval aide at the time. The key figure in the preparations was Eddy, who had been born in Lebanon and was fluent in Arabic. Having won the king's confidence and friendship during his first months as U.S. minister in Jeddah, Eddy was the cultural mediator between the two sides.

The plan called for the king and his advisers to travel overland from Riyadh to Jeddah and board the Murphy for the voyage up the Red Sea to Egypt. Because of wartime security restrictions, the entire plan was kept secret from Jeddah's small diplomatic corps and from the Arabian populace. Eddy accepted social invitations knowing he would not be attending the events; the king put out the word that his caravan was heading for Mecca. When instead he boarded the Murphy and sailed away, there was consternation and grief among the people, who feared he had abdicated or been kidnapped.

Knowing nothing about the king, his country or his habits, Keating and the Murphy's skipper, Commander Bernard A. Smith were understandably nervous about protocol and worried about how their crew would behave; because of the secrecy requirements, they had not been told that Eddy would accompany the Arab party and navigate these issues for them. Their only information came from an encyclopedia, which informed them that the king had many wives and scores of children, and that the consumption of alcohol and tobacco were forbidden in his presence. Their only chart of the Jeddah harbor dated to 1834; no U.S. Navy ship had ever put in there. The Americans knew that Islam prohibited the consumption of pork and that the king liked to eat lamb, but otherwise they knew nothing of his dietary preferences.

The Saudis said the traveling party would consist of 200 people, including some of the king's wives. Smith said the most the Murphy could accommodate was 10. Eddy negotiated the number down to 20, although when the king and his party arrived at the pier there were 48, including the king's brother Abdullah; two of his sons, Mohammed and Mansour; his wily finance minister, Abdullah Suleiman, who had negotiated the oil concession agreement with Standard Oil a decade earlier; and the royal astrologer. It also fell to Eddy to explain to the king's advisers why no women could make the voyage: there was no place aboard the Murphy where they could be sequestered, and they would be exposed to prying male eyes as they negotiated the gangways.

Abdul Aziz spurned the cabin designated as his quarters aboard the Murphy; he and his 39 companions insisted on sleeping outdoors, bedding down where they could around the deck. Because of the king's foot and leg ailments, he could not walk easily on steel, so his retainers spread carpets. The Arabs rejected the sturdy chairs from the Murphy's wardroom as inadequate; aboard came the king's high-backed gilt throne, in which the king sat facing the bow at all times except the hours of prayer, when he and his party bowed toward Mecca—the location of which was plotted for them by the ship's navigators. Most of the Arabs had never before seen a motorized vessel or sailed outside coastal waters, and became seasick, but not the king.

Abdul Aziz brought with him a flock of sheep, which he expected would be slaughtered en route for his meals—and which he insisted the American sailors share as his guests. Smith balked at the livestock, but the Arabs said they would not eat the frozen meat of the Murphy's stores. Eddy negotiated another compromise in which 10 sheep were taken aboard and penned at the fantail, and he told the king that Navy regulations prohibited the Murphy's crew from eating any food other than Navy rations. Surely the king would not want these fine young Americans confined to the brig over such an issue?

The king accepted that argument, but other Navy regulations were thrown overboard to accommodate the Arabs. The Saudis built charcoal fires to brew coffee, including one next to an open ammunition storage room, to the Americans' consternation. When the king asked for names of all crew members, Eddy knew he was preparing to give gifts to all of them, and he persuaded Keating and Smith to accept this breach of the rules rather than offend the king by refusing. "Explain to your superiors that it couldn't be helped," Eddy said.

But if any Americans were inclined to ridicule the Arabs or take the king lightly, they were overpowered by his commanding presence and by the determination of Eddy and Keating to deliver him to his meeting with Roosevelt in a positive frame of mind. When Abdul Aziz boarded the Murphy, Keating wrote, "The immediate impression was one of great majesty and dignity. One sensed the presence of extreme power."

The voyage of the Murphy lasted two nights and one full day, during which Abdul Aziz saw his country's Red Sea coastline for the first time. "The voyage was delightful," Eddy wrote later. "The weather for the most part was fine. The sailors were much more impressed and astonished by the Arabs and their ways than the Arabs were by life on the U.S. destroyer. Neither group had seen anything like their opposites before, but the difference is that any such violent break with tradition is news on board a U.S. destroyer; whereas wonders and improbable events are easily accepted by the Arab whether they occur in the Arabian Nights on in real life. The Arab is by nature a fatalist and accepts what comes as a matter of course and a gift from Allah."

The Americans entertained the king with displays of naval gunnery and navigational instruments, in which he displayed a lively interest. The king ate his first apple and discovered the delights of apple pie à la mode. Abdul Aziz saw his first motion picture, a documentary about operations aboard an aircraft carrier. According to Eddy he enjoyed it, but said he was disinclined to allow movies in his country as they would give the people "an appetite for entertainment which might distract them from their religious duties." His fears on this point would have been confirmed had he been aware of what was happening below decks, where others in the Arab party were delightedly watching a bawdy comedy starring Lucille Ball.

Eddy was the only person on board who spoke both languages. And yet, he wrote, "The Arabs and sailors fraternized without words with a success and friendliness which was really astonishing. The sailors showed the Arabs how they did their jobs and even permitted the Arabs to help them; in return the Arabs would permit the sailors to examine their garb and their daggers, and demonstrate by gestures how they are made and for what purposes. The Arabs were particularly puzzled by the Negro mess-boys on board who, they assumed, must be Arabs and to whom they insisted on speaking Arabic since the only Negroes whom they had ever known were those who had been brought to Arabia as slaves many years ago."

With these cultural shoals successfully navigated, the king was delivered safely to the Quincy, where the president was waiting for him. According to Rigdon, who saw the president's briefing book, Roosevelt had been given this information about his guest: "The king's three admitted delights in life are said to be women, prayer, and perfume...His Majesty has much personal charm and great force of character. His rise to power established order in a country having a tradition of lawlessness, and was partly based on astute policy and on well-publicized displays of generosity and severity according to the occasion...Any relaxation of his steadfast opposition to Zionist aims in Palestine would violate his principles...According to Arab and Moslem custom, the women of his family are strictly secluded and, of course, should not be mentioned...To a visitor of ministerial rank, he often makes a facetious offer of an Arab wife, in addition to any wife the visitor may already have."

Once the king was safely aboard the Quincy, he and Roosevelt almost immediately struck a personal rapport by focusing on what they had in common rather than on their obvious differences. As recounted by Eddy, who was the interpreter for both sides, "the king spoke of being the 'twin' brother of the President, in years, in responsibility as Chief of State, and in physical disability. The President said, 'but you are fortunate to still have the use of your legs to take you wherever you choose to go.' The king replied, 'It is you, Mr. President, who are fortunate. My legs grow feebler every year; with your more reliable wheel-chair you are assured that you will arrive.' The President then said, 'I have two of these chairs, which are also twins. Would you accept one as a personal gift from me?' The king said, 'Gratefully. I shall use it daily and always recall affectionately the giver, my great and good friend.'"

The president also bestowed upon the king another gift that would have great long-term implications for the relationship between the two countries: A DC-3 passenger airplane. That aircraft, specially outfitted with a rotating throne that allowed the king always to face Mecca while airborne, stimulated the king's interest in air travel and was later the first plane in the fleet of what would become—after decades of aviation and maintenance training by Americans from Trans World Airlines—the modern Saudi Arabian Airlines.

After this exchange of pleasantries, the king joined the president for lunch. Following Rigdon's direction, the mess stewards served grapefruit, curried lamb, rice and whatever they could scrounge up as condiments—eggs, coconut, chutney, almonds, raisins, green peppers, tomatoes, olives, and pickles. After some hesitation, "His Majesty fell to, taking several servings and eating with visible pleasure," Rigdon recalled.

When it was time for coffee, the king asked Roosevelt if his ceremonial coffee server could do the honors, to which request the president of course assented. The result was Roosevelt's first taste of the cardamom-scented brew served in tiny cups that is ubiquitous in the Arabian peninsula. He took two cups, with apparent enjoyment; only several days later did he tell the crew that he found it "godawful."

So much did King Abdul Aziz enjoy his repast that he stunned his host with an unexpected request: he wanted the cook for himself. "He said the meal was the first he had eaten in a long time that was not followed by digestive disturbance and he would like, if the President would be so generous, to have the cook as a gift," Rigdon wrote in "White House Sailor." The king meant this as a compliment, but there was consternation among the Americans when Eddy translated his request.

"FDR, always a skillful talker in a jam, explained that the cook on the Quincy was under obligation to serve a certain period of time and that the contract with the Navy, or something of the kind, could not be broken," Rigdon recalled. "He was complimented that His Majesty was pleased with the food and regretted so much that he could not grant his request. Perhaps His Majesty would allow us to train one of his cooks?"

After this exchange, the president and the king retired for a substantive conversation. That Roosevelt was able to engage the king in a lively back and forth exchange that went on for nearly four hours was a tribute to his indefatigable will, because he was ill and exhausted. The arduous trip to Yalta and the equally arduous negotiations there had fatally undermined his already fragile health, and by the time he sat down with Abdul Aziz he was only two months from death.

"Throughout this meeting," Eddy observed, "President Roosevelt was in top form as a charming host [and] witty conversationalist, with the spark and light in his eyes and that gracious smile which always won people over to him whenever he talked with them as a friend. However, every now and then I could catch him off guard and see his face in repose. It was ashen in color; the lines were deep; the eyes would fade in helpless fatigue. He was living on his nerve."

The record of what the two leaders said is remarkably skimpy, considering the importance of the event. The meeting attracted little notice in the American press at the time, Roosevelt described it only briefly in his comments to reporters afterward, and the president's report to Congress about the Yalta conference mentioned his post-Yalta meetings only in passing. The lack of interest in the press is not surprising, considering what was happening in the world at the time. Measured against the climactic campaigns of the war in Europe and the Pacific, the president's brief encounter with an obscure potentate from a little-known desert country did not appear to be a compelling story. Moreover, the participants decided that the delicate issues under discussion did not lend themselves to public ventilation, and they kept silent about the details. The U.S. government's official report on the meeting, published in the Department of State Bulletin of February 25, 1945, said only this: "The discussions were in line with the President's desire that the heads of governments throughout the world should get together whenever possible to talk as friends and exchange views in order better to understand the problems of one another." It did not say what views were exchanged.

Various American officials in Roosevelt's traveling party picked up bits and pieces of the conversation afterward, but most of what is known about it comes from two sources: the brief memoir by Eddy, who as interpreter for both sides was the only American other than the president who heard it all, and an official joint memorandum prepared at the time by Eddy and Yusuf Yasin, a Syrian advisor to the king, which became known to the public only when it was declassified 25 years later.

The president led the discussion; as his guest, Abdul Aziz initiated no topics of conversation, waiting to see what Roosevelt wished to discuss and then responding. Eddy's account emphasizes that the king asked for no economic assistance and the subject was not discussed, even though at the time his country was suffering widespread hardship and even famine because the war had cut off its sources of revenue.

Roosevelt came straight to the most urgent point: the plight of the Jews and the future of Palestine, where it was already apparent that the governing mandate bestowed upon Britain by the League of Nations twenty years earlier would come to an end after the war.

"The President asked His Majesty for his advice regarding the problem of Jewish refugees driven from their homes in Europe," according to the joint memorandum. "His majesty replied that in his opinion the Jews should return to live in the lands from which they were driven. The Jews whose homes were completely destroyed and who have no chance of livelihood in their homelands should be given living space in the Axis countries which oppressed them."

Roosevelt said Jews were reluctant to go back to Germany and nurtured a "sentimental" desire to go to Palestine. But the king brushed aside the argument that Europe's surviving Jews might be fearful of returning to their homes: Surely the allies were going to crush the Nazis, break them to the point where they would never again pose a threat, the king said—otherwise, what was the point of the war?

"Make the enemy and the oppressor pay; that is how we Arabs wage war," he said, according to Eddy's narrative. "Amends should be made by the criminal, not by the innocent bystander. What injury have Arabs done to the Jews of Europe? It is the 'Christian' Germans who stole their homes and lives. Let the Germans pay."

The king—from whose country Jews had been expunged during the lifetime of the Prophet Muhammad twelve centuries earlier—said that "the Arabs and the Jews could never cooperate, neither in Palestine nor in any other country. His majesty called attention to the increasing threat to the existence of the Arabs and the crisis which has resulted from continued Jewish immigration and the purchase of land by the Jews. His Majesty further stated that the Arabs would choose to die rather than yield their land to the Jews." The public record contains no indication that the king saw any contradiction between his belief that the Arabs of Palestine would rather die than give up their land and the fact that some of those same Arabs were selling their lands to Jewish buyers.

Charles E. Bohlen, a prominent American diplomat who was a member of Roosevelt's official party, wrote in his memoirs that the king also raised another point about Palestine that is not mentioned in Eddy's account or the joint memorandum. "Ibn Saud gave a long dissertation on the basic attitude of Arabs toward the Jews," Bohlen wrote in "Witness to History." "He denied that there had ever been any conflict between the two branches of the Semitic race in the Middle East. What changed the whole picture was the immigration from Eastern Europe of people who were technically and culturally on a higher level than the Arabs. As a result, King Ibn Saud said, the Arabs had greater difficulty in surviving economically. The fact that these energetic Europeans were Jewish was not the cause of the trouble, he said; it was their superior skills and culture."

Other American officials traveling with Roosevelt said in their various memoirs that the President seemed at first not to understand the rigidity of the king's opposition to further Jewish migration into Palestine, and brought up the matter several more times, eliciting the same negative response. The President then raised an idea he said he had heard from Churchill—resettling the Jews in Libya, which was far larger than Palestine and thinly populated. Abdul Aziz rejected this notion as well, saying it would be unfair to the Muslims of North Africa.

"His Majesty stated that the hope of the Arabs is based upon the word of honor of the Allies and upon the well-known love of justice of the United States," the joint statement reported, "and upon the expectation the United States will support them."

In response to that, Roosevelt gave the king the famous promise that would become the cornerstone of U.S. policy on Palestine for the next two years, until his successor, Harry S Truman, repudiated it by endorsing the partition of Palestine by the United Nations: "The President replied that he wished to assure His Majesty that he would do nothing to assist the Jews against the Arabs and would make no move hostile to the Arab people" and that his government "would make no change in its basic policy in Palestine without full and prior consultation with both Jews and Arabs."

On April 5, just a week before his death, Roosevelt restated that promise in writing. He sent a letter to the king under the salutation "Great and Good Friend" reaffirming the "full consultation" formula and his promise that he "would take no action, in my capacity as Chief of the Executive Branch of this Government, which might prove hostile to the Arab people."

The king was gratified by Roosevelt's promise, but he also made too much of it. As Eddy noted at the time, Abdul Aziz took it as a commitment of the United States, rather than as a personal pledge from its current leader. "In the conversation the king never seemed to distinguish between F.D.R. as a person and as President of the U.S.A.," Eddy noted. "To an absolute as well as a benevolent monarch, the Chief and the State are the same." The king's failure to understand this distinction accounted for his outrage and disappointment when Truman endorsed the postwar partition of Palestine and recognized the new Jewish state there.

Upon his return to Washington, Roosevelt would tell Congress that "On the problem of Arabia, I learned more about that whole problem—the Moslem problem, the Jewish problem—by talking with Ibn Saud for five minutes than I could have learned in the exchange of two or three dozen letters," but he did not specify exactly what it was he had learned. As one of his senior aides observed sarcastically, "The only thing he learned was what everyone already knew—that the Arabs didn't want any more Jews in Palestine."

After giving the king his "full consultation" pledge, Roosevelt broached the idea of an Arab mission to Britain and the United States to press the argument against Zionist aspirations because "many people in America and England are misinformed." The king replied that such a mission might be useful but "more important to him was what the President had just told him concerning his own policy toward the Arab people."

The conversation then turned to Syria and Lebanon, where the Arabs feared a liberated France would seek to reassert control after the war. Abdul Aziz asked what the U.S. position would be "in the event that France should continue to press intolerable demands upon Syria and the Lebanon." Roosevelt replied that France had given him written guarantees that Syria and Lebanon would be granted independence and he intended to hold the French to their promise. "In the event that France should thwart the independence of Syria and the Lebanon," he told the king, "the United States Government would give to Syria and the Lebanon all possible support short of the use of force."

Then the president turned the conversation in another direction entirely. He raised the possibility that Saudi Arabia could develop agriculturally with irrigation and proper farming techniques—the vision that had inspired his interest in the country during his flight over it after the Tehran summit conference in 1943.

The idea was not so far-fetched as it might have sounded at the time. An American team led by the engineer Karl Twitchell had identified areas of the country where irrigation was feasible, and a team dispatched by Aramco was growing useful crops on the royal experimental farm in al-Kharj, where its pumps were pulling up large quantities of water from underground.

"The President spoke of his great interest in farming, stating that he himself was a farmer," according to the joint memorandum. "He emphasized the need for developing water resources, to increase the land under cultivation as well as to turn the wheels which do the country's work. He expressed special interest in irrigation, tree planting and water power which he hoped would be developed after the war in many countries, including the Arab lands. Stating that he liked Arabs, he reminded His Majesty that to increase land under cultivation would decrease the desert and provide living for a larger population of Arabs."

"I am too old to be a farmer," the king replied. "I would be much interested to try it, if I wasn't too old to take it up." He thanked the president for his interest, but added that "He himself could not engage with any enthusiasm for the development of his country's agriculture and public works if this prosperity would be inherited by the Jews." This was little short of paranoia—there were no Jews in Saudi Arabia and none were proposing to go there. There is no record of what Roosevelt said in response, if anything.

It is evident from the accounts of participants and witnesses to this meeting that the American president and the Arabian king, as different as two men could be in language, religion, education and knowledge of the world, liked and admired each other and struck up a personal rapport. Their mutual esteem delivered to Roosevelt one of the most important and least expected outcomes of their encounter: a tactical and strategic victory over Churchill, who hoped to keep Saudi Arabia within Britain's sphere of influence after the war, despite the king's decision a decade earlier to give the oil exploration contract to an American firm.

Churchill was surprised to learn at Yalta that Roosevelt planned to meet with Abdul Aziz after that conference, and in Eddy's words "burned up the wires to his diplomats" to set up a similar encounter for himself. He got his meeting, and arranged for the king to return to Saudi Arabia aboard a British ship rather than an American one, but the results were counterproductive because the king found Churchill arrogant and disrespectful, on matters great and small.

Whereas Roosevelt had respected the king's wishes and refrained from smoking in his presence, Churchill did the opposite. As he wrote in his memoirs, "If it was the religion of His Majesty to deprive himself of smoking and alcohol I must point out that my rule of life prescribed as an absolutely sacred rite smoking cigars and also drinking alcohol before, after, and if need be during all meals and in the intervals between them." He puffed cigar smoke in the king's face.

On his homeward voyage, the king found the British Navy's food unpalatable and its officers dull; they did not match the Americans' entertaining gunnery displays. And while he was delighted with Roosevelt's gift airplane, he was displeased by the Rolls-Royce automobile he received from Churchill because the steering wheel was on the right. That would have required the king to ride on the driver's left, a position of dishonor, and he never used the car.

Upon Eddy's return to Jeddah, the king summoned him to a private meeting at which, Eddy reported to the State Department, he praised Roosevelt and disparaged Churchill. "The contrast between the President and Mr. Churchill is very great," the king said. "Mr. Churchill speaks deviously, evades understanding [and] changes the subject to avoid commitment, forcing me repeatedly to bring him back to the point. The President seeks understanding in conversations; his effort is to make the two minds meet, to dispel darkness and shed light upon this issue." And the king concluded: "I have never met the equal of the President in character, wisdom, and gentility."

In his report to the State Department about this conversation, Eddy added an important detail about the king's meeting with Roosevelt that was omitted from the joint memorandum. The king asked Roosevelt what he should say to Britons who argued that his country's future lay with them, not with the United States, because America's interest in the region was transitory and would dissipate after the war. He said the British told him they would be responsible for security and international communications in the region and "based on the strength of this argument they seek a priority for Britain in Saudi Arabia. What am I to believe?"

The British had a point; at the time their influence prevailed throughout the Arabian Gulf region, but Roosevelt's vision saw beyond this residual colonialism. He told the king that his "plans for the post-war world envisage a decline of spheres of influence in favor of the Open Door; that the United States hopes the door of Saudi Arabia will be open for her and for other nations, with no monopoly by anyone; for only by free exchange of goods, services and opportunities can prosperity circulate to the advantage of free peoples." That was much more to the king's liking than the British line, for his greatest fear as he opened his country to the foreign technical help he needed was encroachment on Saudi sovereignty and he was suspicious of British designs.

In his audience with Eddy back in Jeddah the following week, the king again brought up his irritation with Churchill, who he said had tried to bully him about Palestine. In his report to Washington, Eddy gave this paraphrase of the king's remarks:

"Mr. Churchill opened the subject confidently wielding the big stick. Great Britain had supported and subsidized me for twenty years, and had made possible the stability of my reign by fending off potential enemies on my frontiers. Since Britain had seen me through difficult days, she is entitled now to request my assistance in the problem of Palestine where a strong Arab leader can restrain fanatical Arab elements, insist on moderation in Arab councils, and effect a realistic compromise with Zionism. Both sides must be prepared to make concessions and he looks to me to help prepare the Arab concessions.

"I replied that, as he well knows, I have made no secret of my friendship and gratitude to Great Britain, a friend I have always been ready to help and I shall always help her and the Allies against their enemies. I told him, how-ever, that what he proposes is not help to Britain or the Allies, but an act of treachery to the Prophet and all believing Muslims which would wipe out my honor and destroy my soul. I could not acquiesce in a compromise with Zionism much less take any initiative. Furthermore, I pointed out, that even in the preposterous event that I were willing to do so, it would not be a favor to Britain, since promotion of Zionism from any quarter must indubitably bring bloodshed, wide-spread disorder in the Arab lands, with certainly no benefit to Britain or anyone else. By this time Mr. Churchill had laid the big stick down.

"In turn I requested assurance that Jewish immigration to Palestine would be stopped. This Mr. Churchill refused to promise, though he assured me that he would oppose any plan of immigration which would drive the Arabs out of Palestine or deprive them of the means of livelihood there. I reminded him that the British and their Allies would be making their own choice between (1) a friendly and peaceful Arab world, and (2) a struggle to the death between Arab and Jew if unreasonable immigration of Jews to Palestine is renewed. In any case, the formula must be one arrived at by and with Arab consent."

However accurate the king's forecast may have been, it was destined to have little impact on events in Palestine because five months later Roosevelt was dead and Churchill had been voted out of office. It would be left to others to decide the fate of Palestine. If anything, the king's entreaties to Roosevelt on this subject had negative results for him, because the president's later comments about how much he had learned from the king stimulated influential American Zionists to redouble their efforts.

Neither the joint memorandum nor Eddy's 1954 account of the meeting, "F.D.R. Meets ibn Saud," contains any specific agreements or commitments by the United States or by Saudi Arabia, yet the impact of their afternoon together was far-reaching.

In the estimation of Colonel Eddy, who knew the Arabs probably better than any other American of his generation:

The Guardian of the Holy Places of Islam, and the nearest we have to a successor to the Caliphs, the Defender of the Muslim Faith and of the Holy Cities of three hundred million people, cemented a friendship with the head of a great Western and Christian nation. This meeting marks the high point of Muslim alliance with the West," he wrote. The people of the Near East, Eddy added, "have hoped and longed for a direct dealing with the U.S.A. without any intervention of a third party. The habits of the past which led us to regard North Africa and the Near East as preserves of Europe were broken at one blow by Mr. Roosevelt when he met the three kings in the Suez Canal in 1945. There were immediate practical results as well, beginning two weeks later when King Abdul Aziz declared war against the Axis powers. Roosevelt and Churchill had told him that doing so was the price of his country's admission to the new United Nations organization that was being formed, but it was not an easy decision for the king. According to H. St. John Philby, his longtime adviser and confidant, "Ibn Saud shrank from the unseemliness, not to say the absurdity, of declaring war on Powers already doomed, with whom his country had no quarrel. Yet in the end he yielded to the diplomatic pressure of his friends; and Saudi Arabia joined the ranks of the belligerent nations in name, if not in fact."

Over the next year or so, the king authorized Aramco to build an export pipeline from Dhahran to the Mediterranean coast to expedite delivery to European markets. He approved an arrangement by which the U.S. Air Force was allowed to operate the air base at Dhahran that the Americans had begun building during the war, and he accepted the deployment of a U.S. military team assigned to train young Saudis in airfield operations and maintenance. As soon as Congress authorized it in 1949, he accepted a full-fledged American military training program. Overcoming his longstanding suspicion of foreigners, he gave Trans World Airlines permission to land at Dhahran on flights from Cairo to Bombay.

And even though Roosevelt died shortly after the meeting, the course he had set of friendship with and assistance to Saudi Arabia continued under Truman. In 1946 the Export-Import Bank lent the Kingdom $10 million for public works and water projects. The U.S. Geological Survey sent a team to look for water and mineral resources. The U.S. diplomatic mission in Jeddah was upgraded to full embassy status. In effect, the strategic and economic partnership that would bind the United States and Saudi Arabia for decades afterward took root and flourished in the aftermath of the landmark meeting of the two countries' leaders.

Roosevelt told his senior advisers after the meeting that Arabs and Jews were on a "collision course" toward war in Palestine and that he planned to meet with congressional leaders back in Washington to seek some new policy that would head it off. He did not succeed before his death two months later, but the strongly favorable impression he had made upon the king of Saudi Arabia limited the damage when that war did break out in 1948. Despite his anger at Truman, the king did not revoke the Aramco concession, terminate the U.S. air base agreement, or take any other action to retaliate against the United States. Under Roosevelt's spell he had cast his lot with the United States, and there it stayed.

THE FLYING CAMEL

In reading what so many have written about the Aramco planes my story was a little different. My Dad was in Kingdom from 1944 in Jiddah and sent to work for early Aramco in 1949. He was in the US and was at Wesley Memorial Hospital for an old wound and met my Mom in 1951. I was born in 1949 and my Mom and Dad had divorced, as they said for "economic reason." Anyhow Mom and Dad fell in love and Dad returned to KSA and Mom and I took the train from Chicago to NYC and boarded a Pan Am Clipper "Flying boat" to Bahrain.

My Dad was waiting along with the Knowles, the Kulpa's and a bunch of others and we went to a hotel and Mom and Dad got married in Bahrain. Then we went by Dhow to Al-Kohbar and drove to Abqaiq. The portable was still on railroad ties with steps and we were right across from where the school was to be built and expanded.

We also flew on the DC-3 s of Aramco with the stopovers except the seating configuration was six rows of two seats and several small cabins like on trains, with fold down beds. I remember actually sleeping on the fold down and then as my family grew I was sleeping on the floor under seat with a blanket. The little cabins had two seats also. So we kids sat on the bunks which when folded out had seat belt to keep us from rolling out of the beds.

I still have in my Aramco collection a tan blanket with Aramco on it. They had brown and blue.

I and my family have certificates of flying around the world on the Pan Am clipper boat ships to many exotic places and I also remember vividly flying on the Aramco "Connie" for at least two trips to the USA from Dhahran.

Jennifer Herbert while riding a horse near Abqaig in later years found an old Aramco B-24 that was WWII issue used by Aramco for oil exploration buried in the sand off and old Abqaiq runway. It has been recovered and is being restored by the Kingdom.

One last story, How many of you remember "The Lady Be Good" bomber found, I belive in the Tripoli desert fully functional and just out of gas. The machine guns still were live and the coffe was supposedly potable. The crew had bailed out and left a rock arrow to point the direction they traveled for help. One was found impacted in the ground with chute still attached. It was thought they were thing they were over water. Amazing enough, one crew member's body was found 27 miles inland in the very heavy dunes by oil explorers years later. Had they walked to the opposite way they were less that seven kilometers from an oil facility and road.

A DATE, THEN A MARRIAGE, THEN ALL HELL BREAKS LOOSE

Hearing from Randa about her escapedes with Vicki Muzika brought back some sneaking out memories I also had with Vicki. We started dating in 9th grade and I saw her as a returning student before her parents left the field and I can relate to the sneaking out bit. One night I went to her house and to her bedroom and knocked on the window.

She answered and we sneak out to her back yard which was dark. We discover puppy love and I really fell for it, and therein lies many adventures best left in the shadows, in particular of Hamilton Hill, rear down slope area....

Anyway I was standing at the window helping her out and didn't notice my feet were tearing her Mom's flowers all to pieces, but you remember our camel boots? Well mine being the size of a camel hoof did a lot of floral rearranging. Anyhow the next day, after sneaking her back in at daylight and knowing I had to go to my first class with Miss Fry, I did pay hardily for these little digressions, but any how I was called out by Mr. Dickerson the vice principal to see my Mom and Mrs. Muzika waiting. We had to go to their house and they matched my hoof prints and I got to replant a lot of what I considered weeds, however Mrs. Muzika considered award winning flowers.

That year Vicki's family left Dhahran and it took me fifteen years later to find her again by Earl Greaves telling me he had seen her at Kent State. I finally found her in a little town in Colorado and ten days later we married. I have another story or two that I had wrote when chat first started, but don't know where they are now. Anyhow one told of our romance which unfortunately ended after a short marriage as she said, "Mike, you still are in love with a fifteen year old cheerleader, and I have changed over the years."

She was right but we had a great 11 months of bliss before reality and the world made the sun go out. None the less, flowers have to this day been a great delight to me when I see real pretty ones. Takes me back to hours of crawling around re-planting what I will never see as flowers.

Such skies and tenderness, never forgotten and never again.

MY BIRTHDAY, OHHH HAPPY DAYS

At 12:01 am, the 16th of May, there rose such a clamor, someone should have taken a hammer.... but I am giving myself credit here. I wrote this in 1996 and since I will be celebrating my birthday I thought Id tell the story again.

It was a wonderful May in 1959. We were living in Ras Tanuara and we always did something to out do each other on ourbirthdays...So, I felt that when I got up that morning, it was PARTY time. Here I was, a stud TEENager, and I knew that it was time to plan the BIG one.

After school, which went quiet for some reason, other than Mr. Goellner hit me with a eraser from the chalk board because I was dropping my pencil repeatedly, trying to peek at something, I dont remember what. Seems they were white tho...anyhow I yelled out "Thats not fair" to which the ever right Mr. Goellner said IN your life, as you know it, Nothing is ever going to be fair . That did it, I bravely shot off my mouth and challenged him to a wrestling match at gym that afternoon. I was a big guy and I knew this old gezzer teacher was going to learn, you dont screw around with a TEENAGER, by golly. The rest of the day was filled with much bravado and how Id kick butt and be a living legend...Gym, somehow that word stills chills me....Miss

Crow was there with the girls class, who were supposed to be playing volleyball and it seemed to me that there were a lot of others around I didnt recognize. I still think Mr. Dickerson bussed in the other districts schools for this World Wrestling Match.

So on to the mat and Mr. Goellner assumed the position, down on all fours, me with one arm on his elbow and the other across his back. He then does something that gave me great cause for some real serious consideration of my wisdom...He put one hand behind his back, grabbed his pants and said With one hand...Some fool, probably Miss Crow, yelled wrestle and BAM!!! I was upside down, shorts around my neck, jock strap to the wind and pinned in a pretzel hold, which gave me room to break wind and die of embarrassment.

To make matters worse, for the next five years, at least once a year I took him on, and lost every time to one hand....

Things rapidly degenerated, Mom had planned a birthday party and so some ten or twelve of us got together at my house and and Mom brought out the cake. Gave Mighty Mike the knife and I went to cut.. I used every way I knew how, wanted to get a chain saw, but to no avail...Mom had made the cake from the foam mattress of a pillow and frosted and decorated it..So much for outsmarting Moms...After that we decided to climb the hedges around our house and chase one another. These hedges were about seven feet tall and three feet wide. Ross Tyler was running, and still claims I pushed him, but off he went into Moms cactus garden..off like a banshee he went around and around the house...Mom trying to tackle him, me in hysterics on top of the hedge and his butt on fire..Finally, after presents and real cake and icecream we all left and I was walking Dick Burgess home when we passed a large penned up area, that ARAMCO had built..

Now you know what that could mean, so over the fence we went...and much to our amazement, there were some fifty cages with all kinds of desert animals. Gazzelles, jackels, large dogs, and a various grouping of others. My immediate thought was this isnt right, so out with the trusty Boy Scout knife I had just gotten for my birthday and I cut holes in all of the fencing and let all of the animals go. Someone sure was pissed as it seemsthese were being made ready to send to a zoo in Riyadh for the King..how wasI to know, put a damn sign up, of course there may have been a no entry sign, but who read all these signs anyway. Would have got clear on this one, but some big mouth friend talked at school the next day and I went round robin to all of the offices of Aramco. I think I had to even apologize to people just coming to Aramco and having just got off the plane.

But, it wasnt quite over.....OH no, I had to go one better..so I called a couple of girls and two guys and we met in the shed out back of my house to play strip poker. Our only knowledge was that every time you got an ace you had to take off something. We boys were smoking cigars and maybe a touch of white. I had mentioned to Mom that the guys and I were going to play cards in the shed, she being an all wise and knowing witch, took all the face cards and aces with out my knowing...So after about four hours, in sweltering evening heat, all still dressed and turning blue from cigar smoke we finally figured out the problem..That was that, we all went home and even now, if I listen carefully I can still hear Mom laughing for hours.....

This birthday, thirty four years later, I toasted Mr.

Gollner in the evening sky, Thanked God for my Mom and Dad, and went to bed, in quiet reflection of my glorious youth....

Thanks Mom, for having me...

POOL HOPPING

When I was a returning student in 1968 there was an incident that I have thought of for years. I have often wondered how I managed to get in so deep by doing nothing, as all know I would never attempt confrontation with Aramco Security.

Seems as if five or six of us decided to do a pool hopping race around Dhahran. Now there weren't a lot of private pools, but we managed to take a phone book and mark the ones we knew about. The idea was to jump the fence, strip down, skinny dip across the pool, dress and dash on to the next pool.

We were going to end up at the main pool at recreation. Well, as one, might expect, bright lad and lassies that we were, no one bothered to actually check and see what, or if these people actually had pools. So off we go and we hit the Lupiens house first, HA!!!!A pool about 20 feet in diameter and five naked Olympic medalists trying to swim it across it and getting all tangled up. With all the confusion of getting dressed a shoe or such got left behind. Tom who was fastest took off up the hill and jumped the next yard hedge. We all followed suit and here was a real pool. Dashing like stalled Dolphins we went across it and lights came on and here we are jumping and dancing for our lives, butt's abare and all and off we go.

By now, someone has called Security and S'aid was hot behind us. We hit two more pools on the hill and started towards 6th street. We knew Polly Robinson had a pool and her house was next. The problem with Polly's pool was that it was tile and slippery. Talk about a ruckus. I do understand that a pair of delicates was found the next day and perhaps we should have realized that we were telling on ourselves as we went around to the drag leading to recreation. One more pool we thought of and over the brick wall down by the Goellners house and the screams of agony were heard in Bahrain like you would not believe. A damn WADING pool??? I am still amazed that no one broke the backs or arms or legs. But we tore it up, that was for sure.

So off we head, now with the lights of Security all around and we are into the game of "starlight, star bright, try to catch us tonight".

Many people never knew that there was a small pool right next door to the Reed girls and we hit it with a vengeance knowing that we were within sight of the big pool at recreation. This pool was about ten feet long and was designed for a person to use as a single lane training pool. What we did know, naked and one after the other we swam it, that the boys were winning. Think a pair of drawers was found at the bottom of the pool the next day.

Suddenly and without warning as we are hopping and jumping around dressing to hit the main pool trucks come from several sides with lights ablaze. We mighty mice caught in the brilliance of their spot lights and bright beams. ZOWIE, we were gone. The girls, being much wiser stayed behind the last fence and snuck home.

We three men of orient bare, headed into the trap of there...ok, so no poet, but we knew no matter what the main pool had to be hit. Over the fence, knocking over the guard house at the gate and whooping like crazed Indians into the pool.

The first shark hit about two minutes later and soon the swarm of feeding frenzy of parents, mad pool owners and Security were upon us. The pool overhead lights are on and here were three are. Rather shamefully in an exposed position and to the merriment of all, many a rude comment on young boys was made. We crawled like a sea turtle on hot sand to the shower room, and there met with Mr. Kieswetter and a few imposing people. We thought we might deny it, but what fools we were to not remember that Mom's always sewed name tags into everything. The evidence was overwhelming and we faced the news of recreation being so far off limits for us for the rest of the summer that we might as well have gone to RT and swam in the gulf.

Best of all, the girls had got home, and when awaked, they looked so innocent and in unison, "Those boys must have stole our things to get us in trouble". I actually heard the skin crack on S'aid's face as he grinned from ear to ear on this one.

So to KK, BB, and another, may you're shorts never be left behind again.

Damm, that was a long summer and my last as a returning student.

A STORY ABOUT
MY FRIEND

I'm not sure when it was…I know the rain and cold were really bad, but we had a swim meet coming up…No, wait a minute, that was another time. It was in reality, hotter that Kennworth engine stacks after a twenty hour drive across the Rub Al'Kahali. And the fools at the school had scheduled a swim meet for all day Thursday. I mean we were all dragging. Hell, the Saluki dogs had to walk slow so as to not step on their tongues it was sooo hot.

"Too damn hot", and so had a little party the night before. Amazing how Mom And Dads just seemed to take off on some weekends. I always thought it was luck, but perhaps knowing me it was their escape. Anyhow, there was a crowd of youngsters there, we being ninth graders and all. I remember that Vicki Muzika, Moe McQuade, Julie Yeager and Pam Leary were all there and Tom Masso and some of us others were setting out to ensure they knew we were "Gods".

Anyhow, that night was legendary for the amount of brown and white that went down, but the girls were only interested in the latest batch of 45's brought back from long leave by Sissy Quick. It wasn't long until the girls reminded us that we had a swim meet the next day. I had practiced with the girls for weeks and was entered in all of the events for ninth graders. The only swimmer even near my outstanding, yet modest ability was Kevin Colgan and some clown named Jeff Yeager.

However, in the girls category, there were two top notch, proud swimmers, Julie and Pam. They were competitors like you have never seen.

OK, so the stage is set. Hot, hung over and woozy we make it to the pool. The girls are lined up behind us and we take our mark, get set, and then, to the great enjoyment of the crowd, Kevin fell in. Not a dive mind you, just a topple. Mr. Goellner wasn't pleased at all and started us again. To this day I am sure That it was either Pam or Julie, or most likely both, as they were behind us. Anyhow, Julie was known for her unbelievable acts and loved a joke. So as we are getting set, she and Pam are edging closer and closer to us. However, we are too far gone and don't catch on. Mr. Goellner blows the start whistle and the girls grab the baggy suit I had on and as I did the perfect belly flop, I lost the suit. Kevin does a perfect racing dive right on top of me and you can hear the hooting and hollering from Julie and Pam in Ras Tanura.

Julie throws my suit to Vicki, who throws it into the deep end and so off I go like a fish. Have you ever tried to put on a suit, swim and not bitch, all under water?

The girls have sat down, unable to stand up. I not only lost, but had to spend ten minutes explaining to Sabistian the life guard that I didn't drop my suit and moon all of Aramco. NO ONE would believe the girls had anything to do with it.

OK, get even time was coming, that was for damn sure. They had these people selling ice cups with crushed ice and flavors, so I got one and had extra blue juice put on it. Revenge is so sweet. I snuck up as the girl's relay was going on, everybody shouting and yelling and no one watching. I grabbed Julie's back of her suit and went to dump the entire icee down her back and she turned on me and yelled so loud that I froze in shock. I did, however, manage to get the icee dropped into my suit, although no one would ever admit to it. So now the crowd has turned around and here I am standing there with blue ice water running down my leg and pooling on the tile. You would think that was enough, but no, not for these gals. They immediately started yelling that Mike Crocker had peed in the pool. Talk about humiliation. I ran like a crazed dog, but not really knowing what to do because of the frozen area and "SPLASH" right into the baby pool and face down. Landed right on top of Mr. Wohlgethan, who proceeded to butt kick me all the way to Rahimia. He was smoking a cigar and I doused him good.

They say all good things come to he who waits. However, the Crockers and Yeagers go way back. It might interest you to know, Billy, that in her future swim meets, Julie held one record after another.

I remember another time in the pool, where I was just minding my own business and here comes the whole bunch, Julie, Vicki, Moe, Janice Cyr and Randa Owens.

As they walked past me, I was standing in the five foot area. They suddenly leapt off the side and do their damndest to drown me. It was a free for all city. They are climbing all over me and trying to dunk me and all of a sudden I hear, loud and clear.."Hey you, you Mr. No Good, you get outta there."

Hours of delicate negations followed with recreation. NO one would believe these girls, who were all perfect angels by then, had jumped me. Something about a reputation I believe. I later learned it was all Julie and Randa's planning.

I remembered a lot of things this past week and the thing I remember the most was that wild laughter and the hee haww of a laugh when ever Julie pulled one off. She was at times more of a menace than I was. Yet I will admit, of all the girls I ever met, Julie had the ability to make everyone have a hell of a good time.

Once when I was a hall monitor and the hall was almost empty, out she and Doral Zadorkin came and slammed at least ten to fifteen steel locker doors. I spent hours telling Mr. Dickerson who it was. Likely story, Crocker…My next safety patrol post was on the south end of the football field, at that time about ten feet from the perimeter fence.

I will tell you something else. Julie had honor and dignity. I don't say this lightly as I am one who has always had a disdain for lessor beings, but Julie Yeager and the entire Yeager family were then, are now and always will be held in the highest esteem by many, many of us.

I wouldn't doubt it for one minute that right now, she is giving another Crocker boy as much of a hard time as she gave his older brother. In fact if I listen…..I can hear the laughter.

God, that blue water was cold…….

Fi'aman'Allah M'hemshaib Julie…

STORY-NEEDLES AND SUCH

Perhaps it was due to Mom being a Nurse, or perhaps it was the initial capitalist beginning to establish itself within me, but immunizations and blood giving were profitable and life threatening to me simultaneously.

I think my brother was about 13 and although we didn't look a lot alike, he being ugly and all, I had conceived a plan that would allow me to make some fa loose and not suffer the needle killers in white. At the time, we got 300 SR for giving blood, but could only go every six weeks, which meant that as a returning student you were limited. My brother, still in school and although now very bright, was easily led astray. Most of the bloodletting was done by three Pakistani Male nurses, or at least I was never able to prove my theory that they were escaped psycho's who loved the draining of small children. Always thought the bottle had a five gallon look to it, rather than a pint.

So I told my brother that he could get 20 SR by just going in and giving a little blood, use my student ID and bring me back the chittie. I therefore sent him in on a Wednesday at 8:00am and he gave a pint, back at 4:30pm, shift change, and gave another. I collected the 600 SR and generously gave him the 20SR. He looked a little weak, but after all, he had the weekend to get up and around. The following week I went in and did it myself after throwing a fit at the Nurse's station about how could I have been there last week, look at me for crying out loud…it was obvious to the American Nurses who had some scorn for their Pakistani counterparts that an error had been made. therefore, I also gave blood, twice, and in a period of five days made a cool 1,200 SR. Less the damn 20SR I had to give up…but hey, sometimes you have to share.

Speaking of sharing brings to light the shots we had to get to leave, once again, like magic I was able to substitute and although he was a little ill for a week, I knew he would survive the double doses….yet, like all good plans of mice and rats, there was a fatal flaw…

Mom was a Nurse and although she normally worked the Saudi side, by chance she was gossiping, how else would she have put it together and thus my defense of heresy, although that too failed. The sky darkened for no reason that day and drums were heard to roll, but I was a brave lad, and had gone on a major shopping spree in Khobar and thus was blissfully unaware that a full confession had been coerced out of my brother, imagine, your own Mother bribing your brother for 5 SR when I had to give him 20SR..I made the mortal mistake, upon returning to the scene of the crime, of first, totally denying the whole thing, then upon hearing that she had paid him, demanding a full refund from my brother, who still looked awful white and pale, but I figured a few hours in the sun would correct that.

Mom figured a few hours in the sun might be good for me, staked out and a Camel fed prune juice standing over me might be a fair description of what her plans were.

Needless to say, I had the full range of shots, and some extra that I think were nothing but sterile water for good measure, yet I seem to recall one of the Pakistani's, who incidently all got in trouble, filing a syringe from a commode, but I'm not real clear on that as I was going in and out of reality what with all the shots, I figured at the time about seventy five…Before this time I never imagined that you could throw a syringe from across the room, or start at a full run and jab like a jousting knight and ride past with a giant grin….

Worse, I had to give up what money was left, my goodies from Khobar were given to my brother and I was once again, inevitably grounded.

To get a shot today requires some form of persuasion, such as a fatal cold or needing a Tetanus shot due to one accident or another.

Another day about "Physicals"……….

418

SUBMARINE

It was very hot the summer of 1960. I lived in House 1-G in Ras Tanuara, and across the street the was a walkway which led to the school. On the left, two blocks was the beach and ergo a story of piracy and daunting do's.

Ross Tyler, and Dick Burgess were my best friends in RT, other than April Harlen and Susan Maloney, from whence I learned spin the Bebsi bottle..However, I digress from the story.(Later perhaps.)

Ross and I and Dick Had been told by somke crazed Aramco adult that right "out there" was a sunken ship, pointing to the whole Persian Gulf,(Yes, youngling's, that's what we called it.)

So we began the plot of building the first submarine so we could go look for this ship. Now we could all swim like fish, Captain Ed having thrown us into the sea at High tide and walked away saying, "swim or drown ". Swim we did.

We found a pile of eight foot long boards and found three old fifty five gallon trash can and started out by getting about twenty gas cans, (Metal Jerry Cans) that we found just laying around, although some seemed attached to big things called trucks.

So, putting the barrels in a row and the laying the boards on them, tying the boards in place with rope we soon had an somewhat cylindrical shaped object, eight feet long. A fifty five gallon drum at each end and one in the middle that we had cut, or hacked out the bottom. Looked very similar to a large bamboo tree lying on the ground. We had hacked out a place in each can and put a diving mask in the holes, for vison ports and a hatch in the top of this thing.

We then tied the jerry cans, now empty(so much for ecology back then) and were using them for flotation devices, with the plan to have one of us out side to open them and let us down a little at a time.. No one though about getting back up...Minor mistake. Now to water proof the whole thing we need to caulk everything. We had this thing on two wagons and so could pull it around and of course Aramco, always wanting to help us young people, had left a tar box going and had gone to prayer call or something... So we used the ladle and poured hot tar over this whole thing, being very careful to pour it in every crack and along every seem. Sealed up the diving masks, and chewed Tar "tobaccy" while we worked..Supposed to be real good to clean your teeth...

Finally we were ready..and off to the beach we went. We got stuck constantly in the sand, and I'm sure little boys weren't supposed to use, much less know such language, but we finally did it and got into the water.

Would you believe it, it floated....So in we climbed and Ross started letting the water into the jerry cans...well, tar doesn't hold well and soon emergency klaxons were going, bells ringing and crash dive was the word for the day...

We went straight to the bottom and fast. Both Dick and I were amazed that it had worked, until we realized we were underwater and filing up fast. One other little fact had slipped our minds, what air ?

So, we managed to get the hatch open, Ross outside diving down and pulling and us pushing. We got out and fortunately we were only about thirty feet from shore...another twenty feet and we would have been at the drop off and most likely would still be there.

Now here we are, on the beach, and covered in tar...do you remember how parents took great delight when you messed up and they had the pleasure of making it worse by "helping you".

Well, going to school the next day, Bald and red from the scrubbing to get the tar off, no eye lashes or even my pride and joy, one chest hair remained..

To say the least…we paid a hearty price..I do believe that that sub is still out there somewhere and that fish die daily from laughter at our efforts.

Lesson for the day….POOL time !!!

SUMMER JOBS

Talking about summer jobs, I had the pleasure of working in Student recreation with Brent Cleaver and Polly Robinson in 66 and I'm not sue who is 67. $ 2.50 per hour.

The biggest event of the summer were the Dhow trips to Bird island. On this trip we had four Dhows and made it to Bird island fine. Then some fool youngster, don't remember who…Hmmmm was Ted there ? Jumped off the Dhow stern in to about three feet of water.

We had to radio in to ARAMCO and they came and picked up whoever it was..Mark, you might remember. On the way back in the sea got rough and our Dhow started falling apart. Boards and planks were ripping off and floating away.

We finally made it back and 18 of us were sent to the hospital with second degree sunburns from our brilliance.

The only dumber thing that I can remember with this senile mind was in December one year when I believe Peter Pestoni and a bunch snuck into the Dhahran Pool and he dove off the diving board…the pool was empty. The fact he wasn't killed still amazes me today.

Have a lot more, but feebleness is setting in and it's time for my nappy…

THANKSGIVING
MURDER-A STORY

Ok, it had to happen..All these stories about Thanksgiving...So let's set the scene. Dhahran in 1962. Mom had put this big bird in a roasting pan type cooker with a glass top piece you could look into, which was removable.. Huge thing that you could thaw out frozen Turkeys and cook or do whatever. It was sitting on a cabinet in the work room off of the kitchen, where the Maytag washer, with roll top hand cranked water squeezer was. Anyone getting warm on the potential here ?

So My Dad comes home at lunchtime and tells this amazing story about the Fire Chief. Barney Robinson, who was the only professional Fireman there at the time and all the rest were Aramco employee volunteers. Well, it seems as if Barney decided to have a major fire drill and had a very large wooden box moved out to an open area. It was about the size of a small house.

Anyway Barney had poured gas on it and lit this thing. The volunteer's all ran, got the fire trucks and made a rush out to this field to show their skills. Meanwhile, back in Administration, Ned Scardino looks out the window and see a huge fire right about where the Dhahran Stabilizer plant is. He gets in his car, races across camp to find Barney and all the Aramcons standing around while this huge box is blazing like crazy. Ned is beside himself and starts screaming at Barney about how dumb can one person be, to start a huge fire next to the Plant. (I will show you shortly how you can be dumber than this). The fire is spreading and Barney yells at the volunteers to put it out. At this point in time, the world of Aramco came to a complete stop and Barney came close to passing away. The head fireman comes over and quite calmly tell's Ned and Barney, "Sir, we didn't fill the trucks with water. There empty !" Ned was looking for a large rock and when Barney finally got everything put out. That night he found a new job description, from which he retired many years later as. Head Custodian of All Aramco Schools. Ned had his ways....

This all leads to a smaller, but much more significant fire at my house. As was usual, I had a couple of stalwart friends there and we decided to play with this washing machine. Now there was a large red button on top, but had no idea what that was for. I managed to convince TP to put his hand in the rollers and I cranked the handle. Well, to say the least, he wasn't responding well and was kicking and screaming and PP was running in circles yelling "Call 211 "and as is with the best of plans, the fool called "211". The emergency number that rang in all volunteers houses, Security and Administration. That number incidently was to be used for major, major issues only, so the whole town was responding. We, of course knew nothing about this but while TP is screaming bloody murder, he manages to kick the Broiler with the turkey off the cabinet and smashes the glass top and knocks the turkey on the floor. Well, I knew that death was imminent and we had to escape and somehow, I think that with banging his head on the top of the washer he managed to hit the red button which popped open the rollers and he was free. So here's the scene, Turkey on the floor, PP running in circles, TP mad as hell and hand mashed. AND worse, he manages to get his foot into the turkey and is hopping around the kitchen, I can no longer stand up from laughter and suddenly the room went dark. Clouds rolled in and thunder hit all of us. Everybody in town was in our kitchen.

Then, as the airborne say, "Death from above" comes walking up the front sidewalk...Mom ! She really hated it when she got embarrassed, but with great diplomacy and nonchalantly, she took the biggest turkey leg off the floor and smacked me right between the yes and as we ran, to a thunderous round of applause from the gathered Aramcons, heaved the turkey leg and caught PP right in the head knocking him down. This wouldn't have been so bad, but now TP's hand is swelling so off to the Dhahran clinic we go.

Since all is quiet, we head back to my house after rancorous treatment at the clinic, they all knew by then, and plan to quiet our nerves with a little White and pepsi. The house is quiet, It has been several hours and things seem calm. On the stove is a smaller turkey as I guess Dad had got an extra one issued from the commissary. I hadn't talked to Mom yet, but thought I'd have Turkey and a drink and leave town for a week or so, perhaps live off handouts in Khobar or some such. We thought that Mom had simply put the old turkey, salvaged, in the large pan on a low heat setting over two burners. So we pull it off, burnt my hand, who knew about pot holders ? Then proceeded to try cutting a piece of it with TP and PP. Well, PP sets his drink down on the top of the stove and the and in the ensuing struggle to cut part of this really stupid bird, we knock over his drink, right into the open burners and FLASH, the room turns into Dante's inferno. This time we really got panicked and called "211' and TP runs in with a garden hose and soaks the kitchen down.

Well, that night we ate at the Dining Hall. The turkey dinner was great. It was rumored that I would never see another Thanksgiving, but Mom softened up as I played the burn on my hand to the max. Couldn't cut my meat etc.

The final end to the day came as the steward brought around the silver coffee pot and sat it on the table, I being the most gracious host and playing it up as much as I could, brown nosing as fast as I could, seeing as how not one word had been said all day about what I had done. Poured Mom her cup and Dad his and then ended the day by dropping the coffee pot into my brother Kenny's lap. His screams were heard for days they say. It slipped, really....

Ohhh, by the way..I have a silver coffee pot with the Aramco Logo on it's side. Think it was given to me alongside my head, but I do have it still..I'll bring it to the reunion and you can judge for yourself if the slight dent in one side could correspond to a solid head.

HAPPY THANKSGIVING TO YOU ALL

THE BLUE FLAME AND OTHER RECREATIONAL PASTIMES

HI, MIKE:

I'm responding to the invite to view images of the sadiqui process, I'm guessing. I would also be interested to know whether you have a copy of the old Blue Flame publication, as my copy is missing a page. Page 17, to be exact. I would be so appreciative If you could complete my copy.

I'ld also like to complement you on the breadth of your contribution to ABI and the general "returning student" spirit that capped off many of our Saudi experiences. I'll bet that you really didn't fully grasp the extent to which people would respond, as they clearly have, when you started down this road.

We're all better off for it. Thanks.

I have to say, it is a side of you I would not have guessed at. You may or may not recall that we have met before several times in Tempe, as I am a peer of your brother Ken. I remember in particular a ride to the airport from your house in Tempe, and a multi-lane changing maneuver to make an off ramp which labeled you forever in my mind as a law enforcement wild-man extraordinaire, to be viewed somewhat askance. It's nice to add depth to that memory. I look forward to chatting with you in Chandler, should you show. That's about it.

Jim Hubbard

THE GREAT
SCORPION HUNT

Imagine this, a large pool of shallow water, scorpions, pellet guns, great white hunters and plenty of horses. Ok, perhaps it might have been a donkey, but the result was talked about for months and certain young boys had a devil of a time. BUT, what a wild two days...so off to Imhoff we go..Ready?

Once again the intrepid hunters of the great Arabia desert, or Hobby Farm to the less imagination challenged, Tom Painter, Peter Pestoni and Indy himself, yours truly, decided that a great hunting trip to the jungles of Imhoff for the great scorpion hunt. Getting our trusty pellet guns out of camp was easy. I volunteered to do a little practice at home on the slide trombone, so borrowed one from Music class, Mr. Danielson.(This is important.)

We put our guns in the case and out the main gate we went. The Hobby Farm VW bus had a few others, namely Heidi Knott and Mary Barger also. This figures into all this too.

So, we slip past the fence at the Hobby Farm and we are in the wild teeming, and I do mean teeming jungles of Imhoff Gardens..Ohhh, for you youngsters, Imhoff Gardens was the sewage pool that Aramco put out behind the Hobby Farm and due to the large amount of furtilizer Aramco generated was like an oasis with date trees and such. Well, we spread out on one end of the "pond" and starting hunting the little red suckers and shooting everything in sight. Peter goes over to one small inlet of sand that leads out into the pool and is shooting across the water at what he thought was a bird or something, but hits Heidi Knotts horse, which must have stung like all get out and it takes off right across the pool, scaring Pete and last we saw, he was diving head first into the "soup" and the next scene was like from the movies. Horse stomping all over where he went in. Evidently he was fine..a little smelly, but mad as a hornet because he now had to fish around in the muck for his gun. To make it worse, he found it and the rather famous Camel incident happened.

For those that have heard this, sorry, but it was just too much not to tell again. Pete see's a large Camel and several smaller ones and decided that will be his trophy. He shoots and shoots the beast, which these little pellet guns just bounce off the hide and the Camel ignores the whole deal. Well, Pete can't take anymore. First, he is covered head to foot and mad, his gun won't even make a dent in the Camel and we are just rolling on the ground with laughter.

So he runs out into the very soft sand, reaches the camels tail, lifts it up and point black shoots the Camel in a tender spot. That Camels head and hump went straight up off the ground and airborne. The look was on of pure surprise, hate and malignant thoughts. It turns around, snorting and furious and there is Pete. He sees the slight problem he is in and starts running like a madman. There are tears rolling off of us and we can no longer even sit up we hurt so bad. Well, the nightmare becomes reality, the camel starts after Pete and Pete is running like a big dog and going nowhere because of the soft sand.

Tom has wet on himself and I am about to bust when the camel catches Pete and it looks like a terrible stomping going on. Pete moving in and out from under the beast and then the fool runs directly at us. OH my God, we all are gonna get killed so we immediately turn and jump. Yea, you got it… right into the sewage pond. I swear the camel laughed for at least ten minutes while we frantic tried to swim. Try swimming in gooey mud..or, ahhh, err, well anyway it wasn't easy.

After about ten minutes we sneak out and decide to go back to the Hobby Farm and wash off. Heidi laughed so hard she fell off the horse into a hay and dung heap. Mary..well I don't even want to remember the comments made.

So we showered off under the horse wash and got a ride back to camp. Some rather rude comments from the driver about "stink Americanee's".

Remember the trombone case? Well, guess what. Yea, left out in Imhoff and destroyed by a mad camel. Mr. Danielson got the whole story from Heidi, who had a little score to settle I guess and he taught us a new musical tune called "Rapping on the knuckles with a ruler".

Now, one would think that was enough. However at the time they were having a Fair at the King's Road ball field and had some donkeys you could ride and a camel. So guess where we went. I think the camel had got a call about us because as soon as Pete went up to it, it turned and spit right on him, which I thought was fantastic, but while laughing at him and my sides hurting so bad I backed into a donkey that a friend was on. The donkey kicked out a little and I took it right in the back lower area. The kid on the donkey was thrown forward and the Arab leading the donkey had to really lay it on to get his donkey in line, and then smacks Tom across the legs with his coup and Tom is screaming, I'm rolling around sore as heck and Pete is yelling he has been spit on.

Nice ride home in the back of Ned Scardino's car. As a special gift from Aramco Security, we got to shovel that whole field the next day. Can you even begin to guess what fifteen donkeys and two camels can leave when they know who has to clean it up? I was only mildly surprised Ned gave us shovels instead of spoons...

Whoops, over the twenty line limit.. Fi'amama'la Sidigi's!

Subject: The Koran

To: Teresa

The Koran

Just some thoughts...

The Koran is by far the finest work of Classical Arabic prose. For Muslims it is the infallible word of God, a transcript of a tablet preserved in heaven, revealed to the Prophet Mohammed by the Angel Gabriel. Except in the opening verses and some passages in which the Prophet or the Angel speaks in the first person, the speaker throughout is God. God speaks in the first person plural, which changes to the first person singular or the third person singular in the course of the same sentence.

The posthumous son of Abdullah Bin Abdul-Muttalib, of the tribe of Ouraysh, Mohammed was born in Mecca about the year AD 570. His mother died and he was brought up by his grandfather and by his uncle Abu Talib. As a youth he traveled with the caravans and married at the age of twenty-five. He married a woman, a widow, fifteen years his senior. Meanwhile he had acquired a reputation for honesty and wisdom, and HAD COME UNDER the influence of Jewish and Christian teachings.

Long before Mohammed's call, Arabia paganism was showing signs of decay. At the Ka'ba the Meccans were worshipping not only Allah, but also a number of female deities whom they regarded as the daughters of Allah. Among these were Al-Lat, Al-Uzzah and Al-Manat, who represented the Sun, Venus and Fortune. Impressed by the Jewish and Christian monotheism, a number of men known as "banifs" had already rejected idolatry for an ascetic religion of their own.

Mohammed appears to have been influenced by them. It was his habit to retire to the mountains to a cave in order to give himself up to solitary prayer and meditation. According to Muslim tradition, one night during Ramadhan about the year 610 as he was asleep or in a trance the Angel Gabriel came to him and said "Recite!. Mohammed replied, "What shall I recite?" The command from the Angel was repeated three times until the Angel said "Recite in the name of your Lord who created, created man from clots of blood." (Incidently, the word "Koran: in Arabic means "The Recital"). "Recite! Your Lord is the Most Bountiful One, who by the pen taught man what he did not know".

When Mohammed woke up, these words were inscribed upon his heart.

Mohammed, who disclaimed power to perform miracles firmly believed that he was the messenger from God, sent forth to confirm previous scriptures. God had reveled his word to the Jews and Christians through chooser apostles, but they had disobeyed God's commandants and divided themselves into schismatic sects. The Koran accuses the Jews of corrupting the Scriptures and the Christians of worshipping Jesus as the Son of God, although God had commanded then to worship none but Him. Having thus gone astray, they (Jewish/Christians) must be brought back to the right path, to the true religion preached by Abraham. This was Islam…absolute submission or resignation to the will of Allah. It is interesting to note that Islam also is awaiting the return of God's Son.

The Koran preaches the oneness of God and emphasizes divine mercy and forgiveness. God is almighty and all knowing, and though compassionate towards His creatures He is stern in retribution. He enjoins justice and fair dealing, kindness to orphans and widows and charity to the poor.

The most important duties of the Muslim are faith in Allah and His apostle, prayer, almsgiving,fasting, and pilgrimage to the Scared House at Mecca, built by Abraham for worship of the One God.

How all the writing and scrips were passed down I'll save for later, but as a historical note, the body of Abraham was taken from burial in Sini and entombed at the Ka'ba.

You mentioned a coveting of another wife, what about in Christian belief of Basheeba ? Where upon the father sent his son to war, in the front lines to be killed so he could have the wife…quite a similarity.

Terry, I know you are on line only during the week, so I hurried this. I apologize for typo's, but was never very good at typing.

Strange how I feel a bonding with you, which if you were a man, I would not. It might be easier to talk with another same sex person, but I have found that most opposites will be more truthful, for we have nothing to gain by deceits. Not that another woman or man would, but there is something….

As far as being open, I too have scary moments after I push "send", but it only for a moment, and it is only that I don't want to lose what is transpiring.

I sent the photo on to the video people to put on the massive tape of Aramco and Arabia I'm working on, but as soon as I get it back, will send it on. I will also look for my writings on comparisons and send it on.

Would we be as open in a room together ? I don't know, but I bet if we were on an Island, alone and no one coming back for ten days to get us, we would learn to be open and develop a trust, by the very aspect of survival…..

Interesting thought.

I've got to send this now or you won't get it. Let me know if you get it before you go home since I have no way to reach you out of the office.

THE SAUDI EXPERIENCE #1

I guess that many of us have felt various emotions over the years about our time in Aramco's communities. I have had several periods that I think many of you may have experienced.

In my writings I always write the humorous and add in several events, with a little poetic license but today I thought I would address my thoughts about 50 years of the Arabian time slice of my life and what I feel. This is not my normal and perhaps it is because I have been doing a lot of reflecting on my past six year history as the President of the ABI. I am going to do a little as I have time and relive the life of emotions that ran the gamuts of hilarity and rage and sorrow.

As a child I went through a lot of emotional times in particular as I was there very young and lived in Abqaiq before it even had a complete perimeter fence, which gave me a sense of vast freedom and even at a very young age, a feeling of freedom not normally felt by most.

I found that being handicapped meant nothing to the local Saudi kids from the vegetable area next to the school. I found my ex-pat young friends more interested in what we could discover in this amazing horizon of openness. Both physical and metaphysical. Old Aramco discarded trucks, aircraft and drums became bombers of the great war to free the world, trucks became convoys of water for thirsty camels and drums became the hiding places and personal "caves" for many of us. Standing on the wreckage of the old tanker that was half buried outside the Abqaiq North end, I can still see the distant far away land that we had to make it to.

The great B-24 that lay on it's belly near the airstrip, now just a memory, but recently dug up for display. It was Aramco's first flying spotter for potential oil formations. When it landed in Abqaiq it broke it's wheels and was pushed off to the sand. We spent so many hours burning every uncovered part of ourselves on the hot metal that I am sure our parents thought, and may still think we were sun addled. I even have photos of this bird bringing Santa in the very early years.

The locust plagues that I have written about before and the taste of a fried one..Crispy critter that was for sure. Reminds me of the TV commercial, "Mikey will eat anything".

Perhaps the memory of friends like the Kulpa's, my classmates like the Romines and the Abbott's and so many others I can't even begin to list. I think that is where I found my first life steps and although my Mom always said I took a step off a cliff and must have hit my head a hundred times, I still see Abqaiq as the stepping stone of my life. I remember the great schmal that took paint off cars, blistered legs and frosted almost the entire Aramco fleet's front windshields. The men and women of those days were true action heros.

I remember the school and the building blocks that the Aramco shops had made for the classrooms. They were all colors, a lot of safety yellow I seem to recall and we built mighty forts in the class room. How I still to this day have a blue mark on my hand where I managed to stick myself with an Aramco blue and green with silver lines pencil that most likely had a safety saying about the misuse of pencils. I remember the lukewarm water from the water fountains and the miracle of flush plumbing. I must have flushed a commode at the school one time for an hour. Yes, I know we had these at home, but one has to realize that I was maybe six or seven and some things were wondrous to me.

I remember when a best friend got badly burned at a birthday party and how much he means to me, even today. I think about how we played baseball on the empty sand lots where a portable was to be put. How the sand burned our feet as we ran for the base. How a bat took most of Mike Reagan's teeth one hot afternoon. How sad it was when his Dad became one, if not the first American civilian advisor killed in the Viet Nam action. His jeep hit a mine as they were building a runway for relief supplies. This so long ago, but his smile still makes me grin. His Mother, still a lifelong family friend used to tell me, "I see your face cracking. It's not made of cement" when ever I pouted. Which, due to my actions was a lot back then. How wonderful it was to dash behind the water truck as it wet down the sand roads. How we would stand along the road at intervals and pretend to be shrubs and the Saudi's who were watering them from the truck would spray us as if we were little shrubs. They were paved eventually, I know.

How my Mom would go out to the alley and pick up a telephone that was on a pole and call my Dad. The whole town was on one phone line. But then, the whole town was less than one mile square. And a lot of that was the large pipe yard right in the, middle of the camp. Do you remember climbing into those pipes and sitting in the shade. Pretending they were tunnels? The seemed so big. In fact, for years the playground had a huge section of pipe half buried that we would crawl through. The swings were huge "a" frame shop built and the slide was even built from pipe and siding. Aramco shops were the makers of magic. I remember a girl named April and the tetter totters at the side of the school. She jumped off as I was at the high part. Quite a butt bumper.

How many know that the Kenworth fleet that was there in 1949 has several that are still running. Many were replaced but the shops built parts and in fact, I believe they rebuilt entire trucks. What about the taste and smell of oleanders?

I leave today with the sound of the noon whistle. I have to get home for lunch. My Dad will be waiting..........

THE STORY

O K, here it is. You must understand that, while Mike C and I spoke briefly at Houston in 95, we had not had the chance to spend any "quality" time together since the summer of '69. This incident occurred when I went to visit our exalted leader in February, while I was rewriting the Bylaws. I wanted to get face to face with Mike to get a better feel for where we had been as an organization, and where we wanted to go, and what the BL's should accomplish. We spent the afternoon in Denny's like coffee shop, then went to dinner that evening. This is a true story! And, Mike, the clamor to re-release this story was just too great to ignore. Like I needed prodding, right??

It begins with a bit of scene setting e-mail:

\>>

DRG referring to something concerning her in the BLs and the fact that MRC and I were meeting:

I am telling you this has to stop—but it doesn't matter because the two Mikes are planning away—I am going to take the position that I don't care anymore.

MJP: The King is dead; long live the King.

You can take that position, but no one will believe it

DRG referencing Mike's then upcoming trip to the Old Country:***** If you are going to be over there for 30 days they surely will find some reason to behead you.

MJP: There was a preemptive strike by a Saudi headman disguised as a mentally disturbed bag lady in a coffee shop in Nutcan'ttouchus, TX .

MRC trying to preempt my telling of the incident:....and under no circumstances believe anything MJP say's about his visit.. We are heading out for Mexican and more work.

MJP: Believe it!!

DRG to MRC: Thought you didn't like Mexican. What are you two working on—another ABI or something equally as dull?

MRC: Rewriting entire bylaws.... I don't like Mex, he does and he is guest in Bedu's home..So...

MJP: Yeah! MC doesn't like Mexican so much that the proprietor of the MEXICAN (not Chinese, not French, not Italian, but MMEEXXIICCAANN restaurant greeted us like Mike is in there three times a week! And then he orders fajitas for two. I lean over, slap him, and request that he kindly order only for himself. He says, "I did." TRUE STORY; fajitas for two!! and a DIET Coke. Hah!!

MRC still in preemptory mode: I will detail his "woman" he forced me to have to deal with at the local coffee shop later.. Hee, Hee, he is at Hotel and I'm changing and preparing for his remarks ahead of time..

>>

DRG: "His" woman or "this" woman—you guys and your typos. What have you done now?

MJP: He meant "his" woman, referring to mine. This man lives in denial. But you won't believe the story about this woman. See below.

Anyway, I'm sitting in this coffee shop with MRC, telling' 30 years of lies, and going over the BLs. Up walks this lady dressed in (you must mentally envision this) a purple ski cap, pink down, thigh-length ski type jacket, baggy calf-length flower print dress sorta thing, under which she had spandex flower print (different print of course) pants, and over-the-ankle Tweety-pie boots. So, obviously,

I figure her to be one MRC's regular lady friends. She starts at MRC wanting him to contact Child Protective Services and tell them that Mr. Mungerson from Evanston, IL was murdered and to not try to pin it on her, and so and so needs to be institutionalized and no, dammit, she's not paranoid, it was that jerk lawyer in the Mundeline County Courtroom, you know, the art therapist.

And MRC is nodding politely, (and I'm taking notes 'cuz this is just TOOO good. Mike offers to call the cops for her. NO! I know the cops' phone number if I want them!! She walks away, and MRC puts on this act like he doesn't know this lady. Of course, after hearing her speak, I know for sure she's one of MRC's babes. You just don't get as screwed up as this lady without having met Mr. Cracker!! Oh but MRC still isn't letting on that she's a lover of his. So I call him on it. Right out! no mamby pamby stuff, I ask him straight, "Now, Mike, I suppose you're going to try to tell me you don't know this woman!?" He's turning red, and all he can mutter is "DJRBRBRG", and something that sounded like, "MJRBRBRP." I knew I had him then! The lady came back three more times.

Talking about the old Mayor Daly (Chicago), the Kennedy's and she was a sex therapist on La Salle St. in Chicago. She goes by Carol Adams but used to be Lynn Taylor. Bill Mitchell lives better than she does (near as I can tell, she thinks Bill murdered Mr. Mungerson. Someone is trying to steal her identity. She's not "..just some little old lady from Dubuque, don't ya know! And some lady is trying to sexually abuse her. She doesn't let anybody touch her lower abdomen, or her "chakra". I've never heard if that before).

Now, I ask you, does this not sound like an MRC bimbo? He lever let on.

But seriously, this lady had problems, but by the way she spoke, somewhere in her background was a hell of an education! Very articulate and well versed. It's just that her verses don't all rhyme.

Life is never dull around MRC.

MJP

Re: To Mike C

At 10:13 PM 4/2/98 -0600, Alva Bryan wrote:

Hi there, never met you but I have just one of many questions, who and where are your parents? Are they in an asylumn somewhere? I'm sure you were a very challenging child (just the kind I like) I ascribe to the saying, "insanity is hereditary, you get it from your kids" Mine call me imature, THANK GOD

By the way, am a retired school teacher, loved Every (almost) day of it.

ANSWER TO THE ABOVE.

Mom and Dad were just released after many years of solitary confinement to the Aramco Betty Ford Clinic. This clinc is designed to allow parents of outstanding, wonderful children to be able to stand the community pressures of famous sons.

My favorite school teacher was Bill Goellner, who was truly an inspiration to me. I know that I was told here recently by a fellow classmate of mine, "I just talked with Miss X and Mrs. Y who had you as a student in 1965 and in 1995 they still claimed you were incorriagable." Now I ask you..is that a fair and impartial teaching process. Why, even now my two Mom's, DRG and SO (Both Brats) and my actual Mom,(if she can find papers to prove it as I am demanding proof that I came from such nice people) tell me all the time to "Strighten up and walk a narrow road".

I, mean, what's a Brat to do??

Humbly (HA!)

Mike Crocker (DH65) AND for causing me such grief, I'm sending out another repeat story so you can all suffer some more from my activities... Ho Ho Ho HO ;>

TOO DUMB TO BE TRUE, BUT IT IS....

Seems as if several young men, bold and true decided to go on a expedition. We thought it would be just a stroll in the park to hike out to Imhoff Gardens and due a little scorpion hunting with our Diana pellet guns. Now as many may remember, guns of most kinds were a no-no for Aramco, although in the very early years, hunting was encouraged.

I know that Peter Pestoni, and Tom Masso, myself and several others went to the fence by the Barger's house on the hill and crawled under a section that was loose. We knew we would be back before sunset and it was only a short walk. Well, a short walk is from the door of my house to a taxi as far as I'm concerned. This turned into a day of infamy as we walked for what seemed like hours and finally reached the blacktop road that led to the Rolling Hill Gulf course, which was half way to Khobar. I had long since tried to shoot to kill both Tom and Peter. The other guy was Tom Painter as I now recall and I think he did shoot Peter.

Anyhow, we went up to the snack bar at the gulf course and had about fifty gallons of Bebsi and then played the one armed bandits that had come from the enlisted men's club at the Dhahran USAF base. Didn't win anything and the guy working there had already called security, which we didn't know. We did however, see them turning off the Dhahran to Khobar road and we hastily made our way to the Hobby Farm, cut thru it and after throwing some horse apples at each other, darted into the Gardens of Paradise. Nobody, and I mean nobody, told me or any of us that Imhoff Gardens was not a natural spring. It was the waste plant from Aramco's communities. In others words, indelicate I know, but still a shit pond...

Being as how we were now the French Foreign Legion and the "Lost Patrol" we quickly stripped and dove head first into the water, which for some reason was only a few feet deep. However, that was not a candy bar that Tom Masso ran into and the shrieks and yells startled even the Camels that were wandering around. However I don't think until that day I have ever seen a Camel laugh. These did and quite heartily I might add. We, naked as jaybirds are scrambling for the shore and really, in the proverbial way, covered in shit. As my Mother do delicately put, "Son, you will always be a shit magnet". However on with it, this of course caused us to look for any source of clean water and we saw a big pipe pumping water into another pool that looked clean. Off we went, leaving behind our clothes, but carrying our monster cannons with us. The water was clean and we managed to get most of the offending offal off of us, although I did accuse Peter of adding to it all as the air about him seemed to turn green a lot.

Now Security in the meantime, Naji of course, drove up and found this pile of clothes, but no one around. Since all of our names were marked in these items, they loaded them up and went back to the main gate. This in itself was reason enough to shoot Tom Masso who's whole idea this trip was, but we were not yet aware of our plight. That is until Hedi Knott comes galloping past our little forlorn group and almost fall's off her horse in lifelong shrieks of hysterical laughter, her being older and all. A few minutes later Mary Barger and a few others are coming and we again are running, shiny butts and all for the pools and shrubs and bushes again. Back into the sewer plant to protect our dignity, of which by now was at the level of an ant's butt.

So finally a little peace and quiet. Back to the main pipe and clean up again and we find a group of camels just standing around, not twenty feet out into the sand. Well, we great white hunters, using our artillery open fire. However, camel hide is equivalent to armour plate and they didn't even notice our pitiful attack. This may be because we weren't allowed real pellets and so we had found we could shoot Rice Kripies since they came, courtesy of the commissary quite hard. After all, being on a ship from the USA for four months had a little something to do with the condition of the cereal. I do know that no amount of powdered milk in those days would affect a bowl of Rice Krispies cereal then. Anyhow, and I have told this part before, Peter Pestoni goes out, butt naked and lifts the tail of the big beast and standing about five feet tall, aims and shoots this camel in a delicate spot. We are mesmerized watching this unfold. That camel went two feet in the air, and as we all know they are somewhat temperamental, came down, turned around and although Peter was running like a wild gazelle, he couldn't get a good start in the soft sand and that camel tore him up. The camel stomped him, spit all over him, kicked him around the sand and finally I do believe, relieved itself right on his mangled remains. I had already wet myself laughing so hard we couldn't move and were all setting down on the sand. We suddenly jumped up and took off for the ponds again as were sitting in a ant colony that had decided to attack. No matter how many shots we got off, all of us got bit. But after cleaning up again we went and got Peter. He was in pretty bad condition. Kept asking why his Dad would drive a Kenworth truck over him. We ran for our clothes and lo and behold. Nothing. Now fear and worry about Peter, who had several bad bites, we turned to shear panic. Grabbing some horse blankets and amid great hilarity from the groups washing and getting horses ready we dashed to the golf club house again and had them call Security. They cam and took all of us in and leaving us at the main gate, took Peter to the "C" Clinic.

Strangely enough the guard at the main gate made us stand some distance away and here comes several cars. Mom's and Dad's who, once they see we are ok, go from worry to intense laughter to a hurricane of anger in seconds. I know Mom broke my pellet gun on my butt. I am sure the others all got the same. Peter turned out ok, but had to take shots and to top it all off, we, without realizing all had damn near third degree sunburns. How many of you guys have ever sunburnt a small appendage? Well, I am here to say that there is little that can match what hot water in a shower will do to a badly sunburnt item. I almost blew the shower curtain off and out into the living room, on fire and screaming at the top of my lungs when I notice the tremendous wall of silence. Mom has the Aramco Woman's group in the living room, and her oldest, most valuable son has just dashed in, screaming and holding onto what must have appeared to these ladies not much. The bellicose laughter made me just about die and I ran for the back. Mom put me in vinegar water and I felt I was in heaven. She did however remind me that the backside would be as sore as soon as Dad got home. A great end to a wonderful excursion.

I guess all in all, I did learn two valuable lessons. One, don't ever hunt with idiots, and two, never, and I mean never dive into unmarked waters.

ANOTHER STORY OF RT

Recall all of this, one must travel back to Ras Tanura and about 1959. It was a dead dog day of heat. The oleanders were leaning way over and hiding in each others shade. Even the gulf seem to be panting as the lips of water hit the blazing hot sand. Seemed to boil a little. The asphalt was way out there in rubbery feel and boards had been laid from the school to the recreation area so that pools of hot asphalt wouldn't get all over people. Well, into the oven mom said and chucked the three, as she said, devils, into the Rub Al Khali of our back yard. Dick Burgess, Ross Tyler and myself. White tee shirts and khaki shorts with sandals.

Bad enough we had gotten into her pies for the Woman's Club, but they were so good looking and little fingers had found a little here, a little there, who thought her evil eye would be able to tell. So here we are. RT, August and bored out of our minds. So over to recreation and into the theater.

For those that remember, there were ac ducts under the stage there and we crawled into one. Me, being just a tad bigger, ok, a lot bigger had a hard time and so Dick and Ross pulled me in. This managed to let me lose not only sandals but also baggy khaki shorts. I am sure the recreation guys howled at the little sandals and pants right by the open grille as they closed it up and put the wing nuts back on the covers. Now of course we are in the tunnels and there is light ahead. We crawl towards it and it is getting mighty chilly on my back end when Dick remarks, rather casually, well, the movie is just about over and we can get out thru the theater.

Unfortunately what Dickie had forgot and we never thought of was that the theater on most Friday mornings was used for Catholic church services. So out we come, by now dirty and me in skives. Needless to say we high-tailed it out of the side exit, and I mean high TAILed it out of there. Susan Maloney, being an all time friend made sure plenty of people saw our three dirty tails leaving. A little point and yell I do recall.

We shot over to the school yard and went to play on the slides. Talk about a blistered butt. Mom couldn't have done more damage that I did sliding down the slide when the metal was most likely 500 degree's hot. And of course right into the blazing desert at the foot of the slide made a wonderful impression also.

Do any of you remember walking the hedges? Great thrill to try to stay balanced on top and walk around a block and try to get on the next set by jumping. So jump we did, hedge leans over, we fall into yard. Not just any yard of course, but one of the seven units back yards that was a bachelors quarters. Running in circles trying to find the gate, the two bachelors soaked us with water from a hose and out we went. At least refreshed, but now how to recover the sandals and pants before Mom finds out and we really get heated up.

So back to recreation and Ross sneaks into the office and there are the clothes. Great success all around and promotions for all of us to smart alecks. We dash home and Ross and Dick are playing in the big Acadia tree we had at 1G in RT and here comes Dad from church. He always went and that usually meant that we had to go to a later service in case of any little flare ups of our behavior. He has a funny look and soon I hear that I am not allowed with 10000 feet of anything for at least ten years. Seems as if he was in the church service and had to do some explaining.

The point of this...well when it's too hot outside, find some shade and wait. It only gets hotter.

TOO QUIET

Well, finally got ahold of cps.. the woman claims I *have * to give my last name.. Said as a teacher I was prosecutable.. When I asked her what I would be prosecuted for she just read the law to me.

I have probably made 20 reports and have never been required to give name or anything other than child's name and where they can find her..

I am very angry.. I told the woman I needed her name and that I had never been threatened with prosecution in spite of many reports made!!! She quickly changed her tune, claimed she had not threatened me. ah well.. I keep thinking about PS.. You will have a wonderful time.

CPS has usually asked for names and contact info, but they keep it confidential. I had a case of a false report made to the 800 # on a friend of mine by who she thought was her best friend. It took about a year but I was finally able to unseal the record and under Freedom of Information act got a copy of her complaint. They had whitened out all reference to who complained, but I found one telephone number where they had mised whiting out and filed charges against the complaint for making a false report. I know this is not what you wanted to hear, but I have a problem with people that make "spite" reports just to cause trouble and then hide behind the "confidentiality law". I know you don't fit in that category, but some do.

Now, as far as your case, why didn't you just report it to the school nurse or Principal and let them report it, and make sure they did? That way you don't have direct involvement. I think that you are such a loving and caring person that you upset yourself and cause yourself grief over controllable matters.

I agree 100 % that these animals need to be prosecuted. I once had a woman come up to my police car and tell me she and her son were scared of her husband, who was abusive and drunk. I asked what she meant and she showed me, right there on the street where he had burned her directly on the most sensitive part of her female lower anatomy and then showed me where he had used cigarettes and a coat hanger to beat the child, who was only four. I sent her to the Sheriff's office in the next county and they radioed me a warrant . I went to the house and the guy was sitting in the living room, watching tv and drunk. Right next to him was a 30-30 rifle that when I told him I was there to arrest him for child abuse and spousal abuse and possible attempted murder, he went for the rifle.

I was still young then and gave him every opportunity to drop the weapon, but he fired it and the bullet tore a two inch gash on my side, so I returned fire wounding him and got him arrested. We went to court the very next day, and he pled guilty to the charges and was given one year and one day in county jail because he was a barber and the sheriff wanted free haircuts for his officers and prisoners. I got her to move to another state, which back then I was making $ 700.00 a month, but I paid for her ticket and start up funds. I then charged him with assault on a police officer, pissed off the Sheriff and got him five years in the State Pen.

Amazingly enough, he was released within a year and the "good ole Boys" told him where she was. He went there, she took him back and about eight months later He was charged with Murder for killing her and the child. Had I known then, what I do now, my returned fire, when he shot me, would have been fatal.

One of the five times I was shot or shot at in Police work. The only time I regret not using lethal force.

So I know how you feel….You need a nursery with babies to look after…pays better and none of the BS like you went thru.

Reading the posts about flying and compartments and the Flying Camel and such rang a few bells in this old Baba Crockers mind. Mayhap warning bells, but a loud ringing nonetheless..perhaps due to my mis-adventures, the smack of Mom's hand is still a memory which causes the ringing sound.

TRAVEL AND OTHER ADVENTURES

Reading the posts about flying and compartments and the Flying Camel and such rang a few bells in this old Baba Crockers mind. Mayhap warning bells, but a loud ringing nonetheless. Perhaps due to my mis-adventures, the smack of Mom's hand is still a memory which causes the ringing sound.

Anyhow, to get sailing here, I went to Arabia via the Queen Mary I, or at least as far as England from New York. Now to me, a ship is a wondrous thing, and as I was but a young lad, there was piracy afoot. My Mother will still roll her eyes and I think there is some wishful thinking that perhaps had some of the events turned out different, she might have had a more restful life.

So the weather is really bad, ice on the decks and heavy seas and I decide that I have found that you can get a running start and slide, like skating down the boat deck and catch the rail at the stern and spin around and be able to use the rise and fall of the ship to slide you back. Great sport, Huh ? Mom had forbidden me to even look out a port hole, which actually did open… and now you know where this leads. As soon as they tuned their backs, I folded my brother up in the cabin fold down bed so that he couldn't get out and tell and out like a flash I went. I did learn that ice is awful cold on bare feet, but the thrill of the slide was worth the cold, or so I thought.

They had strung ropes along the deck and away I went. Sliding like the very devil and yelling at the top of my lungs, and then with a terrific rise of the ship, back the other way I shot...well, as most intelligent people would reason, a rope is there for a purpose, but I thought, Ahhhh! The ultimate challenge. Tie the rope around me and risk it all...slide to the edge and guess if I could catch the rail..right ? Well, let me tell you, the idea was great, the execution perfect and the rail missed....As I sailed out off the boat deck, I knew I was a goner..not because I had gone overboard, but because when Mom found out, it was all over anyway. What I didn't know was that I was simply up three decks and the next deck down was longer than the one I was on, so I fell, attached to the rope straight into the ships stern salt water pool. Which was one cold butt freezing experience. I knew it wouldn't stay cold long when Mom found out, but I was just stuck there.. hanging in the pool on a rope when the deck crew saw me and sounded the alarm. Boy, those ships had loud whistles.

Needless to say, they dragged me out and took me to the ships Doctor, where I'm sure the necessity of pouring rubbing alcohol over my feet and rear was not really necessary, however the evil smirk and seemingly same smirk on the crew and Mom and Dad made me think it was a plan or conspiracy. I really think Mom wanted to cut the rope, but my screams of pure torture when my feet started thawing out got to her kind old heart, however, that didn't seem to extend to my rear to which she added insult to injury with a beating that passing ships sent radio questions about to the Queen Mary...whose kindly old Captain simply smiled and enjoyed the below decks slaughter going on in my cabin. All the while my brother having the time of his life watching justice be administered.

As it was, that and finding out that you are not allowed to go on the bridge and push buttons made for a most memorable trip across the pond....

Tomorrow I'll start with the "Flying Gazelle" and England to Dhahran.. That was a trip worth telling about..at least according to official records which recommended dumping excess baggage, me, at 11,000 feet over Cypress...

TRI-D (RT68) STORY

Well, Dhahran was hotter than the old man's kitchen during a double run.
(Which I had already been to several times to bleed off a little high Quality first run to lead some unsuspecting damsel astray.) After all, it was the day of the big event. RT was having their Tri-District Dance and returning students were foaming at the mouth for the Arabian Nights to come. However my day was a camel of a different color...Mom promised it would be a black one if I tried any shenanigans at all, to which I professed complete and total ignorance of any wrongdoing. Hell, it was just 8:00 am !

In my effort to be very cautious hiding the first run from Mom I came close to going to an orphanage. As the geezers know, first run was about 180 proof. I decided that the only safe place to hide it was in the Listerene bottle in my bathroom. As most remember, it was the cure-all for everything. Oral and antiseptic.

So the first disaster of the day raises it's ugly head. Mom sends my brother in to get the Listerene to pour on my little brothers "Ouchie".

This of course, led to a scream that rivaled Freddy Kruger's murder spree and Mom, wanting to know why my brother was stuck on the ceiling of the bathroom took a large swig to show >him it didn't really burn. Talk about flames of hell coming after me. I heard words in languages I know my mother didn't know or speak. All related to termination of her number one son.

My Dad had gone to the office, sadly shaking his head as if he knew beforehand…I believe he thought the walk from our house to the admin. building was one of those thirteen steps up the gallows sort of thing as he had seen how the day started.

However, never to be daunted by a slight ringing of the head from a solid connection of cast iron skillet, I was up and out the door, making the high jump on to my mighty steed, Honda 50 variety. I think Mom thought the "Hi HO Honda awayyyyy" was a bit much as I know that sandal that passed my head of hers had to be by mistake.

As the day wore on I was able to replenish my supply and used an old camel water bag to put it in as I knew what I had planned was going to require a stealth bomber technique. I had proudly announced to my fellow Dhahran Rats that I was taking my Honda, sneaking under the fence and "Hell's Angeling" to RT. They laughed heartily and I thought, "OK, I'll show you".

Two things come to mind from this..One, always carry water and two, don't mess with camels on the road. So off I rode in shorts and tee shirt, sleeping bag and necessary supplies on board. Now shorts in those days meant really baggy things, that tended to blossom up with air and look as if you had on huge water wings, and being bright yellow was for sure a sight to behold. However the worst part was that they had no substance so that I, about 10 kilometers from Dhahran, had a burnt butt that was legendary. Try riding a Honda 50 to Ras Tanura standing up all the way. Up ahead was a brute of an ugly camel, right in the road. Looked a lot like Mom on a better day was the fleeting thought I had. So I figured, hell, I can smack this beast and get it off the road as I go by. "Pay attention in science class Mr. Crocker" was the voice of Mr. Goellner banging in my head…to top it off, the sweaty shorts had stuck to The blistering seat and I was suddenly in the desert, off the RT road in my g-string and that's when the real humiliation came in. The Camel actually tarted laughing. Called others to join in and a rousing good time was had by all including the yellow taxi full of Pakistani's that went by whistling and clapping. I think I heard the word "Maufy Muk, Maufy Muk" several times.

Well, brushing off the dirt, rearranging shorts and brazenly getting back on my steed. I needed a drink, so out comes the water bottle. Remember my scheme? So a hefty swallow. Tasted pretty good, mixed with bebsi and so another. This in about 140 degree heat and no brains at all.

I'm not in the least bit surprised that some say they saw me riding that Harley Honda backwards as I approached RT, but I seem to have foggy memories of the remainder of that trip. I know that due to the liquid pain killer I was not aware I had almost third degree burns on me. I did beat that damn Kennworth bus tho. 'Course I started at 10:00am and it left Dhahran at 4:00pm, but what can I say.

As might be imagined I went straight to the snack bar and drank three days worth of water and then sat inside the lounge area while the preparations for the night's festivities were in progress. Seems they weren't too impressed with my attempts to help out, something about "Leave the damn chair cushions on the chairs and get the———- out of here." So where else.. why the beach naturally. After all, a sizzling butt has the best chance of cure in salt water.

Well, let me tell you a little about sweaty hot,burned,chafed, abrased skin and salt water. You NEVER just run out and dive in without a Skorsky helicopter right above to grab you as you pass the forty foot mark in altitude when your rear explodes from salt and fire effect. Sharks died in the hundreds from rancorous laughter at the fool dragging his rear up and down the beach.

So, enough is enough. I go to the portable that we had selected to get into, who needed keys? I got in and put my supplies in one of the rooms and thanks to a very benevolent Aramco, we had lights, water and blessedly, AC. About seven thirty the whole gang shows up. There are some twenty of us staying in the portable girls and guys. Let me say one thing about coed portables. Hair dryers and curlers are not compatible with tubs of soapy water. Not so dumb as to drop the hair dryer in the water, but those round VERY prickly hair curlers, Yup. you guessed it. Sat right on one and blasted out of the bathroom and right into about six or seven girls that had just arrived. A quick major flushing and >back into the bathroom and slamming the door. Where the heck is that damn Beach towel anyway?

As always, planning on the goal of all young men of bold, I put my suit on under the pants and shirt I was wearing to the Tri-D. Hey, we can all hope for a moonlight swim you know. Got to the dance and seems as if "Rubber Band" or "Leaky Roof Circuit" was playing, but I remember the song. "Paint it Black" and this has significant meaning here shortly. The night was truly magical for all. The patio doors were open and the ocean was breathing quietly on the sand and we were under an umbrella of stars that made one just know they could reach out and "Touch a Falling Star, put in your pocket...".

However, nefarious plans were afoot. Seems as if certain Abqaiquakers were planning on setting off a huge pile of redwing firecrackers in the lounge and making everybody run. I somehow found out about this and with a trusty band, perhaps even the great Peter and Kevin and others found the dump and in the ensuing hassle with the culprits, we managed to set off this huge box of fireworks. Now, paint it black has a new meaning as my face and arms are as black as the night and I'm standing there, smoke pouring out of my ears and who is there...why Security of course. I cannot to this day understand how they thought I was guilty and went to take me to the recreation office when I broke free and ran for the beach. There were a lot of others so I knew I was covered. I quickly gathered my date, who has one big brother and another and ran down the beach screaming, get out of your jeans and into the Gulf we go. We both had our suits on. Now the bad part was that we were quite a ways from the recreation lounge and so we decided to be romantic. This consisted of me spending two hours of relentless debate on the merits and safety of skinny dipping at night. To prove my honorable intentions I said "I'll go first" So with that brilliant statement I stripped down, made a mad dash to the water and did an amazing belly flop. Right into the largest gathering of gooey sticky jellyfish you have ever seen.

I wasn't hurt, but screamed so load from fear of having jumped into the mouth of the creature from the "Black Lagoon" that I drew attention to us by Security. She ran to safety and I was fished out, sorry state and all and amongst the tremendous round of applause and belly splitting laughing from the crowd, I proudly put on my pants and shirt and slunk around the dunes to dig a large hole and hope a sea turtle would lay eggs on me and bury me forever.

However, about an hour later, I was sitting on the beach, alone, brown and bepsi in hand when the shadow of my heart floated across my vision and I saw her again. My Princess was there in all her radiant glory. She smiled and took my hand and in 1968 we walked into history. The stars that night promised me that one day...

So the next day, back in Dhahran, Honda rode in taxi trunk I got home and without warning was attacked by the mad woman of the house. Had I walked into someone else's house? No, Mom had been on the phone repeatedly all night and most of the day about me. I applied to the French Foreign Legion immediately, but they saw Mom and ran. A tongue that would take paint off of moving cars, a human shamal hit me all at once. I went stone cold deaf. A mistake I assure you. As she soon saw what I was doing, and like a thunderclap, her cast iron pan got my full, albeit slightly groggy, mind into focus. How do you stay grounded until your fifth child is raised? I found out.

I lost my Princess that summer and I have taken some liberty with the story, but of all of my escapades in Arabia, the touch of her lips is still right there. I feel her heart nightly and I know that in a corner, somewhere on this earth, hers trembles a little also.

A BAR OF SOAP

I guess that my familiarity with Lava soap came about differently than most of you. Seems as if I went to the Dhahran Library and found a neat book. This had to be about the eighth grade, and we were all just fascinated by how the Government would censor all the magazines with black magic marker or cut out pages. They did this for anything to do with sex, religion and, of course, Israel. Well, wanting to learn new words, and you can guess the direction this is heading, I managed to find the "FORBIDDEN" book of "American Slang" that was kept on the top shelf of those old steel shelves in the library. Well, these shelves were mighty tall, and myself and another young man (now a damn sight further along into geezerhood than I), decided to climb up the book shelf to get this book of wondrous words. As might be expected, we made it up to the top shelf, and it sure seemed like a mile down to the floor, but in so doing we had managed to push a whole section loose and were not aware of it. So, two little boys sitting on the top shelf with the black leather bound book, and we find the meaning for the word "Sexual Intercourse" (polite way of wording this word of wonders). Many years later I was to learn new ways to use this word, but at the time, the definitions of sexual activity was meaningless to us, BUT, the meaning of how to use it to say "Go away !" was very interesting to me. I was always wanting to impress Mr. Dickerson with my language skills.

I should have known there was trouble brewing because the books we were sitting on suddenly shifted and we fell off the shelf along with about three rows of books. I believe I heard the heart attack gasp at the front desk, although to me, piled up in books and still holding the famous reference, I was more concerned with saving it. I quickly shoved it behind some other books as I heard the slap of sandaled feet moving quickly our way. Well, we dashed out the rear door, which led into the then pool hall and as we thought, HIYO SILVER AWAYYYYY!

I understand this book was placed behind the Librarian's counter after this. However, this led to a very strong and stout learning of the phrase "Wash your mouth out with soap", which to me had never made any sense, although I had heard it plenty of times.

The next day at school, Miss Matthews made the lifetime mistake of asking me to explain some long winded diagram of how a sentence was constructed. I, however, was thinking of others things, and wanting to impress her (I needed the grade) I simply said, loud and clear, FU—Off ! Yes, you might say I made an impression. I think the impact was equivalent to the shot heard round the world. I was looking at Miss Matthews, who was white as a sheet, and the clock on the wall above her seemed to have actually stopped. I know that for a few minutes time stood very still. Pandemonium broke loose as those wiser than I headed for the door, or under desks, waiting for her to explode.

Well, off to the office, propelled as if shot from a cannon, pure bewilderment on my face, I knew I would get a reward for my talented grasp of the language. So there we are, in Mr. Dickerson's office, and he says, "What did you say, Mr. Crocker?" So I told him, "FU—OFF !". Well, evidently, Miss Matthews had not told him what I had said, so he took this a little personal, and asked me again and again, and I kept repeating it thinking that's what he wanted to hear. I think of the smack of what some call one hand "Clapping" (described to me later as the distinct sound of one hand smacking a head).

While I am reeling around, totally amazed at this turn of events, the secretary has called my Mom and she has gotten to the school, as the secretary had heard Mr. Dickerson and I going back and forth, louder and louder with the question and answer. SO with Mom there, and me raising cain about being hit for nothing, my Mom tears into Mr. Dickerson thinking I had been smacked for no reason (a thought which, by the way, she never had again and still doesn't).

Mr. Dickerson calls in Mr. Riley and Miss Matthews, and asks me again. So, I told the whole group, including my Mom, to simply, and I thought quite eloquently, "FU—OFF!"

Talk about manure hitting the fan. I think I got spun in a circle from all the hands that smacked me at once. To make a long story worse, when I got home Mom showed me the true meaning of "Washing Out Your Mouth With Soap", and so my lifelong aversion to lava soap began. I think that by the time Dad got home I was on my third bar, and most likely could have blown bubbles from both ends, but the risk seemed a little high.

Apologies were extended to all known family members of all Aramco, I think. Seemed like I did a lot of writing on the chalk board also, something about "Silence is Golden", one million times. What was stranger was that I had to do it in almost every classroom for a few days. Truly a conspiracy I thought.

Remind me to tell the story about the National Geographic and the school library sometime. I have this urge to go brush my teeth.

TRI-D'S

I don't know when the first was, but I know when my favorite was. RT in 1965. The music was terrific and snaking at the Surf room and then on to the beach with a close friend. We walked barefoot in the warm gulf and found a small tide pool about a mile from the Rec. area.

Being young, and having no fear...skinny dipping we did go. Laying in the warm tide pool and looking at the clear sky and sharp stars I think we counted at lesest three shooting stars. Life was good....

Then, like the Terminator a four wheel Suburban with spotlights lit up our exposed(Double entendre) position and Security was there...

Nothing like running to the dunes for protection, but I'm sure that the Security (Back then American) guy was amazed a the flash of derrere he got. To this day I thank him for the courtesy of politely driving off down the beach. Enemy saboteurs we were not...

My friend of that glorious night has left us, but she is one of those bright starts above today.

Viva La Tri-D's

Old and decrepit, with beachy memories,

Mike Crocker

ANOTHER THOUGHT
ABOUT KC,
MY BROTHER

A very hot day, a long day and a day of personal outrage...that was this day 20 years ago today. I guess you have to know how it was.

He was bright and had a lot of promise. Plans that made even the strong shudder with anticapation. His friends numbered in the hundreds and his family had been in Arabia seemingly forever.

He loved Arabia, travelled it's many paths and made first hand film documentaries of the Bedu and the many Arab villages at a time when most would not venture out from the compounds. He spoke Arabic like a bedu born of the sand. Having been born in Dhahran, it seemed only natural he was part of the singing dunes and the whispering oceans of moving sand. He seemed to flow with the balance of a star studed night and the hundreds of shooting stars offset only by the glow of the ever present flares of our home.

He found a life love there, lost one and found another, but yet always remembering the first. He spoke of her often and today I, who did not know them then, call them friend today.

I remember teaching this youngster to swim and later to stand tall for his beliefs. I led him into the desert and rode on Azziza beach on flying stallions with him, all the while seeing that he was growing with the energy of a powerhouse.

He blazed new trails in the land of sand and he knew his destiny. A friend, a pal, and most of all, my brother.

Twenty years ago today, my younger brother "KC" Crocker met with his maker in tradgedy. He was blessed with 21 years of the sands of Arabia and his love of the desert, I am sure contines in the Great Rub'A'Kahli of God's paradise.

May Allah ride the shores of paradise with him forever...

Till I say "Assalamu Alaikum; kif'al'hal?" to him once again when we meet again, this day I shall always honor.

Fi'Ammam'allah KC...In'sh'allah we meet again..

Your oldest brother,

Michael Crocker (DH65)

So it was Valentine's Day...who cared. Yeah, right. 1965, what a year. Ninth grade, big man on campus going steady with Vicki Muzika, a Cheerleader and just knew I had it all together.

Well, Aramco used to have items like candy and flowers and such at the commissary for people to buy for special occasions. At the very least, Al-Khobar had candy, dated years prior, but it was still candy. So I strut into the teen canteen and there with a bunch of others is Vicki. All smiles and just waiting. Sudden insight almost knocked me out and I had five minutes to live knowing full well that she had told everyone I was bound to surprise her, being such a romantic and all..Ah-huh! Surprise was the word when I saw Kevin Colgan give some other girl a BIG box of candy, Drostle's I think.

He had a grin from hell so I knew he had already set the stage for the slaughter. Calmly, with waves of dread I approached the table and then inspiration set upon me like a pack of rabid Saluki's.

I clamly told her in front of the whole group that I had made SPECIAL reservations at the dining hall for a Valentine dinner and a surprise. Then was taking her to the AEA Valentine's dance at the patio, and that I had tickets and we needed to dress up to be allowed in. Now, thinking on my feet, or perhaps with my feet has never been a bright spot for me, but this time I really outdid myself.

With the calm of a brilliant strategist I sat down to her ohh's and ahh's and compliments from her friends, basking in the knowledge that all's well. I learned shortly the meaning of "All's fair in love and war" and "Hell has no demon worse than an embarrassed women in front of her friends". I made a hasty excuse and told her, with a jaunty attitude, "Baby love, I'll be there at seven to pick you up ." Not even knowing that AL Capone was thinking of a garage he could use for his Valentine's Day workout, and never guessing that Vicki must have been related to him.

I rushed madly to the commissary..nothing, not even chicklets. Out the door like an eraged camel in pursuit of a fleeing Arab with water I went.I shot down to Khobar and at the Green Flag store found a large, actually heart shaped box of chocolates. Man, what a break. I never even asked, just paid many riyals and ran to Eve's jewelry to find a gold anything to tape to the chocolates. She liked charms and I found a charm that looked like a flower. Hell, looked to me like a rose. Down to the corner market and looking at vegetables trying to find something that looked like roses... How the hell do you paint a water mellon to look like a dozen roses, such was my mind. Celery painted red?, Yeah that out to work. Heck, she didn't know roses either, or so the brilliant madman thought. "A dozen you say, sure, with the leafy tops if you will..Shukran" and gone like a flash. Time is of the essence. Need to con Dad out of his tickets to AEA's party and then get to the dining hall. Stop at the house, yelled at Mom, "Get my damn coat and pants ironed," forgot who I was talking too, and had to take about a thirty minute break to clear my head, damn cast iron pans were just too hard.

Much sal'lams and down the hall to Dad's dresser. Where is he..he is out, I know he won't mind, so I rifle his wallet, find the tickets and a 50 SR note. Heck, just an advance on my allowance. Shows what panic will do...I didn't know it, but Dad was MC'ing that night and it was a very special night, being Mom and Dads anniversary and my last day on this earth at the same time.

Up to Ali at the Dining Hall.."No Mr. Mike, no have any room tonight. Big bosses party"...Yeah, well Ali, let me tell you about BIG bosses. MY Dad is a VP and he said "Give Mike a table, WITH a candle." I just knew that Mom and Dad weren't going to this event, they nevcr did. Anyone hear "machine gun Kelly" warming up here? SO, table set, candy and charm in hand, clothes a distinct possibility and tickets, cab fare..all set....Heck, it's only 6:30pm, guess I'll go to the pool and cool off. Man what a day.

At the pool I decided to really push my luck and started rough housing in the water with some other "friends" and suddenly, Naji of recreation is there.

"You, outta the pool, my office you nooo good, NOW!" I think Polhemus had run over there and told on me..always wondered about him...

So I'm at the deadline and in his office with a lot of bellyaching on his part, when he gets a call...Ziiiiiiip, out the door and gone like a flash to the taxi station at the theater and home, clothed and grabbed up all, including my "rose" bouquet and off to get Vicki. Her Dad opens the door, see's the roses and has to sit down with tears in his eyes. Not so damn funny I thought. It got worse when Vicki came out in a beautiful dress and her Mother broke up and almost died of laughter over my "flowers". Vicki at least maintained until we were in the taxi and then really spoke her mind..That took the twenty minutes to the Dining Hall and I don't think stopped for four hours. They have the room all decorated and men in suits and fancy silverware, low lights, really nice.

We are seated at one of the long tables with the likes of Mr. Barger, Mr. Scardino, Mr. Dickerson, etc. No problem, hey, it was romantic right? I give Vicki her charm and she suddenly is all smiles and loving, so I give her the big box of candy, just so proud of myself. She opens it and several large rat droppings fall out on the table, along with what may have at one time, say 1944, been candy and her scream is heard in Houhof.... I make for the door while she is throwing this stuff at me and people are flat amazed and stunned.

After getting as far as I could and spending about an hour on bended knees waiting for her to swing the beheading blow, she finally calms down, after such begging from me that anyone has ever heard. I think I may still have remnants of red painted celery stuck somewhere, but that turned out irrelevant.

I get to the AEA dance, slip right in and we are finally together, in love, in Arabia with the brilliant stars of the desert and love and romance every-where, when the gates of hell open and two of the meanest DoberMoms and Dads known to man appear. I know I had to be unconscious for at least an hour it seemed from the initial attack, but I know of no one that can beat the record I set that night of getting licks from the 3rd street pool to the top of sixth street. I think Mom and Dad recruited other parents to hand off to every few steps as I seem to recall most of Dhahran, Abqaiq and RT getting a few licks in. I even think some Arab caravan passing by got in a few.

Well, grounded until 1999, suspended from recreation until some-time in 2010, the laughing stock of Arabia, BUT, due to the charm and my begging, I saved my love and even through it all, when she finally stepped back and looked at it, I had been trying all along to prove my love. SO, I risked life and limb that night to sneak out (yes, I know…total insanity) and went to her window, knocked and when she opened it, I got a great long kiss and a promise of lifelong love.

Happy Valentines Day to all lovers, past and present of the greatest family and person can have…the Brats of Arabia.

Valentines Day-Kiss me baby!

So it was all about love. Valentines Day is fast approaching and as usual. I waited for the best bargain on goodies at the commissary, and of course, there was nothing left. Now I had been to a spin the bottle birthday party the day before and like the other boys, had offered a dozen various and sundry sacrifices and pleadings with the powers above that I not have the bottle end up pointed at me. To this day I won't drink Bebsi in a bottle. Betrayed by a glass monster and then the humiliation of all, the girl asked for a kiss. A "WHAT!" I screamed…"show me Roberts Rules. the Aramco Safety guide, the Boy Scout handbook that shows me I have to, LET ME SEE THE LAW!" A KISS! are you crazy I yell. Held down by gales of wind from the ferocious blast of laughter, I leaned over and tried to kiss her on the cheek.

Think that was going to happen did ya? She grabbed my face and planted one right on my lips. I went slightly dizzy and lightheaded and was finally able to tear loose and yell for a Medic. I knew I was given the kiss of death. KISS A GIRL! WHAT was I doing? She was quite cute and I was only eleven, and with that lip lock. I was so scared that I may have had a small accident in my cut offs..or was just real sweaty. Mom claims I needed to learn about Hammam's and to find one. Not just walk around saying someone had sprayed me with water.

However, the experience seemed to grow on me I begin to think in strange terms about the young lady and so, it being close to Valentines Day, I thought why not. Might just get another head knocker of a lip smacker. My knees already had trouble holding me when I thought about this strange sensation. Soft pillow cushions shaped like lips was my first polite thought later.

I went home and voiced my great concerns about no Valentines at the store and Mom, with the casualness of one who cares not that I am there or in Bahrain comments, "Well, stupid, make one, you managed to tear down most everything else that isn't locked up." She gave me a sheet of red paper and a set of three crayons. "Hey," I complained, "Where are the rest of the colors?". "Well, perhaps you should have thought about that before you unwrapped each one and broke them" was her retort, said with a smirk.

OK, so I had seen that Valentines were supposed to be shaped like a heart and have some sort of poem. Asking Mom was out of the question so I just went and got her cloth cutting shears, which cut things with a funny jagged pattern. No one explained that scissors was what I needed, not pattern cutting shears. Anyhow I managed to get the rough idea, although to the houseboys great delight, I had a slightly off shaped square with a "v" cut at the top. He rounded it out and told me I needed to get some glue and put a cut out fringe or something to hide the numerous cuts. Sitting in a pile of red scraps from several tries, I look around. What can I use for an edge.

Well, there I see it. the dinner table cloth has an edge that is all frilly. Off like a shot and clip, I had about three feet of lace. Little did I know that Grandma's mother's mother had hand made this cloth and it was very difficult to get things like this in Arabia. Aramco only had plastic sheet material for table cloths. So I put this whole thing on the coffee table, made of bamboo and bought in Hong Kong. I glue it all together, table included and try to pick it up. It would have been a sight me carrying the coffee table to her house, but about that time a great schmal came from the North end of the house. The air was so think and the tongue behind it all could have taken the paint off a moving car. My hair was blasted straight back and I know I had a stupid Cheshire cat like grin on my face, which also was losing color rapidly due to the approaching storm, way beyond the greatest recorded storms called Mom. She had her table cloth in her hands.

Grabbing my valentine, with the original poem, "Roses are Red, I made this for you and I'm dead" I shot out the side door and was gone. Looking back, the house seemed to be puffing and huffing from inside, expanding and contracting. I was off to another foot stomping touch o' lips. I just knew this card was a work of art. Now, to make matters even more interesting, Aramco had one of the finest dental sections in the world. They did however seem to think all kids need metal wire bear traps in their mouths. A little thing called "braces". I only had a short piece on my front teeth and why, well, who knows. Perhaps because In Abqaiq I had been smacked in the mouth while playing baseball, but who cared?

I got there and true enough, my card earned me another smoocher. Also earned me a trip with her Dad to the clinic to get our braces separated. A lot of comments about what my mouth was doing where it was, but all in all, a ray of sunlight. The longest kiss on record I thought. In reality, most likely only a few minutes, the dentist seemed to have a lot of experience with this. The Doctor was a little puzzled when he asked me for my home telephone number as he told me he had called to tell my mom what had happened and she had told him that no one by that name lived there. Strange I thought. I used to live there....

By the by, if anyone knows about this story from having been there at the party, I will find where you live. Her name is forever sealed ..with a kiss.

HAPPY VALENTINES DAY

WHITE AND SWIM MEET

WELL, ONCE AGAIN HERE WE GO

It was in July of 1967 and there was going to be a major swim meet the next day, and as returning students, we helped run these thing and judged them.

So the night before at my house a bunch of intrepid dragon slayers decided to have a little party. Mom and Dad were in RT as Dad was on TDY there for the night.

Managing to get the brown and white out, we proceeded to drown what sorrows there were.

I do recall several events which should give you a good example for rug rats to learn so they don't do these type of things.

Tom Mestrezat was in the bathroom trying to break a light bulb that was floating in the commode with the stick part of a plunger, stabbing at it repeatedly and yelled "Ole". With the help and cheering of many, the light bulb won and Tom broke.

I was outside and Kristy Kay made the comment that she could drink me not just under the table, but bury me.....so as a true Knight of the mason jar we sat out four quart bottles, leaned against a brick wall and started. After about an hour of this, we were unable to stand and she said something to the effect she might be getting sick. I, of course, being gallant, said, don't throw up on Mom's plants, put it in my shirt pocket..thought I was just joking..she did just that..From where I lived at House 639, top of sixth street to where she was staying over a Gail Duell's house was about a block. Since I couldn't walk, I got her on my back and on all fours crawled to Gales house..I have never known how badly that messed up my knees until years later in airborne school.

To make the matter end with more punishments, I had to be at the pool the next day, with the most Gawd awful headache, hangover, pain and my arm in a cast and 115 degree weather, where I stayed most of the day.

Then at 4:00 pm Mom and Dad got home.. life changed dramatically at the moment.. remember the clock stopping.

The moral of the story…don't crawl with a woman on your back..I think…

So, as I have my morning beer. I relate this story.

The expression Walid tabib, maufy bookra comes into mind.

Mike 180 Crocker (DH65)

US Representative to the King Abdul Aziz Foundation (Riyadh, KSA)

KING ABDUL AZZIZ RESEARCH FOUNDATION (USA) http:// www.darah.org

President of Aramco Brats, Inc. http://aramco-brats.com

Author-CHILDREN OF THE SAND http://aramco-brats.com (Click on the "Children of the Sand" link on the front page) author-FOREVER FRIENDS BOOK http://forever-friends.org

Video Producer-King Abdul Aziz Ibn Saud-Vol.I

Aramco-Brats Vol. I

Aramco-Brats Vol. II

All Saudi Arabia Vol. I

"All material in this electronic message is confidential and should not be read by any other than the intended recipient. Should you have received this message in error, no permission is granted for any use and the message should be deleted immediately. All materials on any and all of this message, including links, are copyright and trade marked under US Statutes. All materials remain the property of the sender."

YALLAH,
EMSHEEEEEEEEEEEEE !

So it is New Years Eve, 1965...So cold outside that I am dressed for the extreme..shorts, T-shirt, coolie boots and thoughts of a white and brown Christmas and New Years Eve. I had planned to really bring off the party of my young life. Which, according to some un-named family members would get a lot shorter if I dared embarrass them with their murkily muk party, THAT I wasn't invited to..SO, if they didn't want me at the party, then I would have to just see about a party elsewhere.

Since all the Aramco big shots were going to be at Mom and Dads and then up to the AEA New Years Eve dance with some outfit like "Mitch Miller", talk about music..I can still hear a buzzing sound late at night that seems to say, AHHH One and Ahhhh Two and sing along with Mitch...Man, did I ever hear that nonsense forever. Who cared if the rose was red and the wine was red and the hair was red and the...well it went on and on.

So we decided that the only place for our gathering would be at the school gym. I mean we had sound system, a dance floor and we had socks, Oh yes, we had socks and we were ready to "be bop" all night long. Almost everybody was coming and we had a stash of some five gallon jars of white and at least two of brown as I fuzzily recall. Mom and Dad, HA! were they

477

going to be surprised that their booze had turned to vinegar..well, I had to substitute something right ?

Now after the best laid plans of mighty mouse and boys, we overlooked a few technical details. Such as Aramco Security. We had a record player set up on stage and the lights had been set on the light board so that it was barely light in the gym. Wrestling mats were out and some fools, most likely Jeff Yeager and Peter Pestoni had pulled out the big trampoline and unfolded it. We had hooked into the sound system with our brilliant electrician Tom, for which we were to pay dearly later, but at the start, it was looking goooood man!

So shortly, a large number of kids are shaking and a rattling and twisting the night away, all getting heavily under the influence when several started dancing on the trampoline. Now this wasn't so bad, but a lot of wrestling was going on over on the mats, which had been pulled over to the dark side of the moon and suddenly, Tom hits the flood lights, which I think he fell into, and on the trampoline, Eddie was bouncing with a lady was also bouncing into the air and wham, the trampoline folds up. I thought I was going to die of laughter as it looked as if they had been sandwiched. But due to Kristi I was hardly able to move, something about the volume of white I think. anyhow, here is a bunch of clowns all pulling on the trampoline, Tom is pulling all kinds of switches and suddenly the music sounds as if the combined bands of all three districts has marched into the gym due to the extreme volume and suddenly "POW" out goes the lights, sound, and it is dark.

The tramoline is straightened out and flings Eddie and Leah out into the dark, with amazing sound effects and language suitable for the navy. Talk about basketball floor carpet burns, They had some spectacular ones after that.

Suddenly the emergency lights come on and Tom, with the able assistance of at least ten experts, all seeing various colors of wires at the same time manage to get the music going. The unknown, which always seems to bite hardest, was that we had overloaded the local electric grid and blacked out the major part of Dhahran. Including the AEA dance. I still see little balls bouncing along the music from the roundhouse Mom gave me a little later, but not to get to far ahead here.

Suddenly Security is here and everybody is heading out all the doors, I understand the collection of socks, shoes, other garments found in the gym by Aramco was staggering. Anyhow, about thirty of us headed for the recreation area, planning on skinny dipping in the pool and albeit, we were beyond reality with the effects of booming music, a touch of white and brown and a complete loss of sensibilities.

So to the pool, and soon a huge pile of clothes are stacked by the chairs and almost everybody is in the baby pool. In our excellent Bedouin sense of direction, we thought we were in the big pool, but perhaps that had to do with the fact we were by now to the crawling stage. I didn't know one could drown in about five inches of water, but I damn near did when a lady of size sat on me and I went to the bottom.

Now we do the impossible. Several people have made it to the big pool and they are at the shallow end and there looks to only be about a foot or so of water. However, due to the ultimate strategy of showing off, several have decided to see who can do the biggest cannonball off of the board. So of goes Tom Painter and he hits in about five feet of water. I'm not sure if I heard the smack of water or the smack of his butt hitting the bottom, but in either case it was spectacular. However not as bad as yours truly. I mange to crawl out on the board and fall right off the end. Great style according to those that didn't die of laughter and I managed to do a perfect "belly flop". All I know is that there seemed to be problems getting my breath and then, "BLAM" I am hit and sunk by a cannon ball from what had to be a Golding....maybe not, memory fails me at this point.

I just know that as I stood up, in all the naked glory, all of the pool lights come on and the screaming starts and there are Security men and parents everywhere, Hell, we forgot the AEA dance was on the patio about fifty feet from the pool and that the parents and such were trying to move the portable partition walls AEA had set up to see what was happening. Talk about Custer. Here I am in five feet of water, naked and grinning, dead drunk and I slowly fall forward in to the water, hoping a quiet drowning will suffice for Mom and Dad. Yells, of "Y'allah, emsheeeeeee" scream out and" Kill, Kill, Kill" thunders from the crowd,seemingly led from Mom, but I foolishly and with great aplomb start in, "The rose is red, the wine is red", and I distinctly heard Mom and a chorus of others sing, and "Mike is dead" or so it seemed.

Do you have any idea of a death march? Well, the long walk to the shallow end to climb out of the pool with fifty rabid parents, who by now their little darlings have managed to cover their butts and point at me.."He did it" "Kill him, not me Mommy".

Well, it seems the lights did go out, or at least I did. I don't to this day know if it was the booze or Mom. She denies all knowledge, but with a wicked grin....

It was a long night, or perhaps the night of a thousand lights and it seems that each parent, some thirty three thousand or more walked past with a smack or two for me. I think that Kieswetter simply had them circle around for seconds, but eventually I made it to sanctuary. MY beloved home, the place of rest, the safety of family, and in a strange sounding way, my mind was playing tricks for I kept hearing Miss Crow saying, "No Mike, you are not hearing church bells, but "For whom the bells toll". Something that I think the amount of white influenced me. Who would have even considered the lions den to be safe in a normal state of mind. Then to top it off, Mom say's, "since you like to drink so much, here is a large class of our white we served tonight. Drink it or DIE !" Now do you know what white vinegar will do to your insides? You know where I was for almost twenty four hours straight.

So, I brought in the new and almost last year. Now I wish one final thing for each and all of you.

HAPPY NEW YEAR AND PERSONALLY, 1999 is gonna be mighty fine !

YOUR NEAT
TRIP NARRATION

A t 02:56 PM 3/21/97 EST, you wrote:

HI MIKE

I thought I had the ability to tell a story but you are really good. The color, description and obvious love for the venture made your story one could not be put down—I was sad I had to wait several times for the continuation of the low voltage subscription I have. Anyway much gracias senor for a wonderful and nostalgic trip back to the land of our love and the land we affectionately called "Wajid Maufi".

Since I, a creature of neatness, deleted several of the narrations before I realized I wanted them all, wonders if you could send in total the narration to me at my AOL address/ If so it is Boromgr@aol.com—if not is there a way I could get a copy thru the mail? I will fund the postage and handling. My address is 133 Lancaster Ave Oxford, PA 19363. Lastly I would recommend you have some spares at the re-union as there will be a demand for them I can assure you.

You should consider a avocation of writing if your other profession goes awry or you just want to give it a go—you really are good with the pen.

Looking forward to meeting you at the reunion in May

Jon Walker

DH 51

Jon,

Thanks for the compliment.

Mike

Your Trip Diary

Mike -

Tonight I have spent my evening going over tons of mail in my inbox.

Nestled in the stack was your trip diary from Saudi. I can't thank you enough for this diary! It brought tears several times. Your writting is very vivid ! Your opportunity was once in a lifetime—treasure it well ! We lived in Saudi from 1974 to 1990 and it is my home as well.

A part of us is still back there !

Thanks again for writting and sharing your diary!

Many thanks,

Christy Peters Byrd

DH 87

Subject: VISIT TO SAUDI- Final

Then down to the corner two blocks away and to the toy and water ford crystal store. The owner looked at me and grinned a toothless grin and yelled something about "30 years you no buy anything". Over tea and coffee we talked about the old days when I would use my allowance to buy one toy train car each week and how he would always save me one or two. It was a wonderful feeling to have not been forgotten, and treated as if I was just there a few days before.

I am lost and could easily become lost forever, but reality strikes and tomorrow is Rt and Abq. I have also just been informed that Prince Salman Abd Al-Azziz ibn Sa'ud wants to see me in Riyadh and we will have to go back early, so it will be a very quick trip to RT and Abq. tomorrow. Also another Arab dinner planned for 4:00 pm by Aramco so I'll have to hurry.

We left in a driving rain, very unusual for now and went to Ras Tanura. Upon entering the gate, I knew once again I was in for some pretty heady experiences. We went to Jasmine Street, and to my old house, 1G which has now been made into two homes and yet, the old sidewalk leading to the school was still there, although the houses were gone and the area between Jasmine and the school is like a park. I did find two small girls, one older playing in a yard with a hedge right near my old house, and could swear I heard one say to the Other, "Diana, you better stop or I'll tell Mommy", to which the reply of "Erica, you baby, stop whinnying". I did find some old hedge areas and you can see them here. I went to the beach and the view took me away to the days of Captain Ed and Ross Tyler and Dick Burgess and Susan Maloney all playing on the beach. I filled a bottle with beach sand and shells and small lumps of tar for a friend and then proceeded to walk into the Persian(Arabian)Gulf once again after all this time.

The to the school and to the theater and to the surf house. Coffee and Humos at the surf room and down the hall to the library and out on the patio to join the Trd-D in progress, where Kristi Kay, and Allan Lameier and Greg Larson along with Stanly lightle and Cindy Lundy and Judith Mason and Sharon McQuade. Good Golly Miss Molly, it's Randa Owens and Linda Nicholson with Linda Ozment and Marilyn Perrine all dressed to kill and making the boys wait for a dance. The Kay twins and Candy Rines and Donnie Stephens and Peter Nelson were busy doing the twist. I went to the beach and let the sand of my youth slide between my fingers again.

By special permission of the Prince, I was allowed a quick visit to the old Half Moon Bay, nee Coast Guard Station. I cannot began to tell you of the sights and sounds, but perhaps the posts I have read about the singing dunes best explains the magical moment when I stood fifty feet above the water on the top of a dune that merged with the bay and both the water and the sand were in harmony. I really had to sit down on this one....I just couldn't take the Unbelievable memory flashes that were striking like bolts of pure feeling every microsecond.

My heart saw the hot dogs and burgers and the tin foil blowing down the sand. The remains of watermelon everywhere. The sun slowly setting and the Saudi's thinking I had gone stark raving mad as I sat and rocked myself with the tune of the dune and the dance of the water. I could only think of peace and love and dear, dear friends. So many lost and so many forever gone that I knew if I stayed too long, I might just lay back and die right there of emotion.

For a very special lady I buried a photograph of us in a glass mason type jar with some of the Oleander leaves I talked about earlier and a short poem, and a set of miniature rings with our names in Arabic that I had intertwined so that they would last forever. A short poem which I'll relate to you in person one day. We are there forever. The Saudi Military there used a water drill and dug a hole some fifty to eighty feet deep in the heart of the great dune to the North of Half Moon Bay near the salt water injection plant. I know they thought I was crazy, but we will forever move with the singings sands of love in Arabia now.

In my feeble mind I saw all of us there, not one of you was missing and all of you were as it should be. Friends and buddies, lovers and family. Of all the places, Half Moon Bay replenished my soul and showed me God indeed made this land of sand with magic beneath the surface from which each and every one of us has a bond. As hard and violent as my life has been at times, sitting by the site of the old salt water injection plant, I knew I could only love each and every one of you....

The sun was eaten by the water and the evening started to turn cool and so I left, once again, this place of love and spirits.

As we returned to Dhahran, we went to the Saudi Aramco Public Relations office.

Saudi Aramco Public Relations has acknowledged Aramco-Brats, Inc. and we will get a formal letter shortly. They presented me with a full size Saudi Aramco flag and with at least five full length videos and a complete slide presentation. Also the very latest "Aramco and it's world" with content from our very own Jim Mandiville. This will be coming out soon and is a beautiful book.

Saudi Aramco very much wants an affiliation with Aramco-Brats, Inc. and I feel for the poor slob at ASC after these guys get done chewing. The exhibit they have is nothing compared to the collection and video we have, which I have offered to them as a good faith effort to further develop our two organizations friendship and fellowship.

I was planning on another day, but have been summoned back to Riyadh and we leave very shortly. I will continue later....

Well, the day finally happened. His Majesty King Fahd . I was presented with a solid gold Saudi Sword and his thanks and prayers for our group. I also met with several more of the Royal family and received a solid gold short "Jambilya" or dagger. His Majesty is very soft spoken and extremely gentle.

A very devout and religious man. A man of Honor and Dignity, something we can not claim in our President.

I meet tonight with the Minister Dr. Fahd again for agreements about future endeavors and such. Also again in the morning and tomorrow night I leave the Land of sand and Islam and return to the USA.

I hope to be able to finish this narrative as soon as I return, but it is going to need a lot of additional material as my poor mind will remember it all.

The next day we went back to Jedahriyah as my escorts Kahlid insisted we go. How glad I was he made it so. A section I had not seen was open and was a re-creation of a Saudi town as it was. They had rows of small shops, like Rahema and any and all items were being crafted there. Had this not been my last day, I would have bought hundreds of items and most likely spent a fortune in "Collie Boots". Took a lot of photos and hope to get all this on the home page.

Left that night on Saudia, stopped in Jeddah and then long flight home. Would you believe, the one country with the worlds largest oil and gas resources had a flight that ran out of fuel and we had to make an emergency landing in Gander. Snow blowing and -19 degrees...took on fuel and a hour later off to NewYork. Customs loved me, they had a lot of fun going through all the goodies, but ended up not charging me anything or even questioning. They were just fascinated by the Gold sword and other goodies. I did have to pay extra for one bag that weighed in at 104 pounds and I had six of these monsters.

Should make it home by seven or so tonight..a five day visit that lasted 22 days....The trip of a lifetime and I owe it all to you Brats who have helped gather materials. As a result, each one of you who have or are sending photos, slides, films, etc. should be getting a formal letter of appreciation from the Kingdom, and there are some really GREAT plans being solidified right now. I will be announcing a contest and I will say this much. At least 300 of you will get to return home, at the Kingdoms total cost for a five day visit to Dhahran, Ras Tanura, Abqaiq, Udahliyia and Riyadh. There will also be a competition in writing which I will announce with at least ten people receiving cash gifts of up to $ 1,000.00 each from the Kingdom.

Let me say one final word on all of this adventure..the Saudi's have not lost their generosity in any way shape or form.

SALAAMS

Chatters, If you do not get all this, as it is quite large, please advise. I'll break it up. There will be a book with several hundred photos and the article at the reunion.

Visit to the Kingdom of Saudi Arabia as the Guest of His Royal Highness Prince Salman bin Abd-Al-Azziz Ibn Sa'ud and Minister Dr. Fahd Al-Semmari, Ministry of Higher Education REPEAT OF MY FIRST TRIP HOME AFTER 30 YEARS WORTH TELLING TWICE Left Houston via Confidential Airlines and made New York. Changed from La Guardia at NY and went to JFK and passed through security to Saudi Arabian Airlines. Was sent to First Class lounge. Nice treatment. Flight was on Saudia 747-300 and I must say that when Saudia say's First Class, they mean it !

The flight was very nice and the flight attendants were excellent. We landed at Jeddah airport and were on the ground for about two hours then on to Riyadh. At Riyadh the Minister was there and the Asst. Minister and the Director General of the King Abd-Al-Azziz Research Center. Customs and visa passing was non-existent. Minister showed stamp and off we went. Bags showed up in room at hotel. We had tea and coffee in lounge of Intercontinental Hotel, very nice place and then I went to my room.

2/22/97

The next day I had breakfast of sausage and bacon and eggs, imagine that. Of course they were made from beef..but what the hey...I was picked up and taken to the Maskmak fortress of Riyadh which is the Fortress King Abd-Al-Azziz Al- Sa'ud attacked and captured, thus taking Riyadh, the last main battle to consolidate the Kingdom of Saudi Arabia..They are restoring it to it's original shape and using the exact same construction of mud and sticks and hay. The fortress has several excellent displays and models. Mr. Ibrahim Naser Al-Sabhan is the curator and has done a remarkable job of restoration.

We went to the Sug nearby and I will have to spend the last day there. Unbelievable items and goodies.

On to the Ministers office, and sent e-mail to US. Then back to hotel for short break and then to King Abd-Al-Azziz City for Science and Technology, which was extremely impressive. Met the Vice President, Dr.Mohammed I. Al-Suwaiyel and was introduced to Prince Sultan Salman Abd-Al-Azziz ibn Sa'ud, the Saudi Astronaut. The Vice President/Administrator was very impressed with the AramcoBrat home page.

On to the cities Diplomatic Quarter and visited the main recreation, shopping and sports area of the Quarter. Very much like Dhahran. This is a community of Diplomatic quarters and missions and this very large area was for shopping, banking and all sort of recreational activity.

Met with Minister at 8:00pm and we talked to midnight when he brought me back to hotel. Many, many plans. He is contacting HM and getting Aramco to welcome me for two day visit to Eastern Province. He was impressed with volume of material we have access to. We are drawing up formal plans and a contract between he and ABI for the continuance of our friendship and relationship.

Went to His Majesty King Fahd's palace and had tour. King in Jeddah till weekend.

02/23/97

Expect to see King Sa'ud University and the Disabled Children Association today. Had mysterious note under door, but don't know from who..signed by Adbel Hamid, who says he will call this morning, but I don't know him.

As expected I went to the King Sa'ud University, meet with the Minister of Universities, Minister Fadh I.M. Al-Sanie. The University is a fantastic operation and the building are truly magnificent. The building is "L" shaped and quite large. The University took me to the highly secured Antiquities Department and showed me the restricted materials discovered in one of the excavations being done. Many items of pre-Islamic culture and bronze statues and misc. jewelry from 30 BC. Also a compete tomb burial chamber with the original funeral bed intact. Looked a lot like the couches used in Roman times.

Was then taken to meet the Director of the University who took me on a tour of the entire facility. I saw the fabulous video and visual aids section where they have set up many work stations where Saudi students may learn about other culture, their own heritage, etc. I am proud to say that a new video production, entitled AramcoBrats and utilizing several hundred of the photographs I had sent, collected from so many of you is now being used and according to Dr. Fahad Al-Mohammed, the President of the University, is one of the most popular films they have. It is currently being reproduced for the other schools in the Kingdom. The department has some 2000 work stations, and the Director told me that many days, as many as 50% are utilizing the AramcoBrat video.

I was presented with an Honorary Degree from the King Sa'ud University by the Minister. It is both amusing and honoring that my name is Michael AramcoBrat Crocker on the Degree....

We then left the University and went to the Disabled Children Association, run by Dr Faris H. Saleem (FRCP). The facility is sponsored by HRH Price Salman Abd-Al-Azziz Al-Sa'ud School for Handicapped Children. This school is run entirely by donations and they have done some truly amazing work there in the development and training of the families in how to deal with the handicapped children. A very impressive operation in which Dr. Faris H. Saleem has just told the Saudi Press, as I was standing there, that they are now building 3 more such centers which handle all phases of the child's application in North and South Arabia and in Mecca.

In the evening we went to the Gold Suq here, and may I suffer the curse of a thousand camel flies if I even begin to state the amount of gold and the cost. As my bodyguard/escorts said. "You will have much luck with you lady from this place". Talk about an understatement.......

02/24/97

This morning I met the Minister of Urban Development, Prince Momman

SUBJECT: VISIT TO SAUDI-PART II

This morning I met the Minister of Urban Development, Prince Mommand Al- Jabber and was given a tour and a lengthy discourse by the engineers that are building the King Abd-Al-Aziz Research Center, which I now understand is going to become the National Museum and Heritage Park. A truly magnificent layout with the Kings old Palace as the center piece and the Musmak Fortress . They will begin construction within one week and it is to be finished for the 1999 Centennial of the King. The design is very well thought out and retains a lot of the old, with hi tech new. Several of the Kings cars and others items, numbering in the thousands will be used, including several thousand of the photographs and film that the Brats have provided. These will be identified as such. The model of the layout cost 4 million US dollars alone. The layout is such that a large area is green lands and the buildings meld into the landscaping. Extensive use of vegetation and Palms are planned. Engineers from around the world competed in the design and the final model shows the extensive thought and considerations given to the planning.

The overall size is equivalent to two Smithsonian Museums. Due to photos we have provided, it looks as if a DC 3 and a rather unique Dhow, which the Saudi's were unaware of until the photos we brought will be added to the display and or displayed outside, much like the Space Shuttle was in La. at the Worlds Fair there some years ago. In fact, due to our photos, a search is now on in the Kingdom for many more cars of the King. Also of a DC 3 that will be marked. The Minister was very impressed that we had photos of the Kings Dhow as it is an usual type and the Minister, who knew AbdualAzziz did not know of the dhow. I asked him how did the King get to Bahrain before aircraft, and he suddenly had a big smile and made the remark that we knew more than they did. Actually it was due to a brats family that we had the photos and it showed the King's dhow off the coast of Ras Tanura. Before the surf house had even been built....

Next to the Kings stables, and you Arabian horse lovers will enjoy this. The stables are in downtown Riyadh and once you drive into the compound, you get out of the Mercedes and into a Land Rover to drive about fifty feet in soft sand to the stable yard. They brought out about ten of the horse's, all champions, one having just won the Governors Cup right before Ramadan. They wanted me to show my abilities with a horse of course, and the first two or three I was able to lead about and make trot and run. However the last one had a look in his eye. He was the newest and they said he was spirited..well that sucker pushed me around and the nudged me and finally nipped me playfully on the arm. The Saudi cameraman thought this was great entertainment and was rushing off to send it to be developed.

Incidentally, that crazy horse won the Grand Arabian race that weekend and the purse was 100,000 Saudi Riyals. His owner said the this horse had never been raced before and must have gotten some American strength from biting me..I thought the thing ought to have been dinner, but instead he is now a National Hero, and I get the dubious honor of having been bit by this famous horse. Wonder who is the horses behind now ?

We then all sat and had the traditional coffee and tea and talked about the US and Saudi Arabia and England. Seems as if most of these guys do not like the English.

We talked about the great devil Saddam Hussien and they all were very appreciative of the US Military, but wanted to know why we used such massive force when everybody knew Saddam had only the ragtag bunch actually in Kuwait. I asked if they thought the Saudi forces could have dealt with Hussien alone and they all agreed no, but that with the air power they could have done it. They felt the land force was unnecessary. All claimed to have watched CNN constantly and said that Saddam watched it constantly and bragged that CNN was his "Intelligence" corps.

Tomorrow I meet with Dr. Nasir, who is HRH Salaman bin Abd-Al-Azziz ibn Sa'ud's personal assistant and we discuss my trip to the Eastern Province and to Jeddah. Inshallah, all goes well..

2/25/97

Very exciting day. First to the Society of Protection for animals, which has a fabulous selection of the mammals, snakes and fish of Arabia. The Saudi's have developed four large preserves and have even managed to reestablish the settlement of Gazelles which were almost hunted to extinction. I met the Director and presented him with a video that JM had sent me on the island and his exploration. The director was very impressed and sends his many thanks to JM and the Brats. This display was one of extreme modern layout and Professor Glad A. Nader who is the head of the National Commission for Wildlife Conservation and Development, states that they will be developing a lot more.

We then went to the Palace and met with Dr. Nasir who is the highest lev

SUBJECT: VISIT TO SAUDI-PART IV

florescent lights etc., but plenty of Go wa and Chi, again and again. Strange how here I was in old Arabia and two blocks away, on concrete sidewalks and modern stores, merchants were selling everything, except the real Saudi items. The old suq is on dirt pathways and has small cave like shops, so full that I was hardly able to fit, but the merchants were all Saudi and treated me as if I were a long lost brother. Whereas the newer souvenirs shops were mostly owned by Saudi's but run by Pakistani's. In the old quarter I didn't see one other American after several hours of looking and of haggling over everything.

Tonight I am supposed to go to a State dinner and again tomorrow. I have tomorrow off as it is Friday, the day of rest here as you all remember. However Friday night I have a formal Saudi dinner with the head of Saudi Antiquities Research and Collecting.. He is the titular head of the current Ministry of Antiquities, and will become part of the King Abdualazzi Research Center and National Museum.

Finished another Saudi feast..I think that they want me to take on the position of an affluent Saudi..Big and routound..Since I am 3/4 way there, they are, after all only helping. Lot of questions as to why President Clinton and Prince Bandar Abd AL-Azziz Al-Sa'ud are not friendly. Found out from Prince Mohammed bin Fahd, ibn Al-Sa'ud tonight. Seems as if then Governor Clinton tried to get the Saudi's to donate a sum to a group in Arkansas. Prince Bandar saw this as just another case of some small time official trying to get money out of the Saudi's and sent only a paltry sum.. estimated by the source here to be $ 25,000.00 Mr. Clinton, upon becoming President, reminded Prince Bandar of his lack of what Mr. Clinton thought was sufficent for whatever project it was at the time and has put Prince Bandar on a "distance" position since he took office. This weeks trip by Prince Sultan abd Al-Azziz ibn Sa'ud was to mend the fence under the cover of Military and Peace Accord conversation...Prince Bandar abd-Al-Azziz Al-Sa'ud will be recalled this year and reassigned.

Saw the Saudi form of skiing tonight. They all try to climb very large sand dunes in small Toyota trucks. The crowd had a ball every time one turned around, or over and rolled back. Sand was so soft, they simply righted the vehicle and tried again. This one ought to be popular in USA. I asked if they had thought about using a motorcycle and they thought I was crazy for such a dangerous type of activity. I didn't bring up the fact that Americans jump off bridges on large rubber bands, thought I might be laughed out of Kingdom.

FRIDAY, FEBRUARY 28, 1997

Spent entire day off in bed. Bad head cold and ear stopped up. May not be able to fly. Did visit external area of Islamic University with Minister Of Higher Education tonight on way to Dr. Nasser Al-Wafi's house for Saudi state dinner. Too much humos and fish and chicken again.

SATURDAY, MARCH 01, 1997

Went to ancient ruins of BanBan, Saudi village of over three thousand years of age. Completely abandoned, but had Mosque, school, homes and public buildings. This is a totally restricted area now as over the years much of it has been destroyed by amateur archaeologists and grave robbers. Next to Mesnia in the north, this, other then the newly discovered Jubail Church is the oldest known remains of civilization in Arabia. Took a lot of photos. Went to Saudi Hospital today to get spray for ear infection.. will see.. cost 50 SR, including prescription and one free visit back if necessary in a week...Not bad for medical system. Spent balance of day in bed.

Ordered in tonight.. plain old steak sandwich and french fries..will watch Egyptian TV...quite erotic as they actually have a belly dancing thing on every night. Long ways from HZ 22 TV.

SUNDAY, MARCH 02, 1997

Got started with tour of Museum of History..They had very little from Jawwan Tomb and most of the materials are from pre-Islam and quite interesting. The have complex early Bedu encampment set up in yard.

The on to area where all items made in Saudi are on display. this is current items, such as Clorox, in same bottle but in Arabic, also Coke and Pepsi and believe it or not, Mary Kay Cosmetics......Still not feeling 100% so stayed at hotel this afternoon. Also am planning only one day at Jedahriyah Festival as I truly want to see 1000 camels in a race.

MONDAY, MARCH 03, 1997

Visited the first and only "Social Club" in Saudi Arabia. It is a modern new building and it's purpose is to provide recreation for the elderly(Over 40) group. Everything is in duplicate. One for men, one for women. Several Diplomatic missions use the facility on Fridays as it is closed to the Saudi population.

Very similar to our Court Clubs with all aspects of physical activity involved. This is a first in an Islamic system as it is actually there to provide assistance to the elderly. The old Bedu custom was if they could not fend for themselves, they were left behind. However in more recent times the family has been given the obligation to care for these elders.

It is located out by the old Riyadh airport and we stopped to look at the

SUBJECT: VISIT TO SAUDI-PART V

ircraft that we talked about on chat awhile back. The one that had a fire on board started by someone cooking in the aisle. The nose and crew section and underbelly and tail is all the remained after the fire. The Saudi officer with me stated that the people were trapped inside and that the pilot was still conscious when he started to land, but that they, Saudi Aviation people, feel that he was dead before the plane actually was on the ground. They have left it still on the runway it came in on because to this day they are still sorting out the compensation for the families and here, the law makes it mandatory that the object of the death be retained for examination by the litigators. So it still stands as a mute witness to horror such as can only be imagined.

Tonight we ate at Mcdonalds. Took photos as they have it split into two parts, one male and one female, so if you and your wife enter, you eat on separate sides of a wall. This includes Americans. Took a lot of photos of other restaurants and such for the geezer group....Pizza Hut looks neat in Arabic.

TUESDAY, MARCH 04, 1997

Met with Dr. Faisal M. Al-Rasheed, the Director/Minister of the Royal Commission for Jubail and Yanbu. Was given a complete tour of the operations center and an invite to go to Jubail and Yanbu for a visit, but had to decline as I have been told that I will be in Aramco Saturday, Sunday and Monday. The Royal Commission was quite advanced and predicts that a version of the www will soon be available in both Yanbu and Jubail. E-Mail is already in place as it is in Saudi Aramco. The King Himself is in overall charge of the two cities and they are entirely independent of Saudi Aramco now. They are developed areas that produce a wide variety of products and have many major outside investors such as Shell and Mobil and USS Steel Products. These firms all have factories and family operations. A lot like Aramco, but very advanced. From the presentation I would not hesitate for one moment having a life in either city. You would think you were in a US city, except that in this case, both sites are spotless and extremely well maintained.

It is an early night as the "Jedahriyah" begins tomorrow with the opening at 2:00pm and the first event is the 1000 camel race. A sight I gather I will never see again. Then on to the auditorium to hear poetry and speeches and then to the tradition Saudi dances and many exhibits. We expect to be there from 2 until Midnight.

Well, I'll put this one in the books. I have never seen the likes. One Thousand Camels and racing a spiral track. Fantastic, and those damn things can move...The race was won by a Camel called "Abdul" what else would have been right ? The jockey was a little kid about twelve years old. They all were. What a shock, hell, I won't get near one and I'm just a shade older. He got his prize from Prince Charles. I got to meet the Prince in a form of receiving line. He is quite an ugly duck..Lady Di for me ! Several long poetical speeches and then the most unbelievable light show and operetta style of program. These singers came out on a stage the size of a opera house and, Ohh, this is all indoors and will seat 20,000 people at once. Then the lights and the music and the dancing. Sword dancing, ballet style, rocking and rolling side to side style and in all, about 450 people on stage at once, all in concert with the five lead singers. The the National Guard marched out and did a sword dance with at least 750 men. The laser light show and the huge background was constantly changing with photos of King Abd-Al-Azziz Al-Sa'ud.

The grand finale had the entire troupe of at least 1000 on the floor and all doing various sword dances and playing all native instruments. The Crown Prince and other members went out into the stage area and joined in and the crowd went wild. They were dancing in the bleachers and really getting worked up. I hope to be able to get a video of this.

We, the "Guests" were then taken to the main hall for a traditional meal and we ate like rabid jackals. What a feast. The hall could sit some 2000 at a time and they do this every night until the festival ends. This all started at 2:00pm and we got back to the hotel around mid-night. The line of black Mercedes with the Saudi logo in gold on the door was just staggering. Each of us "Guests" were two to a car and I'll bet there was at least 125 of us...I was interviewed by the Al-Riyadhie Newspaper and will see how that came out. Long way from the humble beginnings of a small town goat herder that I was...So ends "Jedahriyah" for me......InShallah ! Allah Akbar !

WEDNESDAY, MARCH 05, 1997

Going souvenirs hunting today...day off supposedly, but we shall see what happens....Well, I should have known....Saudi's bought all kinds of goodies for reunion..including, and this is partial,

Complete Gutra and Kafia, thobe and outer garment

Complete Coffee cup set with Saudi Logo

Complete Tea set with Saudi Logo

Two complete Bedu Silver necklaces

Two sets of coffee mugs with Arab Coffee pots design

One Brass miniature Riyadh water tower and coffee bean mixer, to be used with incense

One Brass miniature twin palm trees with coffee grinder and coffee mixer 75 Assorted Key chains with Saudi logo, or Arabic. Also about ten Key chains with miniature Coffee pots

Two solid brass small 6"x8" brass table displays with Saudi Arabia, map and swords and palm tree and Saudi Arabia in Arabic.

One brass miniature palm tree with Hubbly Bubbly, coffee pot and coffee grinder

4 Brass small coffee pots with Saudi Logo

Two miniature coffee sets with cups and pot all in brass

One crystal with Saudi Logo on bottom, very nice

One complete coffee serving set

One silver plated dish, Saudi Arabia and Logo

Schedule calls for me to be in Aramco Sat. Sun and Mon. Return to Riyadh, meet on Tuesday with His Royal Highness Prince Salman bin Abd Al-azziz and with the Custodian of the two Holy Mosques, King Fahd bin Abd-Al Azziz ibn Sa'ud. Also am supposed to meet Crown Prince Abd-Allah, although I have already met him at the "Jedahriyah" with Prince Charles in the reception line.

They are sending a Senior Aide from the Prince's office with me to Aramco, I think to make sure that I get to do and go where I want. I plan on hitting high points of Dhahran, Abqaiq, and RT as fast as possible and then meet with Aramco exec's and then out to Riyadh and allegedly leaving

ALL, MY GOD FORGIVE MY RAGE, AND BLESS THIS ANGEL...

We are sitting in the deepest, darkest shadows of the desert. Words can not describe the complete and utter emptiness of the Crocker family. Without warning, our most dearly and beloved Mother, Irene Crocker, passed away in our arms. The Black Camel came and ever so gently looked over our shoulders and knelt on one knee for the Queen of Our Hearts to mount and ride gently into the Kingdom of Heaven. I thank God my brothers were able to tell her to hold on until I arrived. I was able to hold the most wonderful loving person of our lives. She acknowledged all of us and then...ever so slowly, while cradled so hard and soaked with our tears, she stepped into God's hands and went to be with our brother KC and all of the brats on our "in Memory Pages" she loved and took care of for over 30 years in Arabia. She loved so many of you.

We invite all who know of our family to contact us about the service, which we hope to have by Thursday this week. We will announce the name and address of the Funeral Home later today. We are all very lost right now in the greatest of shamals, but we know our Mother, our best friend, our lifeline, has become one of God's Angels.

Our Mother, who knew so many of you, never forgot the warmth and love she and our Dad received when they were at the Chandler Reunion. Mom said then, "t "...the years in Saudi Arabia were the happiest years of her life and wouldn't trade them for anything".

May God hold her so tightly that she feels the presence and light of so many of us who have gently ridden the Black Camel.

CONTINUE WITH PRIOR STORY FELLOW BRATS,

The Black Camel came upon a sleeping figure. A soft woman's voice with the second voice of a young boy spoke to the sleeping figure. "Please come and ride this gentle Black Camel. He has bowed his head for you and we wait here beside him. Come join us and your many friends and family. They are waiting for you in God's arms and His light and eternal love". The sleeping figure smiled I am sure and gently mounted the mighty steed which gently rose and the family rode off into the dark night towards the light of God's blessing.

Our Father, Leo Francis Crocker went home with Mom and our beloved brother KC today.

Goodbye Dad, I know Mom and KC are with you...I miss all of you as do my brothers.

We love you all so much...Mike Crocker

SCHOOL HISTORY

I 'll start in 1965. You had left and there was a lot of anger and hurt in me. I didn't trust women and didn't really care if they got hurt or not after I felt I had been hurt and deserted. I was forced to redo a year due to severe conflict between Mr. Riley and myself and thus went from Class of 64 to Class of 65. Not many people know this. I had excellent grades, but he told Mom and Dad that I needed to mature more. As a result I was an outcast from my class(64) and didn't belong in Class of '65. So in 1965 I was pretty much a loner. However, I did date a lot of the girls there as I was seen to be a "outlaw" by many. I did make his life as miserable as I could and he signed my yearbook with "Good riddance".

Anyhow, about February of 1965 a girl named Vicki Muzika came to Dhahran from the States. I was playing football and she became a cheerleader. I started dating her April 21, 1965 and picked up from where you and I had left off.

I had not progressed sexually because I felt I would only get hurt and my heart couldn't take it again. So she and I started dating and we became infatuated. I was with her constantly and we explored each other, yet never "going all the way" and even tho there were signs she wasn't all real. I chose to ignore them because I felt I was in love.

I was sent into the desert for two weeks on one school break period and when I got back found her on Kevin Colgan's lap. Punched him out and made her leave. She told me that she had seen him because she missed me so much that he was a substitute. I believed it.. On Graduation night she and I went to old incinerator in reclamation as I was leaving the very next day for long leave and then school at San Marcos Military Academy.

At the incinerator we got into heavy petting and actually got completely undressed and just as we were about to complete the act, I stopped and told her "No." That I would not do this until we were married. She was really mad at me for stopping. I didn't know it at the time, and didn't find out until over fifteen years later that she was not a virgin and her plan was to make me believe I was her first. I thought we both were.

This was the summer that I found out I had no real family. All those years I had thought I was a Crocker, but when we all went to the Embassy to swear allegiance, as we used to have to do, they called out all the Crockers but not me. Mom told me to wait.

They then called out Michael Joe Reilly and Mom told me to stand and take the oath. I did so and later she told me that I wasn't Leo Crockers real son, but that she had me three months before she had met Leo. He had been in Arabia hunting with the King and had been shot in the leg by accident and was flown back to the hospital in Chicago where my Mom was a Nurse. They met, fell in love and Dad returned to Arabia in 1949, late. Mom and I flew over and they got married in Bahrain and we went to Abqaiq. My real Father had disappeared after marrying Mom and left us when I was just one month old. She divorced him right away.

This was the start of the problems with my brother Chris as he felt he should have been the oldest and therefore "in charge" and that since IO wasn't REALLY part of the family, I should just leave. The bad part was that Mom and Dad didn't know how to handle this, and so did nothing, leaving me to use brute force to retain Chris.

That night I told Vicki at the third stret playground and she held me and we swore to never tell anyone and it was to be my holiest secret.

When I returned the next summer, she was there and I was back and we started seeing each other again. She told me she hadn't been able to write because of school, and I believed it, even tho I had written every day for 200 some days.

This was summer of 1966. She left on long leave in mid-June and Doral Zadorkin told me all about her dating many guys and having sex and so on. I didn't believe Doral. Anyhow, when I left that summer I wrote back to Vicki and we discussed if you could get pregnant by being in intimate positions without actual sex. She thought she could get pregnant that way and I didn't know. Doral found the letter and gave it to Vicki's Mom, who went ballistic and made her husband quit Aramco and they left.

No one knew where they were and I couldn't find her. I felt as if I had been dumped again by some one I loved and this really took the life out of me. First you, that I never quit loving, and then Vicki who was, as I found later, my first "Gold Digger". Things were really bad at San Marcos, although I excelled at the Military part, I was very anti-social. I was busted from the rank I obtained over and over again for bad conduct. Perhaps the worst part about San Marcos was that at Christmas when everybody got to go home, I stayed on campus because I had no family and no where to go. Aramco didn't bring stateside people out for Christmas. So each day I put the flag up and at night I took it down. All alone on the entire campus and living off the snack machines as no one from the school even knew I was there. All the teachers and such lived off campus and so, there I was.

I know that one time I did go to a friends house for Thanksgiving and it was freezing. All I had was my uniform and while he and his family went into a big family gathering, I stayed in the truck and actually huddled on the floor boards to stay warm. I had been invited, but none told me where to go and I had been asleep in the truck with somebody's uncle who just left me there and they were all in some building. What with the snow and all I was not willing to take the chance that I could find them. From that point on I stayed on campus.

The point of all this was that I was learning to survive and be a loner and learning how easy it was to feel pain. School was ok, but during the year the school was very strict and we weren't allowed to date, and I was still "in love" with Vicki that I wasn't interested. This brings me to the summer of '67 and it was fun as I ran Student Recreation, but I dated no one.

I knew when I saw you the next time that I had never got over you, but you seemed to ignore me and I took it to mean still, from before, that you didn't want anything to do with me, so until the night I walked you home, and that took a lot of courage on my part, I felt that you hated me for some reason. Yes, I wanted very badly to take you out, but the thought that I would once again be pushed away, or so I thought, by you, hurt terribly. Yes we kissed, and yes we got a little intimate (No, I didn't forget), but I thought you were just having fun at my expense, because you never said anything…I was then very confused. I loved you so much and yet, all I knew was that before you had quit talking or having anything to do with me, and I didn't know why, and I had been so trashed by my family that I was waiting for some sign from you that I wasn't going to be trown away again. Martha, I was as shy as you…I felt like I did at the airport in Houston. I wanted to hold you so badly and to kiss you, but knew I was wrong, but still couldn't not try. The only difference is that now I have lived some and if you had slapped me for kissing you, well, so be it. Yet back then, I was afraid I wouldn't be good enough for you. Even so, you still pulled away, and even if I know why I still have to say I wished I had done it better…

I graduated from San Marcos Military school in Mid-year, having skipped a year and my parents wanted me to see what life was like outside of "Privileged" school, so I had to attend the last five months of San Marcos High School and live with a family my parents had found and paid them to keep me. After all I couldn't start college until September anyway. I was not accepted at San Marcos by the kids except that I had a very high bowling average and was able to take their bowling team to the State championship in El Paso, and we won and for that, about fifty people out of five thousand would even talk to me. After all, I was the "snob" from the Academy and was only slumming amongst the High School kids. Not true, but no one wanted to or would listen.

I wrote to many colleges and selected Clarendon Junior College in Clarendon, Texas because the Registrar had sent me a hand written acceptance letter and the personalization impressed me. They met me at the airport and I had two good years there. Was heavily involved with Drama and Speech and History. Fell in love with a girl named Kay Greer, who was with me almost a year when the first Viet Nam guys started coming home that had attended CJC. She fell for one of them and so ended another romance. I was still looking for Vicki and still thought I loved her, and also still had you on my mind. Seems like you were always there somewhere. So I dated a lot of others, and by now was sexually active and a little advanced in that area for this small town so was pretty popular since "I was experienced". Great Huh ? Great sex, so I was "loved". This point is important as you will see later.

At the end of my second year there I was accepted at West Texas State University, about fifty miles from Clarendon . I will pick up here tomorrow night.…

JR COLLEGE

While at Clarendon Junior College I did have the honor of being very active in a lot of new things for me. Drama was an area I was particularly fond of. I acted and was Stage manager and even for the first time in school history was a student Director of a play. I built sets where you could simply move a building to face front, and each side was built like a different place. I won many awards for both Academic and Athletic events. Yet there was a dark side starting to develop. I had become, as far as women went, simply a toy and I liked it. I decided that the best way to never get hurt was to be the best lover any woman had ever found, and thru that, bind them to me and yet never ever let the words "I love you "come from my mouth. I would, quite simply make them feel physically as they had never felt and in effect, make them slaves of their own physical desires. Another side which began to show was the cold blooded side that I didn't know about. I was relentless when faced with an opponent. In Debate at State level I reduced the opposing team to tears by vicious, yet factual and cutting arguments. I had no sympathy.

One area I did do a lot in, and this was a hold over from High School was I worked a lot with the Texas Teens Aid the Retarded. Even in Junior College I would go at least twice a week to teach these young children at the Brown Schools to swim. Even tho I had to re-teach every time I liked it and at the State Convention in Portland, Or. I was elected State President of Texas, seduced the student Rep. from Alaska, and met Vice President Hubert Humphreys who was there for the ceremony. This also is important and he had a friend with him named Barry Goldwater. I spoke with Senator Goldwater for quite some time over the four days of the conference. This was 1969 and the beginning of my schooling at a full university, West Texas State University. I tell you about this as it leads to another tragedy that involved me and a woman.

While at WTSU I was working for the University Police Department and also going to school full time and playing college level football. I really am quite solid under this layer of weight on me now. Being so popular on the campus, Big man and a Sigma Nu Frat member, I was always able to get any girl I wanted to sleep with, and did so. However, I met a girl, red haired yet with temper to match. In the back of the police car, in the dorm, just where ever. I was beginning to like her and had some old feelings that were dead and gone start to retrieve themselves. On day I got a radio call to go to the roadside park, about five miles from the University to check out a report of suspicious activity. This was unusual as Campus Police hardly ever left the campus, but being a commissioned peace officer I knew I had to go. Anyhow, the city and Highway patrol were busy with a major wreck in town and so I went.I got there and there was nothing there, so I radio'ed back in and said I was proceeding to assist the Patrol at the wreck site. The radio was silent, so I figured I was too far out.

Now back to the red haired girl. Her name was Mina and several days before she had told me that she was going to have a baby and I knew I had been her one and only, so I was feeling kind a good about things. I arrived at the wreck site and a tractor trailer rig had turned the corner too sharp and had turned over. Nothing so unusual about that, except that a Dodge Cornet was crushed almost to the ground under the trailer. They told me she had died instantly and that she never felt any pain. That was why they had sent me on a wild goose chase so that they could remove her from the wreckage and I wouldn't see. We buried Mina and little Michael a few days later, it is all a blur to me and I believe that was the day I stopped believing in God. I still send flowers each year, but as I get older, I tend to forget, or perhaps have become so callous that I just don't. I had graduated top of my Police Academy Class to be become certified and decided that I no longer cared so

I went to the US Army recruiter and told him to sign me up for Viet nam. He told me that due to my hands, missing fingers you know, I would have to get some sort of permission. This is where the Senators and VP came in. I called both and thru their intervention I was allowed to be sworn into the US Army as a Second Lieutenant, due to High School ROTC and was sent to Fort Bragg, NC. for basic training.

I guess because I was so determined I placed highest in my class and the Army only requires you to qualify with one or at most two weapons. I qualified with over twelve different types to show I had no handicap. Based on this and my performance, I was approached to join the Green Berets, or Special Forces. I knew by now that war was my home and signed on for 12 weeks of the most grueling training I have ever had. If you want to know who and what I was, check out the John Wayne movie "Green Berets" and it pretty much tells you what I went thru.

Story of a friend, gone now but never forgotten

After boot camp at Ft. Bragg and all kinds of training and learning to survive he got my orders to proceed to the Republic of South Viet-Nam. HeI landed at Tan Sunhut Airforce base and was told. "Take off your officers bars as the life expectancy of an officer with insignia was seven minutes." From time of departure to office complex. Due to VC snipers whose main job was to watch the airport and shoot anyone who looked as if they had authority. Nice way to start the day.

HeI was immediacy processed and sent via Huey Chopper to Na Trang, 5th Special Forces Battalion Hdqtrs. A group of Green Berets had been wiped out at a place called Long Noc and he was being sent to replace them with an "A" team of 18 Special Forces guys and 144 regular army. This was one month after I had got there. I had been processing just routine intelligence reports before this for a civilian agency before meeting him..

We loaded up in a C-140 and proceed to make a night time parachute drop into the old camp and what was referred to as a firebase. Actually a compound with a lot of barb wire and mines and all kinds of nasty devices. However the pilot was evidently high and we were off course some distance. We were supposed to land in an area where there were no VC, but instead he dropped us right on top of a North Vietnamese Regular Army Division. Over 2000 men. The fighting started before we even hit the ground. He was senior officer and had lost 30 men before we got down. Confusion was everywhere, and we started fighting back. A bunch of us made it to the top of a hill and we went in action. The fight went on all night. He was wounded twice and all of us were hurt in one way or another. At daylight I called in air strikes and broke the back of the enemy force who faded away into the brush. On our hill were the only survivors from the fight. There were six of us left. All wounded. 156 men died that night and over 548 of the North Vietnamese died also. Sounds like a victory, but in reality was a major blow to his command and the US Army. He won the Silver Star and Purple Heart from this action as I had been the only one left actually standing and protecting my comrades by hand to hand fighting, knife to knife and finally He was using a shovel to smash and slash and beat them back.

Laid up for two months in the base hospital and was reassigned to firebase Mike Mike Two. This was near the DMZ between the two Viet Nams. We went out on many missions, and one I have sent you about the river and another I think I sent also. This base was a real pain in the NVC side as we were right where they were trying to bring in materials from the North and we were stopping them. So daily they tried to penetrate our defenses. Finally they made an all out attack against us. We had about 420 men and about 35 Green Berets. He wasn't senior officer, but was Intelligence Officer and I had told the camp Commanding Officer that we were fixing to get it. Well, they did it all right. 12 hours of bombardment and then a massive night attack.

They made it over the wire and into the actual compound. The fighting was extremely intense. I can still remember the taste of the blood of the VC soldier who had me down and was pressing a knife into my side as I bit open his throat. The blood was very hot. I staggered up with his knife still in my side and saw that we were being overrun. I jumped in front of two large cannons and using a hammer knocked out the pins which in normal use, kept the gun barrels from depressing too low and the shells hitting right in front of the guns, I then ordered both guns to fire point blank into the oncoming mass, and the resulting blasts caught me between both cannon barrels and blew out both ear drums and knocked me out. However the massive firepower broke the attack and we were ok. I spent three months in the hospital this time, being awarded the the agency Medal of Valor for a civilian. One other mission I'll tell you about I was leading a force of "Phoenix" team men, (we were assinateing the high ranking govt and military officers where ever we found them). The idea being, cut off the head and the snake will die. It was the most successful campaign waged in the entire war. I personally by knife, by high powered rifle and by rope around neck took out fifteen of the enemy ranking personnel. However at the same time I also was forced to kill several women who were lying in bed next to the general or politician that I was to kill. Sins of war. I never killed a child. At one time I had a group of eight high ranking VC officers gather together and we were getting ready to kill them all with silenced weapons when we had crawled within a hundred feet. All of a sudden we heard someone walking up the path less than an inch from where we were lying. It was the outer guard of the camp. Had he seen us, he would have simply machine gunned the bushes and killed all of us. I motioned with my eyes that everyone was to lie very still and the guard stopped less than a foot from me and urinated on me and the guy next to me. The jungle was so thick he didn't see us. I had my knife in my mouth and both hands in front of me, so I couldn't move. Suddenly something bit me on the ear and was ripping my ear. My eyes watered and I was ready to scream. I moved my head just a little and saw a large jungle rat chewing on part of my ear lobe. The guard was still in front of us so I moved my head and managed to stick the rat with the knife in my mouth getting it's blood all over me and thus, blood and urine on my face. The guard walked away and we killed all of them. I found the guard and cut off his male organ and put it in his mouth. The VC feared us more than any other, and whenever they caught one of us, they used to build a coal fire and sit the man down in it nude so that the fire would burn up the back end inside and the coals would eat away at his insides. A very bad and horrible way to die.

Amongst my decorations for this horror is a document giving me "credit" for the death of over 123 of the enemy in this campaign.

I think I told you the story about the prostitute and what she did and what happened so there is one story left and I don't think it is decent enough for you.

I'll stop here as I sure you are sick of this.

End Part IV

PART III-SECTION I

A fter returning from the war zone I knew I had to go back to college. I didn't fit in. First I was older and the free love, peace ideology was still around and I din't understand it. Some amazing encounters with female undergraduates took place as they all seemed to want to prove they could "take down" this "Baby Killer" from the war and wanted to do it sexually. Never worked, but I had a great couple of years. I was proud of my service so never backed down even with Professors or others who spent a lot of time talking, but with very little substance about the war.

I didn't know what to do with my life, so while at school I started a long tradition that has continued right up to now. I overloaded my system with work and play and made it all put terrible strain on myself. I joined the University Police Department and had the 11:00pm shift till 8:00 am and then class from 8:30am till 3:30pm. Used to go to class wearing our uniform which consisted of a blazer with police badge and under the coat a gun belt with weapon and all. This was a turn on for the girls but uncomfortable for me.

I left you in 1977 after my brother died. I came back to the States and went back to college. I seemed kinda lost and finally got my MS and then on to working as a police officer. Once again the girls were fun and college was no challenge it seemed. Grades were easy and I got my MS in a less than two years.

WELL, IF YOU HAVE TO TELL SAD STORIES, THEY MIGHT AS WELL BE INTERESTING AND HAVE A TOUCH OF HUMOR

S O, puppy love in the 9th grade. I was playing Football, GO BEARS, and saw that Dhahran had the most beautiful cheerleaders. As a red blooded boy I found one particularly interesting, new girl in town, who was teaching some new cheers. Well, Steve Reed passed off the ball to Bill Cohea, who gave the damn thing to me. The RT Blue Devils were pressing hard and I thought that the best way to impress this beauty was to run the ball for a touchdown.

So, although the coach had told me to only block, I took off, like a real Bear over to one side of the field where the bleachers used to be, went through the cheerleaders, gave a big smile at the one I was impressing, and flying like the wind charged off to the other side of the field to avoid some-one like DeNunizzo or such. All the while looking over my shoulder at the beauty. We used to have Volkswagen Mini-buses in Dhahran, or I guess it was just a Volkswagen Van, but it had no widows and was parked out of bounds by a good ten feet.

Now for those of you who remember, we played flag football, with uniforms made so tight that it caused us to run funny. But, with great skill I was able to avoid the flag snatchers and was moving on when a couple of RT Devils decided that to stop me, grabbing a flag wouldn't be enough. Seeing that they were getting ready to cream me, I looked over my shoulder, one last look at this beauty, turned left at a full run to dodge those animals and hit the van at full speed. Knocked me plumb out and put a huge dent in the side of the van. To make matters worse I fumbled the ball, Devils got it and ran it back to win the game.

At the "victory" dance that night, amid great revelry in my exploits I met the lady. Our first song was "House of the Rising Sun" and I found a true love in a sweet kiss that lasted fifteen years.

However, not being able to simply let a story go, I'll continue…She lived in a row house near the large playground, and I used to sneak over late and sneak her out and we would go sit on the merry go round for hours. Or sit in her backyard, away from prying eyes, cats mostly, and discovered each other. This wasn't full blown sex, for all you anxious perverts, this was love.

In fact, had I listened to a very dear friend back then, the next fifteen years of my life would have been different. But I didn't and in fact caused her great grief in life, for which I still apologize D.

We got caught by her parents, once half in and half out of her window, which was cause for much humor as I spent days replanting their window flower beds, BUT, along came Graduation, mine. And on that night I promised to marry her one day…and then we would consummate our relationship. Away I went to School and wrote practically daily.

Anyway, her father quit and they moved while I was gone..she didn't write and my heart died. BUT not my belief in love, I just knew it would work. how could it not…It took fifteen years of searching, and finally I called a small town of 150 people that Earl Greaves had told me about that she had mentioned to him while he was at Kent State where she was. The phone rang and rang and turns out it was a public phone. Some guy answered and I asked if this lady lived there. He said "yes". I asked him if he could ask her to answer the telephone the next day, same time. I called and after fifteen years, heard my love's voice again.

She and I talked and I said I'd like to see her.. She said were'e snowed until for the next four months and I asked if there was a lake or something. She told me there was as this town was a fishing resort, but it was frozen. I told her I'd be there the next day, to look for me around 3:00pm and have a fire burning.

I flew to Denver and chartered a small plane, flew to the town and parachuted in. What I forgot was that the town was at 10,000 ft. and I had jumped at 2500 ft. I damn near froze getting down. We stayed in her house that night and I slept on a futon against a wall. Didn't know much about the cold, but should have known this wasn't going to work because during the night my bare butt froze to the wall, and to my humiliation she had to use warm water to free me.

I did marry her, and unfortunately, after so many years, we were 180 degrees apart. She had been married three times, while I had been looking and waiting. She had two children who are wonderful adults.

We ended up divorced, although we now talk, and I still remember that most passionate moment of my life, our first kiss.

Not a lot of humor, but I did have to work off paying for the Volkswagen damage, and coach found many interesting exercises for me for the next few weeks of practice and games.

What I didn't tell the chat was that she had a lesbian affair, and told me it was ok, because I could sleep with the girl also, which I didn't. She then got pregnant twice by different guys, both tubal pregnancies, which I had to pay to correct. This was in 1980 and she thought that an open marriage was ok. Used to tell her friends I had run to Canada to avoid Viet Nam. Even with all this, and having to move every few months because we couldn't survive there, I stayed.

She was in a little theater group in which I participated and ended up doing several plays, directing several and wrote a modern version of "The Elephant Man" which won awards. After the plays we would all go to one of her friends house that had a large hot tub. Everybody nude and drinking Champagne. I was, at this point, ready to call it quits and at the last party had at least eleven different women try me on in the hot tub while the party lasted. Very sick and made me ill. I was drunk, but no excuse. She thought it was great. The next day I told her, "I'm going to Texas to see my folks for Christmas and I'll talk to you Christmas Day." She told me she would call and be sure to be there when she did. I drove 19 hours straight to get home to Texas, and that very afternoon, my parents, not knowing I was en route had left for Illinois. So I was alone for Christmas, as usual, and Vicki called....three years later.

I was unable to find her during that time as she had moved, but when she did call she wanted a divorce, so I wrote it up and filed it. One good thing about our relationship was that while waiting I went to Law School and got my JD. So I wrote my own divorce and filed it. I never heard a word back.

I had dated a few others during that time and built an apartment complex as an investment with some old friends. Here is where I met Dena and things really went wild. This was about 1985. The years between 1982 and 1985 were not interesting and all I did was work and sleep and eat. This next section is very difficult for me, so I'll start on it tomorrow.

Let me know if any of this gets to you.

"MY MOST EMBARRASSING MOMENT"

This memory surfaced after reading all the gymnastics stuff that went around. It hasn't been a buried memory though, if I had one dollar for every time I have thought about this over the years and laughed at myself I could retire today instead of having another twenty years staring me in the face.

After my seventh grade year in Abqaiq, we moved to Dhahran. Although we had lived in DH first, I had been very young, so I did not remember too many people when we moved back. My eighth grade year I was a little insecure, trying to make new friends, trying to fit in, and trying not to miss my friends in AB. Thirteen is such a horrid year for girls anyway, I don't know why the good Lord made it that we had to endure such a thing.

I think it was in the eighth grade, maybe ninth, and we were doing gymnastics in gym. Bear in mind, I am the spectator type when it comes to sports; my big moment in sports in Arabia was being a scorekeeper for the Bruins baseball team in the ninth grade. So I was not overly enthused about this gymnastics stuff, especially the trampoline. If God had wanted me to bounce six feet into the air, He would have given me pogo sticks for legs. I had to be gently led to the thing by the one and only Mr. Goellner, ("You can do it, Madame Curie", which was what he called me).

I started out obviously just jumping, bounce, bounce, bounce, stop. Got that one down with no problem. Well, this one particular day, Mr. G. decided I was ready to get adventurous and do a back drop. There were about four spotters, one of them I think was Mary Barger, and I know for sure Julie Yaeger was one. Imagine if you will how this back drop thing works. You bounce a few times and then drop on your back with your legs pulled up to your chest. (Why would anyone want to do this stuff???)

So I tried it. Bounce, bounce, bounce, legs to chest, drop on back. Hummm, not too bad, let's do it again. Bounce, bounce, bounce, legs to chest, drop on back. Unbeknownst to me, however, all this bouncing and dropping caused a teensy weensy bit of gas to collect somewhere deep in my innards. So, the next try.....you can see this coming a mile away..... bounce, bounce, bounce, legs to chest, drop on back, "poot".

I COULD HAVE DIED

Well, Mr. Goellner (not too successfully) tried his best to keep a straight face and also tried his best to keep all the spotters from laughing. A few of them did just smile and put their hands over their mouths and looked the other way. But Julie Yaeger? I will remember the rest of my life how she hooted and hollered so loudly I am sure they heard her in Abqaiq. Mr. Goellner couldn't do a thing with her, she was having way too much fun. I learned real quickly no special treatment around there for being a sorta new kid, no sir, it was sink or swim, buddy.

I went on to make wonderful friends in Dhahran and consider myself so fortunate to have been one of the "dual district" kids who had friends in two camps. And Julie? I haven't seen her in over thirty years, but in my heart, still consider her one of the best friends I ever had.

TERESA (TERRY) KIERSZNOWSKI DH 66

Hi Jan, I am Betty Collins Stanley Dhahran '51. As you can see I am an OOOLLD Brat or 'Geezer" as one of my Aramco buddies phrased it. But young at heart!! I was with one of the group at the first Brat Reunion in

Monterey. Some of the annuitants weren't too happy with us . We were invading their good time. But I see it has grown and grown. Look at you now!! I lived in Dhahran when it was fenced in, the donkeys roamed around in camp, we would get them and ride them bareback with a stick to guide them. If possible we would try to take them home and tie them to the fence in the backyard. Eventually the braying would get to our parents and Dad would go out and let it go. Boo hoo, we planned on keeping it forever.... In those days we could ride the bus around camp for hours and thats what we did sometimes, driving the bus drivers crazy! We didn't have the freedom to go to Al Khobar alone. But we had lots of fun in camp. The freedom that we had was like nothing else! I think all of us who lived in that time will never forget it. It was special .. Campouts at Half Moon Bay with the Giirl Scouts...Going on trips to Ras Tanura and Abqaiq for football games. A Dhow trip. Trip to Jubail. Riding a camel. Traveling to the States by ship and seeing all the sites along the way...Going to the movies and the Fiesta room. Staying up all night to see a friend off at the airport. The Air Base. If you went out with a soldier you could get a BAD reputation. (they were just kids, too) The library above the movies. The dining hall. The canteen! A bunch of us would get a pack of cigarettes for .10 cents. Then we'd walk around and smoke and get onions (whole ones) from one of the waiters at the Fiesta Room and take turns having bites so our parents couldn't smell the cigarettes on us...We probably knocked them out with that smell. Enough of this rambling. Shorten it as you like. Hope to hear from others who share these memories . Or any memories of early days in SA. Or anything. Bye for now. Betty Khobar could be a grueling adventure. First, we took the 7 A.M. Kenworth monster bus from RT and rode 11/2 hrs. to Dhahran sans AC. We got off at the Dhahran Dining Hall or at the Fiesta Room to have breakfast. After eating we began to feel better BUT...if our sunglasses fogged up as we walked outside, we knew the temp in Khobar was going to be on the wicked side. The taxis lined up for us. We'd have to decide which air conditioned cab to to take to Khobar and then chip in a total of six riyals one way.

Once we arrived, we split up. I shopped at Abdullah's, a sort of big general store and remember buying a pair of Paulette Goddard ballerina style flats. Ugly? Oheeeeeeeeee. I remember that the shoebox had her picture on it. This woman was a semi-glamorous grade B movie star once married to Charlie Chaplin. I knew this because we got Photoplay and Motion Picture magazines every month at the commissary. Anyway, in addition to these beautiful plastic or whatever flats, Clark's Desert Boots were also available at Abdullah's. My dad wore them. For one of my parent's anniversaries, my dad bought my mom a gold and diamond wristwatch at Abdullah's from the second floor display case. For added incentive the salesman assured my parents that this watch was not available in the U.S. It was "for export only." They bought it.

We kids could also buy Smartees there, the British version of M&M's. We ate them and pretended. The Green Flag was another general type store as was Jameel's and Khoogi's (sp)?. THE jeweler in Khobar was Zain. Most of our gold name rings that we loved were purchased there. Zain's salesman was a man with a deep scar on one cheek. When I returned to Saudi in 77, the same man was running Eve's, another Khobar jewelry shop. Zain's was gone. Then there was Stop and Shop, now defunct. S&S made an attempt at air conditioning with one of those window cooler units AND you could get a cold drink! Another store, Ashraf's, had beautiful Daum crystal and Rosenthal porcelain chinaware. I inherited many pieces of "Shadow Rose", the Rosenthal dinnerware pattern that belonged to my parents.

Back in the 50's the Avon and Merle Norman cosmetic lines were available in many of the stores. I haven't been able to figure that one out. Khobar, especially in the summer, was an in and out deal. By 11:00 A.M. we were on our way to melt down. Bad hair day? I've never known a bad hair day to compare with a summer Khobar day. The fly infested beggar women with their suckling babies are no longer there. Well dressed healthy people now walk the streets of Khobar. In the 50's people didn't recognize the housefly as the trachoma carrier. This devastating eye disease was fairly common back then among the populace. In the 60s and/or early 70's a Harvard group researched the disease in the country to help eradicate it. A teacher I worked with in Dhahran told me that her sister had been part of that study team.

Thanks to the Saudi government, education and medical care are replacing the unhealthy conditions that use to exist.

I didn't really mean to write so much, but the vision of green Keds from Green Flag started it all...........Yes, A Real Fashion Statement!

EILEEN WILSON HAYES

RT 59

We all know Crocker can really write…so here goes, had this written just a while ago, but never sent it, guess I needed Mike's recent story that he sent to me to jar the spirit.

Basketball practice was over. The gym was cool and the floor shiny. Big D painted on the floor of the gym, bleachers pushed in today except for one row someone had pulled out to sit and watch practice.

Remember how the curtains hung on the stage. During Sunday School on Friday, when we met on that stage, sometimes we would sneak out around the curtains and listen from the other side. Remember the curtains were drawn during our graduation ceremony that night. We sat on the right side of the stage, as the audience saw it. 4 rows of 15 year olds, unaware of the significance of that night, all that got them there, the trauma of what was to follow in the upcoming days.

Basketball practice was over and I showered and walked outside, it was over 100 degrees, easily, and the humidity was around 80%. I stepped down the 6 steps that led from the entry to the Junior High wing of the school.

How many times had I gone up and down those steps? Going up was harder, sometimes homework wasn't done and I had to find a helping hand, sitting on the cement wall, who would let me see theirs real quick before the bell rang. Did you get all your Algebra done??

We graduated, yeah!! Just got out of the library, where we primped over our hair and the girls told each other how great they looked, the boys stood around with their hands in their pockets and made weird faces at the people taking pictures. How do 15 year olds know what had just happened in the last 10 plus years of their existence? They have no concept of the upcoming events in their young lives. They have no appreciation for what has just occurred to this point. An accumulation of events, classes, teachers and such, as happens to every boy and girl, but there's something else. There were travels, smells, beach happenings, walks around town at various times of day and night, friendships with so many cultures, coolie boots and bangles, houseboys and gardeners, the mail center and teen canteen, things that set us apart from the rest of the world, things only we can talk about, meaningless to millions. Handzus' fence was real low and easy to jump over and hide under, it's grown higher now and Big Tom is gone, Little Tom lives in Calif. and goes fishing in Mexico a lot. He's still the handsome devil he always was. Did you know he bowls better with a cast on his left forearm, and man can he throw those little kids bowling balls fast!!

Basketball practice had been good, twisted an ankle a little trying to make a jump shot like Jim Crawford, but failed miserably. I'll stick to the set shot I guess, Mr. Long says it works just as good most of the time. It'll be ok for Wednesday's game. Then after the game I'll see everyone at the Canteen, wonder who the chaperones are this week, hope not my parents!! I walk across the little road where the busses drove to drop off the kids, where some parents or even taxi's did the same. Then I step over the little 6 inch curb between that road and 3rd street, and I sit down on it, waiting for the bus today, don't want to walk home, too hot and muggy.

They call out our names and we get our diplomas, sit back down and wonder, what now? School somewhere, thousands of miles away perhaps, but that's not the big priority, the moment is, the coming night's events are. Isn't that where 15 year olds live, in the moment? If we had known what was coming we would have panicked. We were being thrown out of the womb. Nothing would be the same, maybe some years of returning studenthood? Maybe a letter or call from Mom or Dad saying their stay where you grew up is over, we'll pass by and see you on our way home to California? Texas? New York? somewhere where you will now live. No more baby pool and ping pong or iodine in baby oil in the sun, no more tri-d's, bus trips to Khobar and hey, I never got to say bye to Karen or Charlie or Lynn or Tom or Bill or Bobby or..............This doesn't sit right with me, feels like I just jumped off the edge of the world and no one is there to catch me. I always had the summer to look forward to, and I was going to be on the tri-D committee this time, and we had our summer bowling team all set, and we were going to watch the guys play softball and then go to the canteen afterwards. This doesn't sit right with me.

Basketball practice had been over for a while. As I sit on the little curb, waiting for the bus, I realize how hot the surface is on my bottom, man it stings. I said to myself, self, we're sitting here through this, on the 3rd St. curb, it will be really hot for a little while, then it will ease and the bus will come soon. Then I said to myself, let's remember this moment for the rest of my life. Don't know why I said that, but I did. The sun is still really hot, but getting a little lower in the sky, haze in the air, as usual, from the dust, high humidity causes beads of sweat to roll down my face. Man is my bottom stinging, but I won't move, never sat through this before but I will today, have to create a memory you know. Can't believe I'm doing this, wonder why?

Graduation is over, had a great night, many of my friends partied all night, I went home, as usual, watched HZ22TV and went to bed around 11, smoky in the house again, both parents smoke and our Swedish prefab is not that big, only one bathroom. Fordo lives across the street from me and Ronnie George just at the end of 7th, Bettencourts in the duplex almost next door, Danee Sullivan is just down the street in that neat brick house. We meet Handzus most every morning and our group walks to school together.

Think one reason I'm really hot today is from Basketball practice, and then this really hot seat doesn't help, neither does the 80+% humidity, but they say it keeps the skin looking young. So................you think you'll remember this for the rest of your life huh?? Maybe. The pain is subsiding. It's tingling a little, but OK. The bus will be here any minute, probably could have walked home just as fast, through that little skinny walkway across from the school, up around the AC plant, bearing rt, passing that circle, then turning rt. up 7th, to 725, big hedge around the front yard. Catepillar droppings on the sidewalk today, where is that guy, there he is, horns on the front of his head, about 3 inches long, eating away. Lets flick him off into the street, he curls up, remember how they did that, don't want to step on it, too much stuff comes squirting out, really gross. Windows at home really dripping today, can't see inside for all the moisture. AC is on almost every minute of every day. Getting a little excited, shipment is coming in a couple days, about 16 boxes this time, Dad takes a couple boards from the boxes up to the Hobby Shop and shaves them down into chips to use to make stuff they drink, course they filter it first to get rid of the small wood stuff floating in the bottle. Lone Ranger on the radio today, along with Inner Sanctum, have the schedule pinned to the wall next to my bed.

THANKS FOR THE MEMORIES

Joel sent this and gave permission to post it. I thought his memories were very important to remind many of us what we do have in common. What does make us a little different and most of all, what our group is all about.

Maybe I'm getting older, but this type of post held my full undivided attention. I was with him in spirit as he put his footprint in the sand and there when the class graduated.

I'm certainly all for the chat being a forum, but boy, doesn't this type of post make all of you, 1946- 1997 realize what a group we are ?

THANKS FOR THE MEMORIES
MIKE

Yesterday I finally logged on to your page with all the pictures of your recent trip and the gallery of old ones. I looked at the recent ones first and had waves of nostalgia sweep over me even though things ha certainly changed in the 30+ years since I had been there—but I still recognized so many things. Maybe it was the atmosphere and ambiance that has changed so little. Then I looked at the old picts of RT. I was pleasantly surprised to find that they were from my generation/time-frame. In fact I thought I recognized my own foot print in the sand in the picture of the old RT Theatre taken just as it opened in 1950 (51?). But what a rush. Wow. And then, of course, I started remembering all those names and faces of people I knew in the Nejma school and hadn't thought about in all these years. I even went so far back in memory as to remember attendind the Second Graduation—held on the pattio of the old Rec Hall down in Camp - and the two graduates Bill Tracy and Nancy Bradfield (Though Jim Manderville will probably tell me they were with him and David Wasson the following year—which may be true—after all that was nearly 50 years ago now, how accurate do you think my memory is, anayway?). But I was amazed at how one thing kept triggering another and like that old mosetrap-pingpong ball demonstration of atomic reaction, my mind was suddenly flooded with mostly appy and plesant memories. Thanks for all the work you have done in maintaining our past as well as keeping us presently in touch and up to date.

Joel Danciangfire Brehm—RT '54

TSI LAW'NEE—FLOWER MOON

In ages past, our old ones were the story-tellers. This was the way things were passed along to the generations that followed. For this reason the aged people make it a point to remember every detail so they could relate it at a later time. They were the word and picture carriers making history and spiritual values alive and important....Age is a grace, and time is too valuable to waste.

HALF MOON/MOTORCYCLE

I guess most of you remember how we used to have picnic's sponsored by Student Rec. etc. at the old Half Moon Bay.

Anyhow, this was also the first summer that ARAMCO had allowed motorcycles in camp, actually only Honda 50's with the big front shield.

Anyhow, if you remember Half Moon Bay you remember the pier that went out into the water and at the end it formed a "T" with the main walkway to the "T" being anchored and the front or top bar of the whole "T" floated up and down with the waves and was hooked on to poles so it could go up and down with the tide also.

Well, there was this little ramp that you walked up or down to get on the "T" top and a this time the water was pretty choppy and was making the floating Top go up and down. Debbie Dirr was sitting there if I recall right. She's a special person. Anyway, Tom Masso, I believe, came roaring down the walkway on his Honda and was planning on scaring the people off the end into the water. Well, he hit the little ramp just as the floating T rose up and that propelled him into the air.

Amazingly enough, I can still hear him changing gears as he went over us and into the bay, about ten feet from the edge. The language used at the time was record setting and I hurt so hard laughing that I was in tears. Anyhow, we finally dove down, got it out and spent a good part of the day drying everything off...and you know, that tuff little machine came to life and was ridden back to Dhahran. Harley's, hurmph !

I do apologize to Tom Masso if it wasn't him, it might have been Peter Pestoni, but the humor of the day has made my senile mind go blank.

Mike, Honda 50 from Hell, Angel (DH65)

AC tower

Chatters,

Sorry about no Daily yesterday...seems we had a tornado and two of my properties were torn up a little, plus we lost power for about six hours. Can't figure out why my computer doesn't run when the lights are out...

Anyhow, in Rodney Burge's tape he goes and shows the cooling tower that is still running.

As might be expected, I have a story about that beast...

It was a very hot day, July 4th, 1967, and I was with Chris Mohlman, Linda Mestrezat, and Peter Pestoni.

We had been standing by the tower and noticed that there was a kinda ladder running up one side...so as if you didn't know, we decided to climb up. Incidently the tower was off, or at least there was no noise. We got about three fourths the way up when we found a little trap door, so in we went... Man, what a neat place for a hangout..

There were wooden floors evey fifteen feet, actually slats that were about four inches wide and then a space of about four inches and then the next slat.

And there was a regular ladder inside that went to the top, so we climbed all the way. At the top they had there two large fans to blow air down thru the slats when the tower was on and water would run and be cooled down this way.

Since it was off, Chris and I and Linda climbed on top and were looking around. We were up pretty high and we could see the school.

I and Chris climbed back in and linda went down the outside all the way to the ground. Suddenly we started getting water pouring down on us...it felt terrific, like being in a warm shower. Well, we decided to get out and dry off and we found that the little trap door was a self latching thing. Linda couldn't hear us because of the water so we decided to climb out the top. No big deal.

We got to the top and Chris wiggled past the fan, which was off, and the I got out and we were helping Peter, when the damn fan started turning.... Now Peter was on the fan blade. These things were like eight feet long and two feet wide each. Peter is going round and round holding on to the fan, we are yelling for help and Linda is waving "Hello" to us, not realizing that ten feet from her was a big red painted emergency stop lever. And not knowing Peter was picking up speed.

The only humor in this is that as the fan went around Peter lost his sandals and then his shorts. In those day Jock-staps were signs of manhood so he had that on and nothing else.

Chris literally jumped from level to level to the ground to get down and try to stop this thing before the speed got going and Peter was killed by the spinning blades.

Well, he managed to do it and we got Peter out and down....he walked real funny and didn't seem to realize that he had only a jock strap on. I think the spinning addled his mind.

So we are trying to get him home and the July 4 th parade starts down King's Row, which we had gotten to in order to cross over by the dining hall to get him home..He is still wacked out from dizziness and all of a sudden there he is in front of the parade walking from side to side dressed to kill.

Needless to say, I along with the Chris, Linda had run home, spent some time being entertained by Aramco Security, Mr. Kieswetter, who could not think of enough things to plan for our immediate future....

Nonetheless, I was truly amazed when I saw that tower after almost thirty some odd years, and immediately saw Peter in a Jock Strap in front of possibly several hundred people in a parade..What a day.

Off to the local Carrier AC man for some memories.

LOCUSTS.....
YUMMMMMM.

In the streets. They were so thick the air was black and the buzzzing was like a dentist drill. I think I even got one stuck up my....opps...My Mom came out and started screaming at me to get inside and they got in her hair and I made the only near fatal mistake of my life..I rat tailed her head to get them off her and the smack was heard in Bagdad. Left a welt the size of the Grand Canyon, at that point, locust no longer mattered to Mom, the death of her first born was all that was on her mind, to hell with bugs.

I know I outran the swarm to the main gate and was on my way to Houfuf and thought I had a good running start, but Mom was like a relentless Kenworth...Just roaring down and the grill was covered in bugs. I knew that I'd never get the locusts out of all the places she was going to stick them in, so I ran into the Camel Sug, right outside Abqaiq and hid behind a camel. The Arabs had covered the camels ears and noses and eyes so the wouldn't panic and get any in their faces, so I covered my head and pretended that If I couldn't see her, she couldn't see me. First time I thought seriously about the French Foreign Legion, and I was only a little tyke, because she had grabbed Doug's Mom's pan and let me have it. MY head ang for hours and I don't know how long my butt rang, but for day's I answered the phone when it wasn't ringing.

The Great Locust Invasion was reapeated several times over the years, but the Saudi Govternment finally got the nesting place killed oof in Africa nd the swarms stopped, however, I will tell an interesting little story about a "Shamal" that took the paint of of a Aramco car and actually flayed some skin off an employee in Abqaiq soon.....

Got to run, got the munchies....

MASH

Talking about the movie "MASH 4077" with a friend of mine reminded me of another time in a far off land and mash...

Seems like it was awful easy to party when there was brown or white available. I had gotten pretty good at sneaking in when Dad would leave his post for a few minutes to go the bathroom or such, turn the little spigot and drain out enough to fill a jar then take off. He used to keep his mash in taped up water bottles in a small closet.

Now he had another closet like box that he had a lock on for the finished product. I would remove the hinge screws, open the door and pour out a half gallon, refill the old mans supply with water and put the door back on and then using model car paint, touch up the screw heads so that there was no sign of then being opened. After all, if a screw is painted over it looks like it has been there for years...so I thought.

Mom and Dad were going to be gone for the weekend and I guess it was in August 1968, which I'm sure the incident had no bearing on, but it was my last visit as a returning student.

I decided that making white was no big deal...I had watched intently for years.. So out comes the big metal still onto the stove and in goes the mash.

Knowing that it was going to take hours, I got into the supply, after all I was making more and I would just substitute it when I was done, right ?

Every thing fitted together just right and I knew that Dad had often used what I thought was a big thermometer and would put it in a sleeve and every so often read it then bleed out liquid gold. I just left the thermometer in the slot and every so often would take the spigot and drip some into a spoon. Now I had been told that first run stuff was highly flammable so I tested the little spoon by lighting it, and sure enough the process seemed to ne working, It caught fire nicely.

A friend had come over, her name to remain secrets due to possible problems with her family today and we went out into the living room to "talk". I know that conversation can drag on, but who would have thought. Three hours later I happen to ask her if she wanted a Bepsi or something and walked into the kitchen..There on the stove was this huge, by now, red metal box I had completely forgot about. The thermometer was broken an the little spigot was red hot. I ran into the other room, gathered things up and told her I need to take care of an emergency and please go on home.... As she got mad and started to leave the kitchen disappeared..She went over to the Cohea's who lived across the alley and called the fire department. I went into the kitchen and with the garden hose was trying to fight this blaze. The still had split and the stove was on fire big time..I just knew Dad would get deported and I would be put to death..Needless to say the fire department got there and everything was under control...they left and damage control was on my mind. It was Thursday night and I had until Friday night to get it all back together or leave the country.

I had no idea that Aramco had contacted Dad in RT and they were already on their way home. I got the parts of the thermometer in the cardboard sleeve and put it on the floor in the closet of his supplies, thinking, OK, he'll think it fell off the shelf and broke, never mind the damn thing was black....

The stove I repainted, they were all white and painted the coils black...I didn't know it took special paint to withstand heat....and the still, well that was a major problem. It was split at one seem and the thing had a rounded look to it. Kinda cute I thought, with no knowledge Death from Rt was approaching.

So I took a hammer and beat the thing into a, I thought, hardly distinguishable, difference from the original and used duct tape to seal the seem, planning on putting it back and hoping dad wouldn't be making any more white until I left for school.

A friend helped me get the water out of the kitchen and Mom had the kitchen painted a light blue, I had only white, so I painted the wall with the most smoke damage white. It seemed like hours, but was really only minutes.. The smell was kinda bad, so we opened all the windows and went out on to the back porch to have a little white and congratulate ourselves on "getting away with it " Suddenly, and to this day I still think I heard the opening strands of Phantom of the Opera, the back door exploded of it's hinges and there was two of the biggest, mean looking adults the world knew. My friend bailed out, over the wall and gone, as I was trying to do, but my feet seemed stuck..Calmly I asked, "Your'e home early, any problems ?" All with the look of total innocence.

Grounded until my fortieth Birthday and asunder other punishments, which included paying for a new still out of summer earnings I never got out of trouble. OH, forgot to mention that the next day Mom was cooking and the stove caught fire and flashed from both my paint and a residue I guess of mash, or mix. I'm fortunate that Aramco only allowed shipments every year or so because I'm sure that after using every belt in the house, going to neighbors and borrowing theirs Mom would have ordered more and calmly waited for the shipment to arrive. I had managed to sizzle her hair, and what was worse than a Mom with fried hair..Being hit by a Kenworth perhaps.

My saving grace was the fact that while riding with my "Uncle John Reagan in his little MG sports car we had been going to Abqaiq, one of the four times I was let out that month, and saw a donkey in the road. Since we had the top down I decided to swat the sucker and make him get off the road, we passed him doing 65 kph and I broke three bones in my hand and two fingers. Hard ass he was. My "uncle" roared for and hour until we got to the clinic in ABq. On the way back the damn donkey was still there, I had a cast and Mom had a new belt given to her compliments of the fire department. No symphony here I can tell you.

ALL IN ALL A FRUITFUL SUMMER

That's about all I know. New Information. About Mr. Earl Greaves, 9th grade art teacher.

Mr. Greaves came to my house after my Mom and Dad had passed away and stayed with me for several months. Wanting to make sure I was ok. Unfortunately he had problems I didn't know about and died in my apartment. I took him, along with six firefighters, he was at 480 pounds and we went to Intensive care where he was revived. The Doctor told me to call the family and I did. Becky flew out immediately while he was still conscious. Nancy made it the next day and she was able to see him, although he was comatose and within 15 minutes he had passed on. I buried him in a very well kept private military cemetery and he know has a cross and has joined his God which he always prayed about. An interesting note as I was disposing all his items, sent some to each daughter, but I found that his mobile home plate was in reality hand painted by this great artist.

CROCKER BOY
IN TAXI

I saw where someone asked about a Crocker being born in a taxi at the police checkpoint and whether it was just some idiot story…I think it was one of my idiot brothers ;>

He wouldn't have been born in a taxi, but while passing thru the Kingdom of Thugba we had to resport to a donkey pulled limo (The Royal transport) and finally found a little yellow Toyota taxi, with thirty five Pakistanis already in it, and went on to Dhahran Hospital, which later became where you could exchange women and cheaply too.

After being born, the Rabbi was called in as he had a funny nose, turned out it was just bent because he had been pressed against the side of the car.

The only problem he has today is that every time he hears "Want a taxi, Baby ?" he gets emotional and wants to hug the cab and call it "Mommy".

I will, of course, deny writing this as someone else has used my terminal while I was waiting for a cab….:)

Mike, err…ahhh…

AWOL AND
A FEW OTHER
COMMENTS ;->

As far as going awol or pulling pranks, I think San Marcos Baptist Academy had a large percentage of such stories. Mayhaps because so many Brats went there. Kevin Colgan was my roommate and we lived in the "fishbowl" dorm called Crook Hall. I always wondered about the name. One of the stories that I well remember was when the Commandant, Col. Archie Buckner came out when we were at moring roll call and parade and announced that someone had stolen underwear from another Cadet and we were going to do a spot check right there. The parade ground was between and in front of several dorms and a lot of females students passed by on their way to breakfast. We normally marched to the mess hall.

So without much ado, we were ordered to drop our pants and the Company Commander was to inspect the labels as we all had our names sewn in. The best part of this was the fact that many didn't have time to get properly dressed and so there were many a shiny hinney showing to the great amusement of the girls and others. The cilprit was not found and I aways thought it was due to a different esecape over Christmas which I'll tell later. I also left the school without permission and was expelled in my

Senior year. I actually graduated from San Marcos High School and even tho I have finanically supported SMA I did not finish there.

As far as fitting in, in 1968 Aramco Security, where I spent my last summer student job in tried to put together a plan to explain the conversion from Aramco to Stateside, Mr. Hank Brentari and I worked on this but at the time Aramco never got it off the ground. Hank was a great Security man and a friend over the years.

I follwed the exploits of many of us for years and there was a very obvious thread of not fitting in and although we, or many did adapt, most seemed to be loners or dropped away from their Aramco heritage and became as the locals.

I have always felt that by not having finished High School in Arabia, many of us never got closure, I found that in the previous reunions, much closure was achieved by being able to once again touch a dear ones face, or shake the hand of a best friend.

Most reunions and in particular Chandler were and are magic. The next reunion will be such I think. I have heard many are concerned about money and cost. Let me tell you, there is no cost or sacrifice that is not worth suffering through in order to once again see the ones we held dear.

The unemployment issue has been brought up and the points of comment are interesting, but I also lost my business and employment, but turned other things to my advantage and although not as happy as I was once, will live just fine in the world of employment, even if it is tenuous at best. I find the extensive reporting about "conditions" in the employment field to be an excuse. I'll put up with a lot to have some security. I can always fuss later. Too many of us are out of work and many of us were close to retiring and many have had to adjust. So we adjust and maybe not make the "standards" a major point.

Iraq eems to be a diversion by the Bushies, he will have his way or as his Dad, go back to hiding. He did the same tactics in Texas, "His way or the Highway" and when the time came, it was the highway, although I feel that we have pushed him out of Texas to the Presidency for which some of us feel may have not been prudent.

All of the above is my own personal opinion, not wanting the typical twenty day debate on words or lines of words, but the most important thing of all is to remember that we are all Americans and we grew up in Arabia and a lot of what happens affects us somewhat deeper than it might a local person.

I think that many Brats have chose to let go of things that were negative in Aramco, and there was a lot more then the few we have heard about. However we, and I am as guilty as others, have made our time there seem to be a fantasy, and in reality it wasn't. Our education may have been the best thing to come from Aramco, but there was also a sense of safety and freedom that we and Saudi Aramco kids today no longer have. Ladies and Gentlemen, the world has changed and we are parting the veils of history to look at a past that seemed much brighter and free, however the dark side was there also. The Aramco I knew is not the Aramco of today, but that is a good thing for Saudi Aramco has achieved many great things and progress always starts small and in this case, grew up fast and furious.

DOES ANYONE
KNOW WHY?
PERHAPS POETRY?

A small boy walks about the sandy ground. his eyes twinkle and his thoughts are of mischief. There are few others and he seems in a daze, but what is happening is the beginning of a great part of his lifes phase. He knows he will travel the land alone but his heart knows he must do it. His mission, to find a friend. His skills, not too finely honed for he is alone. You can tell that he knows but won't accept that dark cloud in a scorching bright day, for its a young adventurer, alone and that way to say.

His Mom is at home, no grass to water, no water to waste. His Dad is working, an office somewhere. He knows not where. His little heart seems surrounded by doubt, but he boldly goes and looks about. There is activity as he looks and the wind is blowing. The sand stings his face and his cherub like features wrinkle from the heavy thought he understands not. He know he is alone, for he sees his tracks. A single pair that run nowhere. What does one do when one has run, and now looks around and sees that he is now fifty three. His tired eyes look around once again. The grass is green and the place is a maze. He walks the path where he trod as a boy, but where did he come from and where does he go. He feels the pain of a thousand alone, yet knows he walks the path of many others before and after his vigil began. He knew as a child he would stand tall, but he knows as a man that he has fallen down and maybe it was that day so long ago…when he looked down the sandy road and felt for the first time, the emptiness and loneliness inside. He knew back then that friends would not come, a loner perhaps without any fun. He grew in his life, but doing not well, his mind accepting he had no one to tell. What did the boy say at the age of one? What does the man do as he passes fifty two?

His mom and his dad, his family and more, he feels the heat but his heart is sore. He doesn't know why, and he starts to cry. But perhaps its best, for young he may be he knows he must die.

Many years later, passing this way, he looks around where he used to play. The ground is now hard, the sand is gone and concrete is the name of the land. His playground of dunes has become the well of progress and his friends all gone, or where they ever there to start with? He looks with eyes that see many a day and his heart hurts as he surly did pay. And now as he sits, in the land of his life, and looks at the people, he knows it is not right. The place has changed and the people have gone, what happen to them and why did he forget. He loved this place, the home of his start. A leap of faith and a thought of his fate, but then he remembers, he loved this place. The taste of the sand, the smell of oil, the water lashing the beach of his youth. He walks the roads and paths of a child, his mind lost in the days of his youth, but where does he go and how does it seem, that fifty years later, the boy still has his dream?

As you have guessed, he is really a mess, but he finds that if he goes back in his mind, his heart does lift, a little as time drains away as the sand from his tilted hand, yet he also knows there is only so much land. His mind is numb from all of the fun, but his heart is cold for it is in a dark place. Someone shut the door to it a long time ago, he never opened it again and now he must go.

However fear not my dears for he shall return, he will do it all again and again. He loves the air, the night above and although much older, he wanders that sandy road and always looks as if he knows, but in reality, the boy is lost. He will one day see this and decide to change, but change is hard and friends are not there, so many are gone and he wonders if it is fair?

At the best he can only say, It is another day and the way is more clear. Yet the pain of the life that lost so much makes him struggle and then shake like a bear. The sand flies off of the storm about his soul and he feels the weather change and knows he must go. He looks around and glances down, the sand is there he has but to touch it and become once more aware. God gave him his life to enjoy as best, but he might have missed it if not for the rest.

Perhaps he thinks this jumble of words has a goal but he knows not what. Just some thoughts from awaking from a dream of the sand. A single tear rips from his eye and thunders down his face and flies into the sky. It strikes the ground and shatters, yet in a way, it is all that matters. His youth is there, in the sand of his soul, but the life he has, he made by his will, now let him start, for he knows he must. He has awakened and lost his touch. But the boy who walked into the sun, shall once again make a rule of fun.

My dad was one of many that had a device that seemed to take up much of the kitchen many days of the month. I was always somewhat interested, but when I asked, it was always a very short communication between he and I. "Leave!"…very simple and direct. Usually meant with a conviction that spoke volumes without the blink of an eye. In fact, to this day his eyelashes seem to have a permanent twist which has always given him the appearance of a devilish sort. Something that a bright young man should, cue word here, "should" have realized they didn't curl like that due to an immeasurable sense of humor. Not when the kitchen was 300 degree's and he seemed stuck to the plastic of the kitchen table chair.

Well, I had heard a discussion between my mom and dad and another friend of theirs and it seems they were planning a large reception. They decided to put two of the devices on the stove and run them in tandem. Now this would have intrigued anyone, much less a very bright young lad with the brain pan of a mouse, as was stated later. My dad had let me see a little of what he was doing, as I was being forced marched out the back door and to impress me, he opened this little spigot and put just a few drops of this, what appeared to me to be water, in a spoon. Holding it out he took a match lit it and "Woof!" the spoon ignited and there was a flash and a little fireball. The point he said was that this stuff was very tricky and I should go out and play dodge the traffic on sixth street. That way I would stay out of the forbidden zone. "What if I get hungry?" I yelled, "Eat Grass" was the rude retort…This comment was a direct reflection on the fact that the day before I had taken the challenge from someone like Tom Painter to eat one of the green caterpillars that were in the hedges. I did and proved that projectile exporting is not just a scientific term. Course Tom wasn't at all happy and his mom had called my mom, thus the smart remark when I said I might get hungry. Now Locust, that was a different story. Not bad when fried by the gardeners...course one has to realize that you don't go up to your mom and, with the back end and feet of a locust in your mouth, ask her opinion. The smack jarred teeth and the locust loose. Didn't do to much for my ego to hear the howls of laughter from the Saudi gardeners who were frying more in the yard.

So after sitting for about an hour, on the curb in front of my house watching the massive New York style traffic flow, I think one donkey cart passed by with shrimp for sale, I was really bored. Now a bored rapscallion is similar to turning a water buffalo loose at a chess match, sponsored no doubt by the local church having a pie sale. Just to make sure I covered the bases here.

Having played with my toy soldiers from the giant Civil War, Blue and Grey set I had for Christmas, I got to thinking that I could most likely build a cannon and play for real. After all, I had the toy one...Inside the hedges were pipes every so many feet. It took several hours to dig one loose, get the wires off it and set it on the ground. Course I was scratched to the hilt from the hedge, but when one is intent on evil ways, you don't notice you look like a neighbors Manchurian tiger pet cat had had you for lunch. Now I needed to mount this pipe and the Cohea's that lived across the alley had some old car springs that were loose on the side of their house. Try dragging that ton of scrap across the alley and into the yard. All of the time with the wailing and tearing of clothes from the hysterical mirth of the Arab gardeners, who by now have called friends over to watch this crazed American sway wahlid.

I finally got the spring upside down to form an arch, used mom's clothes line, just cut a section, she'll never notice, and spend some time tying the pipe to the spring. I actually had a pretty good looking field piece. About a 155 Howitzer compared to me, but still...I had blocked the one end by digging a small hole and setting the pipe in it and now needed to find something to fire. I had a cap pistol and knew the little red caps would go "Bang" when struck, so I put about a years supply down this pipe. At this point one of the Arabs crawled over, stopping to gather his wits ever so often and told me I need to pack it in and find a way to light the caps, which would then make a "bang". So digging up the buried end I put one of mom's dish cloths from the now useless umbrella revolving type clothes line. I mean, come on, who knew all those dumb strings stretched tight made the thing stand out. Not now, but in better days..

I added in a bunch of rocks in the pipe for cannon balls and lit the fuse. Nothing. It just went out. So did several of the Arabs, now about ten, who could no longer stand the laughter and whose sides must have really hurt. No fear, the dauntless one is here. I had a stroke of genius, one which mom has for years refereed to as a complete black out of electrical signals in my brain and I headed inside to the kitchen...Yes, you got it. I remembered the small spoon and ball of fire.

Dad must have gone to the bathroom and I saw a bowl in the sink and so I filled it withe the water from the little spigot tap and grabbed some more Aramco safety matches, a true misnomer if ever there was one according to mom a short while later at Clinic "C". I poured this water down the pipe and put some on the cloth and with a might swipe of the red and blue tipped match, caused Aramco to shudder and I am sure indirectly brought about the near death of ten Arabs who were now semi conscious and almost paralyzed with laughter.

The blast wasn't so bad, but the pipe end that was supposed to be blocked except for the so called fuse, had done what the Doctor later told me, jumped up and "back flashed a huge ball of fire" that got me. It only lasted a second, but I had very little hair left, no eyebrows and a tee shirt that looked as if someone had heaved a pile of camel dung right on me. I think I was almost completely black and still smouldering when mom came out the door like a rocket. The Arabs are by now lying down and uncontrollable and mom must have thought I killed them all. The pipe was about twenty feet down the alley and I was flat, spread out and smoking still.

Well, to say the least, once home from the clinic the sympathy stopped flat dead. Mostly because mom saw her clothes line. To say I was soon smoking again might be an understatement.

HALF MOOOOON BAY

You know, it is not always smart to take on a teacher in a dare. I found this out when I brazenly smarted off to Mr. Goellner that as far as I could see, he was all talk about his scuba diving. Needless to say the challenge was met with a stare that froze the hair on my butt. Yet even worse was the calm, detached voice of impending doom. Which said, "Have you and your buddies at Half Moon Bay at 9:30 Thursday morning and we dive on the old yacht wreck. 60 feet. Got it?"

Having dived many times on the wreck, we called it the "Holy Grail", as someone in the past had struck a sheep skull on the bow and it was eerie coming up on it. Anyway, I knew it well and thought "HA!" the old geezer is in for it now. So bright and early, Tom Campion, Chris Mohlman, James Goellner and Myself were there and preparing for battle. Knives were finely honed, triple rubber "arbelete's" were armed and made ready. Warheads attached and aqualungs bled and swim shorts adjusted. Just never could get the hang of the nylon net inside of swim suits..was there a purpose other than to put you in a strangle hold at 40 feet and hopelessly twist and turn as you buddies died laughing. I don't think you will ever see such a sight as five divers with massive air bubbles heading up as they literally blew up with laughter. Hell, get rid of the shorts, it was easier and who was there but us men…so as you can imagine, here are us mighty men of the deep, two with suits. Real Olympians I'd say.

Down at the wreck Tom see's the mother of all hammour's. Quickly he goes for the kill and Chris takes a long angled shot. Both hit this massive monster and by tugging managed to fill the water with fish parts and, yes, you guessed it, blood.

Now these two are engaged in a death struggle with each other and James Goellner sees something on the bottom and goes over and sticks it with his spear gun. Chris later claimed someone shot at him as he had a spear thru one of his fins. Never was able to prove anything tho….

Suddenly the sand explodes and the menacing shape of what I saw as a fifty foot grey shark darts away and moves around. Mr. Goellner is giving everyone the signal to head up and this shark rips the hammour right in half. Now this pissed both Chris and Tom off to no end. I am more concerned about what may be in the water the shark might decide is tasty and ignoring all diving rules, went to the top, and allegedly beat Mr. Goellner and James to shore only because I was able to run on the water like a bat out of hell, flippers, gun and all going in every which direction.

The visual on this is the group of people under the canopies and the sight they must have seen. Two naked boys, masks and tanks, and moving like enraged camels to the kill trying to get to shore and all the time coming close to drowning by yelling, "Shapppppppp" Salt water in the mouth and throat tends to distort words.

Meanwhile Chris and Tom have attacked the shark with twin spear shots. While we are on the road to Dharan, flippers, butt's and masks running at a heady pace, they are calmly pulling this thing out of the water and hanging it on the old hook scale by the flag pole. I guess it was more like 3 feet, but it looked like "Jaws" to me.

A large crowd is gathered by now, and of course, what does the unflappable Mr. Goellner do, "Hey Crocker, come over here and lets get a picture of this". Yeah, sure, naked glory and a shark about half the size of a Hamoour. He laughed for days and made many points in gym class about our daring "exposure" with the shark. Claimed the shark preyed on shrimp, what ever that was supposed to mean. Yet I do remember a lot of snickering.

What made this event so memorable was that I believe it was the first recorded case of "Mooooning" Aramco employees in the beginning of a long and fine standing tradition carried on bravely by younger Brats in later years.

In particular on the Kenworth buses going to and from the other districts. Must have really done a lot for public relations.

CAN YOU IMAGINE WHERE ALL THE SAND WENT?

By the way, for you that don't know it, Chris and Tom had their photo in the Sun and Flare a little later for spearing a Hammour or Sea Bass that weighed in at over 300 pounds. At the time, the largest ever caught. Speared off the old water injection plant by the massive North dune.

Another fine mess my mouth got me into.

HALLOWEEN THOUGHTS

Just had to jump in here a tad. One Halloween we (me, Jay Johansen, and Barry Knott) egged an outside party at the Cramptons. Just tossed 'em over a big hedge, ran like hell. Caused quite a ruckus, I believe.

Later, we encountered a large dark figure apparently leading a few smaller ones in the conduct of nefarious deeds.

Through yelled conversation, we learned that they had big blocks of wax and were writing neat things on the front windows of houses backwards so they could be read by the owner from inside. Well, we'd never heard of this activity and thought it was darn cool...we wanted to do it too!

I yelled a request for the large kid to toss me part of a block of wax so we could partake of the same type of mischief. He tossed it alright. He sent it over like a major league pitcher. It being a bit dark, I missed catching it, and it hit me square between the eyes; nearly knocking me out.

Who was the "pitcher"? Mike Crocker, of course.

Michael R. Grimler

HELLS ANGELS-HONDA 50 STYLE

Aramco in it's infinite wisdom had banned all motorcycles within the compounds around 1957. By 1963 they had relented and thus was born the Hells Angels, Aramco Chapter, Born to Lose "biker gang"....Course they restricted us to Honda 50's with a two liter engine and automatic shift...not the"Hawg" we wanted, but close enough.

The fact is it was August and 120 degrees and the leather jackets were about 200 pounds heavy and we were most likely the laughing stock of the known world, we knew we were truly lost rebels...Motorcycle boots, nah, coolie boots were all we could bear. So starts the adventure.

To show how impressive we thought we were..here is the mental image. Ten roaring motorcycles, with black leather jackets, chain swinging from every pocket, roaring up to the stop sign on 3rd street going to Recreation.. imagine "Bringgggg-ding-ding-ding, Brinnnng-Ding-Ding", the sound of ferocious motors revving up and the tough, albeit clean shaven faces of the toughest eight and ninth graders in town. Not really tough looking with big wide scooter shields in front on each Honda, but we meant business and you could take that to the bank...

The fun part was roaring past Security and getting them chase us. At 30 mph top speed we were real threats to the peace of the camp, but Security felt obligated to chase us. Might have had something to do with the watermelons we threw at Sayid, but that's just a guess. So off we dash, it's getting dark and several cut down a hedge lined sidewalk on the Hill. Unbeknownst to them, some fool had added a room extension to their house and the end stuck across the sidewalk, allowing for a very skinny person to get by. Well, you can imagine the cal'am that took place when three devils from hell shot down the sidewalk, no lights and shouting remarks such as, "Moonlight, Star bright, Security couldn't catch a tur-le to night ". HA ! the resulting pile up set records for abusive language and commentary. Sayid almost passed out with laughter and owner of the house came out with a garden house and started spraying the guys for their language.

Their ride to fame was short and in great humiliation, they had their Honda's confiscated and were sent home as Sayid roared out loud, and was heard for miles with such soothing words as "Lost, neede ride, wantee go home you toughee guys." Nothing like walking down the road, 200 pound jackets, dragging butts and chains and trying to act like nothing happened. Plus I personally think Sayid threw watermelon at them every fifty feet or so, but I can't prove it.

I, and five others on the other hand had gone home without knowing of this terrible defeat to our collective egos, but the next day, we beat them by far.

A glorious Wednesday and school is out and we roar up to Recreation, hitting the gravel right by the library and piling up. Seems we did a lot of that. Quickly jumping up and making sure no one saw us, we decided that we would head out th Half Moon Bay and camp overnight. The ride was one where the sand was blowing and we were hot as all get out and worse, a donkey cart and Arab passed us..no power at all against a strong wind, but onward we went. Getting there and drinking all the fresh water and even the shower drinking water we finally cooled down. The next day was the Forth of July party and we were all tough as nails and strutting around in out swim shorts and black jackets. We were so bright we had painted on the back of the jackets our club name. I never was good with spelling and somehow came out with "Hels Angles". I just knew the rest were wrong.

Well, the next event is recorded somewhere and may those involved forgive us, but the pier at half moon bay was a "T" shape thing with a floating cross piece at the end with a little ramp that went up and down with the swells…Any ideas here? Well, Tom Masso, sorry old buddy, roared down this pier and just as he got to the end, he was going to go out on the cross piece and turn fast and scare Debbie Dirr and some others into jumping it to the bay. Unfortunately for him, the water lifted the ramp and he instead went airborne. They say they could hear him changing gears as he went over them and down into the bay, gallantly riding his Honda from Hell all the way. He was rather descriptive from what I was told. Anyhow, it took some time to get it up and on shore, must to the collective amusement of the whole gang. And do you know, after it was all wiped down and checked, that little sucker started up.

Once back in town I took Sissy Quick and her sister and I all on the mean machine and started towards their house. That poor little machine had what looked like sand tires on it and I believe a speed bump thru Debbie off and onto a padded, I hope, backside.

I broke the rules for Honda's one last time. We weren't supposed to leave the camps with them..license, what license? But I drove it to RT from Dahahran. I must have lost fifty pounds of sweat and ended up in the clinic in RT with Mom and Dad coming to get me. I think my Honda went into the Gulf, but was a little delirious from the ride, the yelling and the amazing amount of times a small woman can smack a butt while on the run…… was asked to write a poem, and I am no poet but I made this effort. Do you all think I fell off a very large camel while quite young? Remember, in poetry, grammer doesn't count..please!!!!

"The Great North Dune sings it's song of love to the Desert"

The Great North dune slowly puff's it's way across the blazing desert floor, the sand whispers to its neighbor as it crawls to its end the great desert will reach the gulf and the life shall expire

However my heart listens and as the wind blows the wisp's from the top, the dune sings it's mournful song of life and loss, for buried in its heart is the love of two, two who may never touch, two who shall always be entwined as the dune and the desert are.

For their love may not consummate and heads for the end, to fail as the great dune fails to stop the rush to it's death at the hands of the water. The sand stings and whirls, but to no avail the dune sings in a whispering way, It's call, a call to love, but the end is near and the dune has no cheer. The warmth of the dune and the blazing sun of its heart will slowly like life, extinguish in a blaze, or whimper into the night air.

But as the stars reach down, brilliant lights of God, the dune feels the tremor and knows the love will live, for the spirit of the desert may not be put to sleep. It will sing and sing, of love, life and God.

Michael R. Crocker

Copyright 2001 Michael Crocker

HISTORICAL
PERSPECTIVE
(FENCING)

According to the 1947 issue of : "Aramco and World Oil", under "Safety and Identification," the first use of fencing was to protect building sites from materials being misappropriated by other Americans using the materials to build the complex and varied projects throughout the field of operations. This led to individual groupings of fencing and in 1953 when three oil company vehicles were recovered from Yemen, where they had mysteriously appeared, the oil company started protecting it's assets. Until 1950 many facilities had no fencing whatsoever.

Many facilities were located outside of any fencing until 1955 when Aramco, from California ordered all residential areas to be fenced in order to prevent disease infestation from wild donkeys, sheep and wild dog packs. Also the fencing was erected because several personnel had wandered out into the desert during storms and had been lost.

This also was the introduction of "Fish fly traps" in order to prevent infection from flies and mesquitos that abounded within the tribal groups who came to the American facilities to see what was happening. They "are to welcomed and referred to the Safety Department should any employee come into contact with them."

In 1953 the first complete fencing was done around Abqaiq and a set of gates established to protect materials and residential areas. Thus the materials handling gates and the Main gates to the camp facilities.

Incidently, and I quote here "The availability of alcoholic beverages is a privilege of all Americans, but it could be lost to all through serious abuses on the part of a very few......A second condition was that whenever any individual might imbibe too freely, he should remain in his quarters and not pass without or out of the camp into any Arab community." Sounds as if the fence had multiple purpose.

However, nowhere have I found any mention in the 1948, 1950, 1955 Govt.

Relations Handbook, or anywhere that any "Official" reason of separating the two cultures is mentioned. In fact 1949, 1950, and 1955 publications all seem to lean towards mixing the groups as much as possible," with the exception of weekends in which all the local personnel were sent to their homes and Americans lived in seclusion."

This last statement is not found in 1960 or other "Aramco and it's world" publications I have.

There is more, but I'm fenced in right now.

MIKE'S ESCAPADES

I just read the note on Mike & his escapades. Nope, over in RT we were just like Mike! For years, they kept a bulldozer down at the beach in RT. Needless to say, it took a lot of unscheduled trips. Heck, we used to start the thing every Teen Canteen dance (once a month) just to bug Security! Fortunately, both for ARAMCO and us brats, we tended to be very nondestructive. The aim was not to destroy things, but just to have a little fun. Of course, every once in a while things got out of hand. When that happened, the community was so small that the "culprits" usually got caught and punished one way or another. Looking back, I realize that a lot more was "noticed" than I realized at the time. When I was in 6th grade ('67 or '68), Duncan Smith, Phillip Nelson, and I decided it would be a good idea to make a little nitroglycerin. We had the recipe, we had the lab equipment, so all we needed were the acids. Fortunately for us, when we raided the Science Room for them, we took whole bottles, and of course, their dissapearance was immediately noticed. The excitement began when they added up what could be made with that particular combination of chemicals. Just before lunch they called an Assembly, and it was announced that if all materials were returned there would be no consequences. On the other hand, if they were not returned, those responsible, once caught, would be kicked out of

Arabia! We had a conference, and Duncan volunteered to be the sacraficial goat. It turned out that wasn't good enough. He came back and told us he had been told we all had to come in for the deal to work. Man, I still remember that afternoon quite clearly! What impresses me in hindsight is that a few months later Mr. Smith and few other men took us down to the swingsetson the beach (halfway between Rec and the North Fence) and demonstrated dynamite to us. I still remember a 2 ft thick and 5 ft by 5 ft slab of asphault road flying 50 feet up in the air. I lost my enthusiasm for reckless explosives after that. Our parents were smart people Fe mon Allah—Reed Brooks RT

MIKE'S TRIP TO ARABIA

AT 01:40 PM 3/21/97 -0500, JEFF94172@AOL.COM WROTE:

If after reading about Crocker's trip the people from AAAA don't give it up they are really spitting in the wind. In their invite they said they were concerned about hostile takeovers—I would think that at this point anyone can see that the deed is done—there's nothing left to take over except the money I guess. I mean, I don't know where he gets the time but what Crocker has done with this Chat thing is way beyond good. Not to mention the internet thing too. On top of that, this trip to Arabia to get us the recognition and possible benefits from the Saudi Gov.—well all's I can say is AAAA, what have you done that remotely compares to this? I'm not being nasty here—I'm saying he who does the work should get the benefit of it and if Crocker wants to be King of the Brats the pleasure be all mine!! Because he sure has brought me alot of pleasure with this thing. I suppose now he'll want me to kiss his butt when I see him in AZ and although there is a lot to kiss I guess he probably deserves it. To you guys in AAAA, forget about this San Antonio thing, come to AZ prepared to eat a meager portion of poo-poo and then hang with your old friends again—just like when we were kids.

JeffYaeger dh64

MIKE CROCKER RESPONSE

Jeff comments have always been the goal of all of us..to be family and friends. This has been my goal since day one and it is people like the brathood that make it all worthwhile...

PS, Jeff, have reserved spot on ample tail for well planted respect.

Monster Slide

Aramco took care of us kids, but I always felt there was a touch of malicious thought, most likely by parents who had kids who always caused them grief. I, not having any knowledge of that sort of thing, will still plead innocent to all charges. However, the 3rd street playground was being set up and as a jolly young, verrry young pirate, I saw nothing but opportunity.

The main feat was for Aramco to build a dreamland, then surround it with terrible dangers we had to brave to play on the various kill-machines that they bought from some kid hating person. First they build this wonderful playground, then surround it with a foot kill zone of desert sand about thirty feet deep to the first playground equipment. My feet were like that of a Camel after three months of the playground. Flat, ugly and shod. I and do a dancing bear leap to the nearest toy. Which happen to be a series of wooden horses which were mounted on a single large spring and would rock back and forth and side to side and up and down...whew, getting a little dizzy all over again. Anyhow, leaping from about the fourth third degree burn to my poor little piglets, I managed to leap onto the saddle, blister my butt on the really hot wood, and putting my little feet on the wood pegs I rocked forward with the sped of a Gazelle and found out the first devious plan of the evil empire parents. The darn things were only meant for kids that were slightly less my size, so that in going forward, I smacked my face right into the blazing sand. Left a cute imprint and a string of invectives that stood the hair up on my Mom, who was at home three blocks away. To make it worse, the recoil then sent my tail off of the little horse and a really neat back flop onto the sand. Trying to catch my breath I suddenly realize an interesting fact. The darn sand is HOT.

Well, now we all know about the large "A" frame swing sets. At my age, they stood about 100 feet into the air and the seats were a sandpaper leather with chains going into the sky. What a plan. I'll bet that if you swing hard enough and try, you might be able to loop the loop and completely go over the top bar. You know why they refer to the horizontal bars, across more blazing sand "Monkey Bars"? Most of you thought it was because as you cross, you look like monkeys. I am here to tell you that it comes from swinging so high that you get dizzy, the chains are actually whipping a little and suddenly you are airborne, and then engage a set of bars that resemble a latter and like a monkey falling from a tree, you and it become one. Spent two weeks with my hand in a huge bandage and needing a bigger one on my rear end after Mom got me home from the emergency room.

BUT, was I one to quit..ohhhh nooo. Not this mighty adventurer. There was still this funny round machine with a spoke wheel in the center and what parents tried convincingly to call a "Merry go Round." Even the name sounded fishy to me.. Why would Mary want to go round?

Well, a bunch of us got on this beast, and one of the huge guys from a much older age started turning the wheel. Grab on, the beast is awake and we are going round and round. Faster too and slowly we start to slide off the metal railing and no matter what kind of offerings to the older brat nothing works. I even offered my brother into eternal servitude. No avail, this guy intended to make us all seasick or off by centrifugal force. So while once again airborne and reflecting on life in flight, I hit well and only bruised every body part possible. Add to that the ever popular third degree sand burns and my day was just about made. EXCEPT, with a quick run I found this amazing monster. The GIANT slide. Took almost a week to climb the steps, they were even in two levels. One to rest on I guess.

Now many people would say, doesn't he ever learn? Well, nobody told me that metal slides, and bare legs don't work. You STICK, and cook about halfway down. So with a mighty yell and very foul weather language I tried to crawl back up the thing to the top. Only here comes a good friend, sitting on wax paper, he the wise one, and we have a multiple person crash rivaling a downtown Los Angeles freeway wreck. The next person piles into us and of course, who goes over the side, drops like a large stone and smack face down into.. yeah, once again with the sand bit. This time the trip home was even more interesting from the emergency room. Me with a hairline crack in my leg and a cast on my foot. Mom's foot having no cast and very little trouble reaching the only unaffected part of me and I'm out of the playground for two months.

Years later I looked at the that playground, now fenced and guarded. I saw the monster and it seemed so small. I saw the wild ride and the little ponies. Yet deep in my heart, I saw me, and the beast once again jousting for mastership of the playground.

Incidentally, at the ripe old age of 49 on my last visit, one thing you still don't do even after thirty five years, you DO NOT take off your shoes and socks and walk in a dream like state to the slide. The darn sand is still blazing HOT!!!

Made the guards day tho........ The below is one of the articles that I have published in the local media. I also posted this to the group I am President of, the Aramco-Brats and others.

You asked about what I had written and therefore I have put it here.

Thank you for your call. It was if there was an added blessing to my day that I give praise to Allah for.

Mike Crocker

"ISLAMIC BELIEF IN JESUS AND OTHER QUESTIONS"

There is a question that I am asked many times by a lot of people here in town, so I thought I would take this time to address in the newspaper a few thoughts I have learned from my studies and acceptance of Islam as my true path to enlightenment.

I profess my faith in Arabic here and in English for you to understand. ash-hadu an laa ilaahah allallah, Ash-hadu anna muhammad-ar-rasool ullaah

(I bear witness and attest that there is no god worthy of worship but the One God Allaah! I bear witness and attest that Muhammad is the messenger of Allaah)

Now then, to explain as best I can some questions you have asked of me. Praise be to Allah that I am able to answer with His guidance.

Islamic peoples respect and revere Jesus and await his Second Coming as prophesized. They consider Him one of the greatest of God's messengers to mankind. A Muslim never refers to Him simply as "Jesus", but always add the phrase "Upon Him be peace".

The Quran confirms His virgin birth (in fact a chapter of the Quran is entitled "Mary"), and Mary is considered the purest woman in all creation.

Many people ask, Why is it that only Jesus shall return? My answer to this is very simple. Only Allah is aware and knows the wisdom of what He does and why. It is written the when the Angel Gabriel (Quran 3:46) announced to Mary about her son, Jesus, he spoke that Jesus would come and speak as a child and again at maturity. Allah alone knows all and shall decide all.

The Quran relates the Annunciation as follows: "Behold!" The Angel said, "God has chosen you, and purified you and chosen you above the women of all nations. O Mary, God gives you good news of a word from Him, whose name shall be the Messiah, Jesus, son of Mary honored in this world and the Hereafter, and one of those brought near to God. He shall speak to the people from his cradle, and in maturity, and shall be of the righteous."

She said "O my Lord! How shall I have a son when no man has touched me?"

He said, "Even so, God creates what He will. When He decrees a thing. He says to it, "Be!" and it is. (Quran, 3:42-7)

Jesus was born by the same power which had brought Adam into being without a father: "Truly, the likeness of Jesus with God is as the likeness of Adam. God created him of dust, and then said to him "Be!" and he was. (Quran, 3:49)

There is the evidence that Jesus performed many miracles. The Quran (3:49) tells us that he made the statement: "I have come to you with a sign from your Lord: I make you out of clay, as it were, the figure of a bird, and breathe into it and it becomes a bird by God's leave. And I heal the blind and the lepers and I raise the dead by God's leave" However, the miracle of Muhammad is most great because the miracle is the word of Allah, direct and without distortation and has never been distorted or rewritten. It was written at the time of Mohammad and not over a period of centuries, with many revisions, as was the Christian Bible. The Holy Book, the Quran is the final miracle as it is original. What more of a miracle, that can be witnessed today stands true and without versions than Gods word to the Prophet. The most amazing aspect is the fact that the prior prophets made miracles happen that were only short lived or even supernatural. Modern science can make wine from water, but no man has ever been able to write the Holy Book, the Quran. This is the true miracle of Allah. Via his messenger and Prophet Muhammad. It is my humble opinion that Allah created the miracle that would convince all people, everywhere and for all time. Thus Allah did pass to Muhammad the Holy book, the Quran, which addresses mans need and disciplines with great light and direction. Never changing and centuries later, a book of revelation and guidance as it was in the beginning and is today. This is the miracle of the true path, leading to the enlightenment of man by his devotion and love and belief in the one God, Allah.

Muhammad, and not even the Christian Jesus were upon the land to make revision or change the one true path of belief that is the belief in one God.

In the Quran, (Quran 3:50) Jesus is directly quoted as speaking "To attest the law which was before me. And to make lawful to you part of what was forbidden you; I have come to you with a sign from your Lord, so fear God and obey Me." Thus we have full support of the one God and the true path of Allah. The comment by Jesus so fear God and obey me is a direct reference back to the one God and not to fear me being to fear Jesus. For Jesus was a prophet and messenger also.

Prophet Muhammad spoke "Whoever believes there is no god but God alone without partner, that Muhammad is His messenger, that Jesus is the servant and messenger of God, His word breathed into Mary and a spirit emanating from Him, and that Paradise and Hell are true, shall be received by God into Heaven According to the beliefs of Islam, man is not born into original sin. He is God's vicegerent on earth. Every child born has the "fitra", an innate pre-disposition towards virtue, knowledge, and beauty. Islam considers itself to be the "primordial religion" It seeks to return man to his original, true nature in which he is in harmony with creation, inspired to do good, and confirming the Oneness of God. To accept the Angels and to believe in the fact that there is life after death. In Islam, death is but a gate to the life after death. There is a paradise awaiting the believer and the fires for those who chose to follow a path not of oneness with God.

I hope I have cleared up some misconceptions about Islam, I am not an expert on anything, but I am a true believer and my belief brings the light of Allah into my heart and lightens the weight from me whenever I speak of the one God.

Allah Akbar.

Michael Crocker

Subject: Off with a BANG

Seemed to me that the sand was unusually tart about the time I left school. It was one of those wind swept hot summer days and the whirlwinds of sand followed you like an avenging mom. I had worn the usual, shorts, tee shirt and sneakers. Yeah, the old white sidewalls with strings that I always felt the maker of sneakers deliberately made a foot too long so that no matter how you tied them, they still managed to get loose and try to trip you. I always wanted to ask them why they waxed the strings. I must have tied mine a thousand times a day and always at the wrong time. You know, stop suddenly, bend over to tie shoe and Mr. Riley the Principal walks around the corner with his arms full and falls over you. Great way to start the day. In his office before the first bell. Not that that wasn't a usual stop over for me on a normal class day, but this weekend was different. It was the Fourth of July. So I was being extra careful that no dreaded phone call went to my house. I had plans!!

Now I've told the woeful tale of watermelons before but what I haven't spoke about was the Aramco Fire Department and the fireworks display put on by the AEA. As usual, this was planned for the area near the King's Road ball park and Aramco had put out a lot of folding chairs. This was great fun to ride your bike through and knock over and watch the recreation guys go off the deep end. I mean, why would any adult heave a folding chair at a cherub that was innocently passing by, along with a string of invectives I didn't know. I did take notes of the words for future testing on Mom, which usually was a tragedy right up there with wetting your pants in class...

Well as you might guess, we, and the guilty parties are now respectable men of means so I'll save them having to explain to their kids why they say "Don't play with matches", but lurking in their dark corners of the mind is the awful story I'll tell.

In Khobar there were several stores that sold "Black Cat" fireworks in red plastic wrapped packages or you could get just plain handfuls of small "Bangers". While watching the firemen set up the truck and after getting told to ride my damn bike off a cliff by several verbose men, I began to see a way to have a great laugh on all of them. Never one to do anything that might offend Father Roman in confession, I hurriedly gathered up the gang and off we went. We made stops at places along the perimeter fence and at Imhoff gardens and in Khobar. Quick trip to the commissary and we were about ready.

Now back then, Aramco used to turn over 55 gallon oil drums and use them for putting a cloth over and a lamp or smudge pot all around the chairs. For light and for the extra touch of the "Tiki" flare effects. It was the Fourth you know. Now many of you know, a smudge pot is something that only fifty gallons of water, and burying it twenty feet down under sand it might just go out. Chances are there are buried pots still smouldering today. They just wouldn't go out.

Mentioning Father Roman is because I kinda considered him a bank. I would stop by, borrow a little cash loan from this small wooden box, something about "Donations" and then always return it on allowance day. So we hit the jackpot and found about 100 riyals. Well, I knew it would take several allowances to make this up, so I simply signed a IOU with my brothers name. Security blanket you know. This was to be a black day around my house once all the facts were into the kangaroo court Mom held. I mean what idiot misspelled his own name on an IOU. Obviously the hanging judge felt it could only have been someone in the family that knew he had brothers but had long since forgot that they were not there for his convienece.

All day long there had been a parade and a carnival and a lot of fun. We, in the dark alleys and hedgerows were planning and plotting. We had picked up the material I mentioned, about two hundred packages of the Black Cats and from the fence we got some of the two week older rotten fish from the fly killer traps and we had come across some really great beauties of camel and horse, ahhh, spillage at Imhoff. Begin to see light here?

All of this we placed in a bag, after unwrapping hundreds of firecrackers and pouring all this massive firepower into a bag. We then filled the top of the small box with a mixture of the fish and "chips". The fuse was a long string from where? Yup, a well rubbed in powder sneaker string. They did have a use. One small oversight is that to run like a drunken stallion on a desert of soft sand and flash by the world on asphalt that took rubber off tires from the heat was not bright..Why? you say with a slight curl of the lips..well lets say that for lack of a string, there was lack of a sure foot and for lack of a sure foot that was no lack of a sore butt.

Another mistake, one is never enough when dealing with Mom, was to go home and pointedly gripe about smelling like a dead fish and camel sh— and wondering what happened to the high price help around the house not doing anything and where were my clean clothes and so on and so on until the house grew deadly quiet and a cold front blew in and the sky opened and the smack of the fly swatter and resulting scream was undoubted considered by many in the camp to be a familiar sound from the Crockers house and just went about the daily routine with a smirk, knowing full well I had got caught at something.

Now it was a matter of revenge. After all, what right did the Fire Chief have telling Mom I had been helpful all day at Recreation and suggesting that I be tied to my bike and dropped off a Dhow near Bahrain?

We went to recreation and set up our massive, what felt like two hundred pounds of "stink bomb", yeah, you all remember the jokers that got some of those and stomped on them during a movie or once, a poor soul did it during one of Father Romans Mass services and almost met his maker right there, but that's another story .

What we didn't figure on was the fact that we had no real container, just this cardboard box and so that to get any effect, it would have to be against something solid so that the, what we thought, smell would be blown over the group. So we placed it inside the drivers section of the pumper truck that was parked behind the display area and facing the crowd. We knew the wind would spray perfume over all of them. The fuse was laid out ever so careful and we hid behind the truck. The crowd gathered, and to our delight, the front row was filling nicely with big shots, Mr. Kieswetter, Mr. Scardino, Mr. Riley, Mr. Dickerson and all the wives in really nice dresses and a lot of parents. Then the band from school played the National Anthem and the flag was paraded up front by the Boy Scouts and set off to one side in stands and the fire chief begin to light all of the sky rockets, which we always just used a coke bottle, but he was a lot smarter. So we lit our fuse and skulked back out of harms way we thought, and gleefully waited. That darn fuse kept going out and I had to keep running up, slowly relight it and run back. Well, as might be expected, the best laid plans of mice and boys...

SO I open the door, madder then a wet Dhub, and go to re-light this monster and what do I see. The flame disappears into the box..Well, next.. BANG!!!!

I know the truck must have rocked and I was ten feet back, flat out, smouldering and covered in ten pounds of dead fish and camel manure. From head to toe and almost completely black. The white of eyes and the size of them must have been beyond belief and I was on fire I'm sure. Of course some of this wondrous mixture went out the windows and managed to spray just a few in the front row. I didn't know the Fire Chief was manning the foam sprayer on top and to this day I still think he took great delight in foaming me under about forty feet of foam. This of course made the mixture worse and as I said…run? Ha! Lucky to just stumble. Even without hearing I felt the earth tremble as the mass on the other side of the truck realized what was sprayed on them and the ground shook from a thousand high heeled hooves that stampeded to be the first to be in on the kill.

Now history was made that bright starry night as some say a small figure, chunky, maybe, was seen running with a frenzied mob of humanity following, some say with a stout rope, others say a lot of beltless pants were seen as whips cracked the air, but the nomads and bedus still speak with awe at the wails that arose that night from the house at the top of 6th street. The applause was heard in other districts I'm sure and I think the company took the next day off in celebration knowing full well it would be years before I sat down again.

One side note. At the last annuitants reunion, a woman approached me, and with what I saw as a great tenderness gave me a shiny small silver object. It said, "Fire Dept", Aramco logo and the word "Chief". It is in my Aramco collection and when you see it at the next reunion, imagine the aroma of the story….

OKAY MIKE! HERE'S MINE

After reading Mike's story of his valentine experience, I had to tell you about my valentine story that happened a few years after I left Dhahran.

In 1960 I was twenty two, and had just gotten out of the Air Force. I was working in Jacksonville, Florida as a X-Ray Technican at St. Vincents Hospital. I met a cute student there named Kathy King. We started dating, and when her parents came back from Europe on a vaction and found out that we were seeing each other, they tried to do everything possible to break us up. Determined me, I wasn't going to put up with that, so I told her that we were going to elope on February 12th. I would met her at her back door anytime after midnight, and we would drive to Alabama and get married. Well I was there, and about twelve thirty she came to the back door, and told me that her mother caught her packing. I told her to go back to bed, and wait until they went to sleep. After the mosqutoes kept on attacking me, and I had waited a couple of hours, I decided I would be creative. Kathy's house was a large two story brick house on a very seculed lot of the St. Johns River. I went into their garage, and got and aluminum ladder off the wall, and went to her bedroom window and placed it against the house.

The problem was, it was about three feet to short. So I proceeded to get a lawn table and chair, placing the chair on top of the table and the ladder on the chair. Great! it worked, I was able to reach her window sill. I tapped on her window, and she undid the screen, and I removed it, and started receiving her luggage, after making two trip up and down the ladder, her parents light went on in their bedroom. I just lowered my head, and held on to the window sill. Suddenly the table and chair fell over, and left me suspended, hanging from the window sill.

About this time I said to myself "Why Me Dear Lord". The mother came into Kathy's room and asked what the loud noise was, and Kathy told her that she fell out of bed, she went back go bed. To my surprise, I looked down, and the ladder had not fallen all the way to the ground, it was just in the reach of my foot. I tried to reach it, and when I did, it fell very loudly, the rest of the way down to the ground.. Damn, what do I do now. Mrs. King came to the window this time, looking down at me, screaming in the loudest manner possible. I looked up at her, and in a timed way and said "Mrs. King, its me Don, let me in". Where upon Mrs. King proceeded to beat my hands, in order to make me let go of the window sill. I was thinking to myself, what the hell, and I let go of the window, and fell two stories to the ground. I guess I was so frighten that I didn't hurt myself at all, but started running like hell down their long drive way, knowing as the outside lights came on, that I would be shot in the back by her father. Didn't happen! The next day February 13, we spoke on the phone, and decided that when her parents had their big party that night, celebrating their return from their trip to Europe, she would sneak out of the house, and meet me at the end of her long driveway. About ten that night she did, with only a fur coat on a very pretty party dress on. We drove all night to Ozark Alabama. It was a Sunday, on February 14th 1960, but we did find a judge Adams that met us at the courthouse, and married us at 4PM that day. That was a wild one, if I do say so myself, and all of it really happened…Her parents disowned her, and the marriage only last four years.. That's the way it goes, but there were no children. I learned a lot from that experience, and have been married for twenty nine years now to my second, with three beautiful children. But I alway chuckle when I think of my youth and the things I have done over my sixty one years.. Hope you enjoyed that one! See Ya.

Don Raposo dh-51
Atlanta, GA

SUBJECT: PARTLY NON ARABIA -RATED "R"

Thought before I go quietly into the night, albeit perhaps screaming back with a vengence I would relate two non-Arabia or at least post Arabia stories. I must warn that these are real stories and graphic. People ask what happend to a lot of us after Arabia, and so I thought I leave with these. I have writen a lot more that I have been sending only to a very dear, to me, lady and since I have been asked a lot about my brother KC from many who knew him. Story is above.

COLD

Unusually cold for Ras Tanura in 1956, but we had just moved there and lived in house 1-G. Across Jasmine street and straight up the hedged death row to the Senior Staff School. Post office was on the corner and there was the bus stop with the telephone in the grey box. Across the street was the recreation area, but no pool then. Now, behind the snack bar was a hallway and out of it was the RT patio that many a fine talent used to entertain us. There was a small stage located to the front left and on one side double doors that opened up into the lounge. The small window for the snack room was by the front doors in a corner and this was SANTA's place. Holy ground for a 7 year old adventurer.

Now the RT woman's group and AEA had done a bang up job of decorations and the huge tree in the lounge was being worked on. I asked a lady there if I could help, since I needed as many brownie points as possible right before Santa got to Mom. The lady suggested, once she saw it was me suggested I go to the main gate, catch a ride on one of the big trucks and bring her back some sand from the middle of the Rub Al-Kahli…quite helpful of her I thought.

So wandering around I found this large pile of lights, all in a big pile. I thought, ok, here's where I really make Santa happy..I'll layout a long glide path of lights. So grabbing the end I tugged the whole group out into the hall and outside. Heard strange "popping" noise, but wasn't worried, couldn't be anything I was doing. Once out front I started untangling this pile. First I nearly strangled my self and looked as if I were a small Christmas tree and then after what seemed like hours of struggles with this deadly "snake" I was able to lay them out in a long row. In fact almost to the school. Yes, in my brilliance I stretched them across the street. So I hear a lot of commotion and see a white car stopped sideways. Who would ever run over a string of lights, get them wrapped around an axle and then think I had anything to do with it? So after my yelling for him to get off my lights the driver he gave me a hard desert sand boot and threats that were very Un-Christmassy I got things lined out again.

Now Mrs. Killingsworth, a family friend comes out the door at recreation, see's the lights and starts hauling them back in. I see the darn thing start to wiggle across the road and back from I just dragged the beast and my eyes were likely wider than a camel in heat as I was astonished this thing was alive. I had tied them together and so grabbed the end I had. Well, to say the least, the comments that my Mom's good friend said when she came like a tornado across the street were even less Holiday spirit and more like what kind of spirits I might be visiting soon if I didn't "get!".

So back to recreation, and by this time Dick Burgess had joined me. Now he tells me that we can find out if lights work because a friend of his told him that all we had to do was stick our finger in our mouth and then touch the little silver part of the light. Now known to be as a light socket. But we learn....So taking his advice and after being told we could straighten out the lights in a pile and test them, without moving one foot near anything else. I decided to test the light set. Well, to say I managed to have hair standing straight up and a scream from the depths of the Persian Gulf is mild. I caused some guy to turn on a step stool and fall, right into the table with a lot of little colored balls and Dick already heading for safe ground. I was sitting there with a look of pure disbelief on my face when Mrs. Killingsworth grabs me and checks me out. I had shocked myself, but these lights, the gezzer days, ran off a little transformer and so I had got the equivalent of a battery charge that I had also once tested by putting my tongue on it, That too was a blast. Anyhow, once she found I wasn't hurt, the Al-Khobar customs office got a call from Bahrain wondering what the loud smack they had just recorded was. I know that my eyes had to go completely around in my head and I think I was dizzy for about an hour. That was just the beginning of the day as she then took me home. They say that the screams and begging were heard with great pleasure all over Ras Tanura. I do believe people actually brought lawn chairs out in front of our house as Mom, embarrassed beyond rage, was showing me the finer aspects of what a Christmas belt could do as we circled the house. And not an belt of eggnog either......

So sitting in the corner, a butt with the heat of the Arabian sun on it and wrapped in my blankie, I was really ticked off. I didn't mind the clapping and cheers from outside, but the comments from Mom about, "Wait until your Father gets hone, you might as well plan on never sitting again", was a little intimidating. Plus I knew Santa was most likely in the emergency room from histerics over what he had surely seen. Aramco didn't have enough trucks to haul the coal I was getting.

Mom had a really nice tree up and it was all white with red lights. I had got to put my little train set around the base and it was really pretty. I decided to help. Mom was making cookies with occasional comments about "bad seed" and "where the hell did we go wrong" remarks from the kitchen and so I waddled, not quick moves here just yet, too sore, over to the tree. I try to get the little train to go around and it won't. Now I knew it was plugged in and having just learned about electricity the hard way, I wasn't about to touch anything. So I took my Dad's pen from his Christmas card writing list and stuck it into the tree light fixture to wiggle it.

OK, so the whole house went dark, so the kitchen shut down, so the tree was smoking a little, was that any reason for Mom to call Ibn Jawuli? The cookies, several trays were in the oven, Mom flips the electric on, unplugs the tree for fear of fire, calls the hospital and checks to see if they have a bed with restraints and comes looking for me. I thought the dark clouds meant snow, however Mom had other idea's. I think the shot-put of me out the side door was a world record. Then the stern talking too from her was nothing when she smelled the kitchen. Something close to the smell of burning tires. Cookies left in the oven when the lights went out and forgotten while she was determining how to claim the hospital had me mixed up, and soooo, burnt black as camel droppings on the pie tin. Not the smartest time in the world for this youngster to smart off, "Yeah, can tell you are named after Betty Crocker". POW!, the light went out again for me. Never knew you could bend a cookie sheet on a head, but found it can be done.

Banned for life to my bedroom and the back of the house, I found new adventures, which involve hidden presents, a bathtub, Dad's newest golf shoes and my life flashing before me repeatedly in seconds...perhaps before Christmas.

MERRY CHRISTMAS TO BRATS WORLDWIDE

ANOTHER CHRISTMAS TALE

So, locked in the dark passages of the tunnel of the prison, or actually being in the back bedroom. No real chain and ball will ever be effective as a heated up Mothers thrusting rapier of a glare. Yet, I felt that there was treasure afoot. I had heard Mom's instructions to our houseboy, a Pakistani named "Mo". At least that all I could pronounce. She had told him to make sure the wrapped gifts were all hidden in Mom and Dad's room. A place that was so forbidden that the Chinese "Forbidden City" was nothing. Mom had explained that parents rooms were not only off limits, but required an "A" pass from Aramco Security for anyone to ever enter. The door seemed to me to be steel and the lock that of a vault door I had seen at the local merchants shops in Najmah. She even told me of spiny monsters that lurked in the dark closets waiting for a young morsel. This I believed in full, having met some of Mom's demons in person a few times, to the regret of my highly regarded target of opportunity, my butt.

However, knowing the day was going to be very long, I snuck down the hall and just slightly peeped into the bedroom. It didn't look to bad, although the bed had dark areas under it and there did seem to be the hissing of something in there room. Years after this event Mom told me it was a vaporizer for Dad's cold. I experienced a disaster and this infernal machine, I didn't know of, plays a major part. So in I glide, like the proverbial sand viper. All ears and radar going looking for shiny wrapped goodies.

Now Mom and Dad's room had a king bed facing the closet with two of the old Aramco issued metal chest of drawers. I worked my way carefully, seeing the steam breathing monster sitting by a chair and partially hidden. He can't see me, as I can't see him...this from the brain that Mom claims was transplanted from a Hamoor. So in I go, and the room is really dark. I dash behind the chair as I hear Mo going in. He goes to the closet and I see him reach high up and there, lo and behold, the treasure of the Sierra Leone.

Millions of wrapped packages and surely all with my name, but wait, he is leaving and once again the teachings of my religious youth spoke, and in a scream, "Don't do it!!!" At this point, being deaf completely to the noisy Angel, I heed the red robed one with a tail and head into this cavern of Ali Baba.

Up on a chair, in the dark, pulling for the light chain and trying to do this in a vacuum of silence, I suddenly pull lose a large group and I feel the chair shift and down we go. But, without a sound. So here I am. I have about ten packages and they are wrapped. Shake, rattle and roll and I still know nothing. So, just open them and use the Elmers paste to reseal them. I didn't know about scotch tape. Not a single goodie out of the pile..How could Santa be so dumb. A pair of socks? Had he lost his mind? So I climb back up, teetering on the back frame of the chair and "FLASH" on comes the light in the room and Mo yells with glee…M'shaib, Y'allah, sway Muk inta hamman wajid" As he yells I fall and land on Dad's brand new golf shoes with metal spikes. These make a tremendous impression on my already world record sore butt and I throw my self forward, knocking over the vaporizer, and as you geezers remember they had steam with Vicks rub in them. This goes on Mo, he starts tearing off his white shirt and screaming, Mom comes in the door with what looked to be an axe handle, later found it was a rolling pin, and I am spread out in a pile of presents, which have opened and paper is stuck all over me. Some damn glue. The Vicks rub was all over me and what a greasy mess I was. Smelled beyond belief and Mom's says, cool as the glacier ice.."Guess who has Church in ten minutes?" NOWAY," smelling like this I screamed. "Father Roman will knock me out!" Mom's smile said it all…I didn't know that a smile could reach behind a persons ears. Eyes that had a dancing fire in them…Glee, as I found out later.

So into the shower and scrubbing with, what else..Lava soap to be exact. This stuff will take the paint off a moving car. Think I wasn't a bright pink! Well, rushing into my dress clothes, my shoes soaking wet, I decide that Dad's shoes, that are new and shiny and tried to kill me would work. Heck, I knew where to get socks…They were quite large, but no matter. Off and out the door I went. Our Catholic Christmas dinner before Mass was that night and it was also the night a visiting Bishop from Lebanon was in. Well to try and tell you how I managed to step on peoples feet with those spikes, running right out of the shoes and dashing about like a madman, I can tell you today..You never, and I mean never put shoes of any kind with a spike on them on a chair and forget where you put them. As you may find out, certain ladies are very concerned when they sit and get poked by a dozen spikes and the jump up, scream, smack the nearest kid, usually me and yell, for a rope and a tree.

But the best was for last. I had no idea that Mom had bought these special type of shoes, had them flown over in someone's suitcase and hand delivered by the Flying Camel and had hid them around the house for months. How was I to know. I just knew they had to be gone and I ran to the fence close by and heaved them over thinking no one could trace them to me. They had, unbeknownst to me, been marked by Mom with Dad's name.

To say that he was heard in Udaliyiah, before there was a Udaliyiah is an understatement when some sheep herder came to the main gate the next morning and wanted "Backsheesh" for the well chewed up shoes and for one goat that he claimed got sick.

I didn't know there were so many recipes for goat my entire life, but I found out. I think Mo sent to Pakistan for some to help Mom come up with more for me to sample daily. Had to do it standing up of course, but to this day, the thought of those brown topped, lower white bottomed shoes with metal prongs just tends to make me stay as far away from any kind of golf course at all.

ATIVITY MADNESS

Now, one would think that the young experiences that I had would have taught me that Christmas, Santa and I were words not used by most adults in the same sentence. However, remember, Santa tends to forgive little boys and girls. This does seem to be questionable and was raised on more than one occasion around my house, yet...there is always hope for the condemned at the last sweep of the second hand that Mrs. Claus might intercede. Knowing now who that was tends to make me think that I was dropped repeatedly by the Doctors at birth. In fact, there is some proof that Mrs. Claus aka Mom requested the droppings from the Obstetrician. Something about thirty six hours of labor and fat kid...Don't know the details. This would explain why I thought Mrs. Claus might step in and help. I may have had brain damage.

The problem started with the annual Nativity play at King's Road baseball field in Dhahran and that the adults wanted to use real animals. Seems to me that was just looking for trouble when an rapscallion was loose and perhaps a bit curious.

I will start out by commenting that when I offered to help out, I had no idea that Mr. Fairlie, our scoutmaster and a truly knowledgeable man with first hand knowledge of my escapades in scouting, was helping. So the suggestion that I be assigned to shovel the 12 tons of droppings from various beasts of Biblical reference should have been no surprise. I didn't know that a Camel was capable of completely burying me without warning should the ugly beast so decide, which one huge momma camel did. Think she may have been the one that was hunted at Imhoff Gardens in an earlier adventure. Talk about ripping off clothes. Now wonder if she knew my Mom.

I was fascinated by the line of donkeys, while Jeff Yeager seem awful interested in the sheep....

Anyhow, while trying to shovel behind the donkey's, and they aren't too bad I managed to get a shovel into the old wood handled iron wheel wheelbarrow that they had and was supposed to get fresh straw and set it around. So leaving the wheelbarrow behind this old red henna dyed donkey, I head to the straw pile.

Arms full of straw, passing the camels and sticking my tongue out as I ran for my life, I hear this scream and something to the effect, "THAT DAMN CROCKER KID" I was confused. What had I done now? Seems as if Mr Sitar and several ladies were rehearsing a song or something and the donkey kicked the wheelbarrow and some pellets became airborne, landing amongst this fine group of carollers.

I thought sticking the straw where the donkey doesn't shine might be helpful, but by then I was no longer able to catch my breath after out running several ladies with switches. Now these switches are interesting. The donkey and camel herders seem to take great mirth in giving them to the ladies and watching me do a 440 in new world records.

However, as is the norm, Aramco had what I believe were smudge pots, which were like black balls with a torch top. Drop kicked that sucker right into the straw. Fire department was right there of course and wet it down, but did scare some of the sheep. All over the place as a matter of fact. Now sheep are hard to catch. And the wooly little beasts, when scared, do tend to make little messes and those are well renown for causing slippery spots and soon people were falling all around and I swear I heard the Christmas song,

"You better be good, you better be nice, Santa's coming to kill you tonight" but I'm sure that was a figment of my imagination.

Finally all is well, and calm restored. I'm locked in the baseball score-keepers box sorting out the Christmas music and stapling them together. So I staple twenty or so sheets together..no one told me they were two sheets to a person.

Ousted again and told to go home, I head down Kings Road and arrive at a wondrous sight. Christmas Tree Circle. All lit up and music coming from inside and a bright star on top, just memorized me. The signs said "Merry Christmas and Happy New Year to All" One had to admit, inquisitive minds wanted to see the music and how come this particular tree could sing. So I find a cord leading out the bottom of the tree and follow it to one of the sever row houses near by. Looked inside the window and what a place. Tree and gifts everywhere. This made me know that I needed to get home fast as Santa had obviously been there and was early for some reason and I knew he might actually be talked into not stopping if Mom got to him first, so off I shot.

Unbeknownst to me, the house with the presents was a decoration house and wasn't even occupied. Someone had said a lot of prayers that day, or I may have decided to look inside and check it out.

I get home and Mom, from a long day of decorating tells me.."You're wanted in Safanyiah...hurry, you can catch the last bus out" Real welcome I thought.

I got a new bike for Christmas, a American Flyer called the "Hiway Patrol" bike and I flew like magic all over the camp that day.

I wish I had that bike this Christmas.....

PLAYGROUND

We shot over to the school yard and went to play on the slides. Talk about a blistered butt. Mom couldn't have done more damage that I did sliding down the slide when the metal was most likely 500 degree's hot. And of course right into the blazing desert at the foot of the slide made a wonderful impression also.

Do any of you remember walking the hedges? Great thrill to try to stay balanced on top and walk around a block and try to get on the next set by jumping. So jump we did, hedge leans over, we fall into yard. Not just any yard of course, but one of the seven units back yards that was a bachelors quarters. Running in circles trying to find the gate, the two bachelors soaked us with water from a hose and out we went. At least refreshed, but now how to recover the sandals and pants before Mom finds out and we really get heated up.

So back to recreation and Ross sneaks into the office and there are the clothes. Great success all around and promotions for all of us to smart alecks. We dash home and Ross and Dick are playing in the big Acadia tree we had at 1G in RT and here comes Dad from church. He always went and that usually meant that we had to go to a later service in case of any little flare ups of our behavior. He has a funny look and soon I hear that I am not allowed with 10000 feet of anything for at least ten years. Seems as if he was in the church service and had to do some explaining.

The point of this...well when it's too hot outside, find some shade and wait. It only gets hotter.

RED RYDER WAGON

It was a cold and chilly day, unusual for the furnace that I was usually in, but then that may have been the weather of Mom. Never knew so much hot air could bellow at various small innocuous things. Here's why it was cold. Santa flew by, never stopped, dropped coal all over my house and it was now the New Year. If one could call a cold day New Year in Ras Tanura. No going to the beach, although Mom highly recommended it as the water was freezing and potential sharks all over, but I had other plans.

I went by some friends and several had got bicycles from Santa the snake, and I had a red wagon. Now what fool would give a kid, without a driver license a semi motorized vehicle to try on various places. Talking Dick Burgess into going with Ross Tyler and myself, having worked out a deal that we would hook the wagon to the bikes and ride around.

Now near the refinery, there were two unguarded roads back then that traversed the salt marsh and so we went on the side that had the water injection plant water inlet. I mean after all, that water was supposed, note supposed to be warm. Carcogenic ? Didn't know how to spell the word. The intent was to ride the wagon down the sloping cement path that fed the water to the long stone moat to the Gulf. No fences in those days. The water was only a few feet deep and we were men of action. In fact I am sure that action figures for generations to come came from out exploits.. You should remember, "nah, nah nah, Fatman, err, Batman".

No one has to remember that the refinery shut down several days a year then for steam cleaning and high pressure washing and lots of technical things. Who knew or cared. We just knew that the slope was dry and the water out the injection site was low. Who needs more. Cold as a Bears butt in a polar suit, off we went to ride up and down the slope..

Many people knew that these Red Ryder red wagons had wood sides that could be put on and taken off and a metal handle with rubber wheels. Great for holding on to and going down the slope. Not wanting to get our shoes and rather small sized jeans wet, we got down to our little denim jackets, tee shirts and under wear. The following events was what Mom refereed to as the Last Hurrah of a Palm Tree without a single date for brains. Rather unusual and new comment.

All of a sudden there was this huge crash as the main flush valves were re-opened to allow the wash out and the re flow of the intake. We of course went ten feet underwater and tumbled like a sock in a washer, but managed to make it, darn near the end of the intake stone passage to shore. The force had sent the wagon to sail the seven seas with most of our clothing. I still had a tee shirt, but no jacket or underwear. The others were about the same. For a confused moment thought I was looking at a worm, then realized it was in my mind a huge sea snake. Mom didn't think so when all three of us went screaming back to out houses, much to the grand applause of hundreds of classmates and adults. I still won't eat beanies and weenies.

The worst part is that it really was cold. I thought Mom was going to literally die laughing as car after security car pulled up out front. She was just in convulsions and made a strong point to the Night Foremen (Security then) that were had gone fishing with our worms. I saw no such humor and the door darkened even worse as Dad and Mr. Crampton strode in.

Seems we three kids had breached a "red" zone in Aramco security and all wanted to know how. I demanded compensation for my wagon and got a butt blast that rocked most of the Arabian Peninsula and had a hard time sitting for many years, Still limp to this day I think.

The end result was good. Mom took pity after some hundred Management had come in and the volume of yelling was that of the mid day siren going off in my kitchen, but all's well. I got cookies. Of course I understand there was a lot of screaming down the street and across the road and grounded until 99, but still. A way to start a New Year.

A STORY ABOUT MY FRIEND

I'm not sure when it was…I know the rain and cold were really bad, but we had a swim meet coming up…No, wait a minute, that was another time. It was in reality, hotter that Kennworth engine stacks after a twenty hour drive across the Rub Al'Kahali. And the fools at the school had scheduled a swim meet for all day Thursday. I mean we were all dragging. Hell, the Saluki dogs had to walk slow so as to not step on their tongues it was sooo hot.

"Too damn hot", and so had a little party the night before. Amazing how Mom and Dads just seemed to take off on some weekends. I always thought it was luck, but perhaps knowing me it was their escape. Anyhow, there was a crowd of youngsters there, we being ninth graders and all. I remember that Vicki Muzika, Moe McQuade, Julie Yeager and Pam Leary were all there and Tom Masso and some of us others were setting out to ensure they knew we were "Gods".

Anyhow, that night was legendary for the amount of brown and white that went down, but the girls were only interested in the latest batch of 45's brought back from long leave by Sissy Quick. It wasn't long until the girls reminded us that we had a swim meet the next day. I had practiced with the girls for weeks and was entered in all of the events for ninth graders. The only swimmer even near my outstanding, yet modest ability was Kevin Colgan and some clown named Jeff Yeager.

However, in the girls category, there were two top notch, proud swimmers, Julie and Pam. They were competitors like you have never seen.

OK, so the stage is set. Hot, hung over and woozy we make it to the pool. The girls are lined up behind us and we take our mark, get set, and then, to the great enjoyment of the crowd, Kevin fell in. Not a dive mind you, just a topple. Mr. Goellner wasn't pleased at all and started us again. To this day I am sure that it was either Pam or Julie, or most likely both, as they were behind us. Anyhow, Julie was known for her unbelievable acts and loved a joke. So as we are getting set, she and Pam are edging closer and closer to us. However, we are too far gone and don't catch on. Mr. Goellner blows the start whistle and the girls grab the baggy suit I had on and as I did the perfect belly flop, I lost the suit. Kevin does a perfect racing dive right on top of me and you can hear the hooting and hollering from Julie and Pam in Ras Tanura.

Julie throws my suit to Vicki, who throws it into the deep end and so off I go like a fish. Have you ever tried to put on a suit, swim and not bitch, all under water? The girls have sat down, unable to stand up. I not only lost, but had to spend ten minutes explaining to Sabistian the life guard that I didn't drop my suit and moon all of Aramco. NO ONE would believe the girls had anything to do with it.

OK, get even time was coming, that was for damn sure. They had these people selling ice cups with crushed ice and flavors, so I got one and had extra blue juice put on it. Revenge is so sweet. I snuck up as the girl's relay was going on, everybody shouting and yelling and no one watching. I grabbed Julie's back of her suit and went to dump the entire icee down her back and she turned on me and yelled so loud that I froze in shock. I did, however, manage to get the icee dropped into my suit, although no one would ever admit to it. So now the crowd has turned around and here I am standing there with blue ice water running down my leg and pooling on the tile. You would think that was enough, but no, not for these gals. They immediately started yelling that Mike Crocker had peed in the pool. Talk about humiliation. I ran like a crazed dog, but not really knowing what to do because of the frozen area and "SPLASH" right into the baby pool and face down. Landed right on top of Mr. Wohlgethan, who proceeded to butt kick me all the way to Rahimia. He was smoking a cigar and I doused him good.

They say all good things come to he who waits. However, the Crockers and Yeagers go way back. It might interest you to know, Billy, that in her future swim meets, Julie held one record after another.

I remember another time in the pool, where I was just minding my own business and here comes the whole bunch, Julie, Vicki, Moe, Janice Cyr and Randa Owens. As they walked past me, I was standing in the five foot area. They suddenly leapt off the side and do their damndest to drown me. It was a free for all city. They are climbing all over me and trying to dunk me and all of a sudden I hear, loud and clear.."Hey you, you Mr. No Good, you get outta there." Hours of delicate negations followed with recreation. NO one would believe these girls, who were all perfect angels by then, had jumped me. Something about a reputation I believe. I later learned it was all Julie and Randa's planning.

I remembered a lot of things this past week and the thing I remember the most was that wild laughter and the hee haww of a laugh when ever Julie pulled one off. She was at times more of a menace than I was. Yet I will admit, of all the girls I ever met, Julie had the ability to make everyone have a hell of a good time.

Once when I was a hall monitor and the hall was almost empty, out she and Doral Zadorkin came and slammed at least ten to fifteen steel locker doors. I spent hours telling Mr. Dickerson who it was. Likely story, Crocker…My next safety patrol post was on the south end of the football field, at that time about ten feet from the perimeter fence.

I will tell you something else. Julie had honor and dignity. I don't say this lightly as I am one who has always had a disdain for lessor beings, but Julie Yeager and the entire Yeager family were then, are now and always will be held in the highest esteem by many, many of us.

I wouldn't doubt it for one minute that right now, she is giving another Crocker boy as much of a hard time as she gave his older brother. In fact if I listen…..I can hear the laughter.

God, that blue water was cold…….

Fi'aman'Allah M'hemshaib Julie…

Vicki, my future wife, as told by a donkey

Hearing from Randa about her escapades with Vicki Muzika brought back some sneaking out memories I also had with Vicki. We started dating in 9th grade and I saw her as a returning student before her parents left the field and I can relate to the sneaking out bit. One night I went to her house and to her bedroom and knocked on the window.

She answered and we sneak out to her back yard which was dark. We discover puppy love and I really fell for it, and therein lies many adventures best left in the shadows, in particular of Hamilton Hill, rear down slope area….

Anyway I was standing at the window helping her out and didn't notice my feet were tearing her Mom's flowers all to pieces, but you remember our camel boots? Well mine being the size of a camel hoof did a lot of floral rearranging. Anyhow the next day, after sneaking her back in at daylight and knowing I had to go to my first class with Miss Fry, I did pay hardily for these little digressions, but any how I was called out by Mr. Dickerson the vice principal to see my Mom and Mrs. Muzika waiting. We had to go to their house and they matched my hoof prints and I got to replant a lot of what I considered weeds, however Mrs. Muzika considered award winning flowers.

That year Vicki's family left Dhahran and it took me fifteen years later to find her again by Earl Greaves telling me he had seen her at Kent State. I finally found her in a little town in Colorado and ten days later we married. I have another story or two that I had wrote when chat first started, but don't know where they are now. Anyhow one told of our romance which unfortunately ended after a short marriage as she said, "Mike, you still are in love with a fifteen year old cheerleader, and I have changed over the years."

She was right but we had a great 11 months of bliss before reality and the world made the sun go out. None the less, flowers have to this day been a great delight to me when I see real pretty ones. Takes me back to hours of crawling around re-planting what I will never see as flowers.

Such skies and tenderness, never forgotten and never again.

MIKE CROCKER (DH65—"NEVER SNUCK OUT.....WALLAH!!!! WHAT A LIE....LOL")

A LITTLE BOY...

It was strange. I was blasted by the wind and the sand stung my eyes. I thought to myself, where am I? Why did Mom bring me here. I looked around. The place was a playground of sand everywhere. A delight I thought. I mean after all, a telephone on a pole behind a box of a house that had really great flowers. Suck those suckers dry all day. Then down the street was a house that had a huge swing set. I mean the two pipes that joined like a huge "A" were at least 100 feet in the air. At least from the perspective of a rapscallion of six. They had chains the size of a ships anchor chain and canvas seats that when the thin shorts and the seat made contact, a quick jump was all that could save you from a fiery rear end. Had to go early or late to swing.

Now the thought arises, what if one could swing this sucker and do a loop de loop? Ought to be some kind of record. So here we go, a fellow by the name of Doug and myself. Another character named Mike was there beside me also. They push and I pumped, I pumped and they pushed, they pumped and I pushed. The swing was really rocking and rolling now. All I could see was a blur where the sky and the ground came together. I thought this must be like flying. Each peak of the swing arc made my little butt move up and out of the seat just a td. The chains were buckling and jumping a little, for the weight ratio was rapidly changing. I just knew I'd make a complete loop. Well, as fate would have it, some fool yelled, "Watch out, your Mom's coming!" I turned, the seat turned and the A frame and I were formally introduced. Nice to meet you Mr. Pipe I thought as I spiraled to the ground and crashed like a falling star. Surprised I didn't bury myself head first I hit so hard. Who cared. The avenging angel was close and the wail of a siren, or perhaps her wail of the banshee was all I remember. Woke up in a place called Dhahran at a small house. Turned out to be the Dhahran Health Clinic, later to becomes the Woman's exchange, where I thought you went to exchange Mothers. It made sense to me.

Course the three hundred hours of the trip back to Abqaiq, once thought to be the "Friendly City" I thought before having to hear about stupidity on a scale beyond measure. Mom just knew that I had killed myself, and when I didn't, then the promises of a bleak future were dire predictions I can tell you.

Well, walking home the next day, about noon, limping a little we saw where a water pipe had broken. So we jumped across the stream of water that was shooting up about four or five feet. Now don't let anyone tell you that Aramco didn't have hot water. We almost scald ourselves and our shrieks were heard down the small hedgerow that had just been put in. This sidewalk led to my house and Mom was in the front yard. We came dashing like wild camels, wide eyed and flaming red. Mom took one look and exploded. "What happened?" Well, not wanting to get any more torn up then from the night before, I off handily remarked, "Mom, that guy that lives at the end of the street threw hot water on us". Off we went with the enraged paternal instinct and we, thinking we were so smart. We knew no one was home. Wrong. He was watering the yard. Mom took a strip the size of the Rub Al Kahli off of him and when he finally got a word in, he simply pointed down the walkway to the broken water main. I remember to this day the redness that seemed to slowly darken her skin. It was like watching a great Dhub slowly turn mad and the massive head slowly turned. I knew that look and it wasn't pretty. After profuse apologies, we went to the house. Mom never said a word. Soaked me in vinegar and water to take the sting out, asked me ever so politely if I felt any pain, beguiling as she could be, and I, thinking, wow, what a break, got just that. A break of the belt across the already red bare bottom that picked me up about a foot. Down the hall and out the front door right into Mrs. Regan, the other Mike's Mom and her pearls of laughter are often heard in far away places as similar as the shot heard round the world. A naked red butted boy, rare species I'm sure.

The next day was one of intense excitement. The house at the end of the block burned and after all the excitement, and having given more oaths that possible not to go there, off we went. Well, it was eerily quiet. No one had got hurt there but we wanted to look around. I managed to cut myself by the ankle and went running home. Mom wasn't even mad. Took me to the clinic where I got a shot the size of the pipeline of tetanus and Mom ever so tenderly wrapped my ankle. She was a Nurse you know. I also knew that she had a really wrapped sense of hum,or and naturally, she used it to great ability. I did find myself sitting on the floor in the living room, wrapped in my favorite blankey and you may know what a hair pin is, but I had no idea. However I did find out that the little socket that the lamp is plugged into was not for a hairpin. My hair stood straight up, my blanket was on fire and Mom grabbed me and once she made sure I was ok, almost collapsed in horrendous laughter at my hair and black face. I saw no humor at all. Dad saw even less when he got home. The tears from Moms laughter were apparent for many years as she retold the story over and over.

Perhaps the fact that she was my Mom and the only living thing in all of Arabia to love and fear was one of the many reasons that I always was on the lookout. Over the years I remember some of the stunts I got away with, such as the time I thought tar from a tar pot was great for painting sheets hanging on this funny clothes line thing that looked like a wire pyramid on a pole. Do you know how to get tar out of your hair? Mom did. Go to school bald. Always good for a little friendly banter and a black eye or two.

When I was a Scout, who was the Den Mother..who else of course. I went on my first camp out, got scared and Bill Fairle drove me all the way back home and my Mom held me for hours. Years later I roamed the deep desert on horse back and never had a fear of the dark. Back then though, Mom made sure it was ok.

Then on to school, all kinds of devilment, but always knowing the eyes and ears in the back of her head could pick out my remarks, or comments about what I may or may not have been guilty of…she was there. A cloud of warmth or a storm of "Hey you little…!!!"

Broken bones, wounded skin and broken hearts, always mended with the right word and the right touch. At 53 years of age, A phone call a day to cry over split milk or to rejoice over a "Atta Boy!". The dark of life was never black. Mom always managed to make it a little better and the next day was always a little brighter.

I guess if there were a super hero to all of us, it would be our Moms. Mine was and will always be, Last night, in the middle of the darkest night I have seen in awhile, I picked up the telephone to call and get the reassurance all was well within the land….

I miss my Mom….

THIS STORY IS TOLD IN THE BOOK, BUT IT WAS THE SIGULAR MOST DEVASTATING PART OF MY LIFE EXCEPT THE LOSS OF MY MOM AND DAD. SO I AM GOING TO REPEAT IT HIGHLIGHTED AS IT WAS THE MOST DEVASTATING PART OF MY LIFE. OTHER THEN A PASSING OF MY MOM AND DAD, THIS STORY TORE OUT WHAT WAS LEFT OF MY HEART AND THREW IT AWAY.

To the people I know and to those that were there in the land of the whispering dunes, the singing sand and the stars that came to the earth at night so bright and the best welcome any of us ever got upon arriving home from school, the flares from the air.

The Black Camel has visited us once again and this one is too much for me. I have to say that in the summer of 1968 I found a love that blossomed for the summer and disappeared as I went blindly and boldly into a world and life that was like a Spain's Galleon without a rudder. To run ashore with a tearing crash and a horrifying loss on the rocks of the death of love. That wreckage today floats ashore on the Ras Tanura beach, part by part, mostly of my heart.

Can you remember the soft lips of a young kiss, the exquisite touch of a soft caress, the beating of two hearts that knew not what was really happening and the immortal touch of lying and holding one another on the side slope of Hamilton House hill? Well, I do and the memory is what the shell of what I have left will lose any form of feeling of sanity and only live in the the memories of swatches of life in a movie like fashion where I never got to edit and therefore lost most of the movie.

I so vividly remember the smell of Lilacs and Jasmine and the softness of the ground and in particular, the aura of the glow of the softness of her hair, the sweet honey of a kiss and the sweaty grip of life in holding hands,

One time in forty years did I see my Princess and I wrote about it in my Memories of the Chander 1997 Reunion. Those words will be engraved on the crumbling ruins of my heart and soul. At that time we were once again back on Hamilton Hill and the world was alive again. Unfortunately her honor was so very important for both of us that we held hands and softly danced at the reunion, but never was the soul of my dear Princess or her Knight ever compromised.

The last I got was a sweet note telling me that I would always ride the roads of this earthly plain as her Knight in shining Armor and she signed the small scrap of paper, forever in my heart as "Your Princess"

Tonight the tears that flow are a path for the Black camel, bathed in gold and diamonds to follow to her place with our brothers sister and friends who have carved a spot in God's acres called Aramco Heaven. My Mom and Dad, brother and friends will all be there, The Black camel shall walk with pride for he carries the greatest of a man's existence. His love.

She once again is wearing the jeans and tennis shoes along with a golden Abayiah that shrouds her in blazing brilliance as the candle of love in a living heart slowly flickering and dies, leaving only the smell of a wisp of the past.

I, on my knees do not know how to call for the strentgh to stand. The pool of tears is a lake of sorrow and the depth has torn me apart. I once, in 1997 on a trip to home buried a small jar with two gold Arabic name rings intertwined into the face of the great North Dune at the old Half Moon bay. Someday, they will be found and considered the heart of Arabia.

I have repeated the story I wrote back then. So maybe some will understand the foolishness of a broken heart and the why some suffered so much.

ORIGINAL STORY:

Elvis's music still touches me in a way that I can only remember the blazing furnace of true love, puppy love, first love did. I would like to invite you on a trip. A trip of love and loss and hope and despair…So for those of you that are burdened by a hardened heart, or a cold soul, please forgive me as I lay out my "Rose of Arabia" saga. She "Walked like an Angel, Talked like an Angel, and in my eyes, she was my Princess in disguise."

Let me take you back in time, through the mist of life and the patterns of choice and let us once again stand on the heated sands and star blanketed skiesof our youth, in a land of magic and passion like the desert movements.

Singingand whispering through the eons of the loves it has seen come and go, forevertouching the depths of the dunes, and breaking with the crests of the sea as the two meet together, sand and water. Then separate, as I did with my Princess, in the nights of Arabia, only to find and lose again centuries of life later.

For it was the middle of February, the month of love, in the year of 1962, a year blessed by Allah that I first saw her standing there. Her eyes were like saucers and the intensity was unfathomable. You could read her heart, and hear it beat all in the flash of her eyes, which made the moons blaze off of Half Moon Bay pale by comparison. I know, for I never again recovered from the depth of her.

We were but youngsters, and talked throughout the late evening and pass dinner and on into the opening of God's eyes in the form of a trillion stars, a million points of love developing as two small figures, took one anther's hand and the squeeze was felt throughout the land. Even the mighty sands quivered, for it knew. A love was born and a new star rose. My Arabian Rose, My Princess.

What did we know about passion, we were so young? We knew our hands turned sweaty and then, as if a light from afar called our lips together, the lightest brush, for we knew not fully what a kiss was. Yet I do remember the thirst in my heart and the drink of her kiss. Never again was I to feel the heat and coolness, the rush and the excitement, all at once and forever. I don't think either of us knew what had happened.

We didn't have a chance as things were against us, or so it now seems. A childish prank by some of our young friends, they built a "church" and as we walked in they said "Now you have to get married, for you can never be apart again". We quickly parted and said, "Stop", for this is not how we wanted.

The others got mad and told their parents and their Father, being a so-called "good man" called her house and told her Dad. Then called my Dad and the world came asunder for my Princess and I. She was told never to see me and I was told I was placing my Father's job at risk. We never even had a chance as May was upon us and she was away for school the next two years.

I stayed on and finished the ninth grade, then away to Military School having never heard again. Others came and went, but the intensity was always short of the eventful night, when the earth and heavens shook." Catch a falling star and put in your pocket…"

One last time, in the waning days of summer in 1968. An opportunity came and we met again. We walked home from the bowling alley and spoke for hours in her yard. Once again that magic called Arabia worked its spell and her kiss made me feel as if I had fallen into a well of crashing passion and warmth.

For some unknown reason, we were too late; we were separated once again by fate. I traveled far, met the elephant and looked him in the eye, while she walked another road, one less daring than mine. Her life was not perfect, nor mine, for I had become a pirate. I think now, searching for my Princess, but not knowing where to look.

I then found all of you, Houston 1995. I once again came alive and I knew I was home. She wasn't there, but I heard of where. So later that year, when Santa was near I sent a card, but was not to hear. For I did not know it, but she had tried, the call was lost. As this time it was I who was back in my beloved Arabia, and had not looked back into her eyes. Upon my return, the AramcoBrats to form and order to come from chaos. For this chaos was what brought me back and as such, brought me to my Princess once again.

I got in touch through another and found out she was there and we saw one other. Life has its tricks and can deliver mighty hard kicks, and this was one. I was able to talk, and for many months, the marvel of electronics made us as one. Her honor intact, for we never crossed the line, for my Princess's is married and happily, and that's fine.

Chandler 's reunion was a land of Oz. Many remember the land of sand. When the desert of Arizona became the desert of Arabia and one had become the other, we knew. Thus we talked and the events of what happened in our life became clear.

Until the Reunion, we both never knew the story. Each thought the other had done something wrong. I can now shed my tears, because she was still so dear. However Honor and Duty, Integrity and Fidelity remained the order of the day.

For she is happy and that was always our way.

Her Knight will always ride hard, his Princess knows he will always be there. Then the sands of Arabia and the boundaries of life are but a prelude to the future, where all things may come true.

I tell this tale, not looking for anything, yet perhaps to wish each and everyone the chance to experience what I did and the magic of what the ARAMCOBRAT REUNION and the desert song did for me.

This is my reason for all of us, for the Brats to remain alive and the memories to flow, for without this, I feel like I have no soul. So I thank each and everyone of you, for you have given me back what I had lost, and now the beast within me may rest, for it knows it's worth. So come to the reunion, one and all..It is the place of marvels for although life has moved on, for a short while, we may once again be alive in the showdowns of our youth and the agelessness of our time.

To my dear Princess, as I said eons ago, our love will always be there, just as you know.

All I can say now is that I will place a Golden heart with two names by the Kaaba in Mekka and hope that Allah will see the love under His will. I will say good bye now to my Princess, Martha and hope that her life as she choose was a beautiful experience and that she was happy.

For all the rest of you, touch your loves heart once again and remind yourselves, of what you have and will have again if your heart is alive. For in this Princess passing, I did too in my spirit. She had a good husband and good family and instead of being a speck of desert, she will always be a full blown desert sand rose of love.

CAMEL SUQ

Many of you can remember the famous Camel suq in Damman or when the Dhahran County Fair was held on the Kings Road Field. Well, my Mom thought that I as a 12 year old could try to do this. While walking up I thought, how do you tell if a camel is male or female. After all, Donkeys were somewhat obvious as were horses. So I decided to look. No one in their right mind, and according to Mom my mind was never right, I decided to sneak into the group of five or six good sizes camels that were roped off and see. Did you know that a Camel can tell with great accuracy that its tail is lifted? Well, in all fairness, the one I picked was a big mean looking thing and when I lifted, and must have given the tail a hard pull, the ship of the desert must have had bad hay because he/she/it let me have it. I was soaked from head to tee shoes with a combination that had the distinct aroma not of humus. I was in shock and then to add insult to injury the darn killer tried to stomp me flat. Feet the size of Beach balls and me smelling like a camel and I do mean smell.

Well, first the sucker tried to bite me and then spit on me. I spit back, but the camel was not impressed. The Saudi herder came running and instead of smacking the camel with his camel stick, smacked me. That was it. Out I went and ran straight to Mom, who happened to be with about fifty

Aramco wives. First the comments were hurtful, I mean who calls a kid a camelshithead and all in five or six languages? My Dad got Ned Scardino to have the fire truck on the lot spray me down. Evidently this was something that had happened to others for he sure took great pleasure in making sure I sqeeeeeked when I walked away.

Now comes the great time. The have got several camels down to ride and I boldly strode up and after they measured me told me I did not need a co-rider. Well anyone can ride a damn horse right, so what so hard about this. Well first, as you all know Camels do not start out standing. When he leaned forward I went right off the front and flat on my back and the fool Camel spit on me again. That did it.

Back in a flash and on to the beast with the handhold wrapped like a rodeo rider and the beast stands up. First forward and then to one side and then to the other. I thought that was it so I let go my death grip and the sob learned way back to raise up and off I went, this time backwards and into a fresh pile of camel delight. I did not know the Moms and Camels had the same laugh. They do.

I finally get up and the herdsman walks the Camel about fifty feet and turns around and then back.. Whatttt? I went through all that for five minutes. So off I go and Mom put me on a donkey (one of the photos in "Forever Friends book), and I got to ride for about twenty minutes.

Just recently I rode on a herd in column and the sway was wild but I, fifty years later was secure into the desert. Camel my ass. I knew this time.

Story about RT

To recall all of this, one must travel back to Ras Tanura and about 1959. It was a dead dog day of heat. The oleanders were leaning way over and hiding in each others shade. Even the gulf seem to be panting as the lips of water hit the blazing hot sand. Seemed to boil a little. The asphalt was way out there in rubbery feel and boards had been laid from the school to the recreation area so that pools of hot asphalt wouldn't get all over people. Well, into the oven mom said and chucked the three, as she said, devils, into the Rub Al Khali of our back yard. Dick Burgess, Ross Tyler and myself. White tee shirts and khaki shorts with sandals.

Bad enough we had gotten into her pies for the Woman's Club, but they were so good looking and little fingers had found a little here, a little there, who thought her evil eye would be able to tell. So here we are. RT, August and bored out of our minds. So over to recreation and into the theater.

For those that remember, there were ac ducts under the stage there and we crawled into one. Me, being just a tad bigger, ok, a lot bigger had a hard time and so Dick and Ross pulled me in. This managed to let me lose not only sandals but also baggy khaki shorts. I am sure the recreation guys howled at the little sandals and pants right by the open grille as they closed it up and put the wing nuts back on the covers. Now of course we are in the tunnels and there is light ahead. We crawl towards it and it is getting mighty chilly on my back end when Dick remarks, rather casually, well, the movie is just about over and we can get out thru the theater.

Unfortunately what Dickie had forgot and we never thought of was that the theater on most Friday mornings was used for Catholic church services. So out we come, by now dirty and me in skives. Needless to say we hightailed it out of the side exit, and I mean high TAILed it out of there. Susan Maloney, being an all time friend made sure plenty of people saw our three dirty tails leaving. A little point and yell I do recall.

We shot over to the school yard and went to play on the slides. Talk about a blistered butt. Mom couldn't have done more damage that I did sliding down the slide when the metal was most likely 500 degree's hot. And of course right into the blazing desert at the foot of the slide made a wonderful impression also.

Do any of you remember walking the hedges? Great thrill to try to stay balanced on top and walk around a block and try to get on the next set by jumping. So jump we did, hedge leans over, we fall into yard. Not just any yard of course, but one of the seven units back yards that was a bachelors quarters. Running in circles trying to find the gate, the two bachelors soaked us with water from a hose and out we went. At least refreshed, but now how to recover the sandals and pants before Mom finds out and we really get heated up.

So back to recreation and Ross sneaks into the office and there are the clothes. Great success all around and promotions for all of us to smart alecks. We dash home and Ross and Dick are playing in the big Acadia tree we had at 1G in RT and here comes Dad from church. He always went and that usually meant that we had to go to a later service in case of any little flare ups of our behavior. He has a funny look and soon I hear that I am not allowed with 10000 feet of anything for at least ten years. Seems as if he was in the church service and had to do some explaining.

The point of this...well when it's too hot outside, find some shade and wait. It only gets hotter.

Larry Barnes and Aramco Radio For way too many years Larry barnes was THE radio and news man on the Aramco radio station. Sometimes he would even let us kids read part of the news, which was also passed out in a paper form at the mail center.

However Larry got to choose the music that we elevator kids loved so much. There was one thing. I found from a top secret source how to call in on a separate telephone line and it would cancel the song playing and start another. This drove Larry to drink and I think I heard some remarkable commentary that was off record. Anyhow he didn't know for years who was doing it and each time he had the number changed, I would get it and start all over again. The statute of limitations is past now, so I can admit that the head of recreation, Naji, formally of Security was my source. I freely admit I did it this because to be honest, Larry Barnes is one of the finest men I have ever know...Now Gary is another story. ;-)

CHRIS MOHLMAN AND SANDY HOOK

In the olde days, the refinery was open and from the residential area of RT we could go to visit the water outlet area or on the other side we could go to what was called Sandy Hook. A really great beach for spear fishing and in fact there was a large ocean going ship way up on the beach and I never understood how it got there, but we used to wine (brown) and dine the local beauties and they had complete privacy for that perfect tan. No tan lines. Well, Chris and I were out diving there alone one day and I thought I had seen a great whale of a Hamoor and so shot it. Dead square into Chris's oversized foot fin. Well he turned around and I was already headed to shore as I had seen what I did. He camo out of the water chasing me and shot the old boat in frustration. Now we used triple rubber Arbelete spear guns and they packed a hell of a smack. This old boat had been there so long, the dam thing rolled ever so slightly and almost crushed me. Well we made up and decided to head home. Only we had forgot to have the cab come back so we are really struggling to carry all our gear and Chris stops a fuel tanker and we climb on top of the tanker trailer to ride bact to RT and Chris, and I swear I thought we were dead, lights up a cigarette. The little fuel release cap about mid center of the tanker suddenly burst into a flame and we jump, the driver jumped and Chris went down in Aramco history as havin blown up one of the Kenworth trailers. One sad note, or really two. This got Chris a severe probation and due to a couple of other things, he was asked to leave Arabia. I have told that story, but the real killer was when he went into reclaimation and took a sledge hammer and busted out the raditors of about ten Kennworth trucks there, or perhaps it was when he and Gail Duell ran away from home and moved into the cave across from the old incinerator and above the aircraft wreck and bottleland. They stayed there about a week and both caught hell. I, being innocent was found by the District Manager to have smuggled food to them, so I was banned from all recreation until the year 2025.

NEW ONE—DANGEROUS VALATINE

So it was Valentine's Day…who cared. Yeah, right. 1965, what a year.

Ninth grade, big man on campus going steady with Vicki Muzika, a Cheerleader and just knew I had it all together.

Well, Aramco used to have items like candy and flowers and such at the commissary for people to buy for special occasions. At the very least, Al-Khobar had candy, dated years prior, but it was still candy. So I strut into the teen canteen and there with a bunch of others is Vicki. All smiles and just waiting. Sudden insight almost knocked me out and I had five surprise her, being such a romantic and all..Ah-huh! Surprise was the word when I saw Kevin Colgan give some other girl a BIG box of candy, Drostle's I think.

He had a grin from hell so I knew he had already set the stage for the slaughter. Calmly, with waves of dread I approached the table and then inspiration set upon me like a pack of rabid Saluki's.

I calmly told her in front of the whole group that I had made SPECIAL reservations at the dining hall for a Valentine dinner and a surprise.

Then was taking her to the AEA Valentine's dance at the patio, and that I had tickets and we needed to dress up to be allowed in. Now, thinking on my feet, or perhaps with my feet has never been a bright spot for me, but this time I really outdid myself.

With the calm of a brilliant strategist I sat down to her ohh's and ahh's and compliments from her friends, basking in the knowledge that all's well.

learned shortly the meaning of "All's fair in love and war" and "Hell has no demon worse than an embarrassed women in front of her friends".

I made a hasty excuse and told her, with a jaunty attitude, "Baby love, I'll be there at seven to pick you up ." Not even knowing that AL Capone was thinking of a garage he could use for his Valentine's Day workout, and never guessing that Vicki must have been related to him.

I rushed madly to the commissary..nothing, not even chicklets. Out the door like an eraged camel in pursuit of a fleeing Arab with water I went.I shot down to Khobar and at the Green Flag store found a large, actually heart shaped box of chocolates. Man, what a break. I never even asked, just paid many riyals and ran to Eve's jewelry to find a gold anything to tape to the chocolates. She liked charms and I found a charm that looked like a flower.

Hell, looked to me like a rose. Down to the corner market and looking at vegetables trying to find something that looked like roses…How the hell do you paint a water mellon to look like a dozen roses, such was my mind.

Celery painted red?, Yeah that out to work. Heck, she didn't know roses either, or so the brilliant madman thought. "A dozen you say, sure, with the leafy tops if you will..Shukran" and gone like a flash. Time is of the essence. Need to con Dad out of his tickets to AEA's party and then get to the dining hall. Stop at the house, yelled at Mom, "Get my damn coat and pants ironed," forgot who I was talking too, and had to take about a thirty minute break to clear my head, damn cast iron pans were just too hard.

Much sal'lams and down the hall to Dad's dresser. Where is he..he is out, I know he won't mind, so I rifle his wallet, find the tickets and a 50 SR note. Heck, just an advance on my allowance. Shows what panic will do…I didn't know it, but Dad was MC'ing that night and it was a very special night, being Mom and Dads anniversary and my last day on this earth at the same time.

Up to Ali at the Dining Hall.."No Mr. Mike, no have any room tonight. Big bosses party"…Yeah, well Ali, let me tell you about BIG bosses. MY Dad is a VP and he said "Give Mike a table, WITH a candle." I just knew that Mom and Dad weren't going to this event, they never did. Anyone hear "machine gun Kelly" warming up here? SO, table set, candy and charm in hand, clothes a distinct possibility and tickets, cab fare..all set….Heck, it's only 6:30pm, guess I'll go to the pool and cool off. Man what a day. at the pool I decided to really push my luck and started rough housing in the water with some other "friends" and suddenly, Naji of recreation is there. "You, outta the pool, my office you nooo good, NOW!" I think Polhemus had run over there and told on me..always wondered about him...

So I'm at the deadline and in his office with a lot of bellyaching on his part, when he gets a call...Ziiiiiip, out the door and gone like a flash to the taxi station at the theater and home, clothed and grabbed up all, including my "rose" bouquet and off to get Vicki. Her Dad opens the door, see's the roses and has to sit down with tears in his eyes. Not so damn funny I thought. It got worse when Vicki came out in a beautiful dress and her Mother broke up and almost died of laughter over my "flowers".

Vicki at least maintained until we were in the taxi and then really spoke her mind..That took the twenty minutes to the Dining Hall and I don't think stopped for four hours. They have the room all decorated and men in suits and fancy silverware, low lights, really nice.

We are seated at one of the long tables with the likes of Mr. Barger, Mr. Scardino, Mr. Dickerson, etc. No problem, hey, it was romantic right? I give Vicki her charm and she suddenly is all smiles and loving, so I give her the big box of candy, just so proud of myself. She opens it and several large rat droppings fall out on the table, along with what may have at one time, say 1944, been candy and her scream is heard in Houhof.... I make for the door while she is throwing this stuff at me and people are flat amazed and stunned.

After getting as far as I could and spending about an hour on bended knees waiting for her to swing the beheading blow, she finally calms down, after such begging from me that anyone has ever heard. I think I may still have emnants of red painted celery stuck somewhere, but that turned out irrelevant.

I get to the AEA dance, slip right in and we are finally together, in love, in Arabia with the brilliant stars of the desert and love and romance every-where, when the gates of hell open and two of the meanest Dober- Moms and Dads known to man appear. I know I had to be unconscious for at least an hour it seemed from the initial attack, but I know of no one that can beat the record I set that night of getting licks from the 3rd street pool to the top of sixth street. I think Mom and Dad recruited other parents to hand off to every few steps as I seem to recall most of Dhahran, Abqaiq and RT getting a few licks in. I even think some Arab caravan passing by got in a few.

Well, grounded until 1999, suspended from recreation until some-time in 2010, the laughing stock of Arabia, BUT, due to the charm and my begging, I saved my love and even through it all, when she finally stepped back and looked at it, I had been trying all along to prove my love. SO, I risked life and limb that night to sneak out (yes, I know…total insanity) and went to her window, knocked and when she opened it, I got a great long kiss and a promise of lifelong love.

JENAHRIYAH HERITAGE FESTIVAL HOST BY KING

It is an early night as the "Jenahriyah" begins tomorrow with the openning at 2:00pm and the first event is the 1000 camel race. A sight I gather I will never see again. Then on to the auditorium to hear poetry and speeches and then to the tradition Saudi dances and many exhibits. We expect to be there from 2 until Midnight.

Well, I'll put this one in the books. I have never seen the likes. One Thousand Camels and racing a spiral track. Fantastic, and those damn things can move…The race was won by a Camel called "Abdul" what else would have been right ? The jockey was a little kid about twelve years old. They all were. What a shock, hell, I won't get near one and I'm just a shade older. He got his prize from Prince Charles. I got to meet the Prince in a form of receiving line. He is quite an ugly duck..Lady Di for me ! Several long political speeches and then the most unbelievable light show and operetta style of program. These singers came out on a stage the size of a opera house and, Ohh, this is all indoors and will seat 20,000 people at once. Then the lights and the music and the dancing. Sword dancing, ballet style, rocking and rolling side to side style and in all, about 450 people on stage at once, all in concert with the five lead singers. The the National Guard marched out and did a sword dance with at least 750 men. The laser light show and the huge background was constantly changing with photos of King Abd-Al-Azziz Al-Sa'ud.

The grand finale had the entire troupe of at least 1000 on the floor and all doing various sword dances and playing all native instruments. The Crown Prince and other members went out into the stage area and joined in and the crowd went wild. They were dancing in the bleachers and really getting worked up. I hope to be able to get a video of this.

We, the "Guests" were then taken to the main hall for a traditional meal and we ate like rabid jackals. What a feast. The hall could sit some 2000 at a time and they do this every night until the festival ends. This all started at

2:00pm and we got back to the hotel around mid-night. The line of black Mercedes with the Saudi logo in gold on the door was just staggering. Each of us "Guests" were two to a car and I'll bet there was at least 125 of us...I was interviewed by the Al-Riyadhi Newspaper and will see how that came out. Long way from the humble beginnings of a small town goat herder that I was...So ends "Jedahriyah" for me......InShallah ! Allah Akbar !

Assalamu alaikum wa rahmatu Allah

As I stood on the sands of the desert once again recently, I felt a tremor go throughout my body. It was a warmth that can only be described as a sensation of pleasure mixed with deep sorrow. The Brat life blood which pounds like the Ras Tanura surf in my veins was matched only by the Flare in Abqaiq that lit the depth of my soul in my eyes as the way home as we flew the dark skies. Arriving at the main gate at Dhahran the flood of emotions of being safe from the world was once again forming an aura about me. For as the Crown Prince said to me at a meeting in Riyadh, "You are not here Amerike Bedu, you are sailing the Rub Al'Kahli with your spirit. You seem to ride with our father and yours from so long ago. Are you happy?"

The answer must be one that can only come from the spray of fine golden sand from my fingers as it piles on the third street playground. Yes, I whisper, for I have touched the face of my youth and found it to be me. The Great North dune will always sing it's words of sensuality in my heart, if I travel a million miles away. I will always feel the touch of my Arabian Princess who's love can never die,and forever in my mind is the haunting Call to Prayer of the faithful. The touch of the beach, the smell of the shops in Al-Khobar, the sweet taste of the honeysuckle from the hedge. How can one measure all of the feelings and emotions. It is really easy. It is love. For each Brat that I know and each that I may never meet, but will always know, the sands of our youth have touched me.

I am moving on from being your President for the past six years. I am told it is time and as a wise Bedu once said.."Man and the flow of the dune must always move." So be it. For I am alive as I have never been. I have found the Brats and they and I have played the alleys of time once again. We have touched Christmas past and been present for the future. We have grieved for the loss of so many of us, but most of all, I have found, in each of you, a place of heart that may never die.

The greatest gift that God has given me, and He has been generous with me, is you. All 4800 we have brought together. A Brathood of many, with a feeling of one. We have done a lot my friends. For that is our thread of humility..the friendship that life gave us all from a common bond. Let us not forget that we have a purpose, a goal, a responsibility. One of friendship that will last lifetimes.

I wish to thank each and every Brat alive, whether I know you or you know me, for you have given a lost dhow a port of call..The port of friendship.

I hope to be able to see each and every one of you at the reunion, for it shall be my last as your President and I hope we will have pleased you with the efforts of the many that have formed the Aramco Brats, Inc. group. For they truly have fought many a battle and passing the torch of one to another is always hard.

But judge not us hard, for we came from the past and fought through the shifting sands to find a place of magic. A place we can all call our youth for a few days. In Tucson at the Reunion, I will once again be safe and feel the emotions of the past, present and future from you.

I will always be there for my beloved Brats, and I hope that in the future you look kindly at the man who wanders the reunion with the glazed look of a bemused and content camel, for that shall be me seeing each and every time the beauty of you all. My Brats.

Ma'sallam'a siddiqui's

Made in the USA
Lexington, KY
12 March 2012